Sybil, Queen of Jerusalem, 1186–1190

Queen Sybil of Jerusalem, queen in her own right, was ruler of the kingdom of Jerusalem from 1186 to 1190. Her reign saw the loss of the city of Jerusalem to Saladin, and the beginning of the Third Crusade. Her reign began with her nobles divided and crisis looming; by her death the military forces of Christian Europe were uniting with her and her husband, intent on recovering what had been lost. Sybil died before the bulk of the forces of the Third Crusade could arrive in the kingdom, and Jerusalem was not recovered. But although Sybil failed, she went down fighting – spiritually, even if not physically.

This study traces Sybil's life, from her childhood as the daughter of the heir to the throne of Jerusalem to her death in the crusading force outside the city of Acre. It sets her career alongside that of other European queens and noblewomen of the twelfth century who wielded or attempted to wield power and asks how far the eventual survival of the kingdom of Jerusalem in 1192 was due to Sybil's leadership in 1187 and her determination never to give up.

Helen J. Nicholson is Professor in Medieval History, Cardiff University, UK.

Rulers of the Latin East
Series editors
Nicholas Morton, *Nottingham Trent University, UK*
Jonathan Phillips, *Royal Holloway University of London, UK*

Academics concerned with the history of the Crusades and the Latin East will be familiar with the various survey histories that have been produced for this fascinating topic. Many historians have published wide-ranging texts that either seek to make sense of the strange phenomenon that was the Crusades or shed light upon the Christian territories of the Latin East. Such panoramic works have helped to generate enormous interest in this subject, but they can only take their readers so far. Works addressing the lives of individual rulers – whether kings, queens, counts, princes or patriarchs – are less common and yet are needed if we are to achieve a more detailed understanding of this period.

This series seeks to address this need by stimulating a collection of political biographies of the men and women who ruled the Latin East between 1098 and 1291 and the kingdom of Cyprus up to 1571. These focus in detail upon the evolving political and diplomatic events of this period, whilst shedding light upon more thematic issues such as: gender and marriage, intellectual life, kingship and governance, military history and inter-faith relations.

Baldwin I
Susan B. Edgington

Godfrey of Bouillon
Duke of Lower Lotharingia, Ruler of Latin Jerusalem, c.1060-1100
Simon John

The Counts of Tripoli and Lebanon in the Twelfth Century
Sons of Saint-Gilles
Kevin James Lewis

Fulk and Melisende: King and Queen of Jerusalem
Danielle Park

Baldwin of Bourcq
Count of Edessa and King of Jerusalem (1100-1131)
Alan V. Murray

Sybil
Queen of Jerusalem, 1186-1190
Helen J. Nicholson

Sybil, Queen of Jerusalem, 1186–1190

Helen J. Nicholson

LONDON AND NEW YORK

First published 2022
by Routledge
4 Park Square, Milton Park, Abingdon, Oxon OX14 4RN

and by Routledge
605 Third Avenue, New York, NY 10158

Routledge is an imprint of the Taylor & Francis Group, an informa business

© 2022 Helen J. Nicholson

The right of Helen J. Nicholson to be identified as author of this work has been asserted in accordance with sections 77 and 78 of the Copyright, Designs and Patents Act 1988.

All rights reserved. No part of this book may be reprinted or reproduced or utilised in any form or by any electronic, mechanical, or other means, now known or hereafter invented, including photocopying and recording, or in any information storage or retrieval system, without permission in writing from the publishers.

Trademark notice: Product or corporate names may be trademarks or registered trademarks, and are used only for identification and explanation without intent to infringe.

British Library Cataloguing-in-Publication Data
A catalogue record for this book is available from the British Library

Library of Congress Cataloging-in-Publication Data
A catalog record has been requested for this book

ISBN: 978-1-138-63651-4 (hbk)
ISBN: 978-1-032-23466-3 (pbk)
ISBN: 978-1-315-20596-0 (ebk)

DOI: 10.4324/9781315205960

Typeset in Times New Roman
by SPi Technologies India Pvt Ltd (Straive)

Contents

List of Figures	vii
A Note on Names	viii
Acknowledgements	ix
Abbreviations	x
Figures	xi

	Introduction	1
1	**Who was Sybil? Family and sources**	5
	Sybil's cultural and family background 6	
	Sybil the person: personality, appearance and self-representation 8	
	Sybil in contemporary and near-contemporary eyes: the primary sources 10	
	Sybil in modern eyes 15	
2	**Childhood (c. 1159–1171)**	29
	Parents 29	
	Birth and infancy 30	
	Daughter of the king 34	
	Upbringing and education 36	
	Initial marriage negotiations 42	
3	**Adolescence and marriage (1172–1177)**	52
	Family matters 52	
	The minority of King Baldwin IV 53	
	Marriage to William of Montferrat 57	
4	**Widow, countess and second marriage (1177–1180)**	69
	Countess of Jaffa and Ascalon 69	
	Count Philip of Flanders 70	
	Further marriage negotiations 79	
	Second marriage: Guy de Lusignan 82	

vi   *Contents*

5   Wife of Guy de Lusignan and mother of the child king (1180–1186)   92
The shifting balance of power   92
Baldwin IV: building up control   93
Sybil and Guy, countess and count of Jaffa-Ascalon   94
Guy de Lusignan: temporary regent of the kingdom   99
King Baldwin V, 1185–1186   109

6   Queen (1186–1187)   117
Coronation   117
Queen, but not regnant   124
The end of the truce   127

7   Sybil versus Saladin (1187–1189)   134
After Hattin   134
The sieges of Ascalon and Jerusalem   137
Former queen of Jerusalem   142
Reunion with Guy: taking the war to the enemy   148

8   The siege of Acre and the end of the reign (1189–1190)   158
The siege of Acre   158
Sybil's later reputation   165
Conclusion   169

Bibliography   177
Index   194

List of Figures

1 Family tree of the rulers of Jerusalem, 1118–1190 xi
2 Locations in the Middle East mentioned in the text.
   © Nigel Nicholson xii
3 Locations in Europe mentioned in the text. © Nigel Nicholson xiii

A Note on Names

In an historical study drawing on evidence in more than one language, none of them English, it is always difficult to know how best to render names of persons and places, especially as contemporaries were inconsistent. Where there is a general modern consensus on the rendering of a name into English (such as Saladin, Tamar, Jerusalem), I have used that. So, for the name given in Latin as Enfridus and in Old French as Hainfrois I have used Humphrey, which is the modern consensus. Where there is a common equivalent in modern English usage (such as Eleanor, Guy, Henry, or Isabel), I have used it. However, modern scholars working in English do not agree on a single version of the name of King Amaury's eldest daughter, variously rendering it as Sibyl, Sibylla, Sybil or Sybilla. Here I render the name as 'Sybil', as that is the most commonly used modern spelling. Likewise, there is no modern consensus on how to render the name which is given in Latin as Reginaldus or Renaldus, and in Old French as Rainaus or Renaut: I have used Reynald, the version currently most commonly used by English-language scholars. In some cases where there is no consensus on the name of a location I have given the variant versions at first mention and subsequently used the version which I hope is that most familiar to English-speaking readers.

Acknowledgements

I undertook the writing of this book following research on Sybil as part of other projects. I thank Nicholas Morton for commissioning it for Routledge's 'Rulers of the Latin East Series' and thus giving me the opportunity to explore Sybil's life more thoroughly. I am very grateful to Giuseppe Ligato for generously providing me with a copy of his biography of Sybil, *Sibilla regina crociata* (2005), to Richard A. Leson and Chris Mielke for kindly sending me copies of material which would not otherwise have been available to me, and to Tom Asbridge, Myra Bom, Andrew D. Buck, Kelly DeVries, Peter Edbury, Marianne Gilchrist, Rudolf Hiestand, Ben Morris, Alan V. Murray, Jonathan Phillips, Thomas W. Smith, Stephen Spencer and other colleagues and friends researching crusading and medieval warfare for their advice, opinions and comments on various points. Some of the material in this book has been presented at conferences and seminars in the UK and the USA, and I thank all those who made comments and suggestions in response to these presentations. I am also very grateful to my colleagues in the History Department at Cardiff University for granting me research leave in 2020–2021 so that I could complete this study, and to the School of History, Archaeology and Religion for confirming their decision. I am indebted to the staff in Cardiff University Arts and Social Studies Library, especially the staff in Inter-library Loan, and the staff in the library of the Institute of Historical Research, University of London, for their assistance in obtaining copies of research materials during the Covid-19 restrictions. The resources digitised online by the Internet Archive have also been invaluable. Regrettably the Covid-19 restrictions have meant that despite every effort some research material has not been accessible to me. I also thank Cardiff University Optometrists for their support in enabling me to complete this book despite my deteriorating eyesight. My husband has patiently and generously provided computer assistance as required and drew the maps. I drew up the family tree and made all the translations which are not otherwise attributed.

Abbreviations

BD   [Bahā' al-Dīn ibn Shaddād], *The Rare and Excellent History of Saladin or al-Nawādir al-Sulṭāniyya wa'l-Maḥāsin al-Yūsufiyya by Bahā' al-Dīn Ibn Shaddād*, translated by D. S. Richards, Crusade Texts in Translation 7 (Aldershot, 2002)
IA   [Ibn al-Athīr], *The Chronicle of Ibn al-Athīr for the Crusading Period from al-Kāmil fi'l-ta'rīkh*, part 2: *The Years 541–589/1146–1193: The Age of Nur al-Din and Saladin*, translated by D. S. Richards, Crusade Texts in Translation 15 (Farnham, 2007)
'Imād 'Imād al-Dīn al-Iṣfahānī, *Conquête de la Syrie et de la Palestine par Saladin (al-Fatḥ al-qussî fî l-fatḥ al-qudsî)*, translated by Henri Massé, Documents relatifs à l'histoire des Croisades 10 (Paris, 1972)
IP 1 *Das Itinerarium peregrinorum: eine zeitgenössische englische Chronik zum dritten Kreuzzug in ursprünglicher Gestalt*, ed. Hans Eberhard Mayer, Schriften der Monumenta Germaniae historica (Deutsches Institut für Erforschung des Mittelalters) 18 (Stuttgart, 1962)
IP 2 *Itinerarium peregrinorum et gesta regis Ricardi, auctore, ut videtur, Ricardo, canonico Sanctæ Trinitatis Londoniensis*, ed. William Stubbs, vol. 1 of *Chronicles and Memorials of the Reign of Richard I*, Rolls Series 38 (London, 1864), pp. 1–450
LFWT *Die lateinische Fortsetzung Wilhelms von Tyrus*, ed. Marianne Salloch (Leipzig, 1934)
MGH SS *Monumenta Germaniae Historica Scriptores in Folio*, ed. Georg Heinrich Pertz *et al.*, 39 vols (Hanover, etc., 1826–1934)
PL   *Patrologiae cursus completus: Series Latina*, ed. J. P. Migne, 217 vols with 4 vols of indices (Paris, 1844–64)
RRH *Regesta regni Hierosolymitani*, ed. Reinhold Röhricht, 2 vols (Innsbruck, 1893–1904)
RRR *Revised Regesta Regni Hierosolymitani Database*, http://crusades-regesta.com
ULKJ *Die Urkunden der lateinischen Könige von Jerusalem*, ed. Hans Eberhard Mayer, Monumenta Germaniae historica. Diplomata regum Latinorum Hierosolymitanorum (Hanover, 2010)
WT   *Willelmi Tyrensis Archiepiscopi Chronicon*/Guillaume de Tyr, *Chronique*, ed. R. B. C. Huygens, 2 vols, Corpus Christianorum Continuatio Mediaeualis 63, 63A (Turnhout, 1986)

Figures

Family tree of the rulers of Jerusalem, 1118–1190

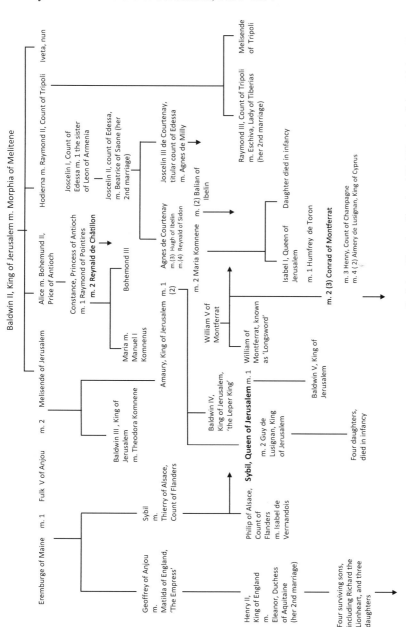

Family tree of the rulers of Jerusalem, 1118–1190, produced by H. J. Nicholson 2021

Locations in the Middle East mentioned in the text. © Nigel Nicholson

Locations in Europe mentioned in the text. © Nigel Nicholson

Introduction

'*Regina, regis Amalrici filia, Sibilla nomine*': the queen, daughter of King Amaury, Sybil by name: so a contemporary described the queen as she set out from Jerusalem after surrendering the city to Saladin on 2 October 1187.[1] Her brief four-year reign was a time of enormous upheaval in the history of the kingdom of Jerusalem. She and her second husband, Guy de Lusignan, had gained the throne as Saladin, ruler of Egypt and Damascus, threatened the very existence of the kingdom. The barons of the kingdom were divided and some refused to do homage to Guy. Following Sybil's and Guy's coronation in autumn 1186, Baldwin of Ramla, one of the leading barons of the kingdom of Jerusalem, withdrew to the principality of Antioch, while Count Raymond III of Tripoli placed himself under Saladin's protection and allowed Saladin's troops into the principality of Galilee.[2] In early summer 1187 Saladin defeated the armies of the kingdom of Jerusalem in two engagements, on 1 May and 4 July. King Guy and many of the leading barons of the kingdom were captured, and Saladin went on to seize most of the cities of the kingdom, including Jerusalem.

Sybil never gave up. She defended her city of Ascalon; she negotiated the release of her husband the king, tried to appeal to the West to obtain aid for her kingdom and began the fightback against Saladin. While she awaited her husband's release she went north to the crusader states of Tripoli and Antioch, which successfully resisted Saladin's forces; then, when Guy was released, she and her husband assembled an army and took the war back to Saladin. Their relatives in Europe responded positively to appeals for help: Guy's brother Geoffrey de Lusignan, a famous warrior; Sybil's Angevin cousins Henry II of England (who died before he could set out) and his son Richard; and her cousin Philip of Alsace, count of Flanders. Sybil died in 1190, fighting to the last to recover her kingdom.

Born between 1157 (when her parents married) and 1161 (when her younger brother Baldwin was born), Sybil was the daughter and sister of kings, granddaughter of Count Fulk of Anjou (and so an Angevin), cousin of King Henry II of England and first cousin once removed of King Richard the Lionheart. She was a contemporary of Eleanor of Aquitaine, Countess Marie of Champagne and Queen Tamar the Great of Georgia, all renowned for their cultural patronage. Her grandmother, Queen Melisende of Jerusalem

DOI: 10.4324/9781315205960-1

(d. 1161), was the owner of the beautiful Melisende Psalter which now graces the British Museum. Sybil herself probably commissioned the lavish tomb of her son King Baldwin V of Jerusalem.

In many respects Sybil's life was typical for a royal princess or noblewoman of her time: educated in an elite women's religious house, married in her mid-teens, widowed and remarried, regularly giving birth and seeing her children die in childhood, seldom mentioned by narrative records but regularly issuing legal documents which indicate that she was active in administering her estates, defending her own estates when they came under attack and negotiating her husband's release from prison after he was captured in battle.[3] Her personal life was dominated by her relatives, who chose her husbands and attempted to force her into divorce. But she was exceptional because from her birth there was always the possibility that she would rule Jerusalem, either as queen of Jerusalem or as regent for her crowned child. She became, as one writer of the late thirteenth century would describe her, *la roine preude femme et bonne dame* – a queen, a valiant woman, and a good lady.[4]

Her contemporaries depicted her as a faithful wife who outwitted her enemies, refused to give up her husband, was prepared to sacrifice her city of Ascalon to recover him alive from Saladin, accompanied him to the dangers of the siege of Acre and died there with their daughters. In contemporaries' eyes her greatest virtue was her fidelity to her second husband. They reported that at Sybil's coronation the barons of the kingdom asked her to divorce Guy de Lusignan and choose a more suitable husband, but when Sybil complied she chose Guy, who was, she said, the best husband she could have and the best king for the kingdom. Perhaps she chose Guy for love but given the divisions among the Franks in autumn 1186 she may have truly believed that there was no alternative and that Guy was the only commander who was trusted by the rulers of Christian Europe, who could attract aid from the West, unite the rulers of the crusader states and defeat Saladin.

Sybil's life was dogged by controversy: before her father, King Amaury of Jerusalem (ruled 1163–74), could be crowned king, he was forced to divorce his wife, Agnes de Courtenay. Sybil and her younger brother Baldwin were legitimated as part of the settlement, but a question remained over their legitimacy to rule. Baldwin's leprosy was interpreted by the pope as God's just judgement. When Sybil's son Baldwin V died, some of the nobles of the kingdom wanted to place her younger half-sister Isabel on the throne instead of Sybil and her husband. Forty years and more after her death, one writer depicted her as if she were a character in one of the new romances, carrying on a long-distance love affair with the nobleman Baldwin of Ramla.[5] If Sybil regarded herself in such terms, perhaps it would have been as the damsel beset by enemies who appears so often in Arthurian romance, welcoming the arrival of the brave young knight from overseas (Guy de Lusignan) to fight for her against her enemies.

Such legends highlight a problem that any study of a medieval queen must face: gender stereotypes in the primary sources. A queen's agency and active involvement in government and military affairs would have been limited by cultural expectations. Contemporary sources do not give us a full picture of women's activity. In a society where respectable women should not be a subject of public gossip, a queen's actions could be omitted from a narrative simply because it would be demeaning to her honour to mention her involvement. All narrative sources from the medieval period had a didactic and moralising as well as an informative role; those writing about the crusades and the kingdom of Jerusalem especially so because the crusades were regarded as Christ's special concern and the kingdom of Jerusalem was His kingdom. The imperative to produce a moralising discourse distorted the depiction of women, recreating them as pious virgins, faithful wives, carers or impious jezebels, with little acknowledgement of their fulfilling wider roles. In addition, each writer had their own perspective on the political disputes within the crusader states and their own views on who was to blame for the disasters of 1187. Depending on each writer's perspective, Sybil became either a faithful wife or a sly schemer, but we have to read very carefully to discover that she also took an active command role in war.[6]

Sybil's reign shows that although twelfth-century queens could have agency and wield power in their own right, not all of them did so.[7] Sybil had plenty of models to follow. Queens Urraca of Castile and Teresa of Portugal had established their authority in their kingdoms in the early twelfth century. Her grandmother Melisende had claimed the right to rule the kingdom in her own right and had opposed her husband and fought her son to enforce this right. Sybil's great-aunts Alice of Antioch, Hodierna of Tripoli, and her first cousin once removed Constance of Antioch all played active roles in government. Her aunt, Countess Sybil of Flanders, twice ruled Flanders while her husband was in the Holy Land. Her aunt-in-law Matilda of England had claimed the throne of England in her own right; although, like Sybil, she had had to contend with nobles who were unwilling to acknowledge her authority and disliked and distrusted her husband, she eventually established her son on the throne. Eleanor of Aquitaine's daughter Marie governed Champagne while first her husband, Count Henry the Liberal, and then her son, were in the Holy Land. Queen Tamar the Great of Georgia, the ancient Christian kingdom on the banks of the Black Sea, showed how successful a twelfth-century queen regnant could be. But Sybil's contemporaries and surviving charters indicate that after she had seized the throne she handed her authority over to her husband and did not attempt to rule in her own name. She confirmed her husband's actions but the evidence indicates she did not initiate policy.

This book could have considered only the period when Sybil and Guy were joint monarchs, tracing Guy's military campaigns in detail and focussing on his response to Saladin. Focussing on only Guy as king is misleading, however, as his authority rested solely on his marriage to Sybil and was challenged on her death. In addition, the problems that Sybil and Guy faced in 1186 did not originate overnight or even in the final years of King Baldwin IV's reign: they began at least as long ago as the coronation of Sybil's father. Rather than focus only on the brief period of the reign of Sybil and Guy, this

4   *Introduction*

study considers the whole of Sybil's life, tracing the development of the situation that Sybil and Guy faced on their accession to the kingdom in 1186 before considering how they attempted to face it and how far they were successful.

Notes

1. *Das Itinerarium peregrinorum: eine zeitgenössische englische Chronik zum dritten Kreuzzug in ursprünglicher Gestalt*, ed. Hans Eberhard Mayer, Schriften der Monumenta Germaniae historica (Deutsches Institut für Erforschung des Mittelalters) 18 (Stuttgart, 1962), hereafter *IP* 1, p. 266; translated as *Chronicle of the Third Crusade: A Translation of the* Itinerarium Peregrinorum et Gesta Regis Ricardi, trans. Helen J. Nicholson, Crusade Texts in Translation 3 (Aldershot, 1997), p. 39 (Bk 1 ch. 10).
2. Malcolm Barber, *The Crusader States* (New Haven and London, 2012), pp. 295–296; Kevin James Lewis, *The Counts of Tripoli and Lebanon in the Twelfth Century*, Rulers of the Latin East (Abingdon, 2017), pp. 260, 264.
3. For comparison, see the lives of her contemporaries and cousins, the daughters of King Henry II of England and Eleanor of Aquitaine: Colette Bowie, *The Daughters of Henry II and Eleanor of Aquitaine* (Turnhout, 2014); and Christine de Pizan's recommendations (written two centuries later) to a royal princess on how to bring up her children, and her own daily duties: Christine de Pisan, *The Treasure of the City of Ladies or the Book of the Three Virtues*, trans. Sarah Lawson (Harmondsworth, 1985), pp. 59–62, 66–68, 76–77, 81–85, 128–130, 133.
4. *Récits d'un ménestrel de Reims au treizième siècle*, ed. Natalis de Wailly (Paris, 1876), p. 14, note 10 (section 28).
5. *Chronique d'Ernoul et de Bernard le trésorier*, ed. L. de Mas Latrie (Paris, 1871), pp. 56–60 (ch. 7).
6. Natasha R. Hodgson, *Women, Crusading and the Holy Land in Historical Narrative* (Woodbridge, 2007); Helen J. Nicholson, 'Queen Sybil of Jerusalem as a military leader', in *Von Hamburg nach Java. Studien zur mittelalterlichen, neuen und digitalen Geschichte zu Ehren von Jürgen Sarnowsky*, ed. Jochen Burgtorf, Christian Hoffart and Sebastian Kubon (Göttingen, 2020), pp. 265–276.
7. On 'female public agency, authority, and power' in this period see now *Medieval Elite Women and the Exercise of Power, 1100–1400: Moving beyond the Exceptionalist Debate*, ed. Heather J. Tanner (Cham, 2019).

1 Who was Sybil? Family and sources

Sybil was queen of Jerusalem for no more than four years. Crowned queen in 1186, probably between 13 September and 17 October in that year, she died in late summer or early autumn 1190 during the siege of Acre in the Third Crusade, possibly just before 21 October.[1] Born between 1157 and 1161, she was no more than twenty-nine when she became queen and no older than thirty-three on her death. As the eldest daughter and oldest surviving child of King Amaury of Jerusalem she was crowned as queen in her own right.

There is very little evidence of Sybil of Jerusalem as an individual. We do not know exactly when she was born or died, or what she looked like. It is not clear exactly how many children she had: one son, and two or perhaps four daughters. We know where she was educated but not what she was taught. For much of her life there is no evidence for where she was living, who were her advisors and companions or how she spent her days. Only one letter that she wrote survives, and that only as a copy in a contemporary German writer's work. We do not have a copy of her seal after she became queen. We do not know where she was buried, or whether she left a will. We have hardly any information about how she may have thought of herself and her role as countess, as royal heiress, as mother, as wife and as queen.

With so much unknown, it is questionable whether a meaningful biography can be written. Certainly it is not possible to write an analysis of day-by-day events which probes its subject's motivations and emotions. Yet enough information survives to enable us to trace the outlines of Sybil's life, piecing together information from a range of different sources – narrative, documentary and archaeological. A few occasions of her life were well recorded by contemporaries, which tell us how her contemporaries regarded her and allow some speculation about her motives.[2]

The contemporary narrative accounts of Sybil's career illuminate her contemporaries' views of women in authority, queenship and government. More significantly, Sybil was queen of Jerusalem at one of the most momentous periods during the history of the crusader states and the kingdom of Jerusalem, and as the crowned head of the kingdom she was its figurehead in the fightback against Saladin and played a part in laying the foundations of the restored kingdom that would continue in existence for another century.

DOI: 10.4324/9781315205960-2

Sybil's cultural and family background

When Sybil came to the throne of Jerusalem in 1186 the 'crusader states' had existed for nearly ninety years, having been created during and following the First Crusade. The polities based around the cities of Antioch, Edessa, Jerusalem and Tripoli were populated by Latin Christian settlers from Europe, who sometimes referred to themselves as 'Latins' and some of whom called themselves 'Franks' and were called *frangoi* or *al-Franj* by Greek and Arabic writers respectively; and by peoples of more local origins, such as Arabs, Turks, Jews, Syrians, Greeks, Armenians and Georgians. They included people of many religions, including the Catholic Christianity of the European settlers; the Byzantine Orthodox Christianity of the Greeks; Armenian, Ethiopian, Georgian, Indian and Syrian Christians of various strands of belief; and Sunni and Shi'ite Islam including Islamic sects such as the Alawites, the Druze and the Nizāris, as well as a Jewish population. Although most of the people living in these polities were not crusaders in that they had never 'taken the cross' in a crusading vow, as polities that had their origins in the crusades and their justification in the crusader ideal, they have long been termed by scholars as 'crusader' states. While acknowledging that the term is inexact, this book will use 'crusader states' as a convenient blanket term for the counties of Edessa and Tripoli, the principality of Antioch and the kingdom of Jerusalem.[3]

The crusader states were established within a network of relations with Greek and Armenian Christians and Sunni and Shi'ite Muslims. Set up during a period of political fragmentation in the Middle East, their initial allies and supporters included both Christians and Muslims, and their leaders married local Christian noblewomen. The First Crusade of 1096–1099 had been prompted by an appeal by Alexios Komnenos, Byzantine emperor, to the West for troops to assist in recovering control over territory recently lost to the Turks: the city of Nicaea – which had passed into Turkish control around 1081 – and Antioch – taken over by Seljuk Turks in 1085.[4] In 1097 the crusaders captured and handed Nicaea over to the emperor, but in the following year they declined to hand over Antioch on the grounds that the emperor had failed to come to their assistance during the siege. Byzantium continued to claim Antioch: in 1108 its Latin ruler, Bohemond, came to an agreement with Alexios by which he would rule the city as the emperor's subject; in 1137 the Latin rulers of Edessa, Antioch and Tripoli did homage to Alexios's son and heir John; and in 1158 John's son and heir Manuel Komnenos gained full overlordship over the city and later married a Latin Antiochene princess – Maria, daughter of Princess Constance and her first husband Raymond of Poitiers, and sister of Prince Bohemond III.[5]

Having captured Antioch in 1098 the crusaders went on to seize Jerusalem, which had been conquered by Caliph Umar in 638, captured by the Sunni Seljuks from the Shi'ite Fatimid rulers of Egypt in 1073, and recaptured by the Fatimids in 1098 while the Turks were distracted by the crusaders. Also in 1098 one of the leaders of the crusaders, Baldwin of Boulogne, gained control of the Christian Armenian-ruled city of Edessa, founding the crusader county of Edessa and going on to marry an Armenian noblewoman.[6] After Baldwin became king of Jerusalem in 1100, succeeding his elder brother Godfrey de Bouillon, he chose as his successor in Edessa one Baldwin de Bourcq, who was related to Baldwin of Boulogne – although the exact relationship is now unknown.[7] When he became count of Edessa Baldwin de Bourcq married Morphia or Morfia, daughter of an Armenian nobleman named Gabriel, who was (according to Archbishop William of Tyre, writing a generation later) a Greek Orthodox Christian. Baldwin of Bourcq succeeded Baldwin of Boulogne as king of Jerusalem in 1118, and his and Morphia's eldest daughter Melisende would go on to succeed them on the throne in 1131. Melisende's younger son Amaury (Amalricus in Latin) would be Sybil's father. From the 1150s, the kingdom developed closer relations with the Byzantines. Both of Melisende's sons married Byzantine princesses and acknowledged Byzantine suzerainty over the kingdom, and in 1169 King Amaury of Jerusalem conducted a joint campaign with the Byzantine fleet against Egypt.[8]

On their mother's side, Sybil and Baldwin were related to one of the great noble families of the crusader states and France. Their mother Agnes de Courtenay was a daughter of Joscelin II de Courtenay, who had been count of Edessa before it was captured in 1144 by the Oghuz Turk Zengi (or Zankī), atabeg of Mosul and Aleppo.[9] Joscelin II's mother had been an Armenian noblewoman, sister of Leon or Levon I of Armenia, so that Sybil and Baldwin were descended from Christian Armenian nobility through both their father and their mother. Joscelin II's father, Count Joscelin I of Edessa, was a son of Joscelin lord of Courtenay in France and his wife Isabel or Elizabeth, daughter of Guy of Montlhéry; her sister Melisende was the mother of Baldwin of le Bourcq, later King Baldwin II of Jerusalem, so Count Joscelin I and King Baldwin II were cousins. Another of Joscelin's and Isabel de Montlhéry's sons, Miles, was the father or grandfather of Isabel or Elizabeth de Courtenay who in around 1150 married King Louis VII of France's youngest brother Peter, founding the Capetian line of de Courtenays – who in the thirteenth century would become Latin emperors of Constantinople.[10]

Nevertheless, despite having an Armenian Christian great-grandmother on both their father's and their mother's side of the family, Sybil's and Baldwin's origins and connections were predominantly western European. Although their exact relationship to the heroes of the First Crusade was unclear, they could claim kinship to Godfrey de Bouillon and Baldwin of Boulogne through their great-grandfather. Their paternal grandfather, Melisende's husband Count Fulk V of Anjou was, through his first wife Eremburge of Maine, also the grandfather of the first of the Angevin kings of England, Henry II (1154–1189), and of Philip of Alsace, count of Flanders (1168–1191). Sybil and Baldwin were thus closely related through their father's father to two prestigious and influential ruling families of Latin Christendom. Having said that, their contemporaries did not stress their descent from the counts of

Anjou but regarded them as the heirs of the family of Godfrey de Bouillon. During their lifetimes Godfrey came to be celebrated as a lay saint, a man of great piety whose mother Countess Ida of Boulogne had foreseen would become a king, and who was commonly believed to have been descended from a swan-maiden – although Archbishop William of Tyre dismissed the last as a '*fabula*' or fairy story.[11]

Sybil the person: personality, appearance and self-representation

Unlike her father King Amaury of Jerusalem, her younger brother King Baldwin IV, or her cousin King Henry II of England, no contemporary who saw her described Sybil's physical appearance, so we do not know whether she was (like her father) tall, overweight, with an attractive face, bright eyes, an aquiline nose and yellow hair, or (like her little brother) simply attractive for her age, or (like her cousin) of above medium height, strongly built, with freckles and blue-grey eyes.[12] We also do not know whether she shared any of her father's or brother's personality traits: whether (like her father) she spoke with a slight speech impediment (*linguam aliquantulum impeditioris*), had a sharp mind and was able to accurately recall what she had heard, enjoyed hearing about history and was always ready to argue a point, or (like her brother) was good at riding, with a tenacious memory and a sharp mind, loving conversation, thrifty, but with a stammer (*verbi impeditioris*).[13] Sybil's contemporaries scarcely ever ascribed any emotion to her: only her tears of submission when she was humbling herself before Saladin to request the release of her husband Guy after the surrender of Jerusalem early in October 1187, and her tears of joy when she met Guy after Saladin released him in early summer 1188.[14] Such tears were an appropriate emotion for a loving wife.

Although no visual depictions of Sybil survive from her lifetime, later artists imagined her appearance, indicating how later generations viewed her and her actions. The thirteenth- and early fourteenth-century artists who depicted Sybil generally showed her at only one moment of her life: her second marriage, to Guy de Lusignan, brought about by her brother Baldwin IV. The depictions suggest that the artists had little knowledge of the text and were simply illuminating a royal wedding. Sometimes Sybil stands on her brother's right (in the place of honour) and sometimes on his left with Guy on his right, but she is usually shown with her long hair loose and uncovered, as if she were an unmarried virgin rather than a widow. In one manuscript – Bibliothèque nationale de France MS Fr. 2754, produced in northern France in around 1300 – Sybil is shown with hair bound up and covered as would be appropriate for a widow, and standing on her brother's right, but in this image the figure on the king's left – presumably Guy – appears to be tonsured like a monk. The corresponding image in Walters Art Gallery MS 142, dating from the first quarter of the fourteenth century, is badly smudged but also appears to show Sybil on the right, with her hair bound up and covered, and Guy on the left, now as a layman. In this image the central figure appears to be a bishop wearing a mitre.[15]

A few artists illustrated other scenes. A Flemish manuscript of Ernoul's chronicle produced in the second quarter of the fourteenth century illustrated Sybil's authority as queen, with illuminations of the barons doing homage to Queen Sybil, Queen Sybil crowning Guy de Lusignan, and Humphrey of Toron doing homage to Queen Sybil and King Guy.[16] A sumptuously illuminated manuscript of the Old French translation and continuation of William of Tyre's chronicle dating from the 1480s included half-page images spanning both columns of text to mark the royal succession from one monarch to the next. These included the death of a king who might be the child Baldwin V alongside Sybil's coronation and her crowning of Guy de Lusignan.[17] Here Sybil was imagined as a tall, slender young woman with pale skin and long red-blonde hair, a contemporary European view of idealised female beauty; she not only receives royal authority from the patriarch but confers it on her husband.

How did Sybil depict herself? In Europe by the middle of the twelfth century one of the markers of authority was the possession of a personal seal to authenticate documents, and the imagery on that seal could indicate the image that the owner wished to project or the basis on which they claimed power and authority. French, German and Spanish royal seals were circular, single-sided and showed the monarch enthroned, with an inscription giving their name. In contrast, from the early twelfth century the monarchs of Jerusalem used a double-sided circular pendant seal, possibly in imitation of Byzantine seals. The obverse of the king's seal showed the king enthroned with his name and the words '*dei gratia rex Hierusalem*' (by the grace of God king of Jerusalem) while the reverse side depicted the three principal buildings of Jerusalem: the Holy Sepulchre, the Lord's Temple and the Tower of David, with the inscription '*civitas regis regum omnium*' (city of the king of all kings).[18] The obverse of Queen Melisende's seal differed, with no image but only the Latin inscription, echoing the seal of her mother Queen Morphia, wife of King Baldwin II, which shows on one side the head and shoulders of the Virgin Mary, Mother of God, and on the other an inscription in Greek. The seal of Queen Theodora, wife of Melisende's eldest son King Baldwin III, followed her husband and the previous kings of Jerusalem with the enthroned figure and inscription on the obverse. Regrettably Sybil's seal as queen does not survive. As in France at least at this time queens' seals were used only for private and domestic matters, and Sybil does not appear to have issued any acts in her own name alone as queen, it is possible she did not have her own royal seal.[19]

However, a reproduction of Sybil's seal as countess of Jaffa and Ascalon does survive. Affixed to a donation to the military religious Order of Mountjoy in 1177, it was circular and showed a fortified city on each side, Jaffa on one and Ascalon on the other, encircled with the inscription '*Sigillum Amal. Regis Filie*' on the obverse and '*Comtissa Iopp. et Ascale*' on the reverse ('the seal of the daughter of King Amaury, countess of Jaffa and Ascalon').

10 *Who was Sybil? Family and sources*

Its design was generally similar to seals of other secular lords of the kingdom, but those showed a mounted warrior on one side and a fortified city on the other; possibly Sybil preferred to emphasise the two centres of her authority, in addition to the fact she was the late king's daughter. Another female lord emphasised her husband's role as military commander in combination with her own authority: the seal of Juliana, lady of Caesarea, from a charter of 1207 to the Hospital of St John, shows on one side a fortified city with her name *Juliana domina Cesaree,* and on the other an armed figure on horseback wielding a lance, with long plumes on its helmet, and the name of her husband, Ademar de Leron. Sybil's and Juliana's seals were circular and double-sided like the seals of their male counterparts, perhaps reflecting Byzantine influence. In contrast many noblewomen's and queen's seals in France and England at the same period were single-sided pointed ovals or lozenge-shaped, similar to the seals of ecclesiastical officials, and showed a standing female figure, perhaps holding a bird or a flower, whereas neither Sybil's nor Juliana's seals showed a representation of their owner.[20] As no other seal of Sybil survives it is not possible to know whether she changed it as her marital status changed.[21]

Sybil in contemporary and near-contemporary eyes: the primary sources

The difficulty of establishing women's actual deeds and authority from contemporary narrative accounts, which insisted that respectable women should not hold authority or take an active role in society except in certain limited roles (typically as devoted wife or mother), is familiar to all historians who have attempted to study the history of women. The narrative commentaries on Sybil's career present modern readers with the additional problem that their gendered expectations were further filtered through the distorting lens of the complex political situation in the kingdom of Jerusalem. Those commentators who wrote after Saladin's victory at Hattin on 4 July 1187 and his capture of Jerusalem on 2 October 1187 also sought to assign blame or credit for these events and adjusted their accounts accordingly.

The main source for Sybil's life to 1185 and for the history of the kingdom of Jerusalem in the twelfth century is the history written by Archbishop William II of Tyre, who was born in Jerusalem in around 1130 and died in 1184, 1185 or 1186.[22] In a short autobiographical section of his work he explained that he had spent nearly twenty years in France (at Paris and Orleans) and Italy (at Bologna) studying first the liberal arts for ten years, then theology for six years, and finally canon and civil law. He returned to the East in 1165, where Bishop William of Acre granted him a prebend in his cathedral. In 1167, at the request of King Amaury of Jerusalem and others, Archbishop Frederick of Tyre granted William the archdeaconry of Tyre. William then worked for the king, initially as a diplomat, and in 1170 he was appointed tutor of Amaury's nine-year-old son and heir Baldwin. William claimed that he was the first to notice that Baldwin had a serious health condition, which was eventually diagnosed as leprosy. After Baldwin succeeded his father in 1174, Count Raymond III of Tripoli, who was acting as regent for the young king, appointed William as chancellor, thereby giving him access to all the documents of government – a great benefit for a historian – and in the following year he was elected archbishop of Tyre. William recorded that King Amaury had told him to write, and also that love of his native land had prompted him; he addressed his work to his fellow-prelates, his 'venerable brothers in Christ', but his work also appears to be intended to present a positive view of the kingdom of Jerusalem and its ruling family to the Latin Christians of Europe. He certainly revised his history as he went. It may be that when he attended the Third Lateran Council in 1179, he became aware of misunderstanding and misinformation about the situation in the Latin East which he wanted to correct and realised that there was a wide potential audience for his writing outside the Latin East.[23]

William's history was an enormous work of scholarship, written in excellent Latin; it would have been an admirable achievement in the eyes of his former tutors in Paris, Orléans and Bologna, and it was read and used by clerical commentators from the early thirteenth century onwards. But its size and its language meant that it was not easily accessible to a wider readership. A French version of William's history was produced by an anonymous translator, probably in France or what is now north-eastern France, in around the years 1219–1223. The French version, a translation and adaptation of William's history, was used by many other writers, and to judge from the number of surviving manuscripts it was very widely known throughout Latin Europe.[24]

It was William's interpretation of events which influenced subsequent generations down to the present day. To first appearance, his work is rational, careful and balanced. Comparison to other available sources, however – such as the work of contemporary Muslim commentators, Latin Christian commentators in Europe, contemporary letters and documentary sources – reveal that William left out some information and presented a one-sided view of some events. He was critical of the papacy and the patriarch of Antioch because the latter claimed jurisdiction over the northern dioceses of the archbishopric of Tyre (Tripoli, Tortosa and Gibelet/Jubail), while the rest of the archbishopric was subject to the patriarch of Jerusalem. As archbishop, William tried to recover control of these dioceses, but the popes supported the patriarch of Antioch. To increase William's bitterness towards the papacy, in 1181 Pope Alexander III, in an encyclical intended to rouse support for the kingdom of Jerusalem, described King Baldwin IV's illness as being due to 'the just judgement of God', implying that God had condemned Baldwin and his dynasty. William always defended the ruling dynasty of the kingdom of Jerusalem, insisting on its legitimacy and emphasising Baldwin IV's military successes to demonstrate his effectiveness as king despite his debilitating illness. Understandably, he was also favourably inclined towards Count Raymond III of Tripoli, who promoted him to chancellor. He also approved of Baldwin's grandmother, Queen Melisende, although he could have had only distant childhood memories of her and the most significant events of her reign occurred after 1145, when he would have left the East for university in Europe. Otherwise he was suspicious of female power and influence in the persons of Melisende's sister Alice, Alice's daughter Constance, and Sybil's and Baldwin IV's mother Agnes de Courtenay; and he mistrusted nobles who arrived from Europe with armies, promising to help the kingdom of Jerusalem but on their own terms. To complicate analysis still further, generations of scholars have interpreted his work with the benefit of hindsight and reached conclusions that are not necessarily supported by a careful reading of William's text.[25]

William's work was continued by various writers. A Latin version may date from the early thirteenth century and was apparently compiled by an English writer from a number of first- and second-hand commentaries in Latin and in French. It takes a positive view of Sybil and credits her with the defence of both Ascalon and Jerusalem against Saladin.[26] French continuations of the French version of William's history were also composed, in France and in the Latin East, the complete work being known as the *Estoire de Eracles empereur* ('History of the Emperor Heraclius') from its opening words. The version of this work known as the 'Colbert-Fontainebleau Continuation', named after previous owners of the manuscripts, was probably compiled in the late 1240s in Acre; it was further developed into the version known as the 'Lyon *Eracles*', so named because the sole manuscript is in Lyon, and dates from around 1250. For the events immediately after William's history ended, 1185–1187, these continuations drew on another prose history of the kingdom of Jerusalem, the so-called *Chronique d'Ernoul et de Bernard le Trésorier* (Chronicle of Ernoul and Bernard the Treasurer), which was generally hostile to Sybil and her husband Guy.[27]

The *Chronique d'Ernoul* is a French prose history compiled in the early 1230s in northern France. The section of the work covering the years 1100–1186 is completely independent of William of Tyre's history, and includes historical narrative, a geographical description of the Holy Land and a pilgrim description of Jerusalem. In the manuscripts of this text that end in 1230 the narrative of the events of 1185–1187 is credited to one Ernoul, *varlet* (literally 'lad' or male servant) of Balian of Ibelin. This account is very detailed and full of exciting incidents, in the style of an Arthurian prose romance of the period, with Balian of Ibelin as the hero, although Saladin is also depicted in a favourable light as a man of integrity and honour. Peter Edbury has argued that the section of this work covering 1185–1187 was indeed based, as claimed in the text, on an account by Ernoul written shortly after events: there is a clear change in style after 1187, and the text does not mention Balian's death in 1193, indicating that it was written while Balian was still alive. At first glance this is a very useful source for the events of 1185–1187, but it is considerably distorted in favour of Balian and his brother Baldwin, presenting them as the only men the Muslims feared and who could have saved the kingdom from Saladin and brushing over or omitting information which would damage them. Moreover, as the version of the text which survives was compiled over forty years after events, there had been plenty of opportunity for material to be adjusted with hindsight, so that the text that we have may preserve only fragments of Ernoul's original. Given that (according to the *Chronique d'Ernoul*) Sybil's coronation in 1186 thwarted the hopes of Balian and his wife Maria to make Maria's daughter Isabel queen, it is not surprising that the *Chronique d'Ernoul* depicts Sybil as capricious, ambitious, untrustworthy and failing to contribute in any way to the defence of her kingdom. Her husband Guy de Lusignan is credulous, easily persuaded to follow bad advice and ineffective.[28]

A range of Latin prose accounts of the events of 1187 written by English clerics took a different view. Roger of Howden and William of Newburgh placed blame for the disasters largely on Count Raymond III of Tripoli and his allies. Roger of Howden, Ralph of Diceto and William of Newburgh noted that Guy de Lusignan was king of Jerusalem only by right of his wife. William of Newburgh noted that many of the nobles thought him unworthy of the crown, while Roger of Howden described an attempt to make Sybil divorce Guy before she could be queen and how Sybil had outmanoeuvred it. Ralph of Coggeshall and Roger of Howden also gave Sybil credit for attempting to defend her city of Ascalon against Saladin.[29] One anonymous clerical account in particular, known as the *Libellus de expugnatione Terrae Sanctae per Saladinum*, effectively presents a sermon setting out to show that the fall of Jerusalem resulted from the sin of the Franks.[30] The anonymous Latin prose account of the years 1187–1190 known as the *Itinerarium peregrinorum* also blamed the Franks' sin for the fall of Jerusalem, specifically the cowardice of the common people in the face of Saladin's siege. The *Libellus* mentions Sybil being crowned in the coup of 1186, as the daughter of King Amaury, and that she made her husband Guy de Lusignan king, but does not mention her again. The *Itinerarium peregrinorum* does not mention the coup and depicts Sybil as the rightful heir to the kingdom (as descendant of Fulk of Anjou) who gives King Guy his title to rule, as one of the defenders of Jerusalem and as a devoted wife. This pro-Angevin stance suggests that the *Itinerarium peregrinorum* is the work of an English cleric, and its stress on the destructive effects of sin suggests that the author was in the entourage of Archbishop Baldwin of Canterbury, who was a Cistercian monk and ardent Church reformer, and took part in the Third Crusade.[31]

Italian, German and French commentators also recorded events in the crusader states during Sybil's lifetime. Some wrote contemporaneously and provide details of events, sometimes distorted, which were overlooked or missing from Archbishop William of Tyre's history. For example, Robert of Torigni, Abbot of Mont-St-Michel in Normandy, recorded that in 1171 Count Stephen of Sancerre carried to Jerusalem the money collected by King Louis VII of France to help the church of Jerusalem, a detail which Archbishop William of Tyre – implacably hostile to Count Stephen – omitted.[32]

However, many of the European commentators wrote after the Third Crusade, sometimes long after. Their interpretation of events would certainly have been influenced by the outcome of the crusade and may have been coloured by Ernoul's views of its beginnings. In Italy, Sicard of Cremona (bishop of Cremona from 1185 to 1215) was a contemporary of the events of Sybil's life but probably wrote that section of his history, which stretches from Adam to 1212, after the Third Crusade. Given his location in northern Italy, he may have had local information on matters relating to Genoa and Montferrat, such as Sybil's first husband William of Montferrat and his brother Conrad.[33] A continuation of Sigebert of Gembloux's chronicle known as the *Continuatio Aquicincta*, produced at the Benedictine abbey of Anchin in Pecquencourt in what is now north-eastern France, covered events occurring between 1149 to 1237, including some information about the crusader states not recorded elsewhere – for instance, that William of Montferrat was poisoned by knights in the Latin East (*a transmarinis militibus veneno extinguitur*) and that one of the battles during the siege of Acre (1189–1191) in late July 1190, in which the non-noble crusaders attacked Saladin's camp without the advice of the leaders of the crusade and were massacred, was instigated by one Elbertus, a priest, dean of Douai (*Duacensi decano*) '*ut relatum est nobis ab his qui interfuerunt*' (as was related to us by those who were there).[34] Writing in the late twelfth and early thirteenth century in his home town of Faenza, the cleric Tolosanus included in his chronicle particular words of praise for Sybil's first husband, describing him as handsome, virtuous, faithful to his wife and sexually abstemious. Uniquely, he called Sybil 'Beneesente', meaning 'Benevolent' or 'well-disposed' (this could feasibly have been William Longsword's pet name for his young wife), but also criticised her for choosing Guy de Lusignan as her second husband.[35] Other contemporary and near-contemporary accounts of the events of 1187 onwards mention Sybil and her affairs only in passing if at all, concentrating on her brother Baldwin IV and her second husband Guy de Lusignan.[36] The later thirteenth-century accounts offer insight into Sybil's historical legacy rather than the actual events of her life.

To put these narrative works into their own context, we should also look beyond the evidence which historians have traditionally taken as factual to literary works which modern readers would consider fictional. The story in the *Chronique d'Ernoul* of Sybil falling in love with Baldwin of Ramla and writing to him while he was in prison echoes thirteenth-century stories of the far-off princess who falls in love with the hero – or he falls in love with her.[37] Likewise, the mysterious and ominous tone of Ernoul's search through the apparently empty castle of La Fève on 1 May 1187, after the massacre of the Frankish force at the Spring of the Cresson, is very like the hero's search though the empty castle in the late twelfth or early-thirteenth century Old French verse continuation of Chrétien de Troyes' story of the Holy Grail.[38] This is not to suggest that the compiler of the *Chronique d'Ernoul* drew on romantic fiction when compiling his chronicle but that he wrote in a literary milieu in which such themes were accepted and even expected by listeners and readers so that including such stories made his work more accessible and acceptable, even if contemporaries knew that they were artistic flourishes rather than actual events.

In addition to the sources from Christian commentators, Muslim historians and commentators provide useful information. Three authors in particular are especially informative: two authors close to Saladin who accompanied him on his campaigns, 'Imād al-Dīn (his secretary) and Bahā' al-Dīn ibn Shaddād (his qadi) and Ibn al-Athīr, a historian writing in the following century in Mosul, who drew on these two authors' work as well as other sources, including his own experience: he had visited Syria in 1188–1189, after Saladin's victories. Unlike the Latin Christian sources these have no political axe to grind for or against Sybil beyond the fact that she followed a despised religion, and so they provide a disinterested view.[39]

In contrast to the plentiful if often unreliable narrative sources, few charters issued by Sybil survive.[40] As the chancery of the kingdom of Jerusalem was lost at the time of Saladin's conquest, only those documents which were kept by institutions and organisations based outside the crusader states have survived. The survivals are skewed towards documents confirming the landholdings and privileges of religious institutions, which retained these records of their rights even after it was clear that they would never be able to return to Syria or Palestine to reclaim them. There are also documents giving or confirming property that later came into the hands of religious orders, forming part of their portfolio of rights that they hoped to be able to claim at some point in the future. Although witnesses to legal documents were not necessarily part of the household of the person issuing the document, when the same individuals repeatedly appear as witnesses to a person's documents it is likely that they were regularly present in their household and were associated with them in everyday life; comparing the lists of witnesses to these charters allows us to build up a picture of those who supported and served Sybil and her relatives. During the years immediately after Saladin's conquests, the Italian communes of Genoa, Pisa and Amalfi, the city of Barcelona and some southern French cities received donations and confirmations of their properties and trading rights in the port cities of Acre, Jaffa and Tyre from both Conrad of Montferrat and Guy de Lusignan and Sybil, in order to ensure these powerful cities' support, especially their naval assistance. These endowments allow us to sketch out an impression of how Sybil and her connections built up a network of supporters.

Sybil in modern eyes

Given how little evidence survives about Sybil and what does survive is contradictory, it is not surprising that since the thirteenth century historians' views of Sybil have been largely shaped by the highly readable depictions in the *Chronique d'Ernoul* and the *Estoire de Eracles*. The strong narrative drive and dramatic content of these works made their version of events much more attractive and palatable than the drier, less dramatic Latin chronicles – quite apart from the linguistic barrier for many readers. Following Ernoul and *Eracles*, scholarship has tended to view Sybil purely in terms of her relationship with her second husband Guy, as she enabled him to come to power, and

16   *Who was Sybil? Family and sources*

has criticised her for selecting an incompetent as king when the kingdom of Jerusalem required a strong military leader.

In the early nineteenth century Joseph-François Michaud, in the second volume of his *Histoire des croisades* (1814), wrote that Sybil was accused of causing the death of her son Baldwin V (an accusation that did not appear in contemporary authors' work, although William of Newburgh accused Count Raymond III of Tripoli of poisoning the child[41]), but insisted that this accusation was unjust, reflecting an '*époque malheureuse, où de pareilles accusations étaient vraisemblables*' (unhappy time, when such accusations were believable). But he added that Sybil did not despise ruses or perfidious promises in order to get the crown, promising to separate from her husband and choose a warrior who could defend the kingdom, but then placing the crown on Guy's head. Developing 'Imād al-Dīd's account preserved in Abū Shāma's 'Book of the Two Gardens', he depicted Sybil leading a procession of widowed women before Saladin after the surrender of Jerusalem to plead for his mercy, and then mentions her presence with Guy during the siege of Acre and her death.[42]

In his long introduction to his edition of the *Itinerarium peregrinorum* (1864), William Stubbs mentioned Sybil's marriages, severely criticised her for her choice of Guy as king and mentioned that Sybil surrendered Ascalon to Saladin in return for her husband's release.[43] Stubbs regarded Sybil's choice of Guy as king as the deed of a devoted but foolish wife:

> When Sibylla bestowed the crown on her husband, she acted as a true wife, and her choice under ordinary circumstances might have been a wise one. But she must have known the prejudice against him which existed in the country, and ought either to have renounced the succession or to have accepted the responsibility of making a fresh choice. The nobles or Palestine would not submit to a French adventurer: the coronation of Guy practically sealed the fate of the colony ... Guy and Sibylla were thus little more than titular sovereigns, the great fiefs and baronies were, with one exception, opposed to them by interest and ambition.[44]

This has remained the predominant interpretation of Sybil's career. For a succession of twentieth-century historians she has been a foolish, love-struck woman who put her feelings for Guy de Lusignan above the interests of the kingdom, a romantic soul with little political sense.[45] However, for Giuseppe Ligato in his biography of Sybil, her devotion to her second husband was condonable. Her actions were sometimes reckless and questionable, but in 1187 she rose to the challenge of events and remained determined to fight alongside him to regain her kingdom, rather than taking refuge in a monastery in Europe. She was the last true queen of Jerusalem, but she lacked men of her calibre to stand at her side. Guy was weak and suggestible, whereas his wife faced the crisis square on and emerged as a figure of dignity and consistency. The question, Ligato asks, is whether Guy was worthy of his wife, rather than the other way around.[46] Alan V. Murray also observed that Sybil remained in the kingdom after Guy's capture by Saladin at Hattin 'rather than seeking safety for herself and her children in the West', indicating 'a real affection for her husband as well as a determination to maintain their rights', the basis of her later depiction as a woman both resourceful and faithful to her husband.[47]

For Christopher Tyerman, Guy de Lusignan was 'an unpopular foreigner', an 'unpopular arriviste', whom Sybil inserted inappropriately into the kingship without due thought or planning. Her actions demonstrated her wifely devotion 'but no political tact'. On the other hand, 'like her father and brother, she understood her rights, knew the law and was prepared to impose her will'. The ruling dynasty was clearly ailing and new blood was essential, yet the baronage resisted all intruders. Although this was a recent dynasty 'without any prior tradition or contemporary authority outside the practical choices of worried men in Jerusalem in 1099 and 1100', by the 1180s – at least partly due to Archbishop William of Tyre – a myth that it was an 'almost sacred dynasty' had developed, based around the heroes of the First Crusade who had become rulers of Jerusalem. In such circumstances, no western rulers or nobles could intervene, and their assistance would not have been acceptable in any case. Yet Guy's opponents in 1186 had no better policies: Count Raymond III of Tripoli's truce with Saladin left him unable to prevent Saladin encircling the crusader states.[48] Kevin Lewis's verdict on Raymond III's policies is damning: in his 'personal history of political errors' he displayed 'an astonishing lack of judgement both in battle and at court'.[49]

For medieval clerical writers, the stories that Sybil chose Guy in 1180 and refused to divorce him in 1186 would have illustrated the recent developments in canon law whereby the consent of both partners made a marriage valid, even where family or lords did not agree. Medieval secular audiences would have accepted these stories because they depicted the world as they wanted it to be, where romantic love and personal choice were essential to making a valid marriage.[50] But, Bernard Hamilton argued, in the real world Sybil was not free to follow a romantic path of her choice because as the king's sister and heiress it was the king and his advisors who chose Sybil's husband for her. She was crowned queen despite Guy's unpopularity because 'there was no real doubt … that Sibylla, as the elder daughter of King Amalric, had the best claim to the throne'.[51]

But was there no real doubt? Even though Sybil and her younger brother had been formally legitimated when their father divorced their mother, Sybil's legitimacy as heir to the throne remained questionable. Sarah Lambert has pointed out that William of Tyre never explicitly stated that Sybil was expected to succeed even though charters of the period recognised her as potential heiress, concluding that this uncertainty may have discouraged potential candidates for Sybil's hand. In 1180, when Baldwin IV arranged Sybil's marriage to Guy, it appears that Sybil was 'a potential heiress', but in 1183 Baldwin IV set Sybil and Guy aside. The problem was not the prospect of a woman succeeding to the throne but the need to exclude her husband

18 *Who was Sybil? Family and sources*

Guy. In the event, however, 'the appeal of primogeniture was ... strong enough to secure coronation for Sibylla'.[52]

Once crowned, Sybil ensured that her husband Guy became king, but – Elena Woodacre has argued – a king who ruled only by right of his wife had even greater barriers to overcome than a queen consort: he was a foreigner or was not born a king, or both, and he had to negotiate his role within the kingdom. Arguably Guy's opponents would have done better to negotiate limits on his authority and role – as was done when Count Raymond III became regent in 1185 – rather than trying to prevent his accession as king.[53]

Scholars' denunciations of Guy as an incompetent military leader were challenged by R.C. Smail, who demonstrated that contemporary depictions of Guy were influenced by political divisions within the kingdom of Jerusalem as much as by Guy's own military expertise or lack of it.[54] The accusation that Guy was an 'adventurer' from a lowly family without any previous connection to the crusades or the Holy Land has been questioned by Jonathan Riley-Smith and, more recently, by Clément de Vasselot, who have shown that the Lusignans took part in both the First and Second crusades, that Guy's father had fought the Muslims in Syria in the 1160s, and that far from lacking noble connections the Lusignans were related to Count Raymond III of Tripoli and to Prince Bohemond III of Antioch. De Vasselot has further argued that the Lusignans held land in the county of Tripoli and that Guy was in Tripoli in 1180 when his brother Aimery summoned him to Jerusalem to marry Sybil.[55]

Although Guy owed his crown to Sybil, it was Guy rather than Sybil who took the initiative in government. The contemporary Muslim historian Ibn al-Athīr recorded that Sybil handed all her power over to Guy.[56] Scholars have argued that because of the constant danger of invasion, the primary role of the ruler of the kingdom of Jerusalem had to be leading the kingdom's military forces in war. As this was (they argue) a purely male function, female heirs did not rule in person, but 'as transmitters of royal blood and kingworthiness' (in the words of Deborah Gerish) they could pass on royal power to a man, acting as regents for their sons or brothers or legitimising their husband's power. They could wield influence but could not exercise power directly in their own name.[57]

This argument would explain why Sybil handed her power to Guy, but against it is the fact that Christian queens and noblewomen of the twelfth century had ruled in their own right and acted as military leaders in the crusader states, in the Iberian Peninsula (also on the frontier of Christendom) and elsewhere. Queen Teresa of Portugal, for example, ruled alone from 1112 to her death in 1128. She was an illegitimate daughter of King Alfonso VI of León-Castile, who arranged her marriage to Henry of Burgundy and endowed the couple with the county of Portugal. After Henry's death in 1112 Teresa continued to rule Portugal by her right as daughter of Alfonso VI. She initially entitled herself 'infanta', but by 1116 was calling herself 'queen', and the title was also used of her by outsiders. Although she had a son who was her heir, she did not rule as his regent but in her own name; as by Visigothic legal tradition daughters inherited equally with sons, and noble daughters who were sole heirs could rule. The clerical author of the *Chronicon Adefonsi Imperatoris*, looking back at Teresa's reign, recorded that even though she was illegitimate King Alfonso VI had particularly loved her mother and this was why he had favoured Teresa; and that she had been acclaimed queen by the Portuguese, thus legitimating her position. As she had been legitimate queen, her son and heir Afonso Henriques was legitimate king.[58]

Teresa's sister Urraca, only legitimate surviving heir of King Alfonso VI, had inherited the throne of León-Castile on their father's death in 1109. She ruled as queen, by her right as her father's daughter and acknowledged heir. The later Muslim historian Ibn al-Kardabus described her as a leader of armies in her wars against her husband Alfonso I of Aragon and against her rebellious magnates. Like Teresa, even though she had a legitimate son and heir from her first marriage, she did not present herself as his regent but as queen in her own right. That said, her position appears to have been strengthened after she established her son Alfonso as her heir. For both Teresa and Urraca their position as daughters of the king was reinforced through their successful military leadership: they defeated their enemies on the battlefield and used their patronage tactically to make allies whose interests lay in maintaining their power.[59]

Urraca and Teresa were not alone among contemporary noblewomen in exercising a military command role. Matilda of Canossa, who inherited her lordship as her father's only surviving heir, was an effective military leader in her wars in support of papal reform and against the western emperors from the 1070s until 1114.[60] Sybil's paternal aunt and namesake, Countess Sybil of Flanders, led military action against Count Baldwin of Hainaut after he invaded Flanders while Sybil's husband Count Thierry was absent on the Second Crusade.[61]

In contrast, Matilda of England was unsuccessful in claiming her right as her father's sole surviving legitimate heir to be queen regnant of England. Although she had been a successful empress to Emperor Henry IV, won over some leading nobles of England to support her, and won a significant military victory at Lincoln in 1141, she failed to convince sufficient lay and ecclesiastical leaders of the realm that their interests lay with her rather than her cousin Stephen of Blois, whose claim to the throne was arguably weaker but who had moved more quickly to seize the throne. On the other hand, she eventually persuaded the political class of England to support the claim of her eldest son Henry as king of England and herself as his representative.[62]

In the crusader states, Sybil's grandmother Melisende had – after an initial struggle to establish her authority – governed equally with her husband Fulk of Anjou in her right as legitimate heir of King Baldwin II of Jerusalem. On Fulk's death she continued to rule, now alongside her eldest son Baldwin. She also commanded military action in defence of her realm. When Baldwin came of age he expected his mother to step aside, which she agreed to do after a brief civil war: Baldwin became sole ruler, but his mother retained control of her own territories and continued to hold considerable influence in the

20 *Who was Sybil? Family and sources*

kingdom.[63] Melisende's younger sister Alice, who was married to Prince Bohemond II of Antioch, on her husband's death in 1130 unsuccessfully tried to establish control over the principality, and in 1135–1136 took control of Antioch with Melisende's assistance. Alice may have led military raids, and may have made diplomatic approaches to a neighbouring Muslim ruler. She claimed authority both as daughter of King Baldwin II and widow of Prince Bohemond. Alice's and Melisende's younger sister Hodierna played an active role in government alongside Melisende and their niece Sybil, countess of Flanders (daughter of Melisende's husband Fulk by his first wife Eremburge), bringing about the appointment of Amaury of Nesle as Patriarch of Jerusalem in 1157, and on her husband's death in 1152 she acted as regent of the county of Tripoli. After being widowed of her first husband, Alice's daughter Constance of Antioch chose her own second husband – rejecting those suggested by her cousin Baldwin III, king of Jerusalem – and after he was captured by the ruler of Aleppo she made a marriage alliance between her daughter and the Byzantine Emperor Manuel Komnenos. Like her aunt Melisende, Constance initially refused to hand over authority to her son when he came of age and only did so at last as part of a settlement with Emperor Manuel.[64]

Sybil's contemporary, Queen Tamar of the Christian kingdom of Georgia (queen 1184–1213), ruled as her father's legitimate heir. The kings of Georgia had modelled themselves on Byzantine rulers, but that did not fit Tamar's case as Byzantium had no fixed tradition of female rulership: as in Latin Christian Europe, idealised feminine virtues were passive and subservient rather than active. Nevertheless, Tamar does not appear to have had any more difficulty in establishing her authority than a male ruler would have done. Although she married – twice – her husband's role was to lead the army, not to wield power; Tamar alone ruled. Tamar depicted herself and was depicted as her father Giorgi III's heir, and she was associated with female saints, particularly the national saint St Nino who converted Georgia to Christianity.[65] During the first half of the thirteenth century there were many examples of women holding positions of power and authority in Georgia, Armenia and in Muslim cities of the Middle East as patrons, builders and regents – but these are beyond the period under discussion here.[66]

These examples show that in twelfth-century Christendom women could legitimately hold authority in their own name and their subjects accepted them as rulers when they were convinced that their authority was legitimate, generally because they were acknowledged as their father's legitimate heir.[67] The argument that women could not act as rulers because they could not be military leaders overlooks that fact that noblewomen did act as military leaders, even if they did not wield arms themselves in the battlefield. Comparing these examples to Sybil, we see that she was crowned as her father's legitimate heir, but she was only partially successful in convincing her subjects to accept her authority. This was partly due to their attitude towards her husband but also to her wider circumstances: the state of the crusader kingdom of

Jerusalem and the wider context of Saladin's conquests and the attitude of the rulers of Latin Christian Europe.

To trace these circumstances, this study begins with Sybil's childhood and follows her life chronologically to the crisis years of 1186–1187 and the Third Crusade. As the events of these years have been thoroughly explored by scholars, rather than completely reworking the ground the present study will take as read the current state of scholarship on many of the issues, discussing them only insofar as is necessary to understand Sybil's career. Its focus will be on Sybil's situation and experiences, focussing on the events and challenges which would have affected her in the crusader states and beyond.

Notes

1 Thomas Vogtherr, 'Die Regierungsdaten der lateinischen Könige von Jerusalem', *Zeitschrift des Deutschen Palästina-Vereins (1953–)*, 110.1 (1994), 51–81, at 68–69.
2 For discussion of a similar case and one of Sybil's female relatives, see Marjorie Chibnall, 'The Empress Matilda as a Subject for Biography', in *Writing Medieval Biography 750–1250: Essays in Honour of Professor Frank Barlow*, ed. David Bates, Julia Crick and Sarah Hamilton (Woodbridge, 2006), pp. 185–194, esp. p. 194.
3 For a discussion of this term see Andrew Buck, 'Settlement, Identity, and Memory in the Latin East: An Examination of the Term "Crusader States"', *English Historical Review*, 135/573 (2020), 271–302. For the various different religious groups in the region see also, for example, Bernard Hamilton and Andrew Jotischky, *Latin and Greek Monasticism in the Crusader States* (Cambridge, 2020), pp. 284, 353; Bernard Hamilton, *The Latin Church in the Crusader States: The Secular Church* (London, 1980), pp. 188–211, 350–351, 363; Lewis, *Counts of Tripoli*, pp. 2, 130–135; Christopher MacEvitt, *The Crusades and the Christian World of the East: Rough Tolerance* (Philadelphia, 2008); Eichanan Reiner, 'Jews in the Crusader Kingdom of Jerusalem', in *Knights of the Holy Land: The Crusader Kingdom of Jerusalem*, ed. Silvia Rozenberg (Jerusalem, 1999), pp. 48–59; Sylvia Schein, 'Between East and West: The Jews in the Latin Kingdom of Jerusalem 1099–1291', in *East and West in the Crusader States: Context, Contacts, Confrontations: Acta of the Congress Held at Hernen Castile in May 1993*, ed. Krijnie N. Ciggaar, Adelbert Davids and Herman G. Teule, Orientalia Lovaniensia analecta 75 (Leuven, 1996), pp. 31–37; Mamuka Tsurtsumia, 'Commemorations of crusaders in the manuscripts of the Monastery of the Holy Cross in Jerusalem', *Journal of Medieval History*, 38.3 (2012), 318–334.
4 Peter Frankopan, *The First Crusade: The Call from the East* (London, 2012), pp. 48–51.
5 Thomas S. Asbridge, *The Creation of the Principality of Antioch 1098–1130* (Woodbridge, 2000), pp. 92–103; Andrew D. Buck, *The Principality of Antioch and its Frontiers in the Twelfth Century* (Woodbridge, 2017), pp. 189–214; Lewis, *Counts of Tripoli*, pp. 140–142; Jonathan Harris, *Byzantium and the Crusades*, 2nd edn (London, 2014), pp. 86–93, 112–115.
6 Susan B. Edgington, *Baldwin I of Jerusalem, 1100–1118*, Rulers of the Latin East (Abingdon, 2019), pp. 38–48. Her name was possibly Arda, but this seems to be a later invention: p. 47. For a wider discussion of intermarriage between the

22 Who was Sybil? Family and sources

Frankish and the Cilician Armenian nobility see Natasha Hodgson, 'Conflict and Cohabitation: Marriage and Diplomacy between Latins and Cilician Armenians, c. 1097–1253', in *The Crusades and the Near East: Cultural Histories*, ed. Conor Kostick (Abingdon, 2011), pp. 83–106.

7 Edgington, *Baldwin I*, pp. 69–70, 74–75 note 32; Alan V. Murray, *The Crusader Kingdom of Jerusalem: A Dynastic History 1099–1125* (Oxford, 2000), pp. 120–123, 171–175, 185–186.

8 Bernard Hamilton, 'Women in the Crusader States: the queens of Jerusalem, 1100–1190', in *Medieval Women*, ed. Derek Baker, Studies in Church History Subsidia 1 (Oxford, 1978), pp. 143–174, at pp. 147, 157–159, 161–163; on Morphia see WT 1: 482 (Bk 10 ch. 23); Harris, *Byzantium and the Crusades*, pp. 115–118.

9 *The Chronicle of Robert of Torigni, Abbot of the Monastery of St Michael-in-peril-of-the-sea*, in *Chronicles of the Reigns of Stephen, Henry II, and Richard I*, ed. Richard Howlett, Rolls Series 82, vol. 4 (London, 1889), p. 194.

10 WT 2: 635 (Bk 14 ch. 3); T. S. R. Boase, 'The History of the Kingdom', in *The Cilician Kingdom of Armenia*, ed. T. S. R. Boase (Edinburgh and London, 1978), pp. 1–33, at p. 9, and Appendix, p. 186; Bernard Hamilton, 'The Titular Nobility of the Latin East: the Case of Agnes of Courtenay', in *Crusade and Settlement. Papers read at the First Conference of the Society for the Study of the Crusades and the Latin East and presented to R. C. Smail*, Peter W. Edbury (Cardiff, 1985), pp. 197–203, at pp. 197–198; John L. LaMonte, 'The Lords of Le Puiset on the Crusades', *Speculum*, 17.1 (1942), 100–118, at facing page 101; MacEvitt, *The Crusades and the Christian World of the East*, pp. 77–78, 202 note 14; Jonathan Riley-Smith, *The First Crusaders 1095–1131* (Cambridge, 1997), pp. 171–172, 248; Nicholas Vincent, 'Isabella of Angoulême: John's Jezebel', in *King John: New Interpretations*, ed. S. D. Church (Woodbridge, 1999), pp. 165–219, at pp. 175, 177, 180, 201–202. Agnes and her brother Joscelin III de Courtenay had a younger sister named Isabel whom in 1142 their father gave as a hostage to Emperor John Komnenos (WT 2: 701, Bk 15 ch. 30). Some scholars report that she married Thoros II of Armenia (died 1168), but see Boase, 'The History of the Kingdom', p. 12.

11 WT 1: 425–427, at p. 427 (Bk 9 chs 5–6); Simon John, *Godfrey of Bouillon: Duke of Lower Lotharingia, Ruler of Latin Jerusalem, c. 1060–1100*, Rulers of the Latin East (Abingdon, 2018), pp. 232–235.

12 WT 2: 867, 962 (Bk 19 ch. 3, Bk 21 ch. 1); Barber, *Crusader States*, p. 234; W. L. Warren, *Henry II* (London, 1973), pp. 78–79, 207–208.

13 WT 2: 865–868, 962 (Bk 19 chs 2–3, Bk 21 ch. 1), quotations at pp. 865, 962.

14 'Imād al-Dīn al-Isfahānī, *Conquête de la Syrie et de la Palestine par Saladin (al-Fatḥ al-qussî fî l-fatḥ al-qudsî)*, translated by Henri Massé, Documents relatifs à l'histoire des Croisades 10 (Paris, 1972), hereafter 'Imād, p. 106; *IP* 1, p. 268 (Bk 1 ch. 11).

15 Paris, Bibliothèque nationale de France MS Fr. 2628 fol. 230v (Acre, circa 1260s and circa 1280); Paris, Bibliothèque nationale de France, MS Fr. 779 (circa 1275) fol. 229; Boulogne-sur-Mer, Bibliotheque municipale, MS 142, fol. 264v (dates from 1280s); Paris, Bibliothèque nationale de France MS Fr. 2754 fol. 136v (northern France, circa 1300); Baltimore, Walters Art Gallery MS 142 fol. 222r (northern France, first quarter of the fourteenth century). For details of these manuscripts see Jaroslav Folda, 'Manuscripts of the *History of Outremer* by William of Tyre: a Handlist', *Scriptorium*, 27.1 (1973), 90–95; Sarah Lambert, 'Images of Queen Melisende', in *Authority and Gender in Medieval and Renaissance*

Chronicles, ed. Juliana Dresvina and Nicholas Sparks (Newcastle Upon Tyne, 2012), pp. 140–164.
16 Camille Gaspar and Frédéric Lyria, *Les principaux manuscrits á peintures de la Bibliothèque royale de Belgique: première partie* (Paris, 1937, repr. Brussels, 1984), pp. 245–246, describing Brussels, Bibliothèque Royale, MS 11142, fols 36v, 37v, 38; Folda, 'Manuscripts', 93.
17 Geneva, Bibliothèque de Genève, MS fr. 85, fol. 217r: online at accessed 2 March 2021), dating from around 1460–1465; Folda, 'Manuscripts', 93.
18 Robert Kool, 'Civitas regis regvm omnivm: Inventing a royal seal in Jerusalem, 1100–1118', in *Crusading and Archaeology: Some Archaeological Approaches to the Crusades*, ed. Vardit R. Shotten-Hallel and Rosie Weetch, Crusades Subsidia 14 (Abingdon, 2020), pp. 245–262, at pp. 250–251, 253.
19 Hans Eberhard Mayer and Claudia Sode, *Die Siegel der lateinischen Könige von Jerusalem*, Monumenta Germaniae Historica, Schriften, 66 (Wiesbaden, 2014), especially pp. 88–90, 92–94, 104–108, 151–153, images 20, 22, 29, 58; Brigitte Bedos Rezak, 'Women, Seals, and Power in Medieval France, 1150–1350', in *Women and Power in the Middle Ages*, ed. Mary Erler and Maryanne Kowaleski (Athens, GA, 1988), pp. 61–82, at p. 64.
20 Mayer and Sode, *Die Siegel*, pp. 151–153, images 58, 69a; Hans Eberhard Mayer, *Das Siegelwesen in den Kreuzfahrerstaaten* (Munich, 1978), pp. 43, 44 and Tafel 3 and 4, esp. nos 23, 25 (from *Codice diplomatico del Sacro Militare Ordine Gerosolimitano*, ed. Sebastiano Paoli, 2 vols (Lucca, 1733–1737), 1: 63, 94–95, Table IV, seals nos 37, 45); Bedos Rezak, 'Women, Seals, and Power', pp. 64, 69–70, 74; Susan M. Johns, *Noblewomen, Aristocracy and Power in the twelfth-century Anglo-Norman Realm* (Manchester, 2003), pp. 127, 203–230; Ralph V. Turner, *Eleanor of Aquitaine* (New Haven and London, 2009), plate 13 (Eleanor of Aquitaine, seal of 1199–1200); *Earldom of Gloucester Charters: The Charters and Scribes of the Earls and Countesses of Gloucester to A.D. 1217*, ed. Robert B. Patterson (Oxford, 1973), pp. 24–25, plate XXXI c and d (Countesses Hawisia and Isabel of Gloucester, seals dating from 1183–1217). The fact that Sybil and Juliana held military fiefs and owed military service does not explain why the design of their seals was like a male lord's seal rather than a woman's seal in western Europe, because the noblewomen in the west with oval seals would also have owed military service for their land.
21 Sybil may or may not have changed her seal in response to her changing status. Throughout her three marriages and widowhood, Countess Isabel of Gloucester (d. 1217) never changed the design of her seal: *Earldom of Gloucester Charters*, p. 24; Johns, *Noblewomen*, p. 132).
22 *Willelmi Tyrensis Archiepiscopi Chronicon/ Guillaume de Tyr, Chronique*, ed. R. B. C. Huygens, 2 vols, Corpus Christianorum Continuatio Mediaeualis 63, 63A (Turnhout, 1986), hereafter WT; Peter W. Edbury and John Rowe, *William of Tyre: Historian of the Latin East* (Cambridge, 1988), p. 22; Bernard Hamilton, *The Leper King and his Heirs: Baldwin IV and the Crusader Kingdom of Jerusalem* (Cambridge, 2000), pp. 199–201; Philip Handyside, *The Old French William of Tyre*, The Medieval Mediterranean 103 (Leiden, 2015), p. 6.
23 Edbury and Rowe, *William of Tyre*, pp. 15–20, 24–29; Hamilton, *Leper King*, pp. 27–28; WT 2: 879–882 (Bk 19 ch. 20).
24 Edbury and Rowe, *William of Tyre*, pp. 3–5; Handyside, *The Old French William of Tyre*, pp. 7, 119; R. H. C. Davis, 'William of Tyre', in *Relations between East and West in the Middle Ages*, ed. Derek Baker (Edinburgh, 1973), pp. 64–76, at p. 71.

24 *Who was Sybil? Family and sources*

25 Edbury and Rowe, *William of Tyre*, pp. 17–18, 29–30, 63, 65, 77, 80–84, 116–123, 128, 173; Peter W. Edbury, 'Propaganda and Faction in the Kingdom of Jerusalem: The Background to Hattin', in *Crusaders and Muslims in Twelfth-Century Syria*, ed. M. Shatzmiller (Leiden, 1993), pp. 173–189, at pp. 183–184; Alan V. Murray, 'Constance, Princess of Antioch (1130–1164): Ancestry, Marriages and Family', *Anglo-Norman Studies XXXVIII: Proceedings of the Battle Conference 2015*, ed. Elisabeth van Houts (Woodbridge, 2016), pp. 81–95; Thomas Asbridge, 'Alice of Antioch: a case study of female power in the twelfth century', in *The Experience of Crusading, Volume Two: Defining the Crusader Kingdom*, ed. Peter Edbury and Jonathan Phillips (Cambridge, 2003), pp. 29–47.

26 James H. Kane, 'Between Parson and Poet: A re-Examination of the Latin Continuation of William of Tyre', *Journal of Medieval History*, 44.1 (2018), 56–82; *Die lateinische Fortsetzung Wilhelms von Tyrus*, ed. Marianne Salloch (Leipzig, 1934), hereafter *LFWT*, pp. 74, 75, 78, 89–90 (Bk 1, chs 15, 16, Bk 2 chs 1, 9).

27 Peter Edbury, 'Ernoul, *Eracles*, and the Beginnings of Frankish Rule in Cyprus, 1191–1232', in *Medieval Cyprus: A Place of Cultural Encounter*, ed. Sabine Rogge and Michael Grünbart, Schriften des Instituts für Interdisziplinäre Zypern-Studien, 11 (Münster, 2015), pp. 29–51, at pp. 30, 33–35; Peter W. Edbury, 'Ernoul, *Eracles*, and the Collapse of the Kingdom of Jerusalem', in *The French of Outremer: communities and communications in the Crusading Mediterranean*, ed. Laura K. Morreale and Nicholas L. Paul (New York, 2018), pp. 44–67, at pp. 45, 56, 62; 'L'Estoire de Eracles Empereur et la Conqueste de la Terre d'Outremer', in *Recueil des historiens des croisades, Historiens occidentaux*, vol. 2 (Paris, 1859); *La Continuation de Guillaume de Tyr 1184–1197*, ed. Margaret Ruth Morgan, Documents relatifs à l'histoire des Croisades 14 (Paris, 1982).

28 *Chronique d'Ernoul*, p. 149 (ch. 12); John Gillingham, 'Roger of Howden on Crusade', in *Medieval Historical Writing in the Christian and Islamic Worlds*, ed. David O. Morgan (London, 1982), pp. 60–75, at pp. 72–73 note 33; Edbury, 'Ernoul, *Eracles*, and the Beginnings of Frankish Rule in Cyprus', pp. 31–33; Edbury, 'Ernoul, *Eracles*, and the Collapse of the Kingdom of Jerusalem'; Edbury, 'Propaganda and Faction', pp. 184–188; James H. Kane, 'Wolf's Hair, Exposed Digits, and Muslim Holy Men: *The Libellus de expugnatione Terrae Sanctae per Saladinum* and the *Conte* of Ernoul', *Viator*, 47.2 (2016), 95–112, at pp. 99, 109–110.

29 Ralph of Diceto, 'Ymagines historiarum', in *Radulfi de Diceto Decani Lundoniensis opera historica: The Historical Works of Master Ralph de Diceto, Dean of London*, ed. William Stubbs, Rolls Series 68 (London, 1876), 1: 291–440, 2: 3–174, at 2: 47; *Radulphi de Coggeshall Chronicon Anglicanum et alia*, ed. Joseph Stevenson, Rolls Series 66 (London, 1873), pp. 21–22; [Roger of Howden] *Gesta regis Henrici secundi: The Chronicle of the Reigns of Henry II and Richard I, A.D. 1169–1192*, ed. William Stubbs, 2 vols, Rolls Series 49 (London, 1867), 1: 358–360, 2: 93; Roger of Howden, *Chronica*, ed. William Stubbs, Rolls Series 51, 4 vols (London, 1868–1871), 2: 315–316, 3: 20; William of Newburgh, *Historia rerum anglicarum*, in *Chronicles of the Reigns of Stephen, Henry II and Richard I*, ed. Richard Howlett, Rolls Series 82 (London, 1884–1889), 1: 255–259 (Bk 3 chs 16–17).

30 Kane, 'Wolf's Hair', pp. 111–112; 'Libellus de expugnatione Terrae Sanctae per Saladinum', in *The Conquest of the Holy Land by Ṣalāḥ al-Dīn: A Critical Edition and Translation of the Anonymous Libellus de expugnatione terre sancte per*

Saladinum, ed. and trans. Keagan Brewer and James H. Kane, Crusade Texts in Translation (London, 2019). The author of this part of the work may have been a resident of the kingdom of Jerusalem, or from Europe: pp. 9–10.

31 'Libellus', pp. 108–111 (ch. I); *IP* 1, pp. 264, 266, 268, 335–336; *Itinerarium peregrinorum et gesta regis Ricardi, auctore, ut videtur, Ricardo, canonico Sanctæ Trinitatis Londoniensis*, ed. William Stubbs, vol. 1 of *Chronicles and Memorials of the Reign of Richard I*. Rolls Series 38 (London, 1864), pp. 1–450, hereafter *IP* 2, at pp. 21, 23, 25, 95–97 (Bk 1 chs 9, 10, 11, 45–46). For a discussion of the authorship of *IP* 1: Hannes Möhring, 'Joseph Iscanus, Neffe Balduins von Canterbury, und eine anonyme englische Chronik des Dritten Kreuzzugs: Versuch einer Identifikation', *Mittellateinisches Jahrbuch*, 19 (1984), 184–190; Helen J. Nicholson, 'The Construction of a Primary Source. The Creation of *Itinerarium Peregrinorum* 1', *Cahiers de recherches médiévales et humanistes / Journal of Medieval and Humanistic Studies*, 37 (2019), 143–165. On Archbishop Baldwin: Christopher Holdsworth, 'Baldwin [Baldwin of Forde] (c. 1125–1190), archbishop of Canterbury', in *Oxford Dictionary of National Biography*, ed. H. C. G. Matthew and Brian Harrison, 60 vols (Oxford: Oxford University Press, 2004), 3: 442–445.

32 *The Chronicle of Robert of Torigni, Abbot of the Monastery of St Michael-in-peril-of-the-sea*, in *Chronicles of the Reigns of Stephen, Henry II, and Richard I*, ed. Richard Howlett, Rolls Series 82, vol. 4 (London, 1889), p. 249.

33 Florian Hartmann, 'Sicard of Cremona [Sicardus episcopus Cremonensis]', in *Encyclopedia of the Medieval Chronicle*, ed. Graeme Dunphy (Leiden, 2010), 2: 1357.

34 'Continuatio Aquicinctina', ed. D. L. C. Bethmann, in *MGH SS*, 6, ed. Georg Heinrich Pertz (Hanover, 1844), pp. 405–438, at p. 415.

35 *Magistri Tolosani Chronicon Faventinum [AA. 20 av. C.-1236]*, ed. Giuseppe Rossini, Rerum Italicarum Scriptores: Raccolta degli Storici Italiani dal cinquecento al millecinquecento, ed. L. A. Muratori, new rev'd edn ed. Giosue Carducci, Vittorio Fiorini and Pietro Fedele, 28.1 (Bologna, 1936), pp. 104–105; Florian Hartmann, 'Tolosanus', in *Encyclopedia of the Medieval Chronicle*, ed. Graeme Dunphy (Leiden, 2010), 2: 1430–1431.

36 'Versus ex libro magistri Ricardi canonici Sancti Victoris Parisiensis', in '*Ein zeitgenössisches Gedicht auf die Belagerung Accons*', ed. Hans Prutz, *Forschungen zur deutschen Geschichte*, 21 (1881), 449–494; 'Monachi Florentini Acconensis Episcopi de recuperatione Ptolemaidæ Liber', in Roger of Howden, *Chronica*, ed. W. Stubbs, 4 vols, Rolls Series 51 (London, 1868–1871), 3: cvi–cxxvi; *L'Estoire de la Guerre Sainte*, ed. Catherine Croizy-Naquet. Classiques français du Moyen Âge 174 (Paris, 2014); *The History of the Holy War: Ambroise's* Estoire de la Guerre Sainte, ed. and trans. Marianne Ailes and Malcolm Barber, 2 vols (Woodbridge, 2003).

37 For instance, the story of Queen Candace of Ethiopia and King Alexander: summary in Julia Rubanovich, 'Re-writing the episode of Alexander and Candace in medieval Persian literature: patterns, sources, and motif transformation' in *Alexander the Great in the Middle Ages: Transcultural Perspectives*, ed. Markus Stock (Toronto, 2015), pp. 123–152, at p. 124; on the romance theme of the love letter sent by the far-off princess see also the discussion in Helen J. Nicholson, '"La roine preude femme et bonne dame": Queen Sybil of Jerusalem (1186–1190) in History and Legend, 1186–1300', *The Haskins Society Journal*, 15 (2004), 110–124, at 114–115.

26 Who was Sybil? Family and sources

38 *Chronique d'Ernoul*, pp. 56–59, 149–151 (chs 7, 12); for the hero searching the empty castle and eventually finding a wounded knight see *The Continuations of the Old French Perceval of Chretien de Troyes*, vol. 1: *The First Continuation. Redaction of Mss T V D*, ed. William Roach (Philadelphia, 1965), lines 14440–14565.

39 [Bahā' al-Dīn ibn Shaddād], *The Rare and Excellent History of Saladin or al-Nawādir al-Sulṭāniyya wa'l-Maḥāsin al-Yūsufiyya by Bahā' al-Dīn Ibn Shaddād*, translated by D. S. Richards. Crusade Texts in Translation 7 (Aldershot, 2002), hereafter BD; 'Imād; *The Chronicle of Ibn al-Athīr for the Crusading Period from al-Kāmil fī'l-ta'rīkh*, translated by D. S. Richards, 3 vols, Crusade Texts in Translation 13, 15, 17 (Farnham, 2005–2008), part 1, *The Years 491–541/1097–1146: The Coming of the Franks and the Muslim Response*, p. 1 (on his travels); part 2: *The Years 541–589/1146–1193: The Age of Nur al-Din and Saladin*, hereafter IA (on Saladin's conquests).

40 On what little is known about Sybil's charters see Hans Eberhard Mayer, *Die Kanzlei der lateinischen Könige von Jerusalem*, 2 vols, Monumenta Germaniae Historica Schriften, 40 (Hanover, 1996), 2: 375–385.

41 William of Newburgh, 1: 255 (Bk 3 ch. 16).

42 Joseph-François Michaud, *Histoire des Croisades séconde partie, contenant l'histoire des seconde et troisième croisades, deuxième volume* (Paris, 1814), pp. 269–270, 304, 363, 378.

43 William Stubbs, 'Introduction' in *IP* 2, pp. i–cxl, at pp. xcviii note 1, ciii–cvi; *Radulphi de Coggeshall Chronicon Anglicanum*, pp. 21–22; Roger of Howden, *Gesta*, 2: 93; Roger of Howden, *Chronica*, 3: 20.

44 Stubbs, 'Introduction', p. cv.

45 Discussion of the opinions of René Grousset, Régine Pernoud and Pierre Aubé respectively in Giuseppe Ligato, *Sibilla regina crociata: guerra, amore e diplomazia per il trono di Gerusalemme* (Milan, 2005), p. 2; Jonathan Riley-Smith, *The Feudal Nobility and the Kingdom of Jerusalem 1174–1277* (London 1973), pp. 105–106; Régine Pernoud, *La femme au temps des Croisades* (Paris, 1990), pp. 147–148, 153.

46 Ligato, *Sibilla regina crociata*, pp. 246–248.

47 Alan V. Murray, 'Women in the Royal Succession of the Latin Kingdom of Jerusalem (1099–1291)', in *Mächtige Frauen? Königinnen und Fürstinnen im europäischen Mittelalter (11.–14. Jahrhundert)*, ed. Claudia Zey, Vorträge und Forschungen 81 (Ostfildern, 2015), pp. 131–162, at p. 151.

48 Christopher Tyerman, *God's War: A New History of the Crusades* (London, 2006), pp. 208–210, 354, 364–365.

49 Lewis, *Counts of Tripoli*, pp. 260, 275.

50 See the discussion by John Gillingham, 'Love, Marriage and Politics in the Twelfth Century', *Forum for Modern Language Studies*, 25 (1989), pp. 292–303.

51 Hamilton, 'Women in the Crusader States', pp. 166, 171 (quotations); Hamilton, *Leper King*, pp. 150–155, 218, 220, 240.

52 Hans Eberhard Mayer, 'Die Legitimität Balduins IV. von Jerusalem und das Testament der Agnes von Courtenay', *Historisches Jahrbuch*, 108 (1988), 63–89; Sarah Lambert, 'Queen or Consort: Rulership and Politics in the Latin East, 1118–1228', in *Queens and Queenship in Medieval Europe: Proceedings of a Conference held at King's College London, April 1995*, ed. Anne J. Duggan (London, 1997), pp. 153–169, quotations at pp. 159, 162.

53 Elena Woodacre, 'Questionable Authority: Female Sovereigns and their Consorts in Medieval and Renaissance Chronicles', in *Authority and Gender in Medieval and Renaissance Chronicles*, ed. Juliana Dresvina and Nicholas Sparks (Newcastle Upon Tyne, 2012), pp. 376–406, at pp. 395–398, quotation p. 396.
54 R.C. Smail, 'The Predicaments of Guy of Lusignan, 1183–87', in *Outremer: Studies in the History of the Crusading Kingdom of Jerusalem presented to Joshua Prawer*, ed. Benjamin Z. Kedar, Hans Eberhard Mayer and R. C. Smail (Jerusalem, 1982), pp. 159–176.
55 Jonathan Riley-Smith, 'The Crusading Heritage of Guy and Aimery of Lusignan', in *Cyprus and the Crusades: Papers given at the International Conference 'Cyprus and the Crusades', Nicosia, 6–9 September, 1994*, ed. N. Coureas and J. Riley-Smith (Nicosia, 1995), pp. 31–45; Clément de Vasselot, 'L'Ascension des Lusignan: les réseaux d'une famille seigneuriale (Xe–XIIe siècle), *Cahiers de civilisation médiévale*, 58 (2015), 123–137; Clément de Vasselot de Régné, 'A Crusader Lineage from Spain to the Throne of Jerusalem: The Lusignans', *Crusades*, 16 (2017), 95–114, at 101, 103–105.
56 IA, p. 316 (vol. 11.527).
57 Deborah Gerish, 'Holy War, Royal Wives, and Equivocation in Twelfth-Century Jerusalem', in *Noble Ideals and Bloody Realities: Warfare in the Middle Ages*, ed. Niall Christie and Maya Yazigi, History of Warfare 37 (Leiden, 2006), pp. 119–144, at p. 137; Deborah Gerish, 'Royal Daughters of Jerusalem and the demands of holy war', *Leidschrift: Historisch Tijdschrift*, 27.3 (2012), 89–112; Sarah Lambert, 'Queen or Consort: Rulership and Politics in the Latin East, 1118–1228', in *Queens and Queenship in Medieval Europe: Proceedings of a Conference held at King's College London, April 1995*, ed. Anne J. Duggan (London, 1997), pp. 153–169, at p. 163; Philippe Goridis, '*Rex factus est uxorius*: Weibliche und männliche Herrschaftsrollen in Outremer', in *Kreuzzug und Gender*, ed. Ingrid Baumgärtner and Melanie Panse, *Das Mittelalter. Perspektiven mediävistischer Forschung*, 21.1 (Berlin, 2016), pp. 22–39.
58 Angel G. Gordo Molina, 'Urraca de León y Teresa de Portugal. Las Relaciones de Fronteras y el Ejercicio de la Potestad Femenina en la Primera Mitad del Siglo XII. Jurisdicción, *Imperium* y Linaje', *Intus-Legere Historia*, 2.1 (2008), 9–23, at 13–14, 19–20; Miriam Shadis, 'Unexceptional Women: Power, Authority, and Queenship in Early Portugal', in *Medieval Elite Women and the Exercise of Power, 1100–1400: Moving beyond the Exceptionalist Debate*, ed. Heather J. Tanner (Cham, 2019), pp. 247–270, esp. pp. 248, 256.
59 Bernard F. Reilly, *The Kingdom of León-Castilla under Queen Urraca 1109–1126* (Princeton, 1982); Therese Martin, 'The Art of a Reigning Queen as Dynastic Propaganda in Twelfth-Century Spain', *Speculum*, 80.4 (2005), 1134–1171; Gordo Molina, 'Urraca de León'; Lucy K. Pick, *Her Father's Daughter: Gender, Power and Religion in the Early Spanish Kingdoms* (Ithaca and London, 2017), pp. 230–231.
60 David J. Hay, *The Military Leadership of Matilda of Canossa, 1046–1115* (Manchester, 2008), especially pp. 247–254. See also on women's leadership roles in warfare in the twelfth and thirteenth centuries, for example, Patrick Corbet, 'Entre Aliénor d'Aquitaine et Blanche de Castile. Les princesses au pouvoir dans la France de l'Est', in *Mächtige Frauen? Königinnen und Fürstinnen im europäischen Mittelalter (11.–14. Jahrhundert)*, ed. Claudia Zey with Sophei Caflisch and Philippe Goridis, Vorträge und Forschungen 81 (Ostfildern, 2015), pp. 225–247, at 239–240; Sabine Geldsetzer, *Frauen auf Kreuzzügen, 1096–1291* (Darmstadt,

28 *Who was Sybil? Family and sources*

      2003), pp. 123, 256 note 13; Jean A. Truax, 'Anglo-Norman Women at War: Valiant Soldiers, Prudent Strategists or Charismatic Leaders?' in *The Circle of War in the Middle Ages: Essays on Medieval Military and Naval History*, ed. Donald J. Kagay and L. J. Andrew Villalon (Woodbridge, 1999), pp. 111–125.
61 Danielle E. A. Park, *Papal Protection and the Crusader: Flanders, Champagne, and the Kingdom of France, 1095–1222* (Woodbridge, 2018), pp. 147–151.
62 The reasons Matilda failed to enforce her claim to the throne of England have been extensively debated by scholars: see, for example, Marjorie Chibnall, *The Empress Matilda: Queen Consort, Queen Mother, and Lady of the English* (Oxford, 1991); Catherine Hanley, *Matilda: Empress, Queen, Warrior* (New Haven and London, 2019). Stephen could have instead sought the throne of Jerusalem through his wife Matilda of Boulogne, niece of Godfrey of Bouillon and King Baldwin I of Jerusalem; but her father Eustace III of Boulogne had renounced his family claim: Murray, *The Crusader Kingdom of Jerusalem*, pp. 120–123, 193.
63 Murray, 'Women in the Royal Succession', pp. 138–144; Hans Eberhard Mayer, 'Studies in the History of Queen Melisende of Jerusalem', in: *Dumbarton Oaks Papers*, 26 (1972), 93, 95–182; Erin Jordan, 'Corporate Monarchy in the Twelfth-Century Kingdom of Jerusalem', *Royal Studies Journal*, 6.1 (2019), 1–15, at 10–14.
64 Asbridge, 'Alice of Antioch', pp. 29–47; Buck, *Principality of Antioch*, pp. 73, 75, 77–85, 132, 135, 191, 201, 210–211, 223–225, 228–229, 235; Andrew D. Buck, 'Politics and diplomacy in the Latin East: The principality of Antioch in historiographical perspective', *History Compass*, 15.9 (2017), 6 of 9; Andrew D. Buck, 'Women in the Principality of Antioch: Power, Status, and Social Agency', *Haskins Society Journal*, 31 (2019), 95–132, at p. 101; Erin L. Jordan, 'Women of Antioch: Political Culture and Powerful Women in the Latin East', in *Medieval Elite Women and the Exercise of Power, 1100–1400: Moving beyond the Exceptionalist Debate*, ed. Heather J. Tanner (Cham, 2019), pp. 225–246; Kevin James Lewis, 'Countess Hodierna of Tripoli: From Crusader Politician to "Princess Lointaine"', *Assuming Gender*, 3.1 (2013), 1–26, at 3; Lewis, *Counts of Tripoli*, pp. 157, 183–186; Murray, 'Constance, Princess of Antioch', pp. 85–86, 91–94.
65 Antony Eastmond, 'Royal Renewal in Georgia: The Case of Queen Tamar', in *New Constantines: The Rhythm of Imperial Renewal in Byzantium, 4th–13th Centuries*, ed. Paul Magdalino (Aldershot, 2994), pp. 283–293, at pp. 289 note 20, 290–293.
66 Antony Eastmond, *Tamta's World: The Life and Encounters of a Medieval Noblewoman from the Middle East to Mongolia* (Cambridge, 2017), esp. pp. 133, 196–202; Zaroui Pogossian, 'Women, Identity, and Power: A Review Essay of Antony Eastmond, *Tamta's World*', *Al-ʿUṣūr al-Wusṭā: The Journal of Middle East Medievalists*, 27 (2019), 233–266, esp. pp. 242–247; Sergio La Porta, '"The Kingdom and the Sultanate Were Conjoined": Legitimizing Land and Power in Armenia during the 12th and Early 13th Centuries', *Revue des études arméniennes*, 34 (2012), 73–118, at pp. 88–89.
67 Heather J. Tanner, Laura L. Gathagan and Lois L. Huneycutt, 'Introduction', in *Medieval Elite Women and the Exercise of Power, 1100–1400: Moving beyond the Exceptionalist Debate*, ed. Heather J. Tanner (Cham, 2019), pp. 1–18, at p. 3.

2 Childhood (*c.* 1159–1171)

Some scholars have questioned the validity of the concept of 'childhood' in Europe before the sixteenth century, but most recent studies have shown that childhood was acknowledged as a distinct period of life in medieval Europe. Then as later it was regarded as a time of training for adulthood, but parents also cherished their children and cared for them, and children had their own cultural activities.[1] In particular, recent studies have considered the childhood and education of noble and royal women contemporary to Sybil and of the previous generation.[2] Taking these as a guide we may make a calculated guess at the upbringing that Sybil would have expected as second in line to the throne of Jerusalem.

Parents

Sybil's parents married in 1157. Her father Amaury had been invested with the county of Jaffa by his mother Queen Melisende earlier in the decade, probably in 1151. Control of this large coastal fief, which dated back to the early years of the new kingdom of Jerusalem in 1108/10, gave its holder control of the southern coastal part of the kingdom of Jerusalem; as such it was essential to the ruler of the kingdom that it was controlled by a loyal, trustworthy and competent person. After King Baldwin III defeated his mother Queen Melisende in a brief civil war in 1152 and took over all the government of the kingdom, he may have taken Jaffa away from his younger brother Amaury to punish him for supporting their mother during the war. However, he later gave the county of Jaffa back to Amaury and added the fortified port city of Ascalon, which the Franks had captured in 1153. To balance Amaury's power, the king could rely on the lands of the Ibelin family – Ibelin, Ramla and Mirabel – which were adjacent to or within the county of Jaffa: as long as the Ibelins supported the king they would ensure that Amaury did not become too powerful in his great fief.[3]

Although Sybil's mother Agnes came from one of the great families of the crusader states, her family had been disinherited in 1144 when Zengi captured their comital city of Edessa. Her father Count Joscelin II then set up his base at Tell Bāshir (or Turbessel) in the west of his county. In 1150 he was

DOI: 10.4324/9781315205960-3

30 *Childhood (c. 1159–1171)*

captured by Nūr al-Dīn, Zengi's son, and imprisoned in Aleppo where he eventually died in 1159. King Baldwin III agreed that the Byzantine emperor, Manuel Komnenos, should take over the remainder of the county of Edessa in return for providing Joscelin's wife Beatrice and their children with an annual income.[4] Countess Beatrice, who had been the widow of William of Saone (or Sahyūn) when she married Joscelin, probably retired to her Saone dower lands in the principality of Antioch. In the late 1140s her daughter Agnes had married Reynald lord of Marash, one of the leading nobles of the principality of Antioch, but he had died in 1149 or 1150. Hence, although in theory as a de Courtenay Agnes was a great noble, because both her natal county of Edessa and her husband's lordship of Marash had been lost she was in fact a landless woman. It is possible that before 1157 Agnes had already agreed to marry Hugh of Ibelin, lord of Ramla, and may in fact have been married to him at the time she married Amaury. If this were the case, and Amaury forced his vassal to give up Agnes and married her while she was still legally married to Hugh, any children who were born from the marriage would be illegitimate.[5]

Birth and infancy

No contemporary commentator recorded the birth of Sybil or that of her younger brother Baldwin a few years later, but this was to be expected. At the time of their birth neither was direct heir to the kingdom, and as the rate of child mortality was high it was likely that neither would reach their first birthday. Even Archbishop William of Tyre, writing his history in retrospect, did not mention their births until he noted under the year 1174, when the children's father King Amaury died, that Baldwin was then aged just thirteen and had an elder sister, *Sibilla* (Sybil).[6] Baldwin, then, was born in 1161, and – if the children were born at equal intervals from their parents' marriage – Sybil was born in 1159. As King Baldwin III had no children, she was then second in line to the throne of Jerusalem, after her father Amaury.

The name 'Sibylle', 'Sebille' and so on, the various spellings depending on the language used and the preference of the writer, was a common woman's name in Latin Christian Europe in the twelfth century. The name is usually taken to derive from the *Sibyllae* of Roman classical tradition, female prophets who authored the Sibylline books, which were consulted at times of crisis in ancient Rome. Writing in France at the beginning of the fifteenth century, Christine de Pizan or Pisan would depict the sibyls as extraordinarily learned and chaste virgins who foretold the coming of Christ. On the other hand, although characters called 'Sebille' who appeared in contemporary epic and romance literature were certainly wise, being enchantresses with knowledge of medicine and the liberal and magical arts, they were also often seductresses, possibly through confusion with the Biblical figure of the Queen of Sheba who visited King Solomon. Hence 'Sibyl' could imply a chaste, pious and wise woman of prudence and foresight, or a rich and beautiful educated woman – possibly not a Christian – who led men astray. Having said that, the name as given to Frankish noblewomen could have derived from a Germanic name such as Sieghilde rather than the classical name.[7]

It was normal practice in western Europe at this period for royal and noblewomen to be named after women of their father's family – his sister, paternal aunt, mother or paternal grandmother – and so the choice of name, rather than implying wisdom, prudence, beauty or any other virtue, simply reinforced a daughter's connection to her father's kindred.[8] William of Tyre recorded that just as King Baldwin III acted as godfather for Sybil's younger brother Baldwin, Countess Sybil of Flanders acted as our Sybil's godmother, indicating that the niece was named after her paternal aunt, half-sister of Amaury of Jerusalem, daughter of Fulk V of Anjou and his first wife Eremburge. Her name explicitly linked baby Sybil to her paternal grandfather's family, while Countess Sybil, as godmother, took on responsibility for baby Sybil's spiritual and physical nurture.[9]

Sybil of Anjou had married Count Thierry of Flanders in 1134. She ruled Flanders as his regent during his pilgrimage to the Holy Land in 1138–1139 and again during his absence on the Second Crusade 1147–1149, when she was also acting as regent for their young son Baldwin. During Thierry's second absence the county had been attacked by Count Baldwin of Hainaut. Countess Sybil was unable to repel the attack because she was about to give birth, but as soon as she could she led her army into the county of Hainaut in a retaliatory raid, and the ongoing hostilities were ended only by papal mediation.[10]

The countess came to Jerusalem in 1157 with her husband Thierry on pilgrimage, leaving their eldest surviving son Philip as their regent in Flanders.[11] This was the first time that the countess had visited the kingdom where her father Fulk V of Anjou had been king and had died. She was evidently welcomed by her family, as she not only stood as godmother to her half-brother Amaury's baby daughter, but also in 1157 worked with her aunts Queen Melisende of Jerusalem and Lady Hodierna, countess of Tripoli, to ensure that Amaury de Nesle, prior of the church of the Holy Sepulchre, was appointed as patriarch of Jerusalem. As William of Tyre – reporting this at least a decade later – stated, Queen Melisende's intervention was against the rule of law.[12]

Perhaps because he was still in Europe at the time of these events, William missed the fact that Countess Sybil did not return to Flanders with her husband in 1159. Clerical commentators writing in the Low Countries and Normandy noted that she remained in the Holy Land and took the religious habit at the Abbey of St Lazarus at Bethany, where her youngest aunt Iveta or Yveta was abbess. William recorded that Count Thierry came to the Holy Land again in 1164, *cum uxore* (with his wife), *religiosa et deum timente femina* (a religious and God-fearing woman), but obviously if Countess Sybil was already at Bethany she would not have accompanied him. Perhaps Thierry came deliberately to visit his wife, and William – who did not return to the East until the following year – was confused into believing that the countess had travelled with him. The countess died in the following year and was buried at the abbey.[13]

William of Tyre recorded nothing about Sybil of Jerusalem between her baptism and her father's death in 1174. Noble babies would normally be brought up within their family household, but despite recommendations from contemporary medical experts that a mother should breastfeed her own child – because the quality of the mother's milk would influence the baby's character – a noblewoman was unlikely to have the time and inclination to breast feed her own child, and was more likely to hire a wet nurse. Countess Agnes of Jaffa and Ascalon would probably have had many demands on her time in administration, patronage and diplomacy that prevented her from breast-feeding her baby daughter and later her baby son or giving much of her personal time to their care. Children were weaned between the ages of one and three, boys perhaps later than girls.[14] Although their parents would have cherished their young children, who represented their dynastic future, they would probably have left the bulk of the day-to-day care of young Sybil, and later baby Baldwin, to nurses and servants.

When William of Tyre noted under 1174 that Baldwin, the heir to the kingdom, was then aged just thirteen and had an elder sister, Sybil, he added that she had been brought up in the convent of St Lazarus at Bethany with her father's aunt Iveta, abbess of that place.[15] According to William, Queen Melisende had founded the Abbey of St Lazarus with the intention that her youngest sister would be its abbess. As a child aged around five, in 1124 Iveta had been given by her mother Morphia as a hostage for the payment of the ransom of her father, King Baldwin II, who had been captured by the Artuqid ruler Nūr al-Daulak Balak. King Baldwin recovered his five-year-old daughter after the ransom money had been paid. Iveta did not marry. Apart from the fact that there was no obvious candidate of sufficient rank among the nobility of the Latin East, her family may have encouraged their youngest child to take up the religious profession to support her family, and she may have preferred the independence and possibility of exercising authority offered by the religious life over marriage. She made a religious profession at the monastery of St Anne (located within the walled city of Jerusalem), mother of the Blessed Virgin Mary. In 1138 her elder sister Melisende decided it was unfitting for a king's daughter to be subject to another as if she was one of the people and built a monastery at nearby Bethany where Iveta could be abbess. This site had belonged to the canons of the Holy Sepulchre, who were given a replacement. As Iveta was only around 18 at this time, an elderly abbess was initially appointed whom Iveta would replace when she was old enough. William did not record the first abbess's name, but King Baldwin III's document confirming the arrangements names her as Matilda. She must have died by 1157, as Iveta was recorded as abbess in that year.[16]

William depicts the abbey as solely Melisende's foundation, but in fact it also had the support of her husband King Fulk, and Pope Celestine II's confirmations of the arrangements to compensate the prior and canons of the

Holy Sepulchre envisaged the foundation as a joint venture of Melisende and Fulk. The pope understood that the queen and king intended to found a house of monks or nuns, which could suggest that Fulk envisaged a double house of men and women like the famous monastery of Fontevrault, which was patronised by the counts of Anjou. Fontevrault was ruled by an abbess but housed both nuns and monks separately. Certainly there was contact between the two houses, as Iveta sent some relics to Fontevrault, including some wood of the Holy Cross. However, as only an outline ground plan of the Abbey of St Lazarus at Bethany can now be ascertained, without indication where various groups were housed, there is no certain evidence that it was a double house. It appears to have been simply a religious house of sisters, ruled over by an abbess.

Certainly the abbey needed some accommodation for priests (required to say mass for the nuns) and possibly for male officials and servants, which would be completely separate from the women's accommodation. Pilgrims to St Lazarus's tomb required accommodation and perhaps housing for the servants who cared for them, but again these were completely separate from the nuns' accommodation. Pilgrims saw two churches or chapels adjoining the abbey, one covering the tomb of St Lazarus, the other dedicated to his sisters Saints Mary and Martha, separated by a courtyard; but although they could visit the tomb and the church of Saints Mary and Martha, they did not enter the abbey itself.[17]

The abbey buildings lay to the south of the pilgrim churches, stretching some forty-five metres south of the two churches and fifty-two metres from east to west. A hall ran along the south side of the courtyard between the two churches, with the nuns' cloister to the south of the west church. Because of the uneven terrain the buildings were terraced into the hillside, which makes it difficult to match the identified remains to any standard monastic layout. However, the upper, western part of the site seems to have housed the nuns' conventual buildings while the lower, eastern part contained the kitchen and storerooms. The nuns' private rooms were well away from any public area; typically their dormitory would have been the most remote of access. The southern and eastern parts of the abbey buildings were surrounded by a wall, including at least two projecting rectangular towers, one of which may be the very strong stone tower which William of Tyre mentioned Queen Melisende had built as a refuge for the nuns in the case of sudden attack.[18]

Melisende (William recorded) endowed her new foundation generously with land to provide a reliable income for the sisters and gave it liturgical vessels of gold with jewels and silver, and priestly vestments of every sort required. When Iveta was made abbess the queen endowed the house with more gifts: chalices, books and other ornaments for ecclesiastical use.[19] Not much is known of the abbey's contents and its landed possessions, as little of its archive has survived. A contemporary reported that it was sacked by Saladin in 1187 after the battle of Hattin, and although the two churches on the site survived at least in part, the nuns abandoned their abbey, setting up a new house at Acre after it was recaptured by the Third Crusade in the summer of 1191. It is most likely that the abbey's cartulary and other documents were lost when Acre was captured and sacked by the army of al-Ashraf Khalil, sultan of Egypt, in 1291. The surviving sisters took refuge on Cyprus. The community survived at least until 1362–65, when it was assessed for tithes, but it was not recorded after this date. Because of these losses we have hardly any information about the abbey's library holdings and only a few names of the women who could have been sisters in the house when Countess Sybil and Iveta lived there, along with some names of the male religious attached to the house.[20]

William of Tyre did not record how old Sybil of Jerusalem was when she went to live in her grandmother's foundation. Although young Sybil must have set eyes on her grandmother – Queen Melisende was probably present at her baptism alongside her niece Countess Sybil – it is very unlikely that she remembered anything of the queen, who died in September 1161 when Sybil of Jerusalem was around two years old.[21] It is possible that her godmother Countess Sybil suggested that her god-daughter come with her to the abbey; it is also possible that Sybil joined her great-aunt and her godmother in the abbey after her father came to the throne of Jerusalem in 1163.

Daughter of the king

King Baldwin III died less than eighteen months after his mother, in February 1163. He and his wife Theodora were childless, and Theodora retired to her dower lands, the important port city of Acre.[22] She remained the only queen in the kingdom of Jerusalem, because Baldwin's brother and heir Amaury was forced to divorce Agnes before he could succeed to the throne.

William of Tyre recorded that the problem was consanguinity: Amaury and Agnes shared a great-great-grandfather, and at the time of their marriage Patriarch Fulcher of Jerusalem had raised objections. As he was still studying in Europe while these events were taking place, William had no direct knowledge of what had happened, and so consulted Stephanie de Courtenay, abbess of the convent of St Mary the Great in Jerusalem and daughter of Count Joscelin I of Edessa by his second wife, the sister of Roger of Salerno, and she confirmed the situation. Amaury had to divorce Agnes, but their children were legitimated so that they could still inherit the kingdom and Baldwin IV, William's later pupil, would be a legitimate king. However, there may have been other factors involved which William did not set down in his history because they cast doubt on the legitimacy of the monarchy and the healthy state of the kingdom.[23]

In the first place, the High Court – the leading nobles of the kingdom of Jerusalem, meeting in formal council – may have worried that if Agnes became queen her brother Joscelin III de Courtenay, titular count of Edessa, would gain even more power and influence in the kingdom than he already had. Joscelin had come south to the kingdom of Jerusalem after Agnes married the king's younger brother, and the king had given him some land and income around Acre.[24]

Although Agnes' and Joscelin's attempts to enrich themselves at the expense of the rest of the baronage could have become a cause for discontent after 1176 – that is, after Baldwin IV had become king and was ruling in his own right – it was not a ground for concern in 1163. Furthermore, the problem was not that Agnes was unfit to be queen: the later accusations in the *Chronique d'Ernoul* that she was an immoral woman were obviously political slurs based on later rivalries and complaints about Agnes's influence over her son. As Archbishop William of Tyre recorded that immediately after her divorce Agnes married the eminent nobleman Lord Hugh of Ibelin, and after his death (while Amaury was still alive) married again, to Lord Reynald of Sidon, she was clearly regarded as a suitable wife for a high-ranking nobleman in the kingdom of Jerusalem.[25]

Rather, Hans Mayer has argued that Agnes had been married to Hugh of Ibelin before Amaury married her in 1157. Her marriage to Amaury was therefore bigamous and invalid, and would bring ecclesiastical censure on the king and on the kingdom. It must be dissolved before he could become king. If Amaury remained in this bigamous marriage he could not be king; but which other heirs were available? Mayer argued that Princess Constance of Antioch, granddaughter of King Baldwin II, would not have been acceptable for a number of reasons, principally that her husband Reynald de Châtillon was currently a prisoner in Aleppo, which would raise the same problem that Amaury's marriage presented: should the heir be forced to divorce before they could inherit? Constance's son Bohemond III was only about fifteen in 1163, just old enough to take over government of his own principality but hardly a rival candidate for the kingdom of Jerusalem. Hence the only feasible alternative heir among the descendants of Baldwin II was the son of Melisende's younger sister Hodierna, Count Raymond III of Tripoli (then aged around twenty-three years old) whom the baronage of the kingdom of Jerusalem apparently regarded as an even less desirable ruler, as they chose Amaury.

On the other hand, if Amaury's marriage were dissolved on the basis of bigamy the two children would be illegitimate as the offspring of adultery, again leaving the succession vulnerable. So instead the marriage was dissolved on the grounds of consanguinity, and Pope Alexander III declared the two children legitimate. Nevertheless, Mayer argued, a question remained in the minds of contemporaries and would arise again after the death of the child king Baldwin V when the baronage had to choose between the rival claims of Sybil, the elder daughter who might be illegitimate, and Isabel, the younger daughter with the indisputable claim.[26]

The surviving evidence leaves the matter unclear.[27] In any case, having been forced to divorce Agnes, Amaury was crowned just eight days after his brother's death.[28] Agnes (whose opinion on these events was not recorded in any surviving evidence) married Hugh of Ibelin, but retained her title of countess. Her children remained with their father.[29] Their younger child, Baldwin, not yet aged two, would have lived at the royal court, where William, archdeacon of Tyre, was appointed as his tutor in around 1170 when Baldwin was nine. But as there was no longer a queen's household at court – and would not be until August 1167 when Amaury married Maria Komnene, the Emperor Manuel's great-niece – this was hardly a suitable place for little Sybil, now aged around four years old. Perhaps her great-aunt Iveta and godmother Countess Sybil proposed that Sybil join them at the Abbey of St Lazarus at Bethany.

Upbringing and education

Some scholars have suggested that being educated in a religious house would have left Sybil underprepared to take on a role in royal government.[30] On the contrary, an abbey was an entirely appropriate place for a king's daughter to be brought up and educated. Royal and noble parents had two options for educating a daughter: to appoint a tutor, female or male, or to have her educated in a women's religious house, one of the functions of which was as a centre of learning for women. Countess Sybil had been tutored by Master Matthew, the future bishop of Angers, while her mother Eremburge was tutored by a *magistra* (a learned woman teacher) named Beatrice.[31] As a young empress, Matilda of England was tutored by Archbishop Bruno of Trier.[32] King William I of England entrusted the education of his daughter Cecilia to Arnoul of Chocques 'who must have taught both at the Abbaye-aux-Hommes and at the Abbaye-aux-Dames' at Caen. The Abbaye-aux-Dames had been founded by William and his wife Matilda and was dedicated to the Holy Trinity.[33] The Benedictine monk and political commentator Matthew Paris of St Albans Abbey, listing the gems held by the abbey, noted that one ring, containing a sapphire, had been given by a Lord Richard Animal who had obtained it from a Queen Eleanor, '*quia conscolares in sua juventute extiterant et sodales*' (because they had been fellow scholars in his youth and comrades) as if they had been at school together or had shared the same tutor: this 'Queen Eleanor' may have been Eleanor of Aquitaine.[34] Eleanor's eldest daughter Marie was probably brought up from the age of eight in the household of the recently widowed Viscountess Elizabeth of Mareuil-sur-Aÿ, near the Benedictine convent of Avenay, 'where she could enjoy the company and educational opportunities of an old aristocratic convent while living with the viscountess'.[35] Eleanor's youngest daughter Joanna was fostered for a short time at Fontevrault Abbey.[36]

In Europe, nunneries were the main providers of education for girls. Local children might attend on a daily basis, but the daughter of a noble family would probably live within the religious house, which provided a secure and stable environment.[37] An abbey presented an additional advantage for the secure education of young noblewomen because it was designed to exclude outsiders. Heiresses were vulnerable to abduction and forced marriage.[38] Within the walls of a religious house, a young heiress would be safe from enemies who might try to abduct her and would be under constant supervision to ensure she stayed away from men until the time came for her to be married. As the Abbey of St Lazarus was enclosed within a strong wall fortified with towers, it was certainly a safe location for the education and upbringing of the king's daughter, second in line to the throne.

As a pupil at the abbey, Sybil would have been taught what every aristocratic woman of twelfth-century Latin Christian society needed to learn in order to run her estates and discharge her other duties to society. She would have been instructed in the Christian faith, to ensure not only that she followed a moral and upright life herself but also that she could give a good example to her servants, subjects, spouse and children. She should have been taught how to read Latin, not only for reading religious literature for her own spiritual benefit but also because as a noblewoman administering her own estates, and possibly as queen if she should inherit the kingdom, she would need to be able to read the documents sent to her and produced by her chancery and possibly to compose them herself – although the act of actually writing them would normally be given to a professional clerk. Noblewomen also wrote letters passing on news or making diplomatic contact; although only one letter sent by Sybil survives (to Emperor Frederick Barbarossa, warning him against Emperor Isaac II Angelos), that single letter is composed in Latin.[39] Sybil would also be expected to be sufficiently educated to carry on informed conversation and debate with nobles and clerics and her own husband and to oversee the education of her own children in the future. As well as Latin, she would learn how to read her own language, French, and possibly to write it. As a noble with estates to administer and protect she would need to learn how to ride. In addition, she should learn women's skills: spinning, embroidery, and even singing; she would be expected to know how to hunt with a hawk and perhaps how to handle a bow.[40]

The skills and knowledge that a French royal or noblewoman required in her everyday work was described over two centuries later by Christine de Pizan; despite the chronological gap, the skills required by a noblewoman in the crusader states were very similar. De Pizan instructed noblewomen with governmental responsibilities to follow a pious lifestyle, beginning their day with personal prayers and hearing Mass, then going to council, listening carefully to what was said and replying wisely. The noblewoman should choose wise counsellors to advise her. After the midday meal she should receive visitors, welcoming each with honour and speaking thoughtfully and appropriately to each. After this she might work with her maidens in her chamber, then hear vespers, go for a walk in her garden and receive petitioners, say her prayers and retire to bed. Baronesses with administrative responsibilities must act wisely and prudently, be well informed about law and local customs, and know how to speak tactfully to those inclined to be rebellious. They should also be familiar with weaponry and able to command military forces if the need arose, know how to launch an attack or defend against one, and keep their fortresses in good repair. A baroness should also understand her financial resources and how to organise them without overburdening her men. De Pizan stressed the importance of managing people carefully and appropriately and knowing when to be firm and when to be generous.[41] Countess Sybil was well versed in all these matters from her experience

38 Childhood (c. 1159–1171)

ruling and defending Flanders and could have instructed her young goddaughter in them.

Like monks, nuns – or at least those in wealthy, well-endowed houses with good libraries – were expected to read a new book from their abbey library every year.[42] Queen Melisende had endowed her abbey with books,[43] but because its records have been lost we have hardly any information about what was available for Sybil to read as part of her education or for her own interest. However, a sixteenth-century biography of Gerard of Nazareth, a former hermit who became bishop of Laodicea by 1140, records that among his works was a sermon or letter *Ad ancillas Dei apud Bethaniam* (to God's handmaidens at Bethany), that is, to the nuns of the Abbey of St Lazarus at Bethany. The sermon itself is apparently lost, but the fact that 'a major literary figure of the Latin East' composed a sermon for the nuns is an indication of the abbey's importance in the religious and cultural life of the kingdom of Jerusalem and of the cultural milieu in which Sybil was brought up.[44]

As second in line to the throne of the kingdom of Jerusalem, Sybil should have learned about the First Crusade, the establishment of the crusader states, and the beginnings of the royal dynasty. There may have been no written French-language story of the First Crusade available when Sybil was a child, but she could have heard oral tales or read one of the Latin histories of the crusade to discover how the kingdom that her father ruled had come into being through God's aid and the courage and virtue of the crusaders. Certainly Archbishop William of Tyre referred to oral tradition in writing his history of the kingdom and also made use of a range of Latin accounts of the First Crusade and its aftermath, showing that there were copies of such books within the kingdom of Jerusalem.[45] At the time of Sybil's birth, laity and clerics of the kingdom had already produced a number of historical and theological works, in addition to those by Gerard of Nazareth already mentioned. The principality of Antioch was also an important centre for manuscript production and for the translation of Arabic medical texts into Latin.[46] It is possible that the Abbey of St Lazarus held copies of such manuscripts produced in the crusader states.

Sybil probably heard stories told in her own language, such as the epics of Charlemagne, Guillaume d'Orange, and Aymeri de Narbonne and his children, set against backgrounds of Muslim invaders fighting Christians in the south of France and Spain and rebellious Frankish nobles challenging the king. In addition to their pious and brave warriors, these epics included strong female characters such as Guibourc, the Muslim noblewoman who converts to Christianity and marries the hero Guillaume d'Orange; or Hermenjart, the Lombard princess who marries Aymeri de Narbonne.[47] Sybil might also have read or heard Geoffrey of Monmouth's famous history of the kings of Britain translated into French by Wace, Wace's hagiographical works, the romances composed in Champagne by Chrétien de Troyes from around 1165–1170 or the poetry of Marie de France composed during the last third of the twelfth century.[48] All these works circulated widely among the noble families of France, England and the Low Countries – the relatives of the Frankish nobility of the crusader states – so it is likely that they were also well known among the nobility of the crusader states, although there is little evidence of their presence in the crusader states until the thirteenth century.[49]

At Bethany Sybil lived in close proximity to her godmother Countess Sybil until the latter's death in 1165, and to her great-aunt Iveta, who may have lived until 1178 – the year after Sybil would have left Bethany to marry William of Montferrat.[50] It would be interesting to know Sybil's great-aunt's and aunt's views on her parents' divorce and what they told her about it after the event, because she would have been too young in 1163 to remember what had happened; their memories could have informed her decision in 1186, when she was confronted with demands that she divorce her husband, father of her surviving children. They could have taught her about the history of her family, both the rulers of the kingdom of Jerusalem and the counts of Anjou, as well as giving her the benefit of their personal experience of rulership, warfare and government, providing all the training she would need if she was to be an effective administrator in the future as wife of a prestigious nobleman, and especially if she were to become queen.[51]

Beyond the obvious connections with her great-aunt and aunt, we do not know what company Sybil kept at the abbey. As a royal foundation, governed by the sister of a former king of Jerusalem and sponsored by the countess of Flanders, and with one of its pupils in line to the throne of Jerusalem, it is safe to say that this would have been the educational establishment of choice for the Frankish nobility who wanted their daughters to develop a good network of contacts and influence alongside their education. Through friendships with daughters of other noble families Sybil could have developed relationships with the noble families whom she would one day rule; but no evidence has survived.

In any case, at the abbey Sybil lived in a community of noblewomen who followed a reasonably comfortable lifestyle suitable to their social station. The nuns may have slept in a common dormitory – although the abbess would have had her own lodging within the abbey enclosure – but novices and girls like Sybil who were educated in the abbey but did not intend to take vows were accommodated separately. The nuns had servants to wait on them and carry out the manual work required to keep the abbey running, such as cooking, cleaning and laundry. As the king's daughter, Sybil could have expected to have her own personal maid or protector-teacher to attend to her needs, but again no evidence has survived.

Although contemporary sources did not mention Sybil during these years, her family outside the abbey must have kept in touch with her to ensure her well-being. King Amaury could have visited his mother's religious foundation on pilgrimage and to pay his respects to his great-aunt and also have seen his daughter. In fact, he needed to maintain contact with her to ensure that she identified with his family interests if he expected her in the future to extend his and their family's power and influence through a prestigious marriage; she could hardly represent a father and a family to which she felt no personal connection.[52]

There was no reason why Countess Agnes should not also visit the abbey on pilgrimage. Her husband Hugh of Ibelin died in around 1169, and as his widow Agnes would have received half the revenues of his fief of Ramla for her lifetime; although, as the couple had no children, Ramla was inherited by Hugh's brother Baldwin. Hamilton pointed out that Agnes should also have been still receiving the pension which the Emperor Manuel was paying her for her family's former lands in Edessa and would have been 'a quite rich woman'. By 1171 she had married again, this time to Reynald son of Gerard lord of Sidon.[53] During this time there is no evidence that she ever visited the royal court or saw her younger child Baldwin; their next certain meeting was after Baldwin became king in 1174. But it is possible that Agnes went on pilgrimage to St Lazarus's tomb, and while there could have visited her daughter.

Meanwhile, on 19 August 1167 Amaury married again. His bride was Maria Komnene, great-niece of Emperor Manuel Komnenos. The marriage was part of a wider diplomatic programme by which the Emperor gave his support to Amaury's invasion of Egypt – a wealthy country whose government was divided and whose caliph, who in theory ruled the country, remained aloof and left government in the hands of his warring ministers – while Amaury took an oath of loyalty to Manuel and aligned himself with the latter's political programme, adopting a Byzantine style of imperial dress on his seal and acknowledging the Byzantine emperor's role as the protector of the Christian holy places. Manuel contributed to the rebuilding of the Holy Sepulchre in Jerusalem and the redecoration of the church of the Nativity in Bethlehem, which included portraits of the emperor. In the Greek inscription recording the completion of the redecoration, Manuel's name was placed first, before Amaury's, while in the Latin inscription Amaury's name appeared before Manuel's.[54]

It is tempting to interpret the Emperor's co-operation with the Franks of the kingdom of Jerusalem and the principality of Antioch as a break with the policy of his father and grandfather, seeking to establish ties of friendship with the Latin Christian descendants of the First Crusade rather than forcing them into submission.[55] In fact he was continuing their policies in extending his suzerainty over the Franks, but in this case peacefully rather than by force. By adopting a conciliatory approach rather than leading his army into the principality of Antioch as his father had done, he won the trust of the Franks and quelled any European and especially papal fears of Byzantine treachery. Manuel had learned in the aftermath of the Second Crusade that traditional Byzantine imperial methods of dealing with the Franks might give him the upper hand but provoked a Latin European backlash in opinion, if not in arms. On the other hand, from the 1150s various opportunities arose for Manuel to intervene in Latin Christian affairs in the role of protector and champion: in Italy (against Frederick Barbarossa) and in the crusader states (against Nūr al-Dīn). There was a new tone at the Byzantine imperial court: an atmosphere of openness to other cultures and efforts to develop good relations with Muslim powers as well as other Christian powers.

Manuel arranged marriages between his relatives and the Latin Christian nobility. Following an approach from King Baldwin III of Jerusalem, he had agreed the marriage of his niece Theodora to the young king in 1158. Baldwin became the emperor's nephew by marriage but also his subject king. After the death of Manuel's first wife, Bertha-Eirene of Sulzbach (sister-in-law of King Conrad III of Germany), Manuel considered as possible brides both Maria of Antioch, daughter of Princess Constance and sister of the young prince Bohemond III; and Melisende, daughter of Queen Melisende's younger sister Countess Hodierna of Tripoli and sister of Count Raymond III. In 1162 he married Maria, alienating Count Raymond in the process.[56]

This marriage continued imperial policy of restoring and maintaining Byzantine control over Antioch. In 1158 Manuel had forced Constance's second husband Reynald de Châtillon, prince of Antioch, to submit to him and subsequently entered Antioch as its lord. Reynald was captured by the governor of Aleppo in 1161 (and remained a prisoner until 1176). Constance's young son Bohemond III then became prince, but he would not come of age until 1163. For Constance the marriage of her daughter Maria with Emperor Manuel assured Byzantine protection for her principality and offered the hope of a long-standing and constructive relationship between the emperor and the city. Another outcome of this alliance was the marriage of Constance's and Reynald's daughter Agnes (renamed Anna) to King Béla III of Hungary, also an ally of Byzantium. Manuel demonstrated the value of his support for his vassal prince by paying Prince Bohemond III's ransom after he was captured by Nūr al-Dīn at the battle of Artah or Harim in 1164.[57] The marriages of kings Baldwin III and Amaury to Byzantine princesses also drew the kingdom of Jerusalem into Manuel's sphere of power, although not so closely as Antioch.

Amaury had already led three military expeditions into Egypt in September 1163 (just over six months after his coronation), 1164 and 1167. The immediate aim of his initial expedition had been to exact tribute from Egypt's Fatimid Shi'ite rulers – which had previously been paid to Baldwin III – and this was successful. Nūr al-Dīn also had hopes of conquering Egypt. In 1163 his general, Shirkuh, led an army to Egypt to help Shawar, the exiled governor of Upper Egypt, against Dirgham, the chamberlain of the Egyptian government. Dirgham was killed, but Shirkuh then tried to take over Egypt. Shawar appealed to Amaury for military support. Amaury's 1164 expedition drove out Shirkuh and left Shawar in control of Egypt. Meanwhile Nūr al-Dīn attacked the northern crusader states, and at the Battle of Artah in August 1164 he captured all the leaders of the Christian army, including Prince Bohemond III of Antioch, his cousin Count Raymond III of Tripoli, Joscelin III, titular count of Edessa (Sybil's maternal uncle) and some Europeans, including Hugh VIII de Lusignan, a cousin of Prince Bohemond and Count Raymond. Although Bohemond was released in 1165 after Emperor Manuel paid his ransom, and Hugh de Lusignan reappeared in the county of Tripoli in 1168, the others endured a long period in prison: Raymond had been released by April 1174 but Joscelin was not released until 1176, at the same time as Reynald de Châtillon.[58]

In January 1167 Shirkuh invaded Egypt again. His forces included his young nephew Yūsuf, who would become known to posterity as Saladin. Yūsuf had already held an administrative post under Nūr al-Dīn in Damascus, and was now developing a military career in his uncle's service. Shawar again requested Amaury's aid to drive Shirkuh out, in return for a generous annual tribute. Amaury's campaign was successful, the tribute was paid, and Amaury returned to Jerusalem in triumph in August and married Maria Komnene. The king and the emperor discussed the desirability of conquering Egypt before it could be taken by Nūr al-Dīn, but in autumn 1168 Amaury set out on another Egyptian expedition without waiting for his new ally's help. William of Tyre, who had been one of Amaury's negotiators with Manuel, considered that this expedition broke Amaury's 1167 treaty with Shawar, although it was also being said that Amaury had acted to pre-empt an intervention by Nūr al-Dīn. Amaury was initially successful but then withdrew, leaving Shirkuh and his army in control of Egypt.[59]

In January 1169 Shirkuh had Shawar killed. The caliph appointed Shirkuh as vizier (chief minister), but in March, Shirkuh died and his nephew Saladin was appointed in his place. While Saladin established himself in his new post, Amaury was planning another campaign in Egypt. The emperor sent a large fleet, and in mid-October a joint Frankish-Byzantine expedition set out by land and sea to besiege the important port of Damietta in the Nile Delta. They were unable to capture it quickly and began to run short of supplies, and Amaury's army retreated to Ascalon. There were bitter recriminations between the allies: Franks complained that Manuel had not sent sufficient supplies while Byzantine writers blamed the Franks. Saladin, on the other hand, came out of the campaign with his position considerably strengthened.[60]

Nevertheless, the alliances held firm. In the summer of 1171, Amaury undertook a state visit to Constantinople.[61] Maria Komnene went on to bear Amaury two daughters. One died in infancy; the other, Isabel, born in around October 1172,[62] would be a rival to Sybil's claim to the throne.

Initial marriage negotiations

But by this time Sybil's father had already started trying to arrange her marriage. In the spring of 1169, he sent an embassy to Europe to ask for military aid from the leaders of Latin Christendom and also to find a husband for Sybil. The ambassadors carried individual and personalised letters to the Emperor Frederick Barbarossa, King Louis VII of France, King Henry II of England, King William II of Sicily and counts Philip of Flanders (whose father Thierry had died in the previous year), Henry I 'the Liberal' of Champagne, Theobald or Thibaut of Chartres, and other leading lords – military leaders who had been involved in crusading personally or were descended from or related to crusaders. The letters set out the pressing danger from Nūr al-Dīn, depicted the crusader states as broken and crushed with pilgrim sites lost to the Muslims and Christian cities under threat, and stressed the need to ensure the security of pilgrims. The initial embassy was driven back by bad weather, but Archbishop Frederick of Tyre and Bishop John of Banyas eventually set off for Europe, carrying the appeals for aid. In July 1169, Pope Alexander III proclaimed a new crusade, adding to the strength of the appeal.[63]

Several considerations could have prompted Amaury to send an embassy to Europe at this time. Shirkuh's capture of Egypt that winter boded badly for the kingdom of Jerusalem. Byzantine aid was very valuable, but Amaury's marriage to Maria Komnene had already given the Byzantine emperor considerable influence in his kingdom, and Byzantine aid always came with strings attached; perhaps Amaury believed that the princes of Europe would be less demanding and more inclined to work with him. It is not clear whether Amaury already knew that his son and heir Baldwin, Sybil's little brother, had a life-threatening condition. William of Tyre claimed that it was he, as Baldwin's tutor, who realised that Baldwin was ill; as Baldwin was then aged at least nine, this realisation did not come before summer 1170, a year after Amaury's embassy had set off. Nevertheless, as Hamilton pointed out, Amaury would have been aware that death could strike at any moment: his father had died in an accident and his elder brother had died of a sudden illness. His son and heir was underage and his Byzantine wife had not yet given birth to a son; in case of accident, the kingdom needed a reliable regent. An obvious solution was to find a husband for Sybil who had military experience and could act as regent if required.[64]

As Sybil would have been around ten years old, it was a reasonable time to start planning her marriage. Although Amaury may not have expected his daughter to be married until she was fifteen (a common age for marriage for noble and royal women), lengthy negotiations would be required to arrange the match.[65] The second in line to the throne of Jerusalem must marry a man who was her equal in rank or at least of excellent noble family and to whom she was not related within the Church's forbidden degrees. But Amaury could not risk upsetting the balance of power within the crusader states by marrying his daughter to one of the local noble families, so he had to look outside his kingdom. So far as is known, he did not approach the Byzantine Empire on this matter: apart from the danger to the kingdom's autonomy from yet another royal marriage alliance with Byzantium, it is possible that no Byzantine prince was prepared to consider Sybil as a wife. In any case, Amaury sought a husband for his daughter among the European nobility.

Through her marriage, Sybil would perform one of the key roles for royal princesses and noblewomen: linking her family to another powerful and influential dynasty which could support her natal family and her kingdom through representing their interests in the West and by sending resources of men and money to the East. As comparison, in the early winter of the same year that Amaury sent his embassy to Europe, Sybil's cousin King Henry II of England received an embassy from Castile requesting the hand of his second daughter Eleanor, born in 1161, for the young King Alfonso VIII. The marriage established a strong alliance between Castile and England and

44 Childhood (c. 1159–1171)

strengthened Henry's hand in his claim (in the name of his wife Eleanor of Aquitaine) to the county of Toulouse.[66] Sybil's position, however, was evidently different from her cousin's: whereas Eleanor of England travelled to her intended husband's court to be married and she then remained in Castile, from subsequent events it appears that Sybil's prospective husband was expected to come to the kingdom of Jerusalem and remain there after the marriage. This indicates that Sybil was already acknowledged as the probable heir to the kingdom and her husband would possibly become king of Jerusalem in due course or in any case would father the future king of Jerusalem. In the meantime, he would hold a position of authority within the kingdom and be a close advisor to the king.

William, at the time of these events archdeacon of Tyre, concluded his description of Amaury's embassy with the brief remark that Bishop John died in Paris and the Lord Archbishop returned after two years with absolutely nothing. However, later on in his history he admitted that the embassy had had one result. Through the archbishop, the king had summoned Count Stephen of Sancerre, '*virum quidem carne nobilem, moribus vero non ita*' (a man noble in flesh, but not so in behaviour), the third son of Lord Theobald of Blois, Chartres and Champagne (and younger brother of Counts Henry I of Champagne and Theobald of Chartres), to marry his daughter.[67]

Stephen had been born in around 1133 (so was aged around thirty-eight when he came to the East) and was a member of 'the largest and most powerful family in France'. To all appearances he was an ideal husband for Sybil, as he would strengthen ties between Jerusalem and the ruling families of northern France. Stephen was the grandson of Count Stephen II of Blois, who had been one of the leaders of the First Crusade, and Adela of Normandy, daughter of King William I of England. He was thus the nephew of Stephen of Blois, king of England, and his wife Matilda of Boulogne, niece of Godfrey de Bouillon and King Baldwin I of Jerusalem. Stephen of Sancerre's eldest brother Henry I, count of Champagne, had taken part in the Second Crusade and would undertake another expedition to the Holy Land in 1179–1181; both Henry and their brother Theobald of Chartres were among the addressees of Archbishop Frederick's embassy. Henry and Theobald had married the daughters of Louis VII of France and Eleanor of Aquitaine, Marie and Alice, and the brothers' sister Adela had become Louis VII's third wife. Their younger brother William became archbishop of Reims. Although Stephen was a third son he held his own patrimony of Sancerre, and – like Fulk V of Anjou in 1128, when he was offered the hand of King Baldwin II's eldest daughter and heir Melisende – his first wife was dead. Unlike Fulk, however, he had not previously visited the crusader states and did not already have personal knowledge of their people and circumstances. William of Tyre did not record how Stephen had come to Amaury's attention or who first suggested that Stephen be offered Sybil's hand. Perhaps one of the noble visitors to the kingdom of Jerusalem had proposed him, such as Count Thierry of Flanders during his visit to the east in 1164, or Stephen of Perche (chancellor of the kingdom of Sicily and archbishop-elect of Palermo) or Count William of Nevers when they came east in the summer of 1168.[68]

Stephen arrived in the kingdom of Jerusalem in 1171 with other eminent nobles, including his nephew Hugh III of Burgundy (who would later be offered Sybil's hand), Stephen II of Burgundy (son of Count William of Saône and cousin of Empress Beatrice, wife of Frederick Barbarossa), Hugh III's seneschal Odo of Champlitte (also a cousin of Beatrice), other lords of Burgundian castles and some Cistercian monks, including the bishop of Verdun. Both Hugh III and Stephen II had married nieces of Frederick Barbarossa. Stephen also brought the money that King Louis VII had collected to help the church of Jerusalem.[69]

William of Tyre wrote that Stephen reneged on his agreements; *turpiter* and *immunde* (disgracefully and foully) he stayed in the kingdom only a few months and then went back to his own land.[70] It is possible that Stephen thought that Amaury was too subservient to the Byzantines or that he was unable to agree with Amaury what authority he would hold as Sybil's husband and whether he would have any claim to the throne.[71] Amaury already had a son and he could still have a healthy son with his second wife, Maria Komnene. Maria may already have given birth to a daughter (who died in infancy) and it is possible that during the time that Stephen was in the kingdom of Jerusalem she became pregnant with Isabel. Stephen would then have realised that he had no guarantee of inheriting anything.[72] It would also have been around this time that it first became clear that young Baldwin was sick.[73] Although the nature of his sickness was not known at that time, Stephen might have been concerned about the health of the family into which he was marrying. Again, no doubt Stephen was aware that Amaury had been forced to divorce Sybil's mother, and perhaps he was worried that Sybil's legitimacy could be challenged. William recorded that after leaving Jerusalem, Stephen travelled towards Constantinople; en route he was attacked near Mamistra by Mleh of Cilician Armenia, and his goods plundered. He reached Constantinople ignominiously with just a small entourage, pursued by the hatred of all the people of the East. William implied that this was due punishment for his bad behaviour in the kingdom.[74]

However, later records from the crusader states suggest that William of Tyre's description of Stephen of Sancerre's time in the kingdom of Jerusalem is misleading. In the mid-thirteenth century Philip of Novara, legal expert and knight, included in his *Livre de Forme de Plait* ('Book on the Method of Pleading in Court') an account of how Count Stephen of Blois, 'a very wise man from the kingdom of France', came to the kingdom of Jerusalem 'for a very long time' and the king and the other leading men of the country made much use of his advice. In particular, he advised on the case of the heirs of Henry le Buffle (Buffalo), who died leaving three daughters as his heirs. Stephen's opinion was that the inheritance should be divided equally between the three, and this established an important legal precedent. The case also appears in one manuscript of another mid-thirteenth-century legal text from the crusader states, John of Ibelin's *Livre des Assises*. As this manuscript was produced in 1369 as a work of reference for the High Court of Cyprus, it appears that the case was still regarded as relevant to late-fourteenth-century Lusignan-ruled Cyprus. This version adds the information that the case was held over for a year and more to await the count of Sancerre's arrival in the East so that he could deliver his opinion.[75]

Even if this later account is exaggerated, it raises a question: if Stephen of Sancerre really was as hated as William of Tyre claimed, how could his legal advice have established such a precedent? Could it be possible that William, suspicious of outside interference in the affairs of the kingdom of Jerusalem and playing down the success of the embassy led by Archbishop Frederick of Tyre – with whom he had quarrelled, although William never recorded the details of their dispute – deliberately misinterpreted Stephen of Sancerre's position?[76] Only William recorded that Stephen of Sancerre had come to the East to marry Sybil. Perhaps his expedition was never more than an armed pilgrimage, similar to that undertaken by Thierry of Flanders in 1164, and the suggestion that he might be a suitable husband for Sybil was never more than that. In fact, Philip of Novara's account suggests that Stephen's value to the king and his nobles lay more in his legal knowledge than in any marital intentions. As William of Tyre had studied civil law at Bologna, he might have resented this intruder into his own realm of expertise.[77] In this context, it is worth noting Benjamin Kedar's suggestion that it was Stephen who informed the royal court and the leaders of the kingdom about the system of taxation used in France in 1166 to raise the money he had brought on behalf of King Louis VII. This tax may have been the inspiration for the general taxation raised in the kingdom of Jerusalem in 1183.[78] Again, this would mean that far from despising Stephen of Sancerre King Amaury and his advisors listened to him and found his advice valuable.

Stephen returned to France early in 1173 and later remarried. He would return to the Holy Land on the Third Crusade, reaching Acre soon after 25 July 1190, and died before 21 October 1190[79] – he would then have been aged around fifty-seven.

In 1171, Sybil was around twelve years of age with no immediate prospect of marriage. There was no immediate urgency: her father was only in his midthirties and could live for many more years; the kingdom was supported by the Byzantine emperor, and clearly the kings and nobles of western Europe were ready to send some limited military aid and money in response to appeals. Nūr al-Dīn was a threat in the East and Mleh of Cilician Armenia was his ally, but in Egypt the vizier Saladin was concentrating on administration and establishing his own dynastic powerbase.[80] For the moment the future of the kingdom of Jerusalem looked secure.

Notes

1 See, for example, Nicholas Orme, *Medieval Children* (New Haven and London, 2001), pp. 4–10; Peter Fleming, *Family and Household in Medieval England* (Basingstoke, 2001), pp. 59–65.

2 Colette Bowie, *The Daughters of Henry II and Eleanor of Aquitaine* (Turnhout, 2014), pp. 57–63; Theodore Evergates, *Marie of France: Countess of Champagne, 1145–1198* (Philadelphia, 2019), pp. 5–6; Kathryn Dutton, 'Ad erudiendum tradidit: The Upbringing of Angevin Comital Children', in *Anglo-Norman Studies XXXII: Proceedings of the Battle Conference 2009*, ed. C. P. Lewis (Woodbridge, 2010), pp. 24–39, at p. 34.

3 Hans Mayer argues that Baldwin III gave Jaffa to Amaury after 30 July 1154: Mayer, 'Studies in the History of Queen Melisende of Jerusalem', 176, and 162–163 and note 98, 175, 178, 181–182; see also Hans Eberhard Mayer, 'The Double County of Jaffa and Ascalon: one Fief or Two?', in *Crusade and Settlement. Papers read at the First Conference of the Society for the Study of the Crusades and the Latin East and presented to R. C. Smail*, ed. Peter W. Edbury (Cardiff, 1985), pp. 181–190. On the lordship of Ramla see Peter W. Edbury, 'The Crusader Town and Lordship of Ramla (1099–1268)', in *Ramla: City of Muslim Palestine, 715–1917*, ed. Andrew Petersen and Denys Pringle (Oxford, 2021), pp. 7–17.

4 Hamilton, 'The Titular Nobility', p. 197; Barber, *Crusader States*, p. 195.

5 Buck, *Principality of Antioch*, pp. 38–39, 148; Hamilton, 'The Titular Nobility', p. 197; Hamilton, *Leper King*, pp. 24–25; Hans Eberhard Mayer, 'The Beginnings of King Amalric of Jerusalem', in *The Horns of Ḥaṭṭīn*, ed. Benjamin Z. Kedar (Jerusalem and London, 1992), pp. 121–135; Edbury, 'The Crusader Town and Lordship of Ramla', pp. 11–12.

6 WT 2: 962 (Bk 21 ch. 2). On child mortality rates – 15–20% in the first year, and 30% by the age of twenty – see Ralph V. Turner, 'The Children of Anglo-Norman Royalty and their Upbringing', *Medieval Prosopography*, 11.2 (1990), 17–52, at 21.

7 Francine Mora-Lebrun, 'Les metamorphoses de la Sibylle au XIIe siècle', *Bien Dire et Bien Aprandre*, 24 (2006), 11–24, at 11–12; Christine de Pizan, *The Book of the City of Ladies*, trans. Rosalind Brown-Grant (Harmondsworth, 1999), pp. 91–95 (II: 1–3).

8 Constance Brittain Bouchard, *"Those of my Blood": Constructing Noble Families in Medieval Francia* (Philadelphia, 2001), p. 120.

9 WT 2:869 (Bk 19 ch. 4). For the role of godparents see Bernard Hamilton, *Religion in the Medieval West* (London, 1986), p. 112.

10 Karen S. Nicholas, 'Countesses as Rulers in Flanders', in *Aristocratic Women in Medieval France*, ed. Theodore Evergates (Philadelphia, 1999), pp. 111–137, at pp. 121–123; Park, *Papal Protection*, pp. 137–153, 169. Alan V. Murray has suggested that our Sybil's name also honoured Count Thierry, Countess Sybil's husband: Alan V. Murray, 'Kingship, Identity and Name-giving in the Family of Baldwin of Bourcq', in *Knighthoods of Christ: Essays on the History of the Crusades and the Knights Templar presented to Malcolm Barber*, ed. Norman Housley (Aldershot, 2007), pp. 27–38, at p. 34.

11 Park, *Papal Protection*, p. 152.

12 WT 2: 840–842 (Bk 18 ch. 20); Barber, *Crusader States*, p. 216; Lewis, 'Countess Hodierna of Tripoli', 17–19; Lewis, *Counts of Tripoli*, pp. 157–158.

13 'Continuatio Aquicinctina', pp. 408, 412; 'Auctarium Affigemense', ed. D. L. C. Bethmann, *MGH SS*, 6, ed. Georg Heinrich Pertz (Hanover, 1844), pp. 398–405, at p. 403; 'Auctarium Aquicinense', ed. D. L. C. Bethmann, *MGH SS*, 6, ed. Georg Heinrich Pertz (Hanover, 1844), pp. 392–398, at p. 398; Abbot Robert stated that the count was not happy about the countess remaining with the abbess of St Lazarus of Bethany, stating that she did so *invito coniuge suo*, but misnames

48 *Childhood (c. 1159–1171)*

   the countess as Mabiria: *Chronicle of Robert of Torigni*, p. 205; WT 2: 876 (Bk 19 ch. 10); for Countess Sybil's death see also Park, *Papal Protection*, p. 169.
14 Nicholas Orme, *Medieval Children* (New Haven and London, 2001), pp. 58–59, 66; S. A. Mays, M. P. Richards and B. T. Fuller, 'Bone Stable Isotope Evidence for Infant Feeding in Mediaeval England', *Antiquity*, 76 (2002), 654–656, at 656.
15 WT 2: 962 (Bk 21 ch. 2).
16 Erin L. Jordan, 'Hostage, Sister, Abbess: The Life of Iveta of Jerusalem', *Medieval Prosopography*, 32 (2017), 66–86; Barber, *Crusader States*, pp. 138, 157–160; Hamilton, 'Women in the Crusader States', pp. 148, 151; Hamilton and Jotischky, *Latin and Greek Monasticism*, p. 232; WT 1: 606, 2: 709–710 (Bk 13 ch. 16, Bk 15 ch. 26). Jordan points out (pp. 72–75) that the accounts claiming that Iveta was abused as a hostage have no contemporary basis; for this reason, they will not be discussed here.
17 Hamilton and Jotischky, *Latin and Greek Monasticism*, pp. 231–235; Barber, Crusader States, pp. 158–159; 'Bethany', in Denys Pringle, *The Churches of the Crusader Kingdom of Jerusalem: A Corpus*, 4 vols (Cambridge, 1993–2009), 1: 122–137, at 124, 127–129 for plans of the site. For male servants and officials at a women's religious house, in this case in the Iberian Peninsula, see María Echániz Sans, *Las Mujeres de la Orden Militar de Santiago en la Edad Media* (Salamanca, 1992), pp. 56–64, 73, 157, 181–222: the community of *Sancti Spiritus* at Salamanca, for example, which had just sixteen sisters, employed in addition to a male chaplain a male water carrier, a male physician, a male sacristan, a male organist, a male mayordomo and other male servants.
18 WT 2: 709 (Bk 15 ch. 26); Pringle, *Churches*, 1: 123, 124, 128–129, 130–134. For the layout of women's religious houses see Roberta Gilchrist, *Gender and Material Culture: The archaeology of religious women* (London, 1994), pp. 163–167; Roberta Gilchrist, *Contemplation and Action: the Other Monasticism* (London, 1995), pp. 119, 129–132, 134.
19 WT 2: 710 (Bk 15 ch. 26); Pringle, *Churches*, 1: 123.
20 Pringle, *Churches*, 1: 124; Hamilton and Jotischky, *Latin and Greek Monasticism*, pp. 232–239; *Cartulaire général de l'ordre des Hospitaliers de S. Jean de Jérusalem*, ed. Joseph Delaville le Roulx, 4 vols (Paris, 1894–1906), 1: 189–190, 446 (nos 250, 664); Ch. Kohler, ed., 'Chartes de l'Abbaye de Notre-Dame de la Vallée de Josaphat en Terre-Sainte (1108–1291). Analyses et extraits', *Revue de l'Orient Latin*, 7 (1899), 108–222, at pp. 148–149, 150–151 (nos 41, 43).
21 Barber, *Crusader States*, p. 363.
22 Barber, *Crusader States*, p. 217; Hamilton, 'Women in the Crusader States', pp. 158–159.
23 WT 2: 869–870 (Bk 19 ch. 4); Barber, *Crusader States*, pp. 232–233.
24 Hamilton, 'The Titular Nobility', pp. 198, 202 note 18; Hamilton, *Leper King*, pp. 24–26; Buck, *Principality of Antioch*, pp. 143–147.
25 WT 2: 870 (Bk 19 ch. 4).
26 Mayer, 'The Beginnings of King Amalric'; Mayer, 'Die Legitimität Balduins IV'. For Bohemond's and Raymond's ages see Buck, *Principality of Antioch*, p. 80; Lewis, *Counts of Tripoli*, p. 183.
27 Edbury, 'The Crusader Town and Lordship of Ramla', pp. 11–12.
28 Barber, *Crusader States*, p. 363.
29 In the same way, Eleanor of Aquitaine's children with King Louis VII of France remained with their father after the dissolution of the marriage on grounds of consanguinity in 1152: Turner, *Eleanor of Aquitaine*, p. 107.

30 Tyerman, *God's War*, p. 358; Andrew Jotischky, *Crusading and the Crusader States* (Harlow, 2004), p. 95. For the contrary opinion, see Hamilton, *Leper King*, pp. 40, 153.
31 Dutton, 'Ad erudiendum, tradidit', pp. 34–35; Bowie, *The Daughters*, p. 59 and note 29.
32 Hanley, *Matilda*, p. 22.
33 Edoardo D'Angelo, 'A Latin School in the Norman Principality of Antioch?', in *People, Texts and Artefacts: Cultural Transmission in the Medieval Norman Worlds*, ed. David Bates, Edoardo D'Angelo and Elisabeth van Houts (London, 2017), pp. 77–88, at p. 79.
34 Bowie, *The Daughters*, p. 58; Turner, *Eleanor of Aquitaine*, p. 32; [Matthew Paris], *Matthæi Parisiensis monachi Sancti Albani Chronica majora*, ed. Henry Richards Luard, 7 vols, Rolls Series 57 (London, 1872–1883), 6: 385.
35 Theodore Evergates, *Marie of France: Countess of Champagne, 1145–1198* (Philadelphia, 2019), pp. 5–6.
36 Bowie, *The Daughters*, p. 41 and note 60.
37 Gilchrist, *Contemplation and Action*, pp. 113–114; David N. Bell, *What Nuns Read: Books and Libraries in Medieval English Nunneries* (Kalamazoo, MI, 1995), pp. 59, 61–62, 77, 81 note 16; Orme, *Medieval Children*, pp. 242, 318.
38 Turner, *Eleanor of Aquitaine*, p. 107.
39 'Sibylla regina Hierusalemitana epistola Friderico Rom. Imp.', in 'Tagenonis decani Pataviensis, Descriptio Expeditionis Asiaticæ contra Turcas Friderici Imp.', in *Rerum Germanicarum Scriptores aliquot insignes*, vol. 1, ed. Marquard Freher, 3rd edn revised Burchard Gotthelf Struve (Strassburg, 1717), p. 410; translated in *Letters of the Crusaders*, trans. Dana Carleton Munro (Philadelphia, 1902), pp. 21–22. For letters written by Sybil's contemporary Eleanor of Aquitaine, see Turner, *Eleanor of Aquitaine*, pp. 187, 291–292.
40 Bowie, *The Daughters*, pp. 59–64.
41 Christine de Pisan, *The Treasure of the City of Ladies or the Book of the Three Virtues*, trans. Sarah Lawson (Harmondsworth, 1985), pp. 59–62, 128–129 (1: 11, 2: 9).
42 Bell, *What Nuns Read*, pp. 41–42.
43 WT 2: 710 (Bk 15 ch. 26).
44 Benjamin Z. Kedar, 'Gerard of Nazareth, a Neglected Twelfth-Century Writer in the Latin East: A Contribution to the Intellectual and Monastic History of the Crusader States', *Dumbarton Oaks Papers*, 37 (1983), 55–77, at 55, 56, 58, 71, 75.
45 Edbury and Rowe, *William of Tyre*, pp. 45–53. For the development of the French epic 'Chanson d'Antioche', which may not have reached its current form until the early thirteenth century, see *The Chanson d'Antioche: An Old French Account of the First Crusade*, trans. Susan B. Edgington and Carol Sweetenham, Crusade Texts in Translation 22 (Farnham, 2011), pp. 3–24.
46 D'Angelo, 'A Latin School?' pp. 80–85. In the following century, Acre (the new capital of the kingdom of Jerusalem) would become a centre for the production of texts in Latin, French and Hebrew on a broad range of subjects and it was a lively cultural centre, despite the constant threat of invasion from its Muslim neighbours: see Jonathan Rubin, *Learning in a Crusader City: Intellectual Activity and Intercultural Exchanges in Acre, 1191–1291* (Cambridge, 2018). As Rubin points out (p. 171) the fact that no university developed in the crusader states does not mean that they were a cultural desert.

50 Childhood (c. 1159–1171)

47 Jean Frappier, *Les Chansons de geste du cycle de Guillaume d'Orange*, 2 vols (Paris, 1955, 1965); Jeanne Wathelet-Willem, 'Guibourc, femme de Guillaume', in *Les Chansons de geste du cycle de Guillaume d'Orange*, vol. 3: *Les moniages; Guibourc. Hommage à Jean Frappier*, ed. Philippe Ménard and Jean-Charles Payen (Paris, 1983), pp. 335–355.
48 Wace, *The Hagiographical Works: The Conception Nostre Dame and the Lives of St Margaret and St Nicholas*, trans. Jean Blacker, Glyn S. Burgess and Amy V. Ogden (Leiden, 2013), pp. 3 (the *Roman de Brut* was completed in 1155), 7 (his hagiographical works were written between 1130 and 1150; he began the *Roman de Rou* in 1160, then stopped working on it, began again in around 1170, but stopped writing around 1174); Chrétien de Troyes. *Les Romans de Chrétien de Troyes édités d'après la copie de Guiot (Bibl. nat., fr. 794) I: Erec et Enide*, ed. Mario Roques, Classiques français du Moyen Âge 80 (Paris, 1981), p. xxvii; Logan E. Whalen (ed.), *A Companion to Marie de France* (Leiden, 2011), p. viii.
49 David Jacoby, 'Knightly Values and Class Consciousness in the Crusader States of the Eastern Mediterranean', *Mediterranean Historical Review*, 1.2 (1986), 158–186; Krijnie N. Ciggaar, 'Robert de Boron en Outremer? Le Culte de Joseph d'Arimathie dans le monde byzantin et en Outremer', *Polyphonia Byzantina: Studies in Honour of Willem J. Aerts*, ed. Hero Hokwerda, Edmé R. Smits and Marinus M. Woesthuis (Groningen, 1993), pp. 145–159; Helen J. Nicholson, *Love, War and the Grail: Templars, Hospitallers and Teutonic Knights in Medieval Epic and Romance, 1150–1500* (Leiden, 2001), pp. 151–152.
50 Jordan, 'Hostage, Sister, Abbess', p. 85.
51 John Carmi Parsons, 'Mothers, Daughters, Marriage, Power: Some Plantagenet Evidence, 1150–1500', in *Medieval Queenship*, ed. John Carmi Parsons (Stroud, 1994), pp. 63–78, at pp. 74–75.
52 See the comments relating to kings' relationships with their daughters in the next generation by Parsons, 'Mothers, Daughters, Marriage, Power', p. 71.
53 Hamilton, 'The Titular Nobility', pp. 199–200, quotation at p. 199.
54 Harris, *Byzantium and the Crusades*, pp. 116–117; Barber, *Crusader States*, pp. 246–247, 363; Hamilton, *Leper King*, pp. 64–67.
55 For what follows see Harris, *Byzantium and the Crusades*, pp. 99–120.
56 WT 2: 856–859 (Bk 18 chs 31, 33); Lewis, *Counts of Tripoli*, pp. 197–201; Buck, *Principality of Antioch*, pp. 209–212.
57 Harris, *Byzantium and the Crusades*, pp. 113–115; Murray, 'Constance, Princess of Antioch', pp. 93–94; Buck, *Principality of Antioch*, pp. 80, 202–208, 212–213, 230.
58 Barber, *Crusader States*, pp. 237–240, 363; Lewis, *Counts of Tripoli*, pp. 206, 209, 219; WT 2: 976 (Bk 21, ch. 10); Hamilton, *Leper King*, pp. 103–104; Vasselot de Régné, 'A Crusader Lineage', 101 (note that 'the master of the Knights Hospitaller' should be 'the commander of the Knights Templar' and in note 44, *PL* 155: 13 should be *PL* 155:1279–1280).
59 Barber, *Crusader States*, pp. 242–252, 363; Malcolm Cameron Lyons and D. E. P. Jackson, *Saladin: The Politics of the Holy War* (Cambridge, 1982), pp. 10–24; Jonathan Phillips, *The Life and Legend of the Sultan Saladin* (London, 2019), pp. 51–53.
60 Lyons and Jackson, *Saladin*, pp. 25–29, 36–38; Phillips, *The Life and Legend*, pp. 54–67; Barber, *Crusader States*, pp. 252–255; Harris, *Byzantium and the Crusades*, p. 118.
61 Barber, *Crusader States*, p. 258; Hamilton, *Leper King*, p. 31.

62 WT 2: 1012 (Bk 22 ch. 5): Isabel was scarcely eight years old in October 1180. For her sister, see *IP* 1, pp. 336–337.
63 WT 2: 926 (Bk 20, ch. 12); Jonathan Phillips, *Defenders of the Holy Land: Relations between the Latin East and the West, 1119–1187* (Oxford, 1996), pp. 170–178, 180–188.
64 Hamilton, *Leper King*, p. 30.
65 For fifteen as the most common age for noble girls to marry see Parsons, 'Mothers, Daughters, Marriage, Power', pp. 66–67; Hamilton, *Leper King*, p. 30, argues for eleven being the age 'when it was considered normal to arrange marriages'. Girls could marry from the age of twelve years, boys from thirteen: James A. Brundage, 'Marriage Law in the Latin Kingdom of Jerusalem', in *Outremer: Studies in the history of the Crusading Kingdom of Jerusalem presented to Joshua Prawer*, ed. B. Z. Kedar, H. E. Mayer, and R. C. Smail (Jerusalem, 1982), pp. 258–271, at p. 261.
66 Bowie, *The Daughters*, pp. 71–73; for the political and other benefits of the marriages of Henry's daughters see pp. 67–97.
67 WT 2: 926, 947 (Bk 20 chs 12, 25).
68 Hilary Rhodes, *The Crown and the Cross: Burgundy, France, and the Crusades, 1095–1223*, Outremer: Studies in the Crusades and the Latin East 9 (Turnhout, 2020), p. 129 (quotation); Phillips, *Defenders*, pp. 178–179; Hamilton, *Leper King*, p. 30; Barber, *Crusader States*, p. 253.
69 Rhodes, *The Crown and the Cross*, pp. 130–133; Theodore Evergates, *Henry the Liberal, Count of Champagne, 1127–1181* (Philadelphia, 2016), p. 151; Benjamin Z. Kedar, 'The General Tax of 1183 in the Crusading Kingdom of Jerusalem: Innovation or Adaptation?' *English Historical Review*, 89 (1974), 339–345, at 345; *The Chronicle of Robert of Torigni*, p. 249.
70 WT 2: 947 (Bk 20 ch. 25).
71 Barber, *Crusader States*, p. 253.
72 Murray, 'Women in the Royal Succession', p. 146.
73 Hamilton, *Leper King*, pp. 27–29, 38; Piers D. Mitchell, 'An Evaluation of the Leprosy of King Baldwin IV of Jerusalem in the Context of the Medieval World', in Hamilton, *Leper King*, pp. 245–258, at 250–252.
74 WT 2: 947 (Bk 20 ch. 25).
75 Hamilton, *Leper King*, pp. 30–31; Philip of Novara, *Le Livre de Forme de Plait*, ed. and trans. Peter W. Edbury (Nicosia, 2009), pp. 21 (date), 141–142, 273–274 (ch. 57) (note that the second daughter married Count Joscelin III of Edessa); John of Ibelin, *Le Livre des Assises*, ed. Peter W. Edbury (Leiden, 2003), pp. 730–731, 763, 766.
76 For the quarrel, see Edbury and Rowe, *William of Tyre*, pp. 16–17.
77 On William's studies in civil law see Edbury and Rowe, *William of Tyre*, p. 15.
78 Benjamin Z. Kedar, 'The General Tax of 1183 in the Crusading Kingdom of Jerusalem: Innovation or Adaptation?' *English Historical Review*, 89 (1974), 339–345, at 343.
79 Evergates, *Henry the Liberal*, p. 151; *Chronicle of the Third Crusade*, p. 98 and note 188.
80 Barber, *Crusader States*, pp. 258–259; Hamilton, *Leper King*, p. 70; Lyons and Jackson, *Saladin*, pp. 45–59; Phillips, *Life and Legend*, pp. 69–77.

3 Adolescence and marriage (1172–1177)

Family matters

The year 1172 saw some changes to Sybil's family. At about this time, her mother Agnes de Courtenay married her fourth husband, Reynald of Sidon, son of Gerald of Sidon.[1] In the autumn Maria Komnene gave birth to her second daughter, named Isabel. William of Tyre did not mention the birth under 1172, only telling his readers under October 1180, when Isabel was about to be betrothed, that she was scarcely eight years old.[2] No information about Isabel's early years survives. William did not even tell his readers where she was educated, although it may have been at the Abbey of St Lazarus at Bethany, like her elder half-sister.[3]

That year also saw another illustrious visitor to the kingdom of Jerusalem, Henry the Lion, duke of Saxony and Bavaria, who, like Stephen of Sancerre before him and Henry I of Champagne later, also visited Constantinople. William of Tyre said nothing of Henry's visit, even though Henry was an illustrious ruler and military leader and married to Matilda, eldest daughter of King Henry II of England and Eleanor of Aquitaine and hence King Amaury's great-niece (and first cousin once removed of Sybil).[4] The fact that William omitted any mention of Henry suggests that, as in his treatment of Stephen of Sancerre, he distrusted and dismissed powerful outsiders.

Another family member returned to public life early in 1174, when Count Raymond III of Tripoli was released from prison in Aleppo, where he had been held since Nūr al-Dīn captured him at the Battle of Artah in 1164. The ransom was paid partly in cash and partly guaranteed by hostages; the Order of the Hospital of St John of Jerusalem, otherwise known as the Knights Hospitaller, paid a large portion of the cash. Hitherto Nūr al-Dīn had refused to release Raymond III on any terms. It is not clear why he changed his mind, but possibly he was happy to allow the crusader states a little more power – by restoring one of their leaders to them – to make them a stronger buffer against the growing power of Saladin in Egypt. Amaury welcomed Raymond home with gifts and confirmed that he was still count of Tripoli. Later that year Raymond married the recently widowed Lady Eschiva of Tiberias, princess of Galilee, whose husband Walter of St Omer had died early in 1174. Eschiva and Walter had had four sons, known to posterity as the Tiberias brothers: Hugh, William, Osto, and Ralph or Raoul – but her marriage to Raymond, which lasted until his death in 1187, was childless.[5]

In 1174 there were also dramatic changes in the political landscape of the Near East. Nūr al-Dīn died suddenly on 15 May. Amaury hoped to exploit the situation to recover territory in Syria which Nūr al-Dīn had captured, but became ill himself and died on 11 July. His only son and immediate heir, Sybil's younger brother Baldwin, was barely thirteen years old; William of Tyre recorded that he was crowned four days after his father's death, on 15 July 1174. In October Saladin took over Damascus, uniting most of the Franks' Muslim neighbours under a single ruler whose power encircled the crusader states.[6]

The minority of King Baldwin IV

Baldwin IV's succession was by no means a certainty. Sole inheritance by the first-born son was not yet the fixed rule among the noble families of western Europe from whom the Frankish nobility were drawn, and at the age of thirteen Baldwin was still too young to govern in his own name; he would need a regent to govern for him until he reached his majority. In addition, the young king's health may have already become a cause for concern, and even though Sybil and Baldwin's legitimacy had been confirmed in 1163, the validity of their dynastic claim to the throne could have been raised in any debate over Baldwin's fitness to rule. When Saladin wrote to his nephew Farrukh-Shah to report the glad news of Amaury's death he noted that the Franks had not yet decided on his successor. But in fact there is no evidence that any candidate other than Baldwin was considered. The same candidates who could have been chosen in 1163, Count Raymond III of Tripoli and Prince Bohemond III of Antioch – both descendants of King Baldwin II and Queen Morphia – were now much older and more experienced men who could have ruled in their own names, but apparently the assembly of lay and ecclesiastical leaders of the kingdom which met to discuss the succession did not consider them for long if at all. Baldwin's succession was agreed and he was crowned as King Baldwin IV of Jerusalem.[7]

The nobles of the kingdom of Jerusalem also needed to decide how the kingdom should be governed, as the king was still underage. Normally in such circumstances in western Europe a regent would be appointed. The customary practice in the kingdom of Jerusalem in 1174 for choosing a regent is not absolutely clear because the surviving records date from the thirteenth century. According to Philip of Novara, writing in the mid-thirteenth century, the written procedures and laws of the kingdom from the period before 1187 had been lost when Saladin captured Jerusalem, but it is more likely that in the twelfth-century kingdom secular law was based on customary practice and was not written down.[8] In any case, the most obvious regent would be the child's mother, but Baldwin's mother, Agnes de Courtenay, was not queen and the queen, Maria Komnene, was not Baldwin's mother. Sybil may have been fifteen by this time and so of age, so would appear to have been eligible.

The next most obvious regent would be the nearest male relation on the father's side, which would bring in Count Raymond III of Tripoli or Prince Bohemond III of Antioch.

In the event – and perhaps because of the difficulty of deciding who had the best claim – the High Court did not appoint a regent, and the responsibility of overseeing government fell on the same person who would hold this responsibility if the king were absent or ill: the seneschal (chief minister) of the kingdom, at this time Miles of Plancy, lord of Transjordan. The seneschal dealt with all administrative matters, while military leadership was the responsibility of Humphrey or Henfrid II of Toron, constable (chief military commander) of the kingdom. Humphrey had been constable since at least 1152 and possibly since 1149.[9] He had gained such a reputation as an exemplar of the noble warrior that by 1190 there was a story in circulation in the Latin East that when Saladin was a young warrior he had come to Humphrey to be knighted.[10]

Miles of Plancy was a relative newcomer to the kingdom of Jerusalem, having come to the East in 1160. As a member of the Montlhéry family, he was distantly related to King Amaury through King Baldwin II's mother Melisende de Montlhéry. He had become a trusted advisor of the king, and had married Stephanie de Milly, daughter of Philip de Milly (lord of Nablus and of Transjordan and briefly master of the Order of the Temple) and widow of Humphrey III of Toron, son of Humphrey II.[11] William of Tyre detested him, criticising the advice he had given Amaury during his Egyptian campaigns, accusing him of 'subverting the king's mind with sinister advice', claiming that he was degenerate in morals, neither feared God nor revered persons and was a shameless, noisy troublemaker.[12] Given that William's criticism of Count Stephen of Sancerre appears to have been based on personal resentment rather than actuality, it is likely that his accusations against Miles of Plancy merely reflect the fact that Miles had the king's ear and controlled access to the king. This would have made Miles extremely unpopular among all those who hoped for favours and promotion from the king – as William himself did.

Nevertheless, despite his high rank and power, Miles was vulnerable. He did not have the network of friends and supporters that he needed to remain in power, and King Baldwin was too young and too lacking in influence and experience to protect him. There were some grounds for complaint against Miles. King Amaury had committed the kingdom of Jerusalem to a joint operation with the Sicilians against Egypt in the summer of 1174: the Sicilians arrived but the Frankish army did not, and the Sicilians had to withdraw. The failure to muster the army when required indicates that Miles and Humphrey were not working together. Indeed, why should Humphrey, a member of one of the oldest families in the kingdom, work with a loud-mouthed newcomer like Miles? Their relationship may not have been helped by the fact that Miles had married Humphrey's son's widow, thus taking for himself all that Humphrey's son had previously gained through his marriage.

Adolescence and marriage (1172–1177)

Humphrey supported Count Raymond III of Tripoli when the latter claimed that he should have the *procuratio regni*, the procuration of the kingdom – that is, he should govern it for the king. Raymond put forward a three-fold justification for his claim: he was the king's nearest male relative, he was the most powerful of the king's vassals (presumably as prince of Galilee, as he was not the king's vassal for Tripoli), and while he was in prison he had instructed his vassals to obey King Amaury in his place as his nearest relative and heir presumptive, so now King Amaury's former vassals should likewise obey him. William of Tyre recorded that Raymond also had the support of Baldwin of Ramla, Balian his brother, Reynald of Sidon and all the bishops. It is not clear why all the bishops should have supported Raymond over Miles, but Baldwin, Balian (also known as Barisan) and Reynald were all members of well-established noble families of the kingdom of Jerusalem who could have resented the newcomer. The Ibelins had been established in the kingdom since the reign of Baldwin II. The father of the family, Barisan the elder, had been constable of Jaffa from at least 1126, married Helvis or Heloïse, daughter of Baldwin lord of Ramla, and was granted Ibelin (also known as 'Ibillin, Yibna, or Yavne) by King Fulk in or around 1141, shortly after its construction. Reynald's father Gerard had held Sidon from at least 1147 – this was a fortified port city, built on a promontory with strong land fortifications, including a castle. All three were related through Agnes de Courtenay: Baldwin and Balian were the younger brothers of her former husband Hugh of Ibelin, while Reynald was her current husband. As mother of the king, Agnes should now have been in a very influential position, although she had no formal role at court and had not been awarded the regency; she may have hoped to exert some influence through Raymond III, with the support of her brothers-in-law and husband, while they in turn could benefit from her relationship to the king. By supporting Raymond's claim the secular and clerical leaders of the kingdom expressed their opposition to Miles's government.[13]

According to William of Tyre, Miles sent an embassy to western Europe with letters and gifts to the kings, and rumours spread that he had sent messages to his friends and relatives in France to come to help him become king. Perhaps Miles hoped that one of the western princes related to Baldwin IV – such as King Henry II of England or Count Philip of Flanders, his first cousins – would claim the regency and establish Miles to rule on his behalf; and certainly Count Philip did take the cross on Good Friday 1175. But whatever Miles's intentions, they were cut short when he was murdered one night in a public street in Acre. The culprit was never brought to justice. The 'Regni Iherosolymitani Brevis Historia', written in Genoa after 1197, blamed the former lords of Beirut. They had lost Beirut to King Amaury, and had possibly expected it to be restored to them at the beginning of the new reign; but Miles would not have been prepared to give up crown lands, especially to a family that believed they had been cheated out of them by his previous master. However, this is speculation, as no one was charged with the murder. After two days of debate the High Court and the senior clergy, presided over by the young king in person, appointed Count Raymond as regent.[14]

William of Tyre generally praised Raymond's policies, not least because it was Raymond who promoted him to chancellor of the kingdom and made him archdeacon of Nazareth in addition to the archdeaconry of Tyre that he already held; Raymond must also have supported his election to the archbishopric of Tyre in May or June 1175. In fact, Raymond was not particularly successful in terms of defending the kingdom. By coming to peaceful agreements with Saladin he allowed him to build up his Syrian empire unopposed, and he offended two allies of the kingdom, Sicily and Byzantium, by negotiating a marriage between Sybil and William of Montferrat, a vassal and cousin of Emperor Frederick Barbarossa (William of Montferrat's mother was the sister of Frederick's father), who was hostile to both Sicily and Byzantium. It is possible Raymond deliberately set out to snub Emperor Manuel, who had insulted Raymond when he had married Maria of Antioch instead of Raymond's sister Melisende; or perhaps this new alliance was intended to counter-balance Byzantine influence in the kingdom of Jerusalem. In any case, Raymond's legacy was not as impressive as Archbishop William would have liked his readers to think. He may even have misdated events in his history to give the impression that Raymond's regency had been more successful than it actually was.[15]

On 13 December 1174, one Aimery de Lusignan, elder brother of Sybil's later husband Guy, made his first appearance in a government document. He was listed as a witness after Baldwin of Ramla's brother Balian of Ibelin. Aimery would marry – if he had not married already – Baldwin's daughter Eschiva. Aimery's brother Peter also appeared as a witness of a confirmation document issued by Count Raymond at around the same time.[16]

Aimery, Peter, and their brothers Guy and William had left Poitou in 1168, where they had been involved in a rebellion against King Henry II of England. Their father, Hugh VIII de Lusignan, had been captured by Nūr al-Dīn at the Battle of Artah in 1164, but he may have been released shortly afterwards, as a Hugh de Lusignan confirmed a donation to the Hospitallers in the county of Tripoli in 1168. If this Hugh was indeed Hugh VIII, still in Tripoli before returning to France in 1171, then it is possible that Aimery and his brothers took refuge in their father's lands in Tripoli after their clash with King Henry. Even if this Hugh de Lusignan was not Hugh VIII he was probably related to the Lusignans of Poitou, as his daughter was named Almodis, an ancestral name for the Lusignans of Poitou. He could have provided Aimery and his brothers with a refuge when they needed one.[17]

During these years we lose sight of Sybil. As she made no appearance in official documents or the writings of contemporary commentators, she was presumably still living in the Abbey of St Lazarus at Bethany, out of the public eye. As far as the surviving evidence indicates, there were no royal women at the king's court at this time. As Maria Komnene was not the king's mother there was no obvious role for her at court, and she probably withdrew to her dower fief of Nablus (an unwalled town with a royal castle and many churches) with her infant daughter Isabel, who would have been a little over eighteen months old when her father died.[18] Despite her apparent support for Count Raymond as regent, Agnes de Courtenay did not apparently come to court to be with her son while Raymond was regent, and seems to have had no voice in the decision to offer William, the junior marquis of Montferrat and son of William V, the hand in marriage of her daughter Sybil, with the towns of Jaffa and Ascalon and the whole county of Jaffa-Ascalon. William of Tyre wrote that the decision to approach the young William of Montferrat was made by the lord king and all the princes of the kingdom, both secular and ecclesiastical, but given the time required for negotiations and ambassadors' journeys the offer must have been made under Raymond's regency.[19]

Meanwhile in spring 1176, in northern Syria, Bohemond III of Antioch concluded an alliance with Gumushtekin, atabeg of Aleppo, against Saladin. In return for his support, Bohemond required the release of the Frankish prisoners held at Aleppo, who included Agnes de Courtenay's brother Joscelin, Sybil's uncle, and Reynald de Châtillon, formerly prince of Antioch in right of his wife Constance. Ransoms were agreed and paid. William of Tyre recorded that Agnes raised her brother's ransom; she would have had some resources of her own, but if the royal treasury made any contribution it must have had Count Raymond's agreement. Reynald de Châtillon's ransom, according to William of Tyre, was paid by his friends, but in fact Emperor Manuel probably paid most of it. In 1158 Reynald had acknowledged Manuel as his overlord for Antioch; Manuel was married to Princess Constance's daughter Maria, he had arranged the marriage of King Béla III of Hungary to Reynald's and Constance's daughter Agnes and taken their son Baldwin into his service, and in 1177 Prince Bohemond III would marry Manuel's niece Theodora. It would have been appropriate for Manuel to contribute towards the ransom of the former prince of Antioch.[20] Joscelin now had no estates of his own, and as Reynald's wife Constance was dead Reynald had no place within the government of his step-son Bohemond III, so both came to the court of the king of Jerusalem.

Marriage to William of Montferrat

Baldwin reached his majority in July 1176 at the age of fifteen and Raymond stepped down from the regency. Soon afterwards Baldwin appointed his uncle Joscelin as royal seneschal, and Joscelin appeared in that capacity witnessing royal documents, followed by Reynald and then Humphrey II of Toron. Humphrey was still constable, but Baldwin himself led the army in the field, even if – at fifteen and physically disabled by his illness – he needed to rely on the constable to carry much of the burden of leadership in battle.[21]

Joscelin and Reynald also gained wealthy brides: Joscelin married Agnes, second daughter of Henry le Buffle, who had inherited a third of her father's property thanks (according to Philip of Novara) to Stephen of Sancerre's advice in 1171.[22] Reynald, who retained his title of 'prince' even though he was no longer prince of Antioch, married Stephanie de Milly, lady of

Transjordan and widow of Humphrey III of Toron and Miles of Plancy. This strategically positioned fief, which controlled the south-east frontier of the kingdom of Jerusalem on the edge of the Arabian desert, was immensely important to the defence of the kingdom and included the near-impregnable castles of Montreal (in Arabic: Shobak or Shaubak) and Kerak (or Karak), which had been constructed during the reigns of Baldwin II and Fulk. The lordship of Transjordan also controlled the caravan traffic across the south of the kingdom, and therefore could potentially block the route between Damascus and Cairo, dividing the two parts of Saladin's domains. These two heiresses were cousins: Agnes' father Henry was a brother of Stephanie's father Philip de Milly.[23]

In October 1176 William of Montferrat, known as 'Longsword' (indicating his military skill), arrived at Sidon in the kingdom of Jerusalem in response to the invitation from the king and all the secular and ecclesiastical princes of the kingdom.[24] Within forty days of his arrival (wrote William of Tyre) the king conferred on him his elder sister as wife and with her the county of Jaffa-Ascalon, as the king and the princes had sworn on oath the previous year. The fact that they had sworn to a time limit could suggest that Sybil's previous prospective husband, Stephen of Sancerre, had failed to marry her in 1171 not because he had changed his mind about the marriage but because the king and leading nobles of the realm had prevaricated, perhaps trying to change the terms of the agreement. William Longsword would then have insisted that the arrangements be carried through quickly before any objections or impediments could be introduced.

Archbishop William's next comment certainly suggests that the leading nobles of the realm were worried about the impact of influential outsiders in the realm. Certain people, he wrote, openly opposed the arrangements, contradicting what had previously been agreed, which William considered made them appear *varii et inconstantis* (fickle and inconstant) people. He did not explain what they were objecting to: the fact that this new arrival had been granted one of the largest and most powerful fiefs in the kingdom, the new arrival's connections to the western emperor, the question of whether his rank was sufficient to marry the daughter and sister of a king, or anything else.[25]

Perhaps they objected to what the promises to William Longsword implied in terms of his future position in the realm. The county of Jaffa and Ascalon had been part of the royal domain since the reign of King Fulk. It had been granted to his second son Amaury while he was heir to the throne but had returned to the royal domain when Amaury became king.[26] The fact that it was now granted to Sybil and her husband William Longsword could be an indication that they were heirs to the throne – and, given Baldwin's illness, were likely to remain so, as he would probably not be able to father children. Bishop Sicard of Cremona, who was a contemporary of the events of Sybil's life but probably wrote this section of his history after 1192, recorded that when the infirm King Baldwin died, he wished to place the crown on Count William. The count refused the crown, but held the whole kingdom in guardianship (*in custodia regnum tenuit universum*). Archbishop William did not state that William Longsword was appointed regent in any capacity, but this may have been the original intention. By the time that William Longsword was invited to marry Sybil, the extent and nature of Baldwin's sickness would have been clearer, and perhaps Baldwin did offer his brother-in-law the regency, or at least asked him to deputise for him when he was too unwell to govern. Located in northern Italy, Sicard might have had access to local knowledge about William Longsword's expedition to the Holy Land and the agreement that had been made.[27]

If it were the case that William Longsword had been invited to the kingdom of Jerusalem to take over Baldwin IV's government, a question might have arisen over whether he should share power with his wife, Baldwin's elder sister, or whether he was governing outright as the appointed ruler. In the case of Sybil's and Baldwin's paternal grand-parents Melisende and Fulk, although the eventual settlement was a joint rulership, it appears that initially Fulk tried to govern alone – and the nobles of the kingdom were not happy with his government. Perhaps in October 1176 some of the nobles of the kingdom feared that William Longsword intended to take over the government in his own name and exclude his wife and the nobles of the kingdom.[28]

The nobles of the kingdom could have wondered how far William Longsword hoped to promote his friends and allies within the kingdom. A document issued at Genoa by William Longsword in August 1176, when he would have been preparing to go to the Holy Land, promises the Genoese consuls and the commune of Genoa that he would do his best to help them keep their possessions and rights overseas and recover those they had lost, although he would not go to war on their behalf and he excluded the county of Jaffa and its appurtenances and the king's possessions from this agreement. The Genoese had played a significant role in the conquest of the Latin East in supplying naval assistance and troops, and the city had been rewarded by King Baldwin II with privileges in the kingdom of Jerusalem. The maritime powers of Pisa and Venice had also received similar rewards. But by the mid-twelfth century the kingdom was no longer so dependent on their assistance, and King Amaury had limited the privileges to merchants who came to the kingdom in person to trade. If the Genoese were now trying to recover the privileges which King Amaury had reduced, the nobles who had supported Amaury's reforms and the other Italian maritime powers could be expected to object.[29]

Archbishop William countered any suggestion that William Longsword was not a worthy husband for Sybil by stressing that Sybil's bridegroom was descended from the highest nobility of Christian Europe on both sides of his family. His father, wrote the archbishop, was the uncle of King Louis VII of France – the brother of King Louis VI's mother (in fact, William V of Montferrat was the half-brother of Louis VI's mother Adelaide of Maurienne; they shared a mother, Gisela of Burgundy) – and his mother was the sister of King Conrad III of Germany (again, a half-sister: they shared a mother, Agnes of Waiblingen). Another point in his favour which Archbishop

60 Adolescence and marriage (1172–1177)

William did not mention was that William Longsword's father, William V, had taken part in the Second Crusade; the family had already demonstrated their dedication to the Holy Land.[30]

In addition, in all physical respects the bridegroom appeared to be the ideal noble warrior: strong, skilled in arms, generous, high-spirited and open with his emotions and thoughts. Archbishop William of Tyre described William Longsword as *adolescens* (a young man), slim and good-looking with yellow hair. He ate and drank too much, but not so much as to affect his mind, and from an early age he had been fully experienced in arms, as was appropriate for the secular nobility; in fact he was unequalled as a warrior or nearly so.[31]

His comments on William Longsword's exuberant high spirits and over-indulgence in food and drink suggest that Archbishop William did not entirely approve of Sybil's husband. In fact William Longsword was hardly *adolescens*; as he had been born in the 1140s, he must have been in his thirties by 1176, but perhaps Archbishop William meant that he still had the energy and uncontrolled impetuousness of youth. As in the case of Stephen of Sancerre, he leaves his readers questioning the moral standards of Sybil's promised bridegroom. However, while the archbishop esteemed self-control in word and deed, William Longsword's fellow-warriors might have preferred him as he was: open, honest and not attempting to conceal his views.

As for the bride: Sybil was now aged around seventeen. Archbishop William gives no indication that she had been consulted on her marriage, but it was the responsibility of her parents and now her brother to ensure that she had the best possible husband, and it was in their interests to ensure that she was content with the match. In addition, it was long established in medical thought that a woman could not conceive unless she experienced pleasure in sexual intercourse; so it would be counterproductive to force her to marry a man she found repulsive. In reality, royal women were not always happy with the marriages their parents planned for them,[32] but as no contemporary commentator recorded any sign of disruption between Sybil and her husband, it appears to have been a happy match.

Their county of Jaffa and Ascalon comprised the ancient fortified port cities of Jaffa and Ascalon. According to John of Ibelin, lord of Jaffa, writing around three quarters of a century later, the county was one of the four baronies of the kingdom of Jerusalem and included the lordships of Ibelin, Ramla and Mirabel, fiefs held by rear-vassals of the count of Jaffa. In fact, it is not certain that there were only four baronies before 1187 and the relationship between the lords of Ramla and the count of Jaffa was complicated by the fact that in 1163–1176 and 1186–1191 the count of Jaffa was also the king, so that in effect the lord of Ramla held their lands directly from the king; the lordship of Ibelin was apparently part of the lordship of Ramla.[33] Ibelin had been a town but had shrunk to a village before the castle was built there by King Fulk. Ramla had been founded in the eighth century AD as a walled city, but by this time only the Frankish castle was fully fortified. Mirabel (also called Majdal Yaba or Migdal Afeg) was a castle built by the

Franks before 1152.³⁴ In the 1170s these lordships were held by Agnes de Courtenay's brothers-in-law, Baldwin of Ramla and Balian of Ibelin. Other fortified sites in the county were held by the military religious orders, such as Bait Jibrin (the Hospitallers) and Gaza (the Templars). As by papal degree these institutions were exempt from secular authority their fortresses and lands were independent of the count.³⁵

Jaffa was the most important port in the kingdom of Jerusalem south of Acre and the port of Jerusalem, although its harbour was insufficiently sheltered to be safe for ships in winter. The town comprised a citadel on a hill, enclosing the parish church of St Peter and the residences of the patriarch and of the count; and the lower town, protected by a wall with two major gates, which contained the Pisans' quarter, where Pisan merchants lived when they came to Jaffa to trade, the houses of the Templars and of the Hospitallers, and churches belonging to the abbeys of St Mary Latin in Jerusalem and St Mary of the Valley of Jehosophat. The lower town also had a parish church dedicated to St Nicolas, while the count's castle had two chapels of its own. Outside the town were gardens, olive groves, vineyards, and orchards growing pomegranates, figs and almonds.³⁶

Ascalon was strategically significant because it controlled the coast road from Egypt. It was noted for its huge outer wall, almost two kilometres in length, with four great gates and punctuated by fifty-three larger and many smaller towers, enclosing a semi-circular area which contained the ancient tell (the mound formed by the original town). The great walls, built of stone and mortar, were constructed on top of an earthwork – which was in fact the ancient town wall of earth, mud-brick and stone constructed in the Bronze and Iron Ages. The stone walls had been constructed on top of the earlier fortifications during the late Roman period and had been periodically rebuilt and improved, most recently by the Fatimid rulers of Egypt during the first half of the twelfth century to strengthen the town's defences against the Franks. The Franks eventually captured Ascalon in 1153; the Fatimids tried unsuccessfully to recapture it later in the 1150s, and Saladin would make another unsuccessful attempt in 1177. The Franks converted the town's many mosques to churches, including a cathedral church dedicated to St Paul. There was also a hospital, belonging to the Greek Orthodox monastery of St Theodosius east of Bethlehem. This was a thriving fortified market town with (according to the Jewish traveller Benjamin of Tudela) over 200 Rabbinic and Karaite Jews and three hundred Samaritans living there, in addition to the Franks and Orthodox Christians. It had a good water supply, provided by wells. In contrast to the strength of its land defences, Ascalon lacked harbour defences and its anchorage was unsafe for ships in winter.³⁷

Although much of the inland region of the county of Jaffa and Ascalon was infertile and unsuitable for growing grain, it was suited to grazing, while areas of poor soils along the coast were planted with vineyards. To judge from properties and incomes listed in charters in addition to contemporary observations, the region could generate considerable income. Archbishop William of Tyre reported that after the Frankish capture of Ascalon crop yields in the region increased sixty-fold, as land which had not been cultivated over the previous fifty years due to the ongoing hostilities was brought into agricultural production. In 1244 there were at least seventy-two villages in the lordship of Ascalon, inhabited by at least 200 families, suggesting that there was a thriving population in the region even after Saladin's conquests of 1187–1188 and the disruption of the following decades. Wine production became a big business under the Franks, who combined European methods of production with local practices. Sugar was also a profitable cash crop in the Near East in this period and grown on an industrial scale by the military religious orders, but as it needs considerable quantities of water to grow well and most of Jaffa-Ascalon was dry land, sugar production would have been limited to the north of the county, in the Jaffa area.[38]

Only three documents issued by William Longsword as count of Jaffa and Ascalon are known; two of these had Sybil's confirmation. The count may, with Sybil's agreement, have donated a piece of land in the Jaffa region to the monastery of St. Mary and the Holy Spirit on Mount Sion near Jerusalem. At Jerusalem he witnessed and confirmed an exchange that Baldwin IV arranged with the canons of the church of the Holy Sepulchre; here the count may have been acting as heir apparent. Count William and Sybil together agreed to a confirmation charter issued by Baldwin IV at Acre, confirming a donation by Prince Reynald and his wife Stephanie and their children Humphrey (IV) and Isabel, to the Leonese Count Rodrigo Alvarez and his recently created military-religious Order of Mountjoy, of a number of casals (villages) and a large stretch of terrain for as long as the brothers of the new order fought against the Muslims. Sybil also later made a donation to this order. The Order of Mountjoy was a military-religious order established on the same basis as the Order of the Temple, whose members took the three monastic vows of personal poverty, chastity and obedience to a superior, followed a monastic lifestyle and wore a monastic-style habit, and in addition to prayer and fasting they fought against the enemies of Christendom. Unlike the Templars, the order was affiliated to the Cistercian Order; but like the Templars it benefitted from royal patronage, in this case from King Alfonso II of Aragon. Probably Prince Reynald and William Longsword believed that this new military-religious order could help them to defend the long southern frontier of the kingdom, Count William's domains being on the west bank of the Jordan and Prince Reynald's on the east.[39]

It appeared that Sybil and William Longsword had a happy future ahead of them; their county was prosperous and as its rulers they held significant power and influence in the kingdom of Jerusalem. Whether or not Baldwin had asked William to take over the government, they were certainly in a position where they could take on this authority if required, and any children they might have would be heirs to the kingdom of Jerusalem. It seems William was working effectively with Prince Reynald, as they were both supporting the Order of Mountjoy. The kingdom was also re-establishing diplomatic relations with the Byzantine Empire. During the winter of 1176–1177 Prince Reynald had travelled to Constantinople; he may have gone to raise the remainder of his ransom from Manuel, but he may also have discussed another joint invasion of Egypt, possibly prompted by the new Montferrat alliance and Reynald's awareness of the need to put pressure on Saladin by invading his southern base. In any case, Manuel responded by sending ambassadors to Baldwin IV to arrange an expedition against Egypt.[40]

Scarcely three months after the wedding, William Longsword fell ill. He struggled on for two months. It is possible that Sybil's donation to the Order of Mountjoy was made during this period, as although she referred to her husband as *incliti viri mei* (my renowned husband) in the opening lines of the donation charter, he did not witness or confirm her gift. Writing as 'Sybil daughter of the distinguished (*egregii*) Amaury king of Jerusalem, by God's grace countess of Jaffa and Ascalon, for the salvation and remedy of my soul and that of my renowned husband Lord William the count', she gave the brothers of Mountjoy one of the great wall towers of Ascalon, the so-called 'Maidens' Tower' (*turris puellarum*), the garden below it, three other towers on the walls, and a hundred bezants (a unit of account which derived from the gold dinar) of annual revenue to be received from the gate tolls at four specified times in the year. Presumably the intention was that the brothers would be responsible for defending as well as maintaining the wall. Sybil attached her seal to this donation charter, the only version of her seal now known. The witnesses were Reynald (former) prince of Antioch, Count Joscelin the king's seneschal (Sybil's uncle), Baldwin of Ramla (her mother's brother-in-law), Joscelin de Semunsac and his brother Baldwin, William Rufus *vicecomes* of Ascalon, and Gerard of Rumeilei, all four of whom would also appear witnessing Sybil's later charters, and a William of Tyre who had witnessed charters for Sybil's father when he was count of Ascalon.[41]

These were all close associates of Sybil and her husband, or members of her staff who had served her father. Joscelin de Semunsac, also spelt Samosac, had been in the kingdom of Jerusalem since at least January 1155, when he had witnessed a charter issued by King Baldwin III at Acre, and in July that year with his brother Baldwin he had witnessed a charter issued by Sybil's father Amaury, then count of Ascalon, at Jerusalem. They had probably come to the kingdom of Jerusalem with Agnes de Courtenay and other refugees from the county of Edessa. William of Tyre described him as *nobilis homo et prudens* (noble and prudent man); he commanded the Frankish troops at the town of Lamonia for three days in the course of King Amaury's 1167 invasion of Egypt. By the end of 1177 he would be castellan of Ascalon, holding overall military command of the town under the authority of the king or count and responsibility for the maintenance of its military garrison and fortifications; unlike Jaffa, at this time Ascalon did not have a distinct 'castle' or 'citadel' that was separate from the town walls, although the massive Jaffa Gate did resemble a citadel.[42] Gerard of Rumeilei, Ramini, or Remille and William Rufus first appeared witnessing one of Count Amaury of Ascalon's charters in June 1157 at Ascalon, a few places further down the witness list from Joscelin of Samosat; Gerard next appeared in the last quarter of 1158, again following Joscelin of Samosat and his brother Baldwin,

64 Adolescence and marriage (1172–1177)

while William Rufus next appeared in a charter of Count Amaury issued in November 1160 at Jaffa, which Joscelin of Samosat also witnessed. William Rufus had become *vicecomes* of Ascalon by April 1165.[43] Their appearances witnessing legal documents indicate that these four men were officials in the service of the count of Ascalon, whoever that person might be.

Count William Longsword died at Ascalon in June, where (as Archbishop William wrote) the young king was also gravely ill; perhaps Baldwin had come to Ascalon to be with his sister and brother-in-law during his sickness. The count left his wife pregnant, and later that year she gave birth to a son who was named Baldwin after his maternal uncle, an indication that he was the king's heir. Count William had a fine funeral at Jerusalem in the vestibule church of the Hospital of St John, at which Archbishop William presided.[44]

The death clearly shocked contemporaries. Archbishop William of Tyre reported it briefly and without comment, as if he were leaving his readers to deduce that William Longsword's intemperate lifestyle, overeating and drinking, and lack of moderation had led to his early death. But some commentators in Europe writing a few decades later suspected that Count William had been deliberately killed.

A continuation of Sigebert of Gembloux's chronicle known as the *Continuatio Aquicincta*, produced at the Benedictine abbey of Anchin in Pecquencourt in what is now north-eastern France and covering events occurring between 1149 to 1237, stated that William of Montferrat was killed with poison by knights in the Latin East (*a transmarinis militibus veneno extinguitur*).[45] Whenever a leading personage died suddenly and unexpectedly some contemporary commentator would suggest poison, but the fact that William Longsword had lingered for two months after his initial illness makes poison unlikely. The cleric Tolosanus of Faenza claimed that the count's early death was caused by witchcraft, blaming his mother-in-law and her daughter (which as Agnes de Courtenay had no other daughters, must mean Sybil's step-mother Maria Komnene and her daughter Isabel, who was then around three years old), saying that they had killed him *eo quod de ipsis curare nullatenus videbatur*, 'because he seemed in no way to care for them'.[46] The story reflects the distrust towards the Palestinian Franks and the Byzantines held by western Europeans, as expressed by Odo of Deuil and several commentators from the Low Countries and Germany during the Second Crusade and the author of the *Itinerarium peregrinorum* during the Third.[47] In particular, its depiction of Maria Komnene is similar to that in the *Itinerarium Peregrinorum*, where she is described as *Graia fece a cunis imbuta ... impia ... mobilis ... fraudulenta* (steeped in Greek dregs from the cradle ... impious ... fickle ... fraudulent).[48] Master Tolosanus's story could be interpreted as meaning that Maria Komnene had made sexual approaches to William Longsword which he had rejected, and she had then cast a destructive spell on him in revenge. Such stories were commonplaces of fictional literature and fitted William Longsword's long and lingering death better than accusations of poison. These European writers may have reasoned that as the nobility of the kingdom of Jerusalem had sabotaged the Second

Crusade and murdered Miles of Plancy, they were clearly capable of any fell deed. In fact, there is no reason to doubt Archbishop William's story that William Longsword's death was due to illness, especially as he mentions that Baldwin IV was also ill at Ascalon at the same time.

Sybil was left a pregnant widow, to administer her county of Jaffa and Ascalon alone. She and her son were not forgotten by their Montferrat relatives, who around ten years later would come to the kingdom to seek them out. In the meantime, it would be easy to forget that Sybil was a Montferrat by marriage, as she was drawn into her natal family's ambitions.

Notes

1 Hamilton, *Leper King*, p. 34.
2 WT 2: 1012 (Bk 22 ch. 5).
3 Murray, 'Women in the Royal Succession', p. 145.
4 Barber, *Crusader States*, p. 253.
5 Lewis, *Counts of Tripoli*, pp. 219–222; *IP* 1, p. 268 (ch. 10); *li frere de Thabarie*: *L'Estoire de la Guerre Sainte*, p. 413 (line 2735); *The History of the Holy War*, 1: 44, 2: 71 (line 2730).
6 Barber, *Crusader States*, pp. 260–264, 364; Hamilton, *Leper King*, pp. 82–83; Lyons and Jackson, *Saladin*, pp. 68–75; Phillips, *Life and Legend*, pp. 94–100; WT 2: 962 (Bk 21 ch. 2).
7 Hamilton, *Leper King*, pp. 32–43; Lyons and Jackson, *Saladin*, p. 75.
8 Peter W. Edbury, 'Law and Custom in the Latin East: *Les Letres dou Sepulcre*', in *Intercultural Contacts in the Medieval Mediterranean: Studies in Honour of David Jacoby*, ed. B. Arbel, *Mediterranean Historical Review*, 10 (1995), 71–76, at 73–75.
9 Hamilton, *Leper King*, pp. 84–86; Barber, *Crusader States*, pp. 197, 404 note 112.
10 *IP* 1, p. 251 (Bk 1 ch. 3); for the date: Nicholson, 'The Construction of a Primary Source', 143–165; for the developing legend: Margaret Jubb, *The Legend of Saladin in Western Literature and Historiography* (Lewiston, 2000), pp. 67–68.
11 Barber, *Crusader States*, pp. 265, 268.
12 '*Sinistro consilio regis mentem subvertit*': WT 2: 921 (Bk 20 ch. 9).
13 WT 2: 963–964 (Bk 21 ch. 3); Hamilton, *Leper King*, pp. 87–89; Barber, *Crusader States*, pp. 265–266; Lewis, *Counts of Tripoli*, pp. 234–236; Peter W. Edbury, *John of Ibelin and the Kingdom of Jerusalem* (Woodbridge, 1997), pp. 4–6; Hans Eberhard Mayer, 'Carving up Crusaders: the early Ibelins and Ramlas', in *Outremer: Studies in the History of the Crusading Kingdom of Jerusalem presented to Joshua Prawer*, ed. B. Z. Kedar, H. E. Mayer and R C. Smail (Jerusalem, 1982), pp. 101–118, at pp. 115–116; Hans Eberhard Mayer, 'The Wheel of Fortune: Seignorial Vicissitudes under Kings Fulk and Baldwin III of Jerusalem', *Speculum*, 65.4 (1990), 860–877, at 862, 871, 872, 873 note 51, 876, 877: Mayer found no connection between the Gerard who held Sidon in 1147 and the Grenier family who held it prior to 1123. On Sidon see Adrian J. Boas, *Crusader Archaeology: The Material Culture of the Latin East*, 2nd edn (Abingdon, 2017), pp. 51–52; Pringle, *Churches*, 2: 317–329, plan on p. 319; Denys Pringle, *Secular Buildings in the Crusader Kingdom of Jerusalem: An archaeological gazetteer* (Cambridge, 1997), pp. 94–95 (no. 201).
14 Barber, *Crusader States*, p. 265; Hamilton, *Leper King*, pp. 89–90, 119; WT 2: 964–965 (Bk 21 ch. 4); Bernard Hamilton, 'Miles of Plancy and the Fief of

Adolescence and marriage (1172–1177)

Beirut', in *The Horns of Ḥaṭṭīn*, ed. B. Z. Kedar (Jerusalem and London, 1992), pp. 136–146; Lewis, *Counts of Tripoli*, pp. 236–237; 'Regni Iherosolymitani Brevis Historia', in *Annali Genovesi di Caffaro et de' suoi continuatori del MXCIX al MCCXCIII*, new edn, ed. Luigi Tommaso Belgrano, Fonti per la Storia d'Italia, 5 vols (Genoa, 1890–1929), 1: 125–149, at p. 135.

15 Edbury and Rowe, *William of Tyre*, pp. 18–19; Hamilton, *Leper King*, pp. 94–95, 100–102, 106; Barber, *Crusader States*, p. 266; Lewis, *Counts of Tripoli*, pp. 239–241.
16 *Cartulaire général*, 1: 320, 321, 336 (nos 467, 468, 487, 488); *ULKJ* 2: 657 (no. 381).
17 *Cartulaire général*, 4: 249 (no. 389 *bis*); Hamilton, *Leper King*, pp. 97–98; Vasselot de Régné, 'A Crusader Lineage', 102–106. For Aimery's career see Philip of Novara, *Le Livre de Forme de Plait*, pp. 179, 304, 325 (section 74).
18 Hamilton, 'Women in the Crusader States', p. 165; WT 2: 986, 1012 (Bk 21 ch. 17, Bk 22 ch. 5). For Nablus, see Boas, *Crusader Archaeology*, p. 55; Pringle, *Churches*, 2: 94–115, plan on p. 969; Pringle, *Secular Buildings*, p. 76 (no. 158).
19 WT 2: 977–978 (Bk 21 ch. 12); Phillips, *Defenders*, pp. 227–228.
20 Hamilton, *Leper King*, pp. 104–106; Barber, *Crusader States*, pp. 267–268; WT 2: 976 (Bk 21 ch. 10); Buck, *Principality of Antioch*, pp. 202–218, 213.
21 Hamilton, *Leper King*, p. 105–107; Barber, *Crusader States*, p. 268; *ULKJ* 2: 670 (no. 390).
22 Philip of Novara, *Le Livre de Forme de Plait*, pp. 142, 274 (section 57).
23 Barber, *Crusader States*, pp. 163, 268; Mayer, 'The Wheel of Fortune', 877. For a recent study of Kerak, see Micaela Sinibaldi, 'Karak Castle in the Lordship of Transjordan: Observations on the Chronology of the Crusader-period Fortress', in *Bridge of Civilisations: The Near East and Europe c. 1100–1300*, ed. Peter Edbury, Denys Pringle and Balázs Major (Oxford, 2019), pp. 97–114.
24 WT 2: 977 (Bk 21 ch. 12).
25 Hamilton, *Leper King*, pp. 109–110; Phillips, *Defenders*, pp. 228–229.
26 Mayer, 'The Double County of Jaffa and Ascalon', pp. 182–183; Mayer, 'The Wheel of Fortune,' 876–877; Mayer, 'Carving up Crusaders', p. 114.
27 *Sicardi Episcopi Cremonensis Cronica*, ed. O. Holder-Egger, in *MGH SS*, 31 (Hanover, 1903), pp. 22–181, at p. 173; Hartmann, 'Sicard of Cremona'.
28 Hamilton, 'Women in the Crusader States', pp. 148–152; Jordan, 'Corporate Monarchy', 1–15.
29 Benjamin Z, Kedar, 'Genoa's Golden Inscription in the Church of the Holy Sepulchre: A Case for the Defence', in *I comuni italiani nel Regno Crociato di Gerusalemme. Atti del colloquio di Gerusalemme, 24–28 maggio 1984*, ed. G. Airaldi and B. Z. Kedar (Genoa, 1986), pp. 319–335, at pp. 331–333; *Codice diplomatico della Repubblica di Genova*, ed. C. Imperiale di Sant'Angelo, 3 vols (Rome, 1936–1942), 2: 235 (no. 105); *ULKJ*, 2: 761–763 (no. 447).
30 WT 2: 978 (Bk 21 ch. 12); Hamilton, *Leper King*, p. 101
31 WT 2: 978 (Bk 21 ch. 12).
32 Parsons, 'Mothers, Daughters, Marriage, Power', pp. 69–71; Christopher N. L. Brooke, *The Medieval Idea of Marriage* (Oxford, 1989), pp. 137–138; Joan Cadden, *Meanings of Sex Difference in the Middle Ages: Medicine, Science, and Culture* (Cambridge, 1993), pp. 126–127; Hanley, *Matilda*, pp. 59–60, 68–71.
33 John of Ibelin, *Le Livre des Assises*, ed. Peter W. Edbury (Leiden, 2003), p. 600 (section 234); Edbury, *John of Ibelin*, pp. 168, 170; Mayer, 'The Double County of Jaffa and Ascalon', 182–183; Edbury, 'The Crusader Town and Lordship of Ramla', pp. 10–14.

34 Boas, *Crusader Archaeology*, pp. 57, 97, 100; Pringle, *Churches*, 2: 28–29, 181–199, 378–384; Pringle, *Secular Buildings*, pp. 52, 67–69 (nos 103, 144).
35 For the extent of the lordships of Jaffa and Ascalon, Ibelin, Ramla and Mirabel, see *The Atlas of the Crusades*, ed. Jonathan Riley-Smith (London, 1991), p. 37, map 1; for the military orders' castles, see Adrian J. Boas, *Archaeology of the Military Orders. A survey of the urban centres, rural settlements and castles of the military orders in the Latin East (c. 1120–1291)* (Abingdon, 2006), pp. 38, 229–230.
36 Boas, *Crusader Archaeology*, pp. 49–51; Pringle, *Churches*, 1: 264–273, with plan on p. 265; Hamilton and Jotischky, *Latin and Greek Monasticism*, p. 164. 169, 174; *IP* 2, pp. 281–282 (Bk 4 chs 24–25); *L'Estoire de la Guerre Sainte*, p. 549 (lines 6933–6934, 6940–6948); *The History of the Holy War*, 1: 112, 2: 126 (lines 6925–6926, 6932–6941). For the roads from Jaffa to Jerusalem see Denys Pringle, 'Templar Castles between Jaffa and Jerusalem', in *The Military Orders*, vol. 2: *Welfare and Warfare*, ed. Helen Nicholson (Aldershot, 1998), pp. 89–109.
37 Boas, *Crusader Archaeology*, pp. 44–45; Pringle, *Churches*, 1: 61–69 (with plan on p. 62); Denys Pringle, 'The Walls of Ascalon in the Byzantine, Early Islamic and Crusader Periods. A Preliminary Report on Current Research', in *Guerre et paix dans le Proche-Orient medieval (x^e–xve siècle)*', ed. Mathieu Eychenne, Stéphane Pradines, and Abbès Zouache (Cairo, 2019), pp. 449–479, at 449, 451–455; Hannah Buckingham and Denys Pringle, 'The Fortifications: Grid 20 Fortification Tower', in *The Leon Levy Expedition to Ashkelon, Ashkelon 8: The Islamic and Crusader Periods*, ed. Tracy Hoffman (Pennsylvania, 2019), pp. 76–90; Denys Pringle, 'The Survey of the Walls of Ashkelon', in ibid., pp. 98–221, esp. 106, 219; Robert Kool, 'Coins', in *The Leon Levy Expedition to Ashkelon, Ashkelon 8: The Islamic and Crusader Periods*, ed. Tracy Hoffman (Pennsylvania, 2019), pp. 523–574, at p. 533; Hamilton and Jotischky, *Latin and Greek Monasticism*, p. 313; *IP* 2, pp. 313, 316–317 (Bk 5 chs 4, 6); *L'Estoire de la Guerre Sainte*, pp. 580–581 (lines 7897–7928, 8023–8058); *The History of the Holy War*, 1: 128, 130, 2: 138, 139–140 (lines 7882–7912, 8008–8043); *The Itinerary of Benjamin of Tudela*, ed. Marcus Nathan Adler (London, 1907), p. 28 (p. 44).
38 Kool, 'Coins', p. 533; WT 2: 810 (Bk 18 ch. 1); Heather E. Crowley, 'The Impact of the Franks on the Latin Kingdom of Jerusalem: Landscape, Seigneurial Obligations and Rural Communities in the Frankish East', unpublished PhD thesis, Cardiff University, 2016, p. 241, figure 4.7 'Agricultural potential: arable', p. 245, figure 4.9 'Agricultural potential: pasture'; Judith Bronstein, Elisabeth Yehuda, and Edna J. Stern, 'Viticulture in the Latin Kingdom of Jerusalem in the Light of Historical and Archaeological Evidence', *Journal of Mediterranean Archaeology*, 33.1 (2020), 55–78, at 59, 71; Rabei G. Khamisy, 'Frankish Viticulture, Wine Presses, and wine production in the Levant: New Evidence from Castellum Regis (Mi'ilyā)', *Palestine Exploration Quarterly*, 153.3 (2020), 191–221; Boas, *Crusader Archaeology*, pp. 79–81; see the map of sugar production sites in Palestine in P. Brigitte-Porëe, 'Les moulins et fabriques à sucre de Palestine et de Chypre: histoire, geographie et technologie d'une production croisée et médiévale', in *Cyprus and the Crusades: Papers given at the International Conference 'Cyprus and the Crusades', Nicosia, 6–9 September, 1994*, ed. N. Coureas and J. Riley-Smith (Nicosia, 1995), pp. 377–510, at p. 459, fig. 2.
39 *ULKJ* 2: 763–765, 843–846 (nos 448, 449 (confirming 393), 450 (confirming 394), Sybil's consent: nos 492 (confirming 448), 494 (confirming 394), Sybil's donation:

493); Alan Forey, 'The Order of Mountjoy', *Speculum*, 46 (1971), 250–266, at 255; Hamilton, *Leper King*, pp. 117–118.

40 Phillips, *Defenders*, pp. 230–231; Bernard Hamilton, 'Manuel I Comnenus and Baldwin IV of Jerusalem', in *Kathēgētria: essays presented to Joan Hussey on her 80th birthday*, ed. J. Chrysostomides (Camberley, 1988), pp. 353–375, at pp. 360–362; WT 2: 982 (Bk 21 ch. 15).

41 *ULKJ* 2: 843–845 (no. 493), quotation on p. 845, and p. 844 on William of Tyre; Pringle, 'The Survey of the Walls of Askheklon', p. 109; Paoli, *Codice diplomatico*, 1: 63 (charter no. 58), image of seal at table IV, no. 37. On Sybil's seal, see Mayer and Sode, *Die Siegel*, pp. 151–153, image 58; Mayer, *Das Siegelwesen in den Kreuzfahrerstaaten*, p. 43 note 132, and Tafel 3 image 23. For the bezant see Peter Spufford with Wendy Wilkinson and Sarah Tolley, *Handbook of Medieval Exchange* (London, 1986), pp. 294–299; the 'saracen bezant' was the principle unit of account in the crusader states (p. 297).

42 For Joscelin *de Samosato*'s early career see *ULKJ* 1: 431 (no. 233), 2: 515 (no. 286); WT 2: 900 (Bk 19 ch. 25); see also Pringle, 'The Survey of the Walls of Askheklon', pp. 108–109, 216–217. The city of Samosata (now Samsat) lies to the north west of Edessa. It had been one of the major strongholds of the county of Edessa. In 1150 Beatrice, wife of Count Joscelin II, sold it and the other remaining strongholds of the former county to Emperor Manuel Komnenos: WT 2: 782 (Bk 17 ch. 16); Hamilton, 'The Titular Nobility', pp. 197, 202 note 2.

43 *ULKJ* 2: 520, 527–528, 532, 546 (nos 291, 298, 305, 312). On the role of the *vicecomes* see Riley-Smith, *The Feudal Nobility*, p. 85.

44 WT 2: 978 (Bk 21 ch. 12); Hamilton, *Leper King*, p. 118; Barber, *Crusader States*, pp. 266–267.

45 'Continuatio Aquicinctina', p. 415.

46 *Magistri Tolosani Chronicon Faventinum*, pp. 104–105 and note 5; Hartmann, 'Tolosanus'.

47 On Europeans blaming the Palestinian Franks and Byzantines for the failure of the Second Crusade, see Elizabeth Siberry, *Criticism of Crusading 1095–1274* (Oxford, 1985), p. 77; Odo of Deuil, *De Profectione Ludovici VII in Orientem. The Journey of Louis VII to the East*, ed. and trans. Virginia Gingerick Berry (New York, 1948), pp. 54–55, 68–69, 72–73, 82–83, 86–87, 90–91, 98–99; 'Annales Palidenses auctore Theodore monarcho', in *MGH SS*, vol. 16, ed. Georg Heinrich Pertz (Hanover, 1859), pp. 48–98, at p. 83; 'Annales Magdeburgensis', in *MGH SS*, vol. 16, ed. Georg Heinrich Pertz (Hanover, 1859), pp. 105–196, at p. 190; 'Annales Rodenses', in *MGH SS*, vol. 16, ed. Georg Heinrich Pertz (Hanover, 1859), pp. 688–723, at p. 719; 'Magni presbyteri annales Reicherspergenses, ed. Wilhelm Wattenbach, in *MGH SS*, vol. 17, ed. Georg Heinrich Pertz (Hanover, 1861), pp. 439–534, at p. 463; *IP* 1, p. 293 (Bk 1 ch. 21).

48 *IP* 1, p. 354 (Bk 1 ch. 63).

4 Widow, countess and second marriage (1177–1180)

William Longsword was dead, and with him died any plan that he would assist Baldwin IV with the government or take over the government as regent. Clearly Baldwin realised that he was too ill to rule alone, as he now appointed Prince Reynald de Châtillon, lord of Transjordan, as his regent. Archbishop William of Tyre described Reynald as '*virum approbate fidei et mirabilis constantie*' (a man of proven faith and admirable steadfastness), perhaps bearing in mind Reynald's many years in a Muslim prison: an ordeal which would have crushed many men but which Reynald had survived. Archbishop William added that if the lord king could not go in his own person, Reynald would administer the business of the kingdom, but he would act with the advice of the lord count of Flanders, Philip of Alsace, when he arrived in the East on his promised crusade.[1]

Countess of Jaffa and Ascalon

Although her husband was dead, Sybil remained countess of Jaffa and Ascalon. According to Philip of Novara's description of legal processes in the kingdom of Jerusalem in the mid-thirteenth century, a widow who owed military service for her lands could have a year and a day of mourning after her husband's death before the lord could require her to marry again. As a woman, she was not expected to provide military service in person, but she should marry a man who could provide it. The lord could not force her to marry any individual but should offer her a choice of three men, who should be the social equals of herself and her late husband, and she should choose the one she preferred. (This certainly appears to have been the procedure following the death of Princess Constance of Antioch's first husband, Raymond of Poitiers, at Inab in 1149: King Baldwin III of Jerusalem suggested three possible husbands who, according to Archbishop William of Tyre, were all suitable candidates, but Constance turned them all down.) If a widow remarried without the lord's permission, opinions differed as to whether – if the new husband was otherwise acceptable to the lord – he could confiscate the fief for a year and a day, or whether he should confiscate the fief permanently.[2] If the process described by Philip of Novara was also the practice in the kingdom of Jerusalem before Saladin's conquests of 1187–1188, then

DOI: 10.4324/9781315205960-5

Baldwin could not require his elder sister to remarry for a year and a day, but after that she could not marry without his permission – and she should marry a man he selected.

In any case, Sybil must administer her county. It is not clear whether as a woman she would preside over her seigneurial court herself or whether social custom in the kingdom of Jerusalem was that she should appoint a male representative to preside. Two centuries later Christine de Pizan, writing in France, expected that a princess and a baroness holding authority to govern would attend council in person and take charge of estate administration herself; it appears that noblewomen in France, Flanders and England in the twelfth century did indeed do this, so perhaps the Frankish society of the crusader states – largely drawn from these regions – would have had the same expectation.[3] As countess of Jaffa and Ascalon, Sybil would have been bound to advise the king alongside other leading secular nobles of the kingdom, but again it is not clear whether she attended the king's council in person or was expected to send a male deputy.

Sybil's authorisation appeared on various legal documents involving her county. In the summer of 1177, Sybil and her brother Baldwin IV agreed to a sale of the 'scribanage' or office of official scribe for the casal or village of Bethduras, which lay on the plains of Ascalon and within the lordship of Ramla. The holder of the office, George of Betheri, had sold it for 250 bezants to none other than the king of France's sister Constance, daughter of King Louis VI of France and Adelaide of Maurienne (and thus a cousin of Sybil's late husband) and former countess of both Boulogne and Saint-Gilles; her purchase had been approved by Baldwin of Ramla.[4] The first four witnesses of Sybil's approval were Archbishop William of Tyre (as chancellor); Prince Reynald de Châtillon (as regent); Joscelin de Samosac, castellan of Ascalon; and Baldwin his brother (whom we have encountered already in the charter issued by Sybil earlier in the year). The last two witnesses were Robert de Piquigni or Picquigny and Geoffrey of Tours, burghers of Jerusalem who had previously witnessed documents for King Amaury and King Baldwin IV and who would later witness for Baldwin V and (in the case of Robert) for the barons at Tyre in the summer of 1187.[5] At the end of 1178 or in 1179 Constance went on to grant the village of Bethduras to the Hospitallers. We might assume from these arrangements that Constance intended to remain in the kingdom of Jerusalem until her death and expected the Hospitallers to make provision for her burial and commemoration, but in fact she had returned to France by the end of 1180.[6]

Count Philip of Flanders

Meanwhile, military assistance had arrived in the kingdom in the person of one of Sybil's and Baldwin IV's cousins. On 1 August 1177, Philip of Alsace, count of Flanders, son of Count Thierry and Countess Sybil, arrived at Acre with his army. As Philip's visit to the Holy Land involved Sybil's interests it merits our close attention.

Philip had a close family connection to the crusader states, as his father had crusaded in the east four times and his mother – Sybil's godmother – had retired to the Abbey of St Lazarus in Bethany and was buried there. As Baldwin's paternal cousin he was an obvious person to take over the regency of the kingdom, and in fact as a descendant of Fulk V of Anjou he could have aspired to be king of Jerusalem himself. However, it appears that Philip was not in a position to remain for long in the kingdom nor to take on any commitments which might jeopardise the interests of his allies in Europe.[7]

In the first place, Philip's brother Peter, who had married the countess of Nevers and was to have acted as Philip's regent in Flanders during his absence, had died in the previous year, leaving only an infant daughter as his heir. Philip could have called off his crusade as a result. In fact he took the decision to continue with his plans, but now his engagement with his cousin's kingdom could be for only a short period.[8]

In the second place, Philip's freedom of action in the East was constrained by their mutual cousin King Henry II of England, who was concerned that Philip's crusade would damage his own interests. Philip had initially taken his crusade vow at Easter 1175 and had expected to set out at Christmas 1176. According to Roger, parson of Howden Minster in Yorkshire and clerk at King Henry's court, writing in his *Gesta regis Henrici secundi* ('Deeds of King Henry the Second'), Henry knew that his cousin Baldwin IV was a paralytic and had lost an arm; and had been told that Philip was going to Jerusalem to be made king in Baldwin's place. Henry asked Philip to defer his crusade until Easter 1177, when he intended either to go to Jerusalem himself or to send knights and sergeants to defend their cousin, the king of Jerusalem. Philip agreed to this request, but in January 1177 he sent Robert V, advocate of Béthune, one of his leading nobles, to Henry to inform him about King Louis VII of France's plans for the marriage of Philip's nieces – daughters of Mary, countess of Boulogne, great-niece and heir of Godfrey of Bouillon and King Baldwin I of Jerusalem – as the marriages that Louis planned for them would give his son and grandson a claim to the throne of Jerusalem. As this obviously threatened Henry's own position, Henry and Philip came to an agreement that Henry would send a contingent of English nobles and knights with Philip, contribute money towards his crusade and make generous donations via the Templars and the Hospitallers 'to sustain the land of Jerusalem', while Philip would not marry his nieces to anyone without Henry's agreement. Philip thus obtained financial support for his expedition, but by contriving Henry's involvement in this way he also allowed his cousin to influence what he could do during his crusade.[9]

Such conflicts of interest within Philip's expedition go some way towards explaining why his actions in the East were 'bizarre and exasperating', to quote Hans Mayer.[10] Philip may also have been uncertain how best to proceed. During his planning for his expedition he wrote to the famous prophetess Abbess Hildegard of Bingen, asking her to inquire from God how he should act to exalt the name of Christianity and crush the ferocity of the Muslims, and whether it would be useful for him to stay in the land or return.

Hildegard reminded him that he was guilty of injustice and homicide, and while urging him to resist through God's grace the faithless who worked to destroy the fount of faith, she also hoped that the Holy Spirit would bring him to repentance so that he would seek God and serve God alone (rather than his own interests). On the assumption that the copies of their letters that survive are complete and were not amended by a copyist in light of later events, Philip's letter suggests that he was in two minds over whether he should take over government of the kingdom of Jerusalem as his cousin's regent or return to Flanders.[11] Perhaps it was Abbess Hildegard's response which persuaded him not to take on the government of the kingdom but to focus on discharging his service to God and then return to his county.

Archbishop William of Tyre recorded that when Count Philip arrived at Acre Baldwin IV was still ill at Ascalon as he had been at the time of William Longsword's death. Very happy at Philip's arrival, he had himself carried to Acre to meet him and sent many of the princes and prelates of the kingdom ahead to welcome him. On the advice of everyone – the lord patriarch of Jerusalem, the archbishops and bishops, the abbots and priors, the masters of the Hospital and Temple, and all the lay princes of the kingdom – Baldwin offered Philip full power (*plena potestas*) and free and general administration over the whole kingdom, both in peace and in war within and without the kingdom, over greater and lesser persons, and allowed him to freely exercise jurisdiction over the treasury and revenues of the kingdom according to his judgement.[12] Archbishop William indicates that Baldwin was appointing Philip as his procurator, his representative in government. As Philip was Baldwin's cousin, it was appropriate for Philip to take on this role. Baldwin was aged only sixteen, inexperienced in government and physically infirm; Philip was more than twice Baldwin's age and an experienced administrator who should have been able to take on his cousin's responsibilities and govern effectively on his behalf.[13]

After taking counsel with his people, Philip replied (echoing his correspondence with Abbess Hildegard) that he had not come to receive any power but to serve God. He did not intend to commit himself to any administration, as he had to be free to return to his own affairs when they recalled him. The lord king should appoint his own procurator over his kingdom, and he (Philip) would obey him as he would obey his lord the king of France. The lord king (wrote Archbishop William), seeing that he had completely refused 'what we had offered him', asked Philip through his *principes* (eminent representatives) to at least take on leadership of the whole Christian army in the expedition against the Egyptians that had been arranged with the emperor of Constantinople. Count Philip's response was the same as before.[14]

When taken in the light of the noble military code of behaviour then current in western Europe, Count Philip's reported response is incredible. The count of Flanders was a leading member of a social-cultural group whose chief value was personal honour, which was gained through demonstrating physical and mental courage and martial skill and endurance; through facing the enemy fearlessly and not turning one's back on any opportunity to prove one's skill in battle. These were the values promoted by epic literature such as the *Chanson de Roland*, the epics of Guillaume d'Orange and of Aymeri of Narbonne, and in the romance literature being composed by Chrétien de Troyes and other, anonymous, poets. Yet, according to Archbishop William, Count Philip declined to lead the Christian forces in battle against the Muslim enemy, as if he were turning his back on the opportunity to win glory and honour in God's name. Such a response would have marked him as a coward, unworthy of the status of a noble warrior, and a traitor to Christ, whose battles he was bound to fight as a Christian warrior.[15] As it is highly improbable that Philip wished to appear to be a coward and a traitor, it is likely that Archbishop William's account omits part of Philip's reply – the part which explained the rationale for his position.

Archbishop William then noted that King Baldwin had already appointed Reynald de Châtillon as his procurator. The king's intention was that Reynald would act as Count Philip's subordinate, but the count advised that the commander of the Egyptian campaign should act independently of the king rather than as his representative, and administer Egypt, if it were conquered, separately from the kingdom of Jerusalem. Possibly Count Philip hoped to rule Egypt himself as king or (more likely, given his previous comments) entrust it to one of his followers, or perhaps he thought it impractical for one person to govern both kingdoms. The king's representatives (who, we now discover, were led by Archbishop William) told him that the king had no intention of treating Egypt as a separate administrative unit. Baldwin and his advisors could have argued that as Saladin could rule both Damascus and Cairo, then Baldwin could certainly rule both Jerusalem and Cairo, which were geographically much closer together.[16]

The count then said that he was amazed that no one had mentioned the marriage of his female cousin. Archbishop William depicted himself and the other representatives as shocked and astonished at the count's presumption and lack of courtesy: after having been so honourably received by the lord king, he was now attempting to supplant the lord king (*in supplantationum domini regis*), against the laws of consanguinity.[17] But was the count's comment really a threat to King Baldwin's authority? Baldwin and his advisers wanted Count Philip to take over the government on Baldwin's behalf; if the count chose Sybil's husband he would be acting as lord of the kingdom, just as Baldwin had requested. Perhaps the count's intention was that Sybil's new husband would take up the responsibility of government on Baldwin's behalf, in which case his own services as regent would not be needed.[18]

This possibility is strengthened by the archbishop's next revelation: the count and his followers had already made plans for the marriage of King Baldwin's sisters. He recorded that 'a certain powerful man', Robert V, advocate of Béthune, had come with the count of Flanders on his pilgrimage and had brought his two adult sons (*filios iam adultos*) with him. The archbishop was dismissive of the advocate's noble credentials: 'this man' (*Hic*), 'it is said, helped by the support of Count William de Mandeville' (King Henry's representative on the crusade), 'who had come with the count on the same journey, got around the count and began to persuade him that he could make great profit for himself in the kingdom.' According to Archbishop William, the advocate reminded the count that he held a very wide patrimony in his county and said that he would give the lord count all his possessions to hold in perpetuity by hereditary right if the count arranged for his two sons to marry the two daughters of King Amaury. Archbishop William concluded that the count gave out that he favoured putting this proposal into effect.[19]

It appears, then, from Archbishop William's account, that Count Philip did not intend to take on authority in the Holy Land himself but planned to marry the king's two sisters to the sons of one of his leading nobles, who would then surrender their lands in Flanders to the count and take over government of the kingdom from his sick cousin. Certainly Isabel was not of marriageable age: she was about five years old, having been born in the autumn of 1172; but there were precedents in western Europe for such child marriages.[20] King Henry II presumably agreed with this plan, as his representative William de Mandeville supported it; Robert V of Béthune held estates in England and was in good standing with Henry.[21]

Having set out this shocking plot to undermine King Baldwin's authority, Archbishop William wrote that the king's delegation told the count that they would consult the king and get back to him on the following day. They returned as promised and reported to the count that the custom in the kingdom was that it was not honourable for a widow, especially one who was pregnant, to marry again within her year of mourning. As it was barely three months since Sybil was bereaved, the count should not think the worse of them for declining to discuss her marriage at this point. But they would be happy to hear his opinion.[22] Count Philip refused to proceed unless all the princes swore in advance to follow his advice, but the king's representatives refused to give this guarantee. The count was very angry, but let the point go.[23]

The archbishop implied that the suggested marriages would have disparaged Sybil and Isabel, but in fact the family of the advocate of Béthune was renowned and influential in Flanders, England and northern France, as well as (as already mentioned) being in good standing with King Henry II of England. It was perhaps Robert V's strong connections with Henry and England that made him unacceptable to Baldwin IV and his barons, who wanted the king of England's money but not his influence in the kingdom's affairs. Isabel's eventual first husband Humphrey IV of Toron was arguably of lower status in Christendom than Count Philip's candidate for her hand, Robert V of Béthune's son William. Sybil's second husband, Guy de Lusignan, was of similar status to Philip's suggested candidate, the later Robert VI of Béthune. If these marriages had proceeded as Count Philip suggested, the kingdom of Jerusalem could have gained substantial military and financial aid from the region which is now north-eastern France. But, as would be apparent when Sybil eventually remarried, the Franks of the kingdom of Jerusalem did not want outsiders coming into the kingdom and taking prestigious positions and power.[24]

A new suitor for Sybil's hand appears at this point in the *Chronique d'Ernoul*, which erroneously places the story of Count Philip's arrival in the kingdom of Jerusalem and the argument over his choice of a husband for Sybil into the narrative before she married William Longsword and before the death of Nūr al-Dīn (1174). According to the *Chronique d'Ernoul*, Baldwin of Ibelin (lord of Ramla) had separated from his wife because he aspired to marry the king's sister. When he heard the count of Flanders's proposal for her marriage, Baldwin of Ibelin asked the count whether he had come to this country to make a marriage, or (as they had heard) to aid and enlarge the land and fight the Saracens (the Muslims). If he came in the army of the kingdom with the king and the nobles to attack the Saracens and returned safe and sound, then he could talk to the king about marriages and the king would take counsel on the matter. The *Chronique d'Ernoul* depicts Count Philip as being so angry at these words that he left the kingdom of Jerusalem.[25]

As Ramla was a rear-fief of the county of Jaffa and Ascalon, Baldwin of Ramla was Sybil's vassal.[26] Sybil had certainly approved one of Baldwin's legal transactions, as a lord would normally do. Baldwin would not have been the first man, and certainly not the last, to aspire to marry his female superior; but the story is unlikely to be true.

First, there is the difference in date: this account of Baldwin of Ramla's pretensions to Sybil's hand was written forty years or so after the death of both parties. Second, there was an obvious motive for the author of the *Chronique d'Ernoul* to invent such a story, being a partisan of the Ibelin family who was attempting to clear their name of accusations of treachery and betrayal during Saladin's conquests of 1187–1188. Baldwin of Ramla had refused to do homage to Sybil's husband King Guy, and this story gave a reason for his refusal.[27] According to the *Chronique d'Ernoul*, Guy had stolen Sybil from Baldwin.

Third, there is no evidence that Baldwin of Ramla had left his wife in order to marry Sybil. His first wife, Richendis of Bethsan, died around 1167/68. He married Isabel (or Elizabeth), widow of Hugh of Caesarea, by 1175, but she had died by 1176 – before Sybil married William Longsword, whereas the *Chronique d'Ernoul* claims it was after. On the other hand, Isabel's death would have left Baldwin free to marry Sybil in 1177; but he would have had to give her a year to mourn her first husband before he could approach her brother to ask for her hand.[28]

Although Sybil was the daughter of a king and held the title of countess whereas Baldwin was only a lord, his brothers had already married into the royal family. His elder brother Hugh had been Agnes de Courtenay's second or third husband, while in the autumn of 1177 Baldwin IV gave permission for the youngest of the Ibelin brothers, Balian (or Barisan) to marry the dowager queen, King Amaury's widow, Maria Komnene. Balian also received the town of Nablus, Maria Komnene's dowry.[29] On this basis Baldwin could aspire to marry Maria Komnene's step-daughter without fear of disparaging the bride. However, as his elder brother had been married to her mother the marriage would have required ecclesiastical dispensation, as canon law prevented a man from marrying his kinswoman, including a relation in-law.[30]

But Sybil, who was supposedly descended from the saintly Godfrey de Bouillon and was both mother of the prospective heir to the throne of the holy city of Jerusalem and an heir to that throne herself, stood far above the Ibelins in spiritual terms; and in any case she could not marry anyone without the permission of her brother, who was her liege-lord and the king. If she married without his consent, her fief and her husband's fief would be forfeit. For the same reason that her father had looked for a husband for her outside the kingdom, it is highly unlikely that Baldwin IV would have agreed to his sister marrying one of the lords of the kingdom. Marriage to Baldwin of Ramla would have made the Ibelin family intolerably powerful within the kingdom, upsetting the balance of power between the noble families, and would have aroused great resentment from the other leading nobles. Baldwin IV could not afford to offend any of his nobles by favouring the Ibelins so far above them. The author of the *Chronique d'Ernoul* dwelt on tales of frustrated marriage hopes, but outside the pages of romance personal wishes were of little importance.[31]

Sybil's marriage prospects aside, the next instalment in Archbishop William's tale of grievances against Count Philip was the arrival of noble ambassadors from Emperor Manuel. As the count had arrived in the East, it was time for the joint expedition that had previously been agreed against Egypt; Archbishop William indicates that this had all been previously agreed with the count, but he had now suddenly changed his mind and refused to take part. Possibly the agreement between the Franks and Byzantines was that the Byzantines would take over any Egyptian conquests, putting paid to any ambitions Count Philip may have had of acquiring land in Egypt for himself or his companions or even of ruling it as king. Possibly he considered that the kingdom's southern frontier was already well protected by the forces of Prince Reynald of Transjordan and Countess Sybil of Ascalon, and his own troops could be better employed elsewhere in the crusader states. In any case, the Byzantine fleet which had sailed south to Acre to take part in the joint expedition returned to Constantinople, and at the beginning of October 1177 Count Philip and his army set off for the principality of Antioch. Archbishop William of Tyre remarked that some people blamed the prince of Antioch (who had been present in Jerusalem when Count Philip arrived) and the count of Tripoli for Count Philip's opposition to the Egyptian campaign and that they had enticed him north to join their own campaigns. Perhaps they hoped to take advantage of Saladin being occupied in Egypt fighting the Franks and Byzantines to make territorial gains in the north.[32]

In November, while Count Philip and his northern allies were occupied besieging strategic locations in the north, Saladin invaded the kingdom of Jerusalem and marched on Ascalon. As the constable, Humphrey II of Toron, was ill, Reynald de Châtillon led the Frankish army, although Archbishop William depicts King Baldwin as being in overall charge. As an indication of the gravity of the situation, the famous holy relic of wood which was believed to have come from the Cross on which Christ died was brought from the church of the Holy Sepulchre to act as the army's standard and talisman. It comprised a fragment of wood set in precious metal and embedded in a larger piece of wood shaped like a cross. The patriarch of Jerusalem remained in Jerusalem to lead the defence of the city while the bishop of Bethlehem carried the Cross into battle.[33]

The Frankish army reached Ascalon before Saladin but withdrew into the town when it became clear that their army was not yet large enough to engage him. Saladin besieged Ascalon for three days, but then moved his army away towards Jerusalem. With their reinforcements still arriving, the Frankish army followed. On 25 November 1177, the Frankish army attacked Saladin at a hill which Archbishop William of Tyre called Mont Gisard, and which the Arabic commentators described as being near Ramla. Saladin was unable to draw up his united force before the attack and the Frankish cavalry charge broke through his lines while his forces were still deploying on the field. Saladin initially claimed that the battle was a victory, but his supporters knew it had been a terrible defeat. In the West, Abbot Robert of Torigni recorded that a small Christian army had defeated an 'innumerable army of pagans' through the virtue of the Holy Cross, while Ralph of Diceto, dean of London, would later record a magnificent charge led by Odo (or Eudes) of Saint-Amand, the master of the Templars, which sent Saladin fleeing for his life on a racing camel.[34]

Where was Sybil while these dramatic events were taking place? Apparently she remained in Ascalon throughout. She did not lead her county's contribution of knights to the army of the kingdom; she would have appointed one of her male military officials to take on this responsibility. Two documents which she issued after Balian of Ibelin's marriage to her stepmother in October 1177 but before 28 April 1178, confirming a loan agreement between Balian lord of Nablus and the Hospitallers, were witnessed by Joscelin de Samosac castellan of Ascalon, Roger de Verdun and Gerard de Rimeilleio or Remille. The first and last of these had already witnessed other documents she had issued, and the fact that the first witness was castellan of Ascalon and the agreement involved property at Ascalon indicates that it was made at Ascalon.[35]

Sybil's and William Longsword's son Baldwin would have been born between late summer 1177 and winter 1177–1178.[36] After childbirth, a woman should not go out in public for some weeks: Leviticus 12:1–5 set this at forty days after the birth of a boy and eighty days after the birth of a girl, but – depending on local practice – it may have been simply a standard month.[37] If Sybil was in Ascalon in October 1177 and had just given birth or was in the late stages of pregnancy, she probably remained there despite the danger from Saladin. It would have been more dangerous for her to try to move to another fortress than to stay where she was behind Ascalon's formidable defences. She would certainly not be the last Latin Christian noblewoman to give birth while the fortress where she was staying was under attack by Muslims.[38]

78   *Widow, countess and second marriage*

Meanwhile, Count Philip, Raymond of Tripoli and Bohemond III were campaigning in the north. They had attacked Homs and Hama, and then spent some weeks besieging Harim, a significant fortress which guarded the approach to Antioch and which had been captured by Nūr al-Dīn in 1164 following the Battle of Artah. Eventually Prince Bohemond received a large sum of money from as-Salih, prince of Aleppo, to withdraw and as-Salih then took over the castle. Compared to King Baldwin's (actually Reynald of Châtillon's) achievements in the south, they seemed to have gained nothing.[39]

William of Tyre indicated that Count Philip wanted to celebrate Easter in Jerusalem and then return home. He travelled via Constantinople, where he opened negotiations on behalf of King Louis VII of France for a marriage between one of the king's daughters and Manuel's son Alexios, son of his marriage to Maria of Antioch. The negotiations eventually led to the marriage of Louis's daughter Agnes (thereafter known as Anna) to Alexios in March 1180.[40]

Archbishop William's account of Count Philip's crusade appears to have been carefully crafted to put the count firmly into the wrong, blaming him for the failure to make any great territorial gains. It defended the leaders of the kingdom and discredited the count. According to the archbishop, the crusade achieved nothing apart from disrupting the alliance between the kingdom of Jerusalem and the Byzantines (although going on to promote an alliance between the kingdom of France and the Byzantines) and enabling as-Salih of Aleppo to get control of the fortress of Harim. At the same time, King Baldwin and the nobility of the kingdom of Jerusalem had shown that they could win a decisive victory in the field against Saladin without western help, which boosted their morale and military prestige.

On the other hand, the count and his noble companions – such as William de Mandeville, King Henry II's friend, and Count Robert V of Béthune – could have reported on their return to Europe in October 1178 that it was impossible to work with the king, the nobility and the higher clergy of the kingdom of Jerusalem, who had deliberately misinterpreted the count's words, taken offence at everything he said or attempted to achieve, and were obstructive and hostile to outsiders. None of the commentators in Europe recorded such criticisms, but by stressing the Franks' victory against Saladin they gave western leaders an excuse to postpone planned expeditions to the East, as clearly they were not urgently needed.[41]

Archbishop William did not record whether Sybil ever met her cousin while he was in the East. Given that his mother had been Sybil's godmother, it would have been appropriate for Count Philip to visit her to offer his respects, and given that as countess of Ascalon she was responsible for the defence of the south-western frontier of the kingdom, as a military leader and crusader it would have been appropriate for him to discuss the defence of this frontier with her or her commanders. Instead the archbishop depicted the count as a threat to Sybil, attempting to force her and her half-sister into disparaging marriages. As it was entirely fitting for the count to express an opinion on his cousins' marriages and the marriages he suggested would not have disparaged them, the archbishop's narrative principally shows his fierce opposition to any outsider being involved in the kingdom's affairs and his suspicion of any man who married or proposed to marry Sybil. We have already seen his tirade against Stephen of Sancerre and his more subtle criticism of William of Montferrat; having dismissed Count Philip's proposed husband for Sybil, he would go on to deprecate Duke Hugh of Burgundy for failing to come to the East and was unsparing of his criticism of Sybil's second husband Guy de Lusignan.

In any case, Sybil would have continued to administer her county during this time, and she also acted as a formal witness to some of the public acts of her brother King Baldwin which were not obviously connected to her county, possibly because she was Baldwin's designated heir. On 1 July 1178, she agreed to a gift of land made by her brother King Baldwin to one Baldwin of Cyprus in recognition of his service for King Amaury; possibly this was within her county, or possibly it fell into her sphere of authority because the debt was owed by her father.[42]

Further marriage negotiations

After a few months when little occurred in the kingdom of Jerusalem that Archbishop William thought worthy of recording in his history, October 1178 was busy. First, Archbishop William recorded that he, with Archbishop Eraclius of Caesarea, Bishop Joscius of Acre and other leading ecclesiastics of the kingdom of Jerusalem had set off for a general synod at the Lateran in Rome to which all the leaders of the Latin Church were summoned. Bishop Joscius also had another task: he was to carry out an embassy to Lord Hugh (whom William called 'Henry') duke of Burgundy to ask him to come to the East, for it had been unanimously agreed (wrote William) 'that we should concede to him in matrimony the lord king's sister, whom first the marquis (of Montferrat) had had, on the same conditions'. Although Archbishop William had never recorded what those conditions were, to judge from William of Montferrat's experience Duke Hugh would become count of Jaffa and Ascalon and take over the burden of government from King Baldwin. However, unlike William Longsword, Duke Hugh would not be the immediate heir to the throne of Jerusalem because the direct heir was now Sybil's baby Baldwin; the best he could hope for would be to act as his stepson's regent. Archbishop William recorded that the duke received both the message and the bishop gratefully and confirmed on oath that he would come.[43]

Duke Hugh had already visited the kingdom of Jerusalem on crusade with his uncle Stephen de Sancerre in 1171. Born in around 1148, he was now aged around thirty. His mother Marie was the sister of counts Henry I of Champagne, Theobald V of Blois and Stephen of Sancerre, and of King Louis VII of France's third wife Adela. His father was Duke Odo II of Burgundy. In 1164 or 1165 Hugh had married Alix, daughter of Frederick Barbarossa's sister Bertha and Duke Matthew of Lorraine. At some point in the late 1170s or early 1180s Hugh and Alix separated and by 1184 he was married to Beatrice of Albon, daughter of Guigues V, count of Albon.[44] It is possible, then, that in 1179–1180 he was free to marry Sybil. But Archbishop William concluded his record of the embassy with the comment that 'for certain reasons still unknown to us' the duke failed to fulfil his oath.[45]

In the same month that the kingdom of Jerusalem's delegation set out for the Third Lateran Council – due to begin on 15 March 1179 – King Baldwin IV began constructing a fortress at Vadum Iacob (Jacob's Ford). This was a Muslim holy site and arguably not even within his territory, but in military terms it was strategically important, being on one of the main crossing points from Palestine to Syria and on the main road from Cairo to Damascus. Saladin objected to the construction of the castle on military and religious grounds and tried to get the building stopped but eventually decided it would be better to capture and destroy the castle himself. In August 1179, he brought up his army, besieged and captured the partly completed castle and killed or captured the garrison.[46]

This was Saladin's second significant victory against the Franks in 1179. The first was on 10 June, when he had defeated the Frankish army at Marj Uyun. The army was without a constable or a marshal (the second in command), as Humphrey II of Toron had died in April after a long illness and the marshal had died in May. King Baldwin was carried to safety, Count Raymond III of Tripoli escaped to Tyre, and Reynald of Sidon – Sybil's stepfather, husband of Agnes de Courtenay – rescued many other Franks; but many were captured, including Brother Odo of Saint-Amand, master of the Templars; Baldwin of Ramla; and Hugh of Tiberias, son of Eschiva of Tiberias and stepson of Raymond III of Tripoli. Among the dead was Archbishop William of Tyre's brother Ralph. William blamed Brother Odo for this defeat (and hence for his brother's death) and reported that he died in prison mourned by none.[47]

Noble crusaders had come to the kingdom that summer, including Louis VII's brother Peter de Courtenay, a distant relative by marriage of Sybil's mother, and Count Henry I of Champagne, elder brother of Stephen of Sancerre. But, wrote Archbishop William, they achieved little. They joined King Baldwin's army at Tiberias to go to the assistance of the Templars at Vadum Iacob when Saladin attacked but arrived too late.[48] Archbishop William noted that through Count Henry of Champagne discussions were reopened with his nephew Duke Hugh III of Burgundy, with the hope that the duke would soon come East, yet he did not.[49]

Meanwhile, government must continue. On 22 October 1179 at Acre, Baldwin IV, king of Jerusalem, with the assent of his sister Sybil, countess of Jaffa and Ascalon, confirmed with his seal to Joscelin, his uncle and seneschal, two casals which Joscelin had bought for 4,500 bezants from Petronilla, vice-countess of Acre. The witnesses were Reynald of Châtillon, Balian of Ibelin, Reynald lord of Sidon, Walter of Beirut, Guy his brother, Pagan of Haifa (all great lords of the kingdom) and Balian of Jaffa (castellan of Jerusalem); further witnesses included Gosohuin (or Gotsuin) Boccus and

William de Molembec (or Molembucca; both witnessed many other royal charters); Gerard de Ridefort, the new royal marshal (and later master of the Temple); Giselbert de Floriaco, *vicecomes* of Acre; and four burghers of Acre, including Anthelm of Lucca and William de Furcis, who would appear again in 1183, witnessing a document for the king.[50] Through confirming their uncle's purchase, Baldwin and Sybil were assisting him to build up his landholdings around Acre, and their mother's current husband Reynald of Sidon and other leading nobles of the kingdom supported them in this. With Saladin a growing danger and Duke Hugh of Burgundy not yet arrived, the siblings would need their uncle's support over the months to come.

Their mother also now began to exercise her influence more publicly. Although she may have been present at court since Baldwin IV reached his majority in 1176, when she contributed towards her brother Joscelin's ransom, Agnes de Courtenay had not previously been mentioned in any legal records. In December 1179, before Christmas, Countess Sybil of Jaffa-Ascalon, 'daughter of the illustrious Amaury of Jerusalem', agreed to William Rufus, former *vicecomes* of Ascalon, leasing property to the Hospitallers. The first witness was the countess of Sidon, that is, Sybil's mother; followed by the count of Sidon, her stepfather. The next few witnesses were members of Sybil's administration at Ascalon: Joscelin, castellan of Ascalon and 'Baldus' his brother; Girard de Ruinehaco or Remille; then Curginus (or Turginus), Roger de Verdun (who had also witnessed an earlier document for Sybil), Bertrand of Jaffa and his brother Guibert (who would witness another document for Sybil in 1183), Robert de Pinqueni or Picquigny, William *vicecomes* of Ascalon, and seventeen more.[51] Although the document does not state where it was authorised, the fact that many of the witnesses were involved in the administration of Ascalon suggests that it was drawn up at Ascalon and that Sybil was living at Ascalon at that time.

Sybil's baby son Baldwin may have been with her, as the wardship of an underage heir was usually held by one or both parents. According to the Latin continuation of William of Tyre's history, probably compiled in the early thirteenth century, he was brought up in royal magnificence at Ascalon (*nutriebatur apud Aschalonam prout regia exigebat magnificentia*).[52] However, as Sybil was also an heir to the kingdom in her own right, her brother Baldwin may have thought it better for his nephew to be raised by a person who had no right to inherit the throne. According to Philip of Novara, writing in the middle of the following century, this was normal procedure to avoid a conflict of interests.[53]

Hugh III of Burgundy was expected to arrive in the kingdom of Jerusalem in time for Easter 1180, on the spring sailing. But he did not set sail. Possibly he had second thoughts about leaving his young son, Odo III, as his regent in Burgundy, as the youth was aged only around thirteen. It now being clear that King Louis VII of France was ailing, Hugh may have decided it was unwise to leave his duchy during the confusion that was already breaking out in France and which could only get worse when the old king died and his only son Philip, who would be aged only fifteen, succeeded him. In view of his failing health, King Louis had had Philip crowned king of France on 1 November 1179, but Philip and his mother Adela were soon in dispute. Far from this being an auspicious time for Hugh III to leave France, the young King Philip II apparently wrote to his uncle Count Henry of Champagne asking him to hurry home.[54]

Count Henry set off home early in 1180. He initially headed north for Constantinople, possibly intending to attend the wedding of his niece Agnes, daughter of his sister Adela of Champagne and her husband King Louis VII, to the young Alexios Komnenos, due to take place early in March. But travelling through Anatolia en route for Constantinople his party was attacked by Turks and he was taken prisoner. He missed the wedding, but Manuel Komnenos paid his ransom. Henry had met the emperor many years before, when the Second Crusade passed through Constantinople, and had apparently made a good impression on him. He was probably still in Constantinople when Manuel died late in September 1180 and Alexios and Agnes succeeded as emperor and empress. Henry continued his journey home at the end of September, but did not arrive until 8 March 1181, dying of illness eight days later.[55]

Second marriage: Guy de Lusignan

A year earlier in the kingdom of Jerusalem, King Baldwin, Countess Sybil and the royal council had been waiting for Duke Hugh of Burgundy to arrive, marry Sybil and take over the burden of government from the sick king. But he did not come. Yet again there had apparently been miscommunication and misunderstanding between the Latin Christians of Europe and the crusader states. Archbishop William recorded that no explanation was ever given. He was in Constantinople on a diplomatic mission in spring 1180, so he would have been absent from Jerusalem at the crucial time and had to rely on second-hand information.[56]

According to Archbishop William's account, Baldwin IV received news that his cousins Prince Bohemond III of Antioch and Count Raymond III of Tripoli were coming to Jerusalem for Easter 1180 with their armies. There was nothing strange in this, as pilgrims flocked to Jerusalem from all over the crusader states and the whole of Christendom for the Easter ceremonies. Sybil, and possibly her baby son, would have been in Jerusalem too for the ceremonies; Reynald of Sidon was certainly there (as he witnessed a donation charter a week after Easter), so most likely the queen mother Agnes de Courtenay was also with her husband. But (according to Archbishop William) Baldwin, gravely ill, believed that Bohemond and Raymond intended to remove him from the kingship and take over the kingdom themselves. Realising that he needed to secure the succession and find an alternative regent – clearly he was not prepared at this time to accept Count Raymond III as regent again – he unexpectedly (*ex insperato*) gave his sister to 'a certain adolescent, sufficiently noble, that is, Guy de Lusignan, son of Hugh le Brun, from the diocese of Poitou', and – contrary to normal usage (*preter morem*)

– had the marriage carried out during the feast of Easter. Prince Bohemond and Count Raymond, realising that that their arrival was not welcome to the king or his people, stayed in Jerusalem for the Easter feast and then returned home.[57]

After all the lengthy negotiations which had preceded Sybil's previous marriages or non-marriages, this sudden resolution of the problem of Sybil's marriage was certainly unexpected. For Archbishop William it remained inexplicable. Writing half a century later, the compiler of the *Chronique d'Ernoul* had a different story. According to this, Countess Sybil had written to Baldwin of Ramla while he was in Saladin's prison (after he had been captured at Marj Ayun, so in the summer or autumn of 1179) telling him that when he was released she would persuade her brother to let them marry. Baldwin convinced Saladin to release him with the promise that he would pay a large ransom, but the countess told him to pay the ransom before she talked to her brother, because she did not want to mortgage her property to pay his ransom. Baldwin went to Constantinople, where Emperor Manuel received him kindly, partly because Baldwin's brother Balian was married to Maria Komnene. Manuel gave Baldwin the money for his ransom. But when Baldwin returned to the kingdom of Jerusalem he found that one of his sons-in-law, who was also royal constable, and who was the lover of the king's mother – through whom he had got the post of constable – had persuaded the countess and her mother that the countess should marry his brother '*un des beaus chevaliers del mont*' (one of the fairest knights in the world). This royal constable then sent for his brother, Guy, and they talked to the king, and the king gave his sister to Guy and made him count of Jaffa. When Baldwin saw this, he married the daughter of the constable of Tripoli. It later becomes clear in the *Chronique* that Baldwin never forgave Guy for this. The author of the *Chronique d'Ernoul* explained that Guy was a very fair knight (*mout beaus chevaliers*), which would normally mean that he was extremely skilled as a knight; but as he added that he was neither *preus* (doughty) nor *sages* (wise), he appears to have meant that Guy looked good but nothing more.[58]

The compiler of the *Chronique d'Ernoul*, however, was not an objective writer, denigrating Guy de Lusignan (and also Sybil for agreeing to marry him) in order to defend the Ibelins against accusations of treachery and of actively contributing to the fall of the kingdom of Jerusalem to Saladin in 1187. But, once again, the compiler of the *Chronique d'Ernoul* falsified the chronology of events.[59] Easter in 1180 fell on Sunday 20 April. Just over a week later, on 28 April 1180, Baldwin of Ramla was in Jerusalem making a donation to the Hospitallers, witnessed by Reynald de Châtillon, Count Joscelin the royal seneschal, Reynald lord of Sidon and Baldwin's brother Balian.[60] So Baldwin was in Jerusalem, not Constantinople, at Easter 1180. Moreover, this group of witnesses suggests there was no breach at that time between the king's supporters – Reynald de Châtillon, Count Joscelin, and Reynald of Sidon, Agnes de Courtenay's husband and stepfather of the king – and the Ibelin brothers. The claim that Guy's brother Aimery de Lusignan, son-in-law of Baldwin, was royal constable at Easter 1180 cannot be verified;

the earliest documentary evidence of him as constable is from almost a year later, 1 March 1181.[61] Nor is there any contemporary evidence that he was got this post through the favour of Agnes de Courtenay.

The contemporary commentator Abbot Robert of Torigni recorded that King Baldwin of Jerusalem gave his sister 'to a certain best knight, brother of Geoffrey de Lusignan' (*cuidam optimo militi, fratri Gaufredi de Lizenun*).[62] Robert recorded nothing about Guy's looks but stressed his military skill. Unlike Archbishop William, he mentioned Guy's famous elder brother rather than his father, but Hugh le Brun of Lusignan had been to the East on crusade and so was known to Archbishop William and his compatriots by repute if not personally.

If Clément de Vasselot is correct in deducing that Guy's father Hugh did not die in Nūr al-Dīn's prison after he was captured at Artah in 1164 but was released, spent some time in the county of Tripoli where he acquired land and remarried, and then returned to the West, then Guy could have been living on his family's lands in Tripoli before he came to the kingdom of Jerusalem. This would account for the long gap in Guy's known movements between his leaving Poitou in 1168 after killing Earl Patrick of Salisbury in the course of a rebellion against King Henry of England and reappearing at the royal court of Jerusalem at Easter 1180. He could have taken refuge in the county of Tripoli, and then followed his brother Aimery to Jerusalem to serve King Baldwin IV. In the county of Tripoli he could have served Count Raymond, who was a distant cousin, descended from their mutual ancestor Almodis de la Marche. Clément de Vasselot suggested that the Lusignans of Poitou anticipated taking over the county of Tripoli if Raymond died without an heir.[63] We can only speculate whether Raymond's dislike for Guy was due to his regarding Guy as a possible rival for his county as well as the throne of Jerusalem.

The *Chronique d'Ernoul*'s claim that Sybil married Guy for his looks had support from the English commentator Roger of Howden. Like the *Chronique d'Ernoul*, Roger's chronology was incorrect: he placed these events at least two years too late, after the accession of Pope Urban III to the papal throne in 1182, after Patriarch Eraclius of Jerusalem's embassy to Europe in 1184–1185, and following an apparently fictional story of a renegade Templar named Robert of St Albans who defected to Saladin, married his sister's daughter, and led an attack on Jerusalem. According to Roger, William, son of the Marquis William of Montferrat, count of Jaffa, had just died; and the king took his sister into his own household to be looked after with her mother. Guy de Lusignan was one of his household knights; he was *decorus facie et probus in armis* (good looking in face and doughty in arms) and closer to the king than other royal familiars (*inter familiares regis caeteris familiarior*). Sybil, '*videns ... quod Gwido iste decorus esset*' (seeing that that Guy was good-looking), decided to marry him, not daring to tell the king what she wanted, and they slept together. When this became known the king wanted to stone him, but after much torture (*post multos cruciatus*), with the prayer and counsel of the Templars and other wise people, he let them both live (*utrique vitam donavit*). As his sister was his only heir, he allowed her to marry Guy, and gave him the county of Jaffa on condition that the son which she had from her earlier marriage would succeed him (the king) in the kingdom, which was done. Not long after, Baldwin IV, king of Jerusalem, died and his sister's son succeeded him in the kingdom.[64]

Roger of Howden was clearly writing this section of his work after Baldwin IV's death, possibly during the summer of 1191 when he was at Acre and could have heard gossip and stories about the past few years from local people in the royal army, but the information he had gathered was muddled and distorted by hindsight. Perhaps Roger himself realised this, as he omitted the story from his later *Chronica*.[65] Sybil was probably not living at the royal court in 1177–80; all her charters were witnessed by the officials of Ascalon, indicating that she was at Ascalon. Archbishop William of Tyre, a direct contemporary of events, did not like Guy de Lusignan and so would probably have mentioned the story of a secret affair and clandestine marriage if such a story was circulating at the time; as he did not, there was probably no such story. What is more, although he thoroughly disliked Agnes de Courtenay, later in his history calling her *mulier plane deo odibilis et in extorquendo importuna* (a woman plainly hateful to God and unreasonably persistent in extorting what she wanted),[66] he did not mention that she had any role in Baldwin's decision, which suggests that she did not.

There is no evidence that Sybil had a choice in this marriage. A woman who was a fief-holder could not marry whomever she liked; she could wed only with the consent of the lord of the land.[67] In particular, as Hamilton pointed out: 'the marriage of the king's sister and heir was a matter of state'.[68] King Baldwin IV would not have allowed his sister to marry a member of the Ibelin family because the family was already immensely powerful in the kingdom and (as would be seen later in the year with the betrothal of his younger half-sister Isabel) he could not afford to allow any one family to gain substantially more power than the rest. What is more, as Sybil's step-uncle, Baldwin of Ramla would have required ecclesiastical dispensation to marry Sybil. In addition (again, as Hamilton pointed out), at Easter 1180, Sybil was still betrothed to Duke Hugh III of Burgundy and was not free to engage herself to anyone. Her brother changed his mind and broke the betrothal only under threat of invasion and overthrow.[69]

So the romanticised stories told by the *Chronique d'Ernoul* and Roger of Howden cannot be true, but one point mentioned by Roger of Howden could have some basis in actuality. According to Roger's informants, Guy de Lusignan was a close friend of King Baldwin, one of his closest household knights, although the fact that Guy did not witness royal documents until after he became count of Jaffa and Ascalon suggests that he had only recently arrived in the kingdom. It is possible that Baldwin did see Guy de Lusignan, younger brother of one of his most faithful ministers Aimery de Lusignan, as a trusted friend. He was a skilled knight who would be able to lead the army of the kingdom in the field for many years.[70] He was from a noble family with a crusading heritage. As he was a distant relation in the male line of both

Prince Bohemond III of Antioch and Count Raymond of Tripoli, all descendants of Almodis of La Marche by her first and second marriages, Bohemond and Raymond could hardly complain about the match, which also avoided giving excessive influence to the Ibelins. No ecclesiastical dispensation was required. Altogether, Guy de Lusignan looked like the ideal match for Sybil. The fact that Archbishop William did not directly criticise the king's judgement in his choice of Sybil's husband suggests that it was the king's own decision. Unlike his attitude towards other leading figures in the kingdom, the archbishop was always very reluctant to criticise Baldwin IV, his former pupil, for whom he appears to have had great affection and respect.

Regardless of this, Archbishop William indicated that there were grave problems with this marriage. It had taken place *preter morem*, he wrote, contrary to normal usage. In fact the marriage was illegal under canon law, which held that marriages should not take place during Lent or Easter. The thirteenth-century law of the kingdom of Jerusalem as laid out in the *Assises de la Cour de Bourgeois* (written down around 1240) would state this explicitly, '*Bien sachés que dés le dimanche de Careme prenant, jusques à huit jours après la Pasque, ne doit ni ne peut nus hons espouser*' (Be certain that from the Sunday before Lent to eight days after Easter, no one must nor can marry) and continued:

> '*Et c'il avenist, par aucune aventure, qu'aucun houme espousast en ces jors qui sont defendus et par la lei et par sainte Yglise, la raison coumande que celuy mariage ne vaut, ni les enfans qu'il auront ne seront mie dreit heir d'aver ce que eschier lor devret. Et est tenue sainte Yglise par dreit de partir celuy mariage*' (and if it happens by some chance that someone marries during these days which are forbidden both by the law and by holy Church, reason commands that that marriage is worthless, and the children that they may have will not be legitimate heirs to any property that should fall to them. And the holy Church is bound by right to separate that marriage).[71]

This may not yet have been secular law in the kingdom of Jerusalem in 1180, but it was certainly canon law.

The validity of the marriage was also questionable because (to judge from Archbishop William's description of it as 'unexpected') it was carried out too quickly for any banns to be proclaimed. At this time the reading of banns on a series of days before a wedding took place was the practice in England, Paris and north-eastern France. Although it did not become a requirement on the whole of the Latin Church until the Fourth Lateran Council of 1215, the absence of banns could suggest that something was amiss in the marriage, as it had taken place without due consideration and publicity.[72]

The fact that King Baldwin IV had married his sister to Guy de Lusignan at a time when a marriage ceremony was canonically invalid and without public notice being given indicates that he acted in a great hurry because he was extremely concerned about his cousins' intentions. But did Prince

Bohemond III of Antioch and Count Raymond III of Tripoli really intend to overthrow King Baldwin IV at Easter 1180, and if so whom did they intend to promote as Sybil's husband? There were some possible grounds for concern. In 1177 when Count Philip of Flanders had abandoned the planned joint campaign with the Byzantines in Egypt in favour of campaigning with Bohemond and Raymond in Syria, Archbishop William of Tyre had indicated that Bohemond and Raymond may have deliberately sabotaged King Baldwin's military plans by persuading Count Philip to depart from the Egyptian campaign. Possibly in 1180 they had decided that after the defeats of 1179 Baldwin was no longer fit or able to act as king of Jerusalem. Perhaps, as Hamilton suggested, they were concerned about the power of the de Courtenays in the kingdom and wanted to stop Sybil's marriage to Duke Hugh III of Burgundy – a very distant relation of the de Courtenays of Edessa.[73] The most straightforward means of doing this was to marry Sybil to someone else. Roger of Howden wrote later that Raymond III of Tripoli had wanted to marry Sybil himself and gave this as the reason for Raymond's alleged betrayal of the Christian people to Saladin; but Raymond was already married to Lady Eschiva of Tiberias.[74] Bohemond was not free to marry either; he was married to Theodora Komnene at this point; although he repudiated her later that year. In any case, both men were too closely related to Sybil to marry her. Raymond had no sons of his own to marry Sybil, and Bohemond's sons were, like their father, too closely related to Sybil. Hamilton suggested that Baldwin of Ramla was their preferred candidate; but Baldwin of Ramla was also related to Sybil, as he was her step-uncle.[75]

Whatever his cousins' intentions, King Baldwin pre-empted them. Sybil was married to a man he was confident that he could trust, who owed his position to King Baldwin's own patronage, but who was also of noble birth and who had a good reputation as a warrior. If there had been a crisis and the whole affair was not simply a sick man's paranoia, the crisis was over for the moment.

Notes

1 WT 2: 979–980 (Bk 21 ch 14); Hamilton, *Leper King*, p. 118.
2 Philip of Novara, *Le Livre de Forme de Plait*, pp. 161–164, 290–293 (section 68) and note 265; Peter W. Edbury, 'Women and the customs of the High Court of Jerusalem according to John of Ibelin', in *Chemins d'outremer: Études d'histoire sur la Méditerranée médiévale offertes à Michel Balard*, ed. D. Coulon, C. Otten-Froux, P. Pagès, and D. Valérian (Paris, 2004), pp. 285–292, at p. 287; reprinted in Peter W. Edbury, ed., *Law and History in the Latin East* (Farnham, 2014), article IV; WT 2: 785–786 (Bk 17 ch 18).
3 Edbury, 'Women and the customs of the High Court of Jerusalem', p. 291; Christine de Pisan, *The Treasure of the City of Ladies*, pp. 59, 128–129 (1: 11, 2: 9); for noblewomen's active involvement in administration in France and Flanders see the articles in *Aristocratic Women in Medieval France*, ed. Evergates; Park, *Papal Protection*, pp. 136–170; for England see, for instance, RāGena C. DeAragon, 'Power and Agency in Post-Conquest England: Elite Women and the

Transformations of the Twelfth Century', in *Medieval Elite Women and the Exercise of Power, 1100–1400: Moving beyond the Exceptionalist Debate*, ed. Heather J. Tanner (Cham, 2019), pp. 19–43, esp. pp. 30–33.

4 *Cartulaire général*, 1: 336, 337, 341 (nos 487, 488, 489, 491, 495); Riley-Smith, *The Feudal Nobility*, pp. 57–58. On Constance see Myra Miranda Bom, *Women in the Military Orders of the Crusades* (Basingstoke, 2012), pp. 69–70.

5 *Cartulaire général*, 1: 351–353 (nos 516, 517, 518); *ULKJ* 2: 678–679, 846–847 (nos 396, 495, 496), and 4: 1637, 1679 for Geoffrey of Tours's and Robert de Piquigni or Picquigny's appearances as witness.

6 *Cartulaire général*, 1: 373–374 (no 551). The evidence for Constance's return to France in 1179–1180 was set out by Dr Myra Bom in her paper 'Constance of France (Countess of Saint-Gilles)'s Travel to the Latin East: Motivation and Strategy' at the Leeds International Medieval Congress, Monday 5 July 2021, session 304, and in email correspondence to me on 12 July 2021. I am very grateful to Dr Bom for her help with this point.

7 Hamilton, *Leper King*, pp. 119, 122.

8 Barber, *Crusader States*, pp. 268–269; Hamilton, *Leper King*, p. 119; *Chronicle of Robert of Torigni*, pp. 271–272.

9 Hamilton, *Leper King*, pp. 120–121; Roger of Howden, *Gesta*, 1: 116, 133, 136, 158–159 (Philip did not keep this promise: Roger of Howden, *Chronica*, 2: 119, 131); David Crouch, 'At Home with Roger of Howden', in *Military Cultures and Martial Enterprises in the Middle Ages: Essays in Honour of Richard P. Abels*, ed. John D. Hosler and Steven Isaac (Woodbridge, 2020), pp. 156–176; Hans Eberhard Mayer, 'Henry II of England and the Holy Land', *English Historical Review*, 97 (1982), 721–739, at 725–726.

10 Mayer, 'Henry II of England and the Holy Land', 727.

11 Miriam Rita Tessera, 'Philip Count of Flanders and Hildegard of Bingen: Crusading against the Saracens or Crusading against Deadly Sin?' in *Gendering the Crusades*, ed. Susan B. Edgington and Susan Lambert (Cardiff, 2001), pp. 77–93.

12 WT 2: 979 (Bk 21 ch 13).

13 Hamilton, *Leper King*, p. 23 (for Baldwin's age); Park, *Papal Protection*, pp. 152–158 (for Philip's age and experience).

14 WT 2: 979 (Bk 21 ch 13).

15 See *La Chanson de Roland*, ed. F. Whitehead, 2nd edn (Oxford, 1946), for instance at lines 1007–1016, 1073–1081, 1088–1123.

16 WT 2: 980 (Bk 21 ch 13); Hamilton, *Leper King*, pp. 123–125.

17 WT 2: 980 (Bk 21 ch 13).

18 Hamilton, *Leper King*, p. 125.

19 WT 2: 980–991 (Bk 21 ch 14).

20 For example, see Warren, *Henry II*, pp. 72, 90 (marriage of Henry the Younger of England, aged five years, and Margaret of France, aged around two); William Clay Stalls, 'Queenship and the Royal Patrimony in Twelfth-Century Iberia: the Example of Petronilla of Aragon', in *Queens, Regents and Potentates*, ed. Theresa M. Vann (Dallas, TX, 1993), pp. 49–61, at pp. 49–51 (betrothal of Petronilla of Aragon, aged one year, to Count Ramon Berenguer IV of Barcelona, aged around twenty-four).

21 Eljas Oksanen, *Flanders and the Anglo-Norman World, 1066–1216* (Cambridge, 2012), pp. 88–89.

22 WT 2: 981 (Bk 21 ch 13).

23 WT 2: 981 (Bk 21 ch 13).
24 Hamilton, *Leper King*, pp. 126–127; Edbury and Rowe, *William of Tyre*, pp. 63–64; Mayer, 'Henry II of England and the Holy Land', pp. 727–729; Oksanen, *Flanders and the Anglo-Norman World*, pp. 88–89; E. Warlop, *The Flemish Nobility before 1300* (Courtrai, 1975–1976), vol. 1, pp. 156, 264, vol. 2, p. 528, note 295, p. 518, note 132, vol. 3, pp. 660–661. I am very grateful to Dr Paul Webster for his help with this point.
25 *Chronique d'Ernoul*, pp. 32–33 (ch 4); Hamilton, *Leper King*, pp. 125–126; Edbury, 'Ernoul, *Eracles*, and the Beginnings of Frankish Rule in Cyprus', pp. 31–33; Peter W. Edbury, 'Ernoul, *Eracles*, and the Collapse of the Kingdom of Jerusalem', 44, 46.
26 Edbury, 'The Crusader Town and Lordship of Ramla', pp. 10–14.
27 *Chronique d'Ernoul*, pp. 137–139 (ch 11).
28 Hamilton, *Leper King*, pp. 125–126 and note 71; *Chronique d'Ernoul*, p. 48 (ch 6).
29 WT 2: 986 (Bk 21 ch 17).
30 James A. Brundage, *Medieval Canon Law* (London, 1995), p. 75.
31 John, *Godfrey of Bouillon*, pp. 232–235; *Chronique d'Ernoul*, pp. 48, 56–60, 114 (chs 6, 7, 10).
32 WT 2: 985 (Bk 21 ch 17); Barber, *Crusader States*, pp. 269–270; Hamilton, *Leper King*, pp. 127–132; Lewis, *Counts of Tripoli*, pp. 242–243; Buck, *Principality of Antioch*, pp. 52, 236–237.
33 Hamilton, *Leper King*, pp. 133–136; Alan V. Murray, '"Mighty Against the Enemies of Christ": The Relic of the True Cross in the Armies of the Kingdom of Jerusalem', in *The Crusades and their Sources: Essays Presented to Bernard Hamilton*, ed. John France and William G. Zajac (Aldershot, 1998), pp. 217–238, at pp. 221–222, 236.
34 Steven Tibble, *The Crusader Armies 1099–1187* (New Haven and London, 2018), pp. 300–313; Hamilton, *Leper King*, pp. 135–136; Barber, *Crusader States*, p. 271; Lyons and Jackson, *Saladin*, pp. 121–126 (p. 123 on the battle site); Phillips, *Life and Legend*, pp. 117–122; BD, p. 54 (section 53); IA, pp. 253–254 (vol. 11.442–443); *Chronicle of Robert of Torigni*, p. 276; Ralph of Diceto, 'Ymagines historiarum', 1: 423–424.
35 *ULKJ* 2: 849–851 (nos 500, 501).
36 Archbishop William of Tyre recorded that Baldwin V was scarcely five years old (*vix annorum quinque*) in November 1183, suggesting that he was born in 1178: WT 2: 1058 (Bk 22 ch 30); but the later writer Arnold of Lübeck recorded that he was in his ninth year at the time of his death in summer 1186, indicating that he was born in 1177: Hamilton, *Leper King*, p. 139, note 47.
37 Henrietta Leyser, *Medieval Women: A Social History of Women in England, 450–1500* (London, 1995), p. 130.
38 Margaret of Provence, queen of France, gave birth to three children during her husband Louis IX's first crusade (1248–1254); during the same crusade her sister Beatrice, wife of Louis IX's youngest brother Charles of Anjou, gave birth to a son, and her sister-in-law Matilda of Brabant, wife of Count Robert of Anjou, also gave birth to a son; while her niece-in-law, Eleanor of Castile, gave birth to a daughter while she was at Acre in 1272 during her husband's crusade: Sabine Geldsetzer, *Frauen auf Kreuzzügen, 1096–1291* (Darmstadt, 2003), pp. 195, 213–215.
39 Barber, *Crusader States*, p. 269; Hamilton, *Leper King*, pp. 136–137; Buck, *Principality of Antioch*, p. 52; Lewis, *Counts of Tripoli*, pp. 203–204, 243; IA, p. 256 (vol. 11.445–446); BD, p. 54 (section 53).

40 WT 2: 989–990 (Bk 21 ch 24); Hamilton, *Leper King*, pp. 137–138.
41 *Chronicle of Robert of Torigni*, p. 276; 'Continuatio Aquicinctina', p. 417; Roger of Howden, *Chronica*, 2: 132–133.
42 *ULKJ* 2: 685–686, 847–848 (nos *402, *497).
43 WT 2: 996–997 (Bk 21 ch 25); Phillips, *Defenders*, p. 240; Rhodes, *The Crown and the Cross*, pp. 135–137.
44 Rhodes, *The Crown and the Cross*, pp. 127–128.
45 WT 2: 997 (Bk 21 ch 25).
46 Barber, *Crusader States*, p. 272; Hamilton, *Leper King*, p. 142; Ronnie Ellenblum, 'Frontier Activities: the Transformation of a Muslim Sacred Site into the Frankish Castle of Vadum Iacob', *Crusades*, 2 (2003), 83–97; WT 2: 997–998 (Bk 21 ch 25); Phillips, *Life and Legend*, pp. 126–133.
47 WT 2: 1001–1002 and note on 28, lines 40–46 (Bk 21 ch 28); Hamilton, *Leper King*, p. 143; Barber, *Crusader States*, p. 273. Hugh of Tiberias had been ransomed by September 1181: Lewis, *Counts of Tripoli*, p. 248.
48 WT 2: 999, 1003 (Bk 21 chs 26, 29); Hamilton, *Leper King*, pp. 145–146.
49 WT 2: 1004 (Bk 21 ch 29).
50 *ULKJ* 2: 706–707, 848 (nos 413, 498), and see p. 707 lines 5–7 on William de Furcis and Antelm de Luca, pp. 658–659 on Radulf de Nigella or Nela and 4: 1617 on Balian of Jaffa, 1640 on Gotsuin Boccus. The document states it is 'given by the hand of William, archbishop of Tyre and king's chancellor' – although William was still in Europe at this time: for discussion, see Mayer, *Die Kanzlei*, 1: 231–232, note 176. I am very grateful to Peter Edbury for his comments on this point.
51 *ULKJ* 2: 849 (no 499), and see 2: 790 on Bertrand of Jaffa/Caruana; Hamilton, 'Women in the Crusader States', pp. 163–164.
52 *LFWT*, p. 50 (Bk 1 ch 1).
53 Philip of Novara, *Le Livre de Forme de Plait*, pp. 66–69, 227–229 and notes (sections 20–21).
54 Rhodes, *The Crown and the Cross*, pp. 135–136; Hamilton, *Leper King*, pp. 144–145, 149–150; John W. Baldwin, *The Government of Philip Augustus: Foundations of French Royal Power in the Middle Ages* (Berkeley, 1986), pp. 3, 6–7, 15–17; Jim Bradbury, *Philip Augustus, King of France 1180–1223* (London, 1998), pp. 38–42.
55 Evergates, *Henry the Liberal*, pp. 22, 24, 162–164.
56 For William's travels in 1179–1180, see Hamilton, *Leper King*, pp. 147–148; Edbury and Rowe, *William of Tyre*, pp. 19–20; WT 2: 1009 (Bk 22 ch 4).
57 '*Cuidam adolescenti satis nobili, Guidoni videlicet de Liziniaco, filio Hugonis Bruni, de episcopate Pictavensi*': WT 2: 1007–1008 (Bk 22 ch 1); Hamilton, *Leper King*, pp. 150–159; Barber, *Crusader States*, pp. 274–275.
58 *Chronique d'Ernoul*, pp. 56–60 (ch 7).
59 Hamilton, *Leper King*, p. 153.
60 *Cartulaire général*, 1: 395–396 (no 582); *A Handbook of Dates for Students of British History*, ed. C. R. Cheney, revised Michael Jones (Cambridge, 2000), p. 214.
61 *ULKJ* 2: 719–720 (no 423).
62 *Chronicle of Robert of Torigni*, p. 291.
63 Vasselot de Régné, 'A Crusader Lineage', 101–102, 104.
64 Roger of Howden, *Gesta*, 1: 343.
65 Roger of Howden, *Chronica*, 2: 308 mentions only in passing Sybil's marriage at the death of Baldwin IV. For the writing of the *Gesta* and *Chronica* see David

Corner, 'The *Gesta Regis Henrici Secundi* and *Chronica* of Roger, Parson of Howden', *Bulletin of the Institute of Historical Research*, 56/134 (1983), 126–144.
66 WT 2: 1019 (Bk 22 ch 10).
67 Edbury, 'Women and the customs of the High Court of Jerusalem', pp. 286–287.
68 Hamilton, 'Women in the Crusader States', p. 166.
69 Hamilton, *Leper King*, pp. 153–154.
70 Guy's birth date is not known, but on the assumption that he was at least eighteen when he killed Earl Patrick in 1168, he was probably born by 1150 and so was aged around thirty in 1180. He was around nine years younger than Baldwin of Ramla.
71 'Assises de la cour des bourgeois', ed. Le Comte Beugnot, in *Recueil des historiens des croisades: Lois*, vol. 2 (Paris, 1843), p. 120 (ch 180); Brundage, 'Marriage Law', p. 262.
72 On the requirement for marriage banns see Mia Korpiola, 'Introduction: Regional Variations and Harmonization in Medieval Matrimonial Law', in *Regional Variations in Matrimonial Law and Custom in Europe, 1150–1600*, ed. Mia Korpiola (Leiden, 2011), pp. 1–20, at pp. 9–10; Carole Avignon, 'Marché matrimonial clandestin et officines de clandestinité à la fin du Moyen Âge: l'exemple du diocèse de Rouen', *Revue historique*, 312.3/655 (2010), 515–549, especially p. 522.
73 Hamilton, *Leper King*, p. 154.
74 Roger of Howden, *Gesta*, 1: 359–360.
75 Hamilton, *Leper King*, pp. 154–155; Buck, *Principality of Antioch*, p. 238.

5 Wife of Guy de Lusignan and mother of the child king (1180–1186)

The shifting balance of power

Having dealt with the problem of his elder sister's marriage, Baldwin went on to make a two-year truce with Saladin, covering both land and sea. Archbishop William claimed that the truce was humbling for the kingdom of Jerusalem, because unlike previous occasions the Muslims did not pay tribute in return for a truce. Saladin's administrator the Qadi al-Fādil wrote that the Franks no longer needed to be bribed to make truces; they had been forced by the sword. The truce did not include the county of Tripoli, but Saladin launched a naval assault from Egypt, combined with an attack by land, and forced Count Raymond III also to negotiate a truce.[1]

In late summer 1180, the balance of power in the eastern Mediterranean changed dramatically with the death on 24 September of Emperor Manuel Komnenos, who had been a valuable ally and protector to the crusader states. His successor was his son Alexios II, married to Agnes/Anna, youngest daughter of King Louis VII of France. As Alexios was underage his mother Maria of Antioch, sister of Bohemond III of Antioch, ruled as regent, sharing the government with the patriarch of Constantinople and Manuel Komnenos's nephew Alexios Komnenos, who held the office of protosebastos. However, conflict soon broke out between them and Manuel Komnenos's daughter Maria the Porphyrogenita (that is, 'born in the purple'), who was married to Renier, son of William V, marquis of Montferrat, and brother of Sybil's first husband.[2]

In the principality of Antioch, Prince Bohemond III may have taken the news of Manuel's death as an opportunity to throw off the yoke of Byzantine overlordship in the person of his wife Theodora, Manuel's niece whom the emperor had bestowed on his vassal as bride in around 1177. He married a woman named Sybil, whose background is unclear but whose sister was married to the lord of Barziyya and who was in correspondence with Saladin, so probably came of a good local family.[3] The ecclesiastical and secular leaders of the principality vigorously protested against Bohemond's divorce and remarriage, and a team of negotiators was sent from the kingdom of Jerusalem to try to resolve the dispute. Bohemond may have temporarily separated from his new wife, and some of his closest advisors left his court

DOI: 10.4324/9781315205960-6

and went to the court of Prince Rupen III of Cilician Armenia while some new men took up positions in the government of the principality of Antioch. Clearly the nobles of the principality of Antioch believed that they had the right to be consulted over the prince's marital arrangements.[4]

Meanwhile, in October 1180, Baldwin IV took the advice of one of his most loyal nobles, Reynald of Châtillon, and betrothed his younger half-sister Isabel, who was 'scarcely eight years old' (*vix annorum octo*) to Reynald's stepson Humphrey (or Henfrid) IV of Toron, son of Humphrey III of Toron and Stephanie de Milly. Archbishop William described Humphrey as both *adolescens* (young) and *puer iam puber* (a boy who had already reached puberty), and as Bahā' al-Dīn ibn Shaddād would still describe him as a 'youth' ten years later he was probably aged no more than fifteen in 1180. The archbishop added that Prince Reynald, third husband of the boy's mother, had worked very hard to arrange the betrothal, implying that he had proposed it to the king.[5] As a vassal of Manuel Komnenos, whose son had served the emperor and whose daughter's marriage the emperor had arranged, Reynald was a suitable father-in-law for Queen Maria Komnene's daughter. The betrothal removed any risk that Baldwin's paternal relatives – Prince Bohemond of Antioch or Count Raymond of Tripoli – might try to marry this Byzantine princess to one of their own supporters.

Baldwin IV: building up control

As part of the betrothal agreement, Humphrey had to surrender to the king the lands he had inherited from his father *in finibus Tyri* (in the area of Tyre) – Toron (now Tibnin in Lebanon), Chastelneuf and his claim to Banyas. He received in return a money fief of 7,000 Saracen bezants. King Baldwin must have decided that as young Humphrey was the heir to the lordship of Transjordan through his mother and was now betrothed to marry the third in line to the throne, he could not be allowed to hold the lordship of Toron as well. Subsequently, Baldwin granted Toron to his mother Agnes de Courtenay: according to the traveller Ibn Jubayr or Jubair from al-Andalus, who was passing by on his way from Damascus to Acre in mid-September 1184, the king's mother held it.[6]

The election of the new patriarch of Jerusalem was probably also controlled by Baldwin IV. Patriarch Amaury of Nesle died on 6 October 1180. Archbishop William reported simply that Archbishop Eraclius of Caesarea was elected in his place. In contrast to his description of Amaury's election in 1157, he did not accuse the dowager queen or her female relatives of influencing the election.[7] The much later account of the election set out in the *Chronique d'Ernoul* and developed in the even later *Estoire de Eracles* accused Agnes de Courtenay of using her influence to obtain Eraclius's election as patriarch.[8] Clearly it was normal procedure for secular princes to have the final say in the election of prelates in the crusader states, as Queen Melisende did in 1157 and as Pope Celestine III complained in 1191 in his bull *Cum terrae, quae*, in which he condemned the practice. Archbishop William did not hesitate to condemn Agnes for her intervention against Count Raymond in spring 1182, but on this occasion he mentioned nothing of the kind.[9] The most likely secular prince to have chosen Eraclius as patriarch, whose actions Archbishop William seldom if ever questioned, was King Baldwin.

Eraclius was well educated and well connected; like Archbishop William he had studied at Bologna, and had friends among prominent ecclesiastics in Europe. As a native of the Auvergne he was not tied into the kingdom of Jerusalem's social and political networks, and he went on to be an effective patriarch working for what he saw to be the kingdom's benefit irrespective of royal or noble interests. Just as Baldwin IV had married his elder sister to an outsider, perhaps the king thought it best to appoint an outsider to the highest ecclesiastical position in the land. In contrast, the later story in the *Chronique d'Ernoul* and the *Estoire de Eracles* of Agnes's intervention was devised to imply that Eraclius was never truly patriarch because he was irregularly elected, and by extension discredited everything he did, including crowning Sybil and Guy in 1186.[10]

By the end of 1180 Baldwin IV was in a much stronger position than he had been at Easter. His elder sister was married to one of his household knights, his younger sister was betrothed to the stepson of his loyal former regent, he had taken control of a powerful lordship which he would soon entrust to his mother, and he had appointed a highly competent patriarch of Jerusalem. He was now much more secure against any attempt by his cousins of Antioch and Tripoli to overthrow him. He was even ruling alone, without a regent: Reynald de Châtillon no longer appeared in this position, while the royal seneschal Joscelin of Courtenay was absent for several months on a diplomatic mission to Constantinople.[11]

Externally, matters did not look so good. The papal view of Baldwin's regime, as expressed by Pope Alexander III in his crusading bull *Cor nostrum* of 16 January 1181, was that Baldwin was 'scourged by the just judgement of God' (*justo Dei judicio flagellatus*) and that his realm needed outside help to survive.[12] Baldwin's Byzantine allies could no longer be relied upon, as civil war had broken out between the regency government led by Maria of Antioch, and her step-daughter and son-in-law, Maria and Renier of Montferrat.[13] On the positive side, in 1181 Prince Rupen of Cilician Armenia married Humphrey IV of Toron's sister Isabel, renewing ties between the leading families of Cilicia and Jerusalem.[14]

Sybil and Guy, countess and count of Jaffa-Ascalon

Even if the plan had been for Sybil's new husband to take on the burden of government from the king, Guy de Lusignan did not immediately do so. Instead, it appears Countess Sybil and her husband Guy were administering their county of Jaffa-Ascalon, as the surviving documents that they issued related to their own lordship.[15] Sometime between Christmas 1180 and 10 September 1181, Guy and Sybil confirmed a sale of a casal to the Hospital of St John of Jerusalem which had previously been agreed by Baldwin, lord of

Ramla, and was also confirmed by the king. Reynald, lord of Sidon and husband of Sybil's and Baldwin's mother Agnes, was first in the witness list to the king's confirmation charter.[16]

Sybil's and Guy's first child could have been born early in 1181 – that is, nine months after their marriage. The author(s) of the *Itinerarium peregrinorum*, writing in the crusader camp outside Acre in late 1190 or early 1191, recorded that Sybil and Guy had four daughters; as contemporaries reported that two died with Sybil in autumn 1190, two must have predeceased her.[17] Contemporaries did not record the dates of their daughters' births, but if we suppose the children were born at equal intervals throughout Sybil's marriage to Guy then a child was born around every thirty months, meaning there was not much time when Sybil was not either pregnant or recovering from childbirth – and there could also have been still births and miscarriages in between. The couple may also have had the care of Sybil's son Baldwin, but – as already noted – as Sybil also had a claim to the throne, it was customary in the kingdom to entrust the child heir to the care of an independent third party. As William of Tyre depicted Baldwin IV having his nephew crowned in November 1183 without reference to Sybil, it appears that at that time the little boy was not living in his mother's household.[18]

By March 1181, Guy de Lusignan was taking a more active role in the government of the kingdom. He appeared as first witness in a document issued by Baldwin IV at Acre with his elder brother Aimery de Lusignan in second place as constable of the kingdom, then followed by Geoffrey Tortus or Le Tor (a crown vassal), Reynald lord of Sidon and Gillebert or Gislebert de Flori (*vicecomes* of Acre).[19] But Guy's role was not consistent. In November 1181, in a document issued at Tyre, Guy and Aimery were nowhere to be seen: the first witness was Joscelin de Courtenay, the royal seneschal; followed by Reynald lord of Sidon; Raymond of Scandalion; Miles de Colouardino (or Colaverdo); Symon de Vercinni, castellan of Tyre; and John Lombard, castellan of Toron.[20] And Guy and Sybil did not witness Baldwin's agreement made at Acre in November 1181, approving repayment terms for a loan his uncle Joscelin had made there.[21]

As holder of one of the two most southerly fiefs of the kingdom whose southern frontier bordered Saladin's territory, Guy could also have co-operated with Reynald de Châtillon's raids south during the winter months, when the rains had allowed grass to grow in the desert regions so that the Frankish cavalry had fodder for their horses. Archbishop William never mentioned Reynald de Châtillon's winter campaigns except to indicate that they were lawless raids that broke King Baldwin's truces with Saladin, but in fact they had a considerable impact and were strategically valuable to the crusader states.[22] In the winter of 1181–82, Reynald's raid towards Eilat, which reached Tabuk on the Damascus–Mecca road, effectively prevented Saladin from moving against Aleppo following the death of its ruler as-Salih (whom we last met capturing Harim early in 1178) early in December 1181. Saladin's nephew Farrukh-Shah, governor of Damascus, was unable to follow his uncle's instructions because he had to deal with Reynald's raiders. 'Izz al-Dīn Mas'ūd of Mosul was able to pre-empt Saladin and take over Aleppo instead.[23]

Reynald was back in the kingdom of Jerusalem by 6 February 1182, when Guy, count of Jaffa and Ascalon, was first witness of King Baldwin's confirmation of a gift of sugar made by his uncle Joscelin to the Hospital of St John of Jerusalem at Acre. Reynald followed Guy in the witness list, followed by Count Joscelin himself, Aimery the constable, and Joscelin de Samosat, castellan of Ascalon.[24] On 22 February, Baldwin gave Chastelneuf (which had previously belonged to Humphrey IV of Toron) to his uncle Joscelin, with incomes from the *fondo*s of Acre and Tyre (the customs houses that collected taxes on land trade), and Maron (now Maroun er-Ras) with other properties. Joscelin would owe the king the service of six knights, plus the service owed by his rear-vassals. Count Guy de Lusignan and Countess Sybil of Jaffa and Ascalon gave their agreement to this gift, which was witnessed by Prince Reynald de Châtillon, Reynald lord of Sidon, Baldwin lord of Ramla, Balian his brother, Aimery the constable, Geoffrey Tortus and Miles de Colouardino.[25]

The effect of these donations to Joscelin de Courtenay, together with Agnes de Courtenay's possession of Toron, was to give Sybil's and Baldwin's maternal relations control of the region around Acre and Tyre.[26] It is likely that Baldwin gave them this power so that they could block any further attempt by his paternal cousins to take over the kingdom. When Count Raymond III of Tripoli travelled south to the kingdom of Jerusalem in spring 1182 – according to Archbishop William he wanted to visit his wife's lordship of Tiberias – King Baldwin was warned that the count had sinister intentions and should not be allowed into the kingdom. According to Archbishop William, the king, '*aurem nimis credulam prebens*' (lending an excessively credulous ear) to these insinuations, forbade the count to enter and he returned to Tripoli. The archbishop was infuriated by this insult to the count and accused his denigrators of trying to take advantage of the king's illness to control the government of the kingdom. First on his list of those responsible was the king's mother, 'a woman hateful to God and unreasonably persistent in extorting what she wanted', and her brother the royal seneschal with a few of their followers, whom he called '*viris ipiis*' (impious men) as if criticising the count was tantamount to attacking God. But other princes, wrote the archbishop, intervened and the king agreed to allow Count Raymond back to the kingdom. He was persuaded to take Raymond back into his favour only because the truce with Saladin was about to expire and Raymond's forces would be needed for the military campaigns to come.[27]

In his determination to defend Count Raymond, who had supported him early in his career, Archbishop William came close to criticising the king. Although King Baldwin was ill, he was not as incapable as the archbishop implied. He was able to lead the army, and he was well able to form his own judgements and reach his own decisions. If he listened to warnings against his cousin it was because he himself was very concerned about his cousin's past behaviour and present ambitions.

In the past, Agnes had approved of Count Raymond. In 1174, when Baldwin had come to the throne, her husband and former brothers-in-law had supported Count Raymond's claim to the regency. But in autumn 1177, Count Philip of Flanders had campaigned with Count Raymond and Prince Bohemond III of Antioch rather than joining the joint campaign with the Byzantines which her son had negotiated. Then at Easter 1180, her son had feared that his cousins were about to overthrow him. If we did not have Archbishop William's opinions to steer us, the obvious conclusion to draw from Agnes's opposition to Raymond in spring 1182 would be that she believed he still intended to overthrow her son.

Some modern writers have depicted Agnes and Joscelin and their supporters as newcomers to the kingdom and ignorant warmongers, while their opponents were from long-standing families who knew the need for peace.[28] Certainly Agnes and Joscelin were outsiders in the sense that they were born in the county of Edessa rather than in the kingdom of Jerusalem and were of mixed Frankish-Armenian heritage – but Queen Melisende of Jerusalem and her sisters, ancestors of Prince Bohemond, Count Raymond and King Baldwin, had also been of mixed Frankish-Armenian heritage and were born in Edessa, not Jerusalem. Agnes and her brother Joscelin had lost their family inheritance and their father to Zengi of Mosul and his son Nūr al-Dīn and were under no illusions about the costs of war. Joscelin, royal seneschal and one of the leading men of the kingdom since 1176, had served King Baldwin III, had personally experienced the risks of war and the costs of failure – having suffered Nūr al-Dīn's prison in Aleppo for twelve years (two years longer than Count Raymond) – and had negotiated on behalf of the kingdom with the Byzantines. He was experienced and respected in international affairs. If it were not for Archbishop William's accusations, it would be natural to assume that it was Baldwin who was anxious to see his uncle and mother in positions of power and influence within the kingdom against the machinations of his paternal kin rather than that Agnes and Joscelin were trying to hold on to their power for their own selfish interests.

Archbishop William did not record who supported the king's mother and uncle in suspecting Count Raymond's intentions and who counselled peace. It would be interesting to know the views of Patriarch Eraclius of Jerusalem, who advised Baldwin to make peace with Count Guy early in 1184, and the opinions of Baldwin's sister Sybil and her husband Guy of Lusignan. Although they held one of the major fiefs of the kingdom and were prospective heirs or regents to the kingdom, Archbishop William did not mention them between their marriage and September 1183.

When the truce with Saladin expired in spring 1182, Count Guy would have led his county's contingent to the kingdom's army, which was normally commanded by Baldwin IV and often accompanied by the Cross. As Saladin's brother al-'Ādil in Egypt co-operated with Saladin in Damascus, attacking the south of the county of Jaffa-Ascalon when Saladin attacked the north of the kingdom, Guy would also have been active defending his own lands.[29] In previous years the Franks might also have tried to negotiate a joint venture with the Byzantines against Egypt, but this ceased to be an option following the usurpation of Andronikos Komnenos in April 1182. Andronikos murdered Maria of Antioch and her opponents (and in autumn 1183, murdered the young emperor Alexios II and married his thirteen-year-old widow Agnes/Anna), and his troops murdered the Italian merchants in Constantinople, their families and other Latins. Unsurprisingly, the Franks were unwilling to work with him.[30]

Guy may also have supported Reynald de Châtillon's raid to the south early in 1183. Reynald had pre-constructed ships carried in sections on camels hired from the Bedouin to the Gulf of 'Aqaba on the Red Sea, where they were assembled and embarked on a naval campaign. Saladin's admiral Husām al-Dīn Lu'lu managed to destroy them before they could attack Medina, but the raid was a blow to Saladin's prestige as he was away campaigning against Muslims (of Mosul and Aleppo) while it took place. As Reynald's territory had no ports where ships could be built, it is possible that his ships were originally constructed at one of Guy de Lusignan's ports. Reynald also attacked Eilat by land, and Guy could have given assistance.[31]

The only clear evidence of Sybil's and Guy's activities during this period is in the surviving documents they issued. At some point between Christmas 1182 and 1183, they gave one Torgis and his heirs some property which Guy and Sybil had bought in the casal of Gesehale from George the Syrian, their scribe. The witnesses were first Joscelin de Somesac, castellan of Ascalon and Baldwin his brother, followed by some new names: Seignoreit *vicecomes* of Ascalon (replacing William Rufus, the previous *vicecomes*); Rainald of Mongisard (later a witness for Sybil's son Baldwin V); Rainald of Soissons (later one of Guy's vassals on Cyprus); Girard or Gerard of Remille (whom we have met before witnessing documents for Sybil); Bertrand Caruana and Guibert his brother (who had also witnessed a document for Sybil in 1179); and six others who did not appear elsewhere.[32]

The documentary evidence also shows Sybil and Guy taking a role in Baldwin's government. On 19 March 1183, Sybil and Guy gave their consent to another concession by King Baldwin to his uncle Joscelin at Acre. Baldwin also gave his uncle a house at Chastelneuf, and one John, the dragoman of Chastelneuf. The witnesses were first Guy count of Jaffa and Ascalon, then Aimery the constable, Baldwin of Ibelin (lord of Ramla), Balian his brother, Geoffrey Tortus, Gotsuin Boccus and William de Molembocca. As this was not land that fell within the county of Jaffa and Ascalon, Sybil's and Guy's role in confirming the donation must have been in their roles as Baldwin's heirs apparent.[33]

But Count Raymond of Tripoli also held a prominent position at court, and on the same day his name was listed before Guy's on a confirmation by King Baldwin to his uncle regarding fourteen casals that Joscelin had bought from Geoffrey Tortus. Guy's name was followed by Prince Reynald de Châtillon and then the same witnesses as the other document on that day, except for Geoffrey Tortus, and followed by further officers and burghers of

Acre and Jerusalem, including William de Furcis and Antelm of Lucca, whom we have met witnessing a document for Baldwin in October 1179.[34]

In spring 1183, then, Sybil's husband held a similar position at court to Count Raymond. It was unclear which of them would take over from King Baldwin in the event that he became unable to govern. Matters came to a head in autumn 1183.

Guy de Lusignan: temporary regent of the kingdom

In June 1183, Saladin at last gained control of Aleppo – by negotiation rather than conquest – so that his domains now surrounded the crusader states. He made a truce with Prince Bohemond of Antioch while he established himself in Aleppo, and then in September he moved his troops south.[35]

Baldwin IV mustered his army at 'the spring of Sepphoris' (also known as Saffūriyya or Saforie) in Galilee, but then fell ill at nearby Nazareth – so ill that Archbishop William wrote that his life was despaired of. He summoned his princes and in the presence of his mother and the patriarch, he appointed 'Guy de Lusignan, his sister's spouse, count of Jaffa and Ascalon' as procurator of the kingdom, 'saving for himself the royal dignity and reserving to himself only Jerusalem with 10,000 gold pieces to be paid annually', and he conferred on Guy the general and free administration of the remaining parts of the kingdom (*reliquarum regni partium generalem et liberam ... administrationem*), ordering his faithful people and all the princes generally that they were Guy's vassals and should show him their fealty with hands (*ei manualiter exhiberent fidelitatem*). But before this was done, Guy had to swear that he would not aspire to the crown while the king was alive, and he would not transfer anything from the cities and castles which he held as the king's representative to another or alienate anything from the fisc. This may have been simply laying out some ground rules, but it does suggest that the king and his advisors suspected that Guy intended to hand out royal castles and revenues to his supporters. Archbishop William indicated that many were not happy about these arrangements either because they thought Guy was not equal to the task or because they thought they could do it better.[36]

These arrangements did not last long; within four chapters of his history, Archbishop William was recounting that Baldwin had taken the administration of the kingdom back from Count Guy and also any hope of Guy's gaining the kingdom. The reason for his decision, he implied, was Guy's conduct of the campaign against Saladin.

So far as evidence survives, this was Guy's first major military command. His strategy was cautious but sound. On 30 September 1183, he led the army to a location where he had an excellent water supply and from which the army could easily move to face the enemy, but he did not attack. The army, raised with the funds gathered from a general tax levied in February that year, was much larger than usual: Archbishop William wrote that such a great army had never before assembled from the whole of the East, with up to 1,300 horsemen (*equites* – but William probably meant knights) and over fifteen thousand infantry. What is more, he wrote, it had illustrious leaders: Bohemond III of Antioch; Count Raymond of Tripoli; Duke Henry of Louvain, a prince of the German Empire; and Ralph de Mauleon, a nobleman from Aquitaine. The princes of the kingdom were also there: as well as Count Guy, there was Reynald de Châtillon, Baldwin of Ramla, Balian of Nablus his brother, Reynald of Sidon, Walter of Caesarea and Joscelin the royal seneschal. The Cross accompanied the army.[37]

But this great army failed to engage the enemy in a full-scale battle. Saladin – with even greater forces – tried to force the Franks out of their defensive position and bring them to battle, but although there were skirmishes the Franks did not budge. On 5 October, Saladin withdrew to Damascus, leaving the Franks in control of the region. The strategy of non-engagement had been successful, but it is not clear whether it was deliberate or whether Guy had been forced into it because he was unable to persuade the other princes of the army to work with him.[38]

For outsiders who had come to the East to win honour and renown in battle against the Muslims, the failure to engage the enemy would have been frustrating. Perhaps they had been hoping for another battle of Montgisard to wipe out Saladin's army once and for all. But Saladin's strength had grown considerably since November 1177. The Franks had won military successes in autumn 1182 while Saladin was concentrating on taking Mosul and Aleppo, but in autumn 1183 the victorious Saladin, the greatest general in the Middle East, came fresh from conquering Aleppo to engage the crusader states and been forced to withdraw. The Frankish army had won a victory.

Judging from the Muslim commentators' views, if the Franks had attacked Saladin's larger army they would probably have suffered a heavy defeat. But Archbishop William recorded that King Baldwin, who had now recovered from his illness, considered that Guy had been cowardly and foolish and that his incompetence had almost led to the kingdom's destruction. William added that Baldwin also wanted to change the agreement over his personal conditions and income to have the city of Tyre rather than Jerusalem.[39]

Perhaps the king considered that Tyre, on the coast, would be a healthier and more pleasant place to live than Jerusalem, which was inland, far from the cooling sea, and much further south in more arid countryside. Situated on a triangular-shaped peninsula, surrounded on three sides by the sea, Tyre was well fortified, connected to the mainland only by an artificial isthmus. In addition to its natural protection it was surrounded by a double wall with towers around the part of the city facing the sea, and a triple wall on the part facing the land, with massive towers and a ditch which could be flooded with sea water to block an enemy's advance. Its harbour was protected by two towers built into the sea, with a chain stretched between them which could be raised to block the entrance. The city contained the archbishop's cathedral, the royal castle, the properties of the Venetian, Pisan and Genoese merchant communes, houses of the Hospitallers and Templars, and many other churches. In short, it was a fine city and a suitable place to which the sick king could retire.[40]

Guy refused Baldwin's proposal, perhaps unwilling to lose direct control over this valuable port. Baldwin then changed his mind about the whole arrangement. He took the administration of the kingdom back from Guy and with it any hope of inheriting the realm. With the common counsel of the princes (wrote Archbishop William), especially Prince Bohemond of Antioch, Count Raymond of Tripoli, Reynald of Sidon, Baldwin of Ramla and his brother Balian, with Count Guy present but not daring to contradict, on the suggestion and with the full encouragement of the king's mother, the king had his nephew Baldwin, *adhuc puerulus vix annorum quinque* (still a little boy scarcely five years old – in fact he must have been aged around six), anointed and solemnly crowned king. This was done (the archbishop wrote) in the church of the Holy Sepulchre, with the universal vote of the people and the assent of the clergy who were present. All the barons gave their oaths of fealty to the boy without delay; only the count of Jaffa (wrote Archbishop William) was not invited to give his oath of homage. The archbishop added that it was unanimously agreed that only the count of Tripoli should be procurator with the responsibility of leading the army against the enemy. However, as Baldwin led the next campaign himself, Count Raymond was not actually given command at that point.

The archbishop recorded that this took place on 20 November 1183.[41] This was a Sunday, the fifth Sunday before Christmas, which in the kingdom of Jerusalem was the start of Advent and so the beginning of the liturgical year. In the church of the Holy Sepulchre the day was marked with a unique liturgy which celebrated the Lord's Resurrection with full solemnity just as on Easter Day.[42] It was an auspicious day for a royal coronation, marking a new beginning of hope. The fact that this day was selected for the coronation suggests that this was not the sudden decision that Archbishop William implies but had been planned well in advance.

Archbishop William's explanation for this sudden change of royal policy is inadequate. He implied that all the secular lords of the kingdom were deeply critical of Count Guy's handling of the military campaign. In fact, one of the leading military commanders, Prince Reynald de Châtillon, was not present: he was at Kerak, overseeing the defence of his castle against Saladin.[43] William did not record what the masters of the Hospitallers and Templars thought about Count Guy's military leadership, although they were well placed to judge, and the fact he did not mention them at this point suggests that they had no complaints to make. Certainly early in the following year they urged the king to make peace with Count Guy.[44]

The change in royal policy was clearly not the result of an argument between factions at court. Whereas in spring 1182 Archbishop William had depicted Sybil's and Baldwin's mother and maternal uncle intervening to block the influence of Count Raymond of Tripoli, he now stated that the queen's mother supported Count Raymond as regent and supported – even initiated – the coronation of her grandson Baldwin and the exclusion of her son-in-law Guy from government. He did not mention Count Joscelin by name, but implied that he was included with the other princes of the kingdom.

It is possible that it was not Count Guy's handling of the military campaign which led to a break in relations but the argument over King Baldwin's income and place of residence – Tyre or Jerusalem.[45] Alternatively, perhaps (despite Archbishop William's claims) Baldwin had only ever intended to delegate his powers as a temporary measure, until he was well enough to take up the government again. If this were the case, William would have resented the fact that King Baldwin had appointed Count Guy as temporary procurator, as he believed that Count Raymond should have been given that role, and so he deliberately misrepresented King Baldwin's actions to make it appear that Count Guy had been disgraced. In contrast, the *Chronique d'Ernoul* wrote nothing about Guy's appointment or removal, depicted the campaign at Saffūriyya as a success (but confused it with the battle of le Forbelet in 1182), and then moved straight to describing Saladin's siege of Kerak. The next event in the history of the kingdom, according to this writer, was the council called by King Baldwin IV at which Count Raymond was made regent, followed by the coronation of Baldwin V and all the nobles doing homage to the child just before Baldwin IV's death in spring 1185.[46] Given that the *Chronique d'Ernoul* generally took every opportunity to make Guy appear an inadequate leader, it is odd that it does not mention his fall in autumn 1183 – unless, in fact, his position as procurator was never intended to be permanent and so his appointment and removal were not as significant as William of Tyre implied.

Baldwin IV was never quick to hand over power to others, always preferring to govern and to lead the army himself, even when he had to be carried in a litter because he could no longer ride and even when his illness had rendered him blind. He had good reason for this: whenever he stepped back from government the nobles divided; but they all united under his leadership.[47] He could, then, have decided to appoint Count Guy as his procurator when he believed himself to be dying, but having recovered he judged that it would be better to lead the government himself. Rather than appoint a permanent procurator to govern in his place, he would follow a practice used by the Byzantine emperors, the Capetian kings of France and his cousin King Henry II of England and crown his successor in order to ensure a smooth succession, with procurators appointed temporarily as required.[48]

Baldwin's action in crowning his nephew as king did not necessarily affect his elder sister's rights, as Sybil could expect to act as regent for her son if Baldwin IV died before her son came of age. Contemporary commentators in Latin Christendom accepted that women who held royal authority by hereditary right could rule on behalf of their son and heir and then step aside when he came of age: this was a legitimate use of power by a female ruler.[49] However, Baldwin IV went on to block any possibility of his sister and her husband gaining power in this way by appointing his male relatives as regents for Baldwin V. Perhaps he feared that allowing Sybil to act as her son's regent would lead to the civil war in the kingdom, as had occurred during the reign of their grandmother Melisende when she acted as regent and then co-ruler with Baldwin III and did not step aside when Baldwin came of age; moreover, their first cousin once removed, Constance of Antioch, who ruled Antioch as regent for her son Bohemond III from 1161 to 1163, may have tried to remain as co-ruler or with Bohemond as sub-ruler of Latakia-Jabala, although she eventually stepped aside – perhaps as part of an agreement with Manuel Komnenos.[50]

What was Sybil's view of her young son's coronation? As no contemporary recorded that she protested at not being appointed regent for her son or tried to obtain physical custody of him, it appears that she agreed to the coronation and accepted that she would not act as regent. Count Guy, on the other hand, may have objected – at least, in the early thirteenth century the Latin continuation of William of Tyre's history portrayed Guy complaining about the situation.[51] Sybil must have given fealty to her son as countess of Jaffa and Ascalon. Archbishop William implies that Guy was no longer a great fief-holder in the kingdom after 20 November 1183, because he was not called on to do homage to the child Baldwin. Nevertheless, Guy accompanied the army of the kingdom on its next expedition: even if he were no longer count of Jaffa and Ascalon, he would have gone with the army as leader of his wife's knights.

The next military expedition was to relieve the castle of Kerak in Transjordan from Saladin's siege. Shortly before King Baldwin had decided to take back the reins of government and crown his nephew, Kerak had hosted the wedding of Sybil's and Baldwin's younger half-sister Isabel to Humphrey IV of Toron. As Isabel had been (according to Archbishop William) 'scarcely eight years old' in October 1180, in autumn 1183 she was only eleven, a year too young for marriage.[52] Reynald de Châtillon had been forewarned of Saladin's attack and had garrisoned Kerak against a siege, but (wrote Archbishop William) on the same day as the wedding had taken place, Saladin began his siege with 'an innumerable multitude' and a variety of siege engines.[53]

Baldwin IV led his army to relieve Kerak, bringing the Holy Cross as well, but during the course of the march he handed over command to Count Raymond, making him *preceptor* (as Archbishop William put it). Saladin raised his siege of Kerak on 4 December 1183: according to William this was because he had heard that Count Raymond was at the head of the Frankish relief force. It is more likely that he did not want to commit his troops to a battle because the fast of Ramadān was approaching.[54]

Archbishop William now portrayed Count Guy as an enemy of Baldwin IV. Every day (he wrote), the hatred between the king and Count Guy grew greater and greater.[55] The king decided that he had sufficient cause to divorce his sister from the count, and he publicly called on the patriarch to set a day to carry it out. The archbishop did not explain what the grounds for divorce would be. Perhaps Baldwin claimed that he himself had forced his sister to marry Guy de Lusignan when she already betrothed to Duke Hugh III of Burgundy. Moreover, the marriage was canonically invalid because it took place at Easter and questionable because it took place without any banns being called. As Sybil's marriage had never been legitimate, it may have only ever been a stopgap measure to meet the emergency of Easter 1180. Baldwin may always have intended to separate his sister from Guy de Lusignan if it suited him to do so – for example, if Duke Hugh III of Burgundy arrived to marry her.[56]

Nevertheless, even though the marriage was not canonically valid it was still a marriage between consenting partners and could not be dissolved without their agreement. According to Archbishop William, Count Guy was not prepared to give up his wife, nor she him. Having been informed about what was happening, as Guy was returning from the expedition to Kerak he took a shortcut to Ascalon, sending a message to Sybil – who was then staying at Jerusalem – to leave the city and proceed to Ascalon, because he feared that Baldwin would not allow her to leave the city.[57]

This is the first time during his account of the events of 1180–1183 that the archbishop mentioned Countess Sybil's location. To judge from the witness lists to her charters, Sybil was usually resident at Ascalon, but she would have had to go to Jerusalem in November 1183 to attend the coronation of her son and to do formal homage with the other nobles of the kingdom. Archbishop William did not describe Sybil's reaction to her husband's message, but to judge from what followed she must have left Jerusalem and joined Guy at Ascalon.

Archbishop William continued his account, stating that King Baldwin sent a messenger (*nuntius*) to Count Guy, summoning him and setting out the reason for the mandate. Count Guy refused to come, claiming that he was ill. When he was summoned again, he again delayed, saying that the king should come himself in person and issue his command with his own voice.

The king arrived at Ascalon (according to Archbishop William), accompanied by some of his princes, and found the city gates locked. Placing his hand on them, he ordered three times that they should be opened. All the people of the city, having heard of the king's arrival, had placed themselves on towers and on the walls to watch, waiting to see the outcome of the affair, but no one opened the gates. When he found that no one obeyed him, the king angrily withdrew and went straight to Jaffa, where he was admitted at once. Here he set up a procurator to manage the town.[58] King Baldwin had acted within his rights as king in depriving Count Guy and Countess Sybil of Jaffa, because they had defied his summons and refused to open the gates of Ascalon to him; but they still held Ascalon.

Archbishop William continued: then King Baldwin reached Acre and summoned a general council (*curia generalis*) to meet there, at which the princes of the realm (except, apparently, for Count Guy and Countess Sybil) assembled on the day stated, although William did not give the date. The patriarch and both of the masters of the Temple and Hospital interceded on bended knee for Count Guy, calling on King Baldwin to put aside his rancour and restore the count to his grace. When Baldwin refused to respond immediately, they indignantly left the court and the city. A proposal was made among the assembled princes to send *nuntios* (messengers) to the kings and the rest of the princes 'over the mountains' (*ultramontanos*) to invite them to aid

Christianity and the kingdom. But the patriarch wanted to make peace between the king and Count Guy first, and when this was rejected, he left Acre.[59] The choice of word here is odd, as '*ultramontanos*', over the mountains, might imply that the princes of the kingdom of Jerusalem intended to call on the Cilician Armenians or the Byzantines for help, whereas the reference to kings and princes suggests that William meant *ultramarinos*, overseas.

Archbishop William did not record that, following up the suggestion made at the council at Acre, in spring or early summer 1184 Patriarch Eraclius and the masters of the Temple and Hospital set off on a mission to the West. The ambassadors kept in touch with King Baldwin: the patriarch wrote to let the king know that they had arrived safely at Brindisi, and in mid-September the king wrote back to the patriarch to give him an update on events that summer: Saladin had launched an unsuccessful attack in July and August on Kerak and had raided Nablus, Sebaste and properties of the military orders including the Hospitallers' castle of Belvoir. Sybil, as countess of Ascalon, would have contributed knights to the army of the kingdom when it marched to relieve Kerak, and her husband Count Guy should have been with the army leading her troops, as he had when Baldwin IV had relieved Kerak early in December 1183; but Archbishop William and the *Chronique d'Ernoul* made no mention of these campaigns.[60]

They also failed to mention the embassy, although it made a considerable impression in Europe. The master of the Temple died in Verona in September 1184, but the patriarch and the master of the Hospital continued on their way, visiting Pope Lucius III and Emperor Frederick Barbarossa in Verona in autumn 1184, King Philip of France in Paris in January 1185 and King Henry of England during February to April 1185. European commentators reported that they offered the crown of Jerusalem to one ruler after another, presenting their requests in the names of the nobility of Palestine, the Templars and Hospitallers and all the clergy and people. They did not claim to speak in the name of the king of Jerusalem, and unlike earlier embassies they did not offer Sybil's hand as an inducement; she was now married to Guy de Lusignan and the attempt to divorce her from him had failed. The implication was that the current ruling dynasty had reached a dead end and a new ruling family was needed. Mayer suggested that 'the patriarch was aiming at the removal of King Baldwin IV and of the whole dynasty'. Whatever the patriarch's intentions, they were disappointed. Although they gave promises of money and soldiers, no ruler was prepared to come in person to rule the kingdom.[61]

Ignoring the patriarch's embassy, Archbishop William's account moved straight from the general council at Acre early in 1184 to sometime after 6 October 1184, with a report that Guy de Lusignan attacked a Bedouin camp near Darum which was under the king's protection. In response, the king summoned the princes of the kingdom and committed the 'care and general administration' of the kingdom to the count of Tripoli. All the people and princes were satisfied by this action, according to William; and he ended his history at this point.[62]

William presented Count Guy's assault on the Bedouin as an act of destructive vindictiveness which demonstrated that Count Guy was unfit to rule the kingdom. However, the Bedouin were not quite the harmless pastoralists that he portrayed them. Saladin's advisors regarded the Bedouin as unreliable. They could act as spies for Saladin, but also for the Franks; they acted as guides for the Franks, helped them with water and transport and helped escaping Frankish prisoners; but on other occasions they helped to track down escaping Franks.[63] In short, the Bedouin followed their own policies to their own benefit.

It may be that these particular Bedouin were working for Saladin. Following on from the summer campaigning, Count Guy's attacks on the Bedouin could have been part of a winter campaign against Saladin's territory to the south of the kingdom of Jerusalem, just as Reynald de Châtillon had raided south in the winters of 1181–1182 and early in 1183, and possibly also in September 1184. As Saladin was at Damascus in the late autumn of 1184 and then moved north against Mosul in January 1185, the winter of 1184–1185 was an opportune time for Guy to invade his southern territory.[64]

Even if Sybil and Guy were unwelcome at the king's court in the winter of 1184–1185, they maintained relations with Sybil's wider family. On 1 February 1185, they issued a charter stating that they had sold to Joscelin III of Courtenay, titular count of Edessa and seneschal of the kingdom of Jerusalem, the casals of Kabul, Kaukab and Tall Kisan with all their appurtenances for 5,000 bezants. This was property that Sybil's mother Agnes de Courtenay had purchased, and the fact that Sybil and Guy sold it to Agnes's brother indicates that Agnes had recently died and Sybil had inherited her property. Regrettably the original document has been lost and only a thirteenth-century summary survives, so the exact titles that the couple used in this document are uncertain: whether they were still calling themselves count and countess of Jaffa and Ascalon or this was simply assumed by the author of the later summary. On the basis that the date and the titles given in the summary are correct, Sybil and Guy were still in control of at least part of their county on 1 February 1185, just before King Baldwin IV's death. Sybil should also have inherited Toron from her mother, but her brother and Count Raymond appear to have blocked this and given Toron to Joscelin, as she and Guy did not acquire Toron until they gained the crown in 1186.[65]

Archbishop William implied that King Baldwin's appointment of Count Raymond of Tripoli as his regent followed immediately on Count Guy's attack on the Bedouin. The traveller Ibn Jubayr, who was at Acre from mid-September to early October 1184, heard that at that time the king's uncle (Joscelin de Courtenay) was the royal chamberlain and regent with control of the treasury, while the count who was lord of Tripoli and Tiberias was the most powerful of the Franks, holding authority in the realm and qualified to be king. But Hamilton suggested that the formal transfer of power to Count Raymond probably took place in early or spring 1185, as 'a stopgap measure' until the patriarch's embassy could return with a king or prince from Europe to take over the government of the realm.[66] Early in April 1185, Count Raymond sent messengers to Saladin's nephew Taqī al-Dīn, lord of Hama, to request an extension to Saladin's truce with the principality of Antioch – indicating that by this time he was acting as Baldwin IV's regent. Saladin arranged a general truce with Raymond that included Antioch, Tripoli and the kingdom of Jerusalem. He also made a treaty with Emperor Andronikos of Constantinople and a truce with Cilician Armenia, which freed him to concentrate on the conquest of Mosul.[67]

The *Chronique d'Ernoul* – which is based on a contemporary and sometimes eyewitness account from this point to late 1187[68] – describes a council between the dying Baldwin and all the barons of Jerusalem, which may record the process whereby Count Raymond was appointed regent. The count of Tripoli was asked to take on the role of *bailleus* for ten years, until the child Baldwin V came of age.[69] Count Raymond responded that he would accept responsibility for the realm (the *baillie*) but not responsibility for the child king, then around seven years old. If the child died before the ten years were up, Raymond did not want to be blamed for his death. (The fact that this was a concern suggests that the child Baldwin may already have been in poor health but may also reflect the bitter divisions and mutual mistrust between the Frankish nobility and a fear that whoever was regent would be scapegoated for any accident.) He wanted the Templars and Hospitallers to take charge of the castles of the kingdom, so that no one would suspect him of plotting anything. He wanted his expenses to be underwritten, because there was currently no truce with Saladin (so, this council took place before Raymond finalised a truce with Saladin in April 1185) and there would be a considerable cost in raising an army to fight the Muslims. He demanded that if the child Baldwin died within ten years, he himself would continue to hold the *baillie* until the pope, the emperor of Germany, the king of France and the king of England judged which of the two sisters should have the kingdom.

The reason for the doubt over which of the sisters should inherit, according to the *Chronique d'Ernoul*, was that as King Amaury had divorced Sybil's mother before he became king, she was born of a king alone, whereas her younger sister was born of a king and queen. In the 1240s the question was taken further by the compiler of the *Estoire de Eracles*, who stated that when Sybil's mother left her father the children were not declared legitimate – contradicting the assertion by Archbishop William of Tyre that they had been. Of course, if Sybil was illegitimate, so was Baldwin IV himself; but raising this question of legitimacy enabled this writer to justify the actions of Guy de Lusignan's opponents in 1186.[70]

Count Raymond may have indeed raised questions over his appointment, but they may equally have been asked by other members of the council. The questions listed by the *Chronique d'Ernoul* suggest that there was considerable concern among the barons over whether they could trust Count Raymond to act in the kingdom's best interests. In response to the first point, Count Joscelin (Baldwin V's great-uncle) was given custody of the child-king. On the question of expenses, it was agreed that Count Raymond could have the port of Beirut to contribute towards his outgoings as regent. Beirut was the most northerly port in the kingdom of Jerusalem, standing on the border with the county of Tripoli. Having control of Beirut would ensure Count Raymond's access to and from the kingdom of Jerusalem and would mean that the de Courtenays' power bloc around Acre and Tyre was no barrier to his moving between the county of Tripoli and the lordship of Tiberias, owned by his wife.[71]

However, the succession arrangements were effectively unworkable, because it would take several months to consult the four rulers in Europe, and they were unlikely to agree on a candidate. On the death of King Baldwin I the nobles of the kingdom of Jerusalem had chosen not to summon his designated heir, his elder brother Count Eustace of Boulogne, to the East to become king of Jerusalem, preferring to select a candidate who was on the spot and who could take over the government at once rather than risk a period of interregnum.[72] If this were the case in 1118 it was certainly so in 1185. It is possible that the compiler of the *Chronique d'Ernoul* muddled an instruction from King Baldwin IV to await the return of Patriarch Eraclius and the master of the Hospital from Europe and the results of their mission to these four rulers. If the embassy had succeeded in persuading one of the four rulers to come to the East, then the succession problem would be solved.[73]

The *Chronique d'Ernoul* then has Baldwin IV organising a formal crown-wearing ceremony for the child Baldwin V and requiring all the barons to do him homage as their lord and their king. They also had to do homage to the count of Tripoli as *bail*, and swear that if the child died before ten years were up they would keep to the arrangements about taking legal advice on the respective rights of the two sisters. Balian of Ibelin, lord of Nablus, carried the young Baldwin V from the church of the Holy Sepulchre to the *Templum Domini* (the Lord's Temple, that is, the Dome of the Rock) where a banquet was held after the crown-wearing ceremony. The *Chronique d'Ernoul* stated that Balian carried the king 'because he was little', so that he would not be lower than others; but as Balian was King Baldwin IV's stepfather (as husband of the dowager queen Maria Komnene), he was an appropriate stand-in for King Baldwin IV and could represent both King Amaury and the royal heir Isabel. The fact that he and not Count Guy carried the young king indicated that he had replaced Count Guy (and, by implication, Countess Sybil) at court.[74]

Although the *Chronique d'Ernoul* states that all the barons of the land were at these events, given that Countess Sybil's claim to the throne was questioned during the council it appears that Count Guy and Countess Sybil were not present – even though they governed at least part of one of the greatest fiefs of the kingdom, and Sybil was the child king's mother. If King Baldwin had not summoned them to this council, this would suggest that they were no longer in control of the county of Jaffa and Ascalon and had been totally excluded from contact with the court and any power in the realm. However, the charter issued by Sybil and Guy in February 1185 indicates that they were still in *de facto* control of at least part of their county and in contact with Sybil's uncle Joscelin de Courtenay, seneschal of the kingdom.

King Baldwin V, 1185–1186

Baldwin IV died in spring 1185, possibly on 15 April, aged around twenty-four years old. He was buried in the chapel of the Latin kings in the church of the Holy Sepulchre.[75] Baldwin V was now sole king, and there is no evidence that Sybil and Guy had any role in royal government. Despite the assertion in the Latin continuation of William of Tyre's history that Baldwin V lived at Ascalon, the charters issued in his name support the *Chronique d'Ernoul*'s statement that he was living at Acre. As he was in the care of his great-uncle Joscelin de Courtenay, whose properties lay in the Acre region, Acre would have been a more convenient home for the young king and his guardian than Jerusalem.[76]

The royal residence at Acre was shown on Matthew Paris's map of the city of 1250–1259 as the 'chastel le roi', located on the northern city wall. Matthew's drawing shows a three-storied castellated tower, possibly circular, surrounded by a ditch and an outer castellated wall with two large castellated towers, but as Matthew had never visited Acre himself this may be simply a conventional image.[77] It was built during the reign of King Baldwin I. After the crusading army recaptured Acre from Saladin's forces in July 1191, Richard lodged his wife Queen Berengaria, his sister the dowager queen Joanna of Sicily, and their young ladies and maids there, indicating that it was a secure, luxurious and spacious residence.[78] Located on the city wall, the royal castle stood at a distance from the busy port and the quarters of the Venetians, Genoese, Pisans, Templars and Hospitallers.[79]

The earliest extant charter of Baldwin V was issued at Acre on 16 May 1185, with the assent of Raymond count of Tripoli, procurator of the whole kingdom, and Balian of Nablus, and confirmed a sale of land to the abbey of St Mary of the Valley of Jehoshaphat. On 1 June, again at Acre, the king, with the assent of Count Raymond, gave his great-uncle Joscelin de Courtenay freedom to produce sugar and to sell the product at Acre. The witnesses included the leading nobles of the realm and men familiar from witness lists of documents issued by King Baldwin IV, and the documents were drawn up by the new royal chancellor, Peter archdeacon of Lydda (replacing Archbishop William) – but Count Guy was conspicuously absent.[80] Guy's absence from both witness lists indicates that he was not at court and had no role in advising or supporting the young king, his stepson.[81]

In July, Patriarch Eraclius and the master of the Hospital returned from the West, with promises of men and money but with no European prince to take over the government.[82] Some crusaders did come to the East as a result of the embassy; some of these went home when they discovered that there was a truce with Saladin, but others remained to fight when it ended. One prominent figure who had responded to the patriarch's embassy was Baldwin of Forde, recently elected archbishop of Canterbury, who took the cross in March 1185 while the patriarch and the master of the Hospital were in England; but he did not set out on the crusade until spring 1190.[83] William Marshal came to the East at around this time, having left the West in early 1184; he returned home in spring 1186.[84] Roger de Mowbray, one of the great magnates of England, arrived in 1186; he had already come to the East on the Second Crusade and possibly in 1177 with Count Philip of Flanders and remained despite the truce, fighting and being captured at the Battle of Hattin in 1187. The Templars ransomed him, but he died shortly afterwards.[85] The English noble Hugh de Beauchamp also came, and later fought and was captured at Hattin.[86]

Another arrival was William V, marquis of Montferrat, Sybil's father-in-law by her first husband and grandfather of King Baldwin V. He had also taken part in the Second Crusade and would remain to fight at Hattin and be captured by Saladin. According to the Lyon *Eracles*, the king and Count Raymond endowed him with the castle of St Elias (al-Taiyiba, 20 kilometres north-north-east of Jerusalem). This had previously been held by Count Joscelin, who had returned it to King Baldwin IV in February 1182 with other properties in exchange for Chastelneuf. William V, as grandfather, was more closely related to Baldwin V than either Count Raymond of Tripoli (first cousin twice removed) or Count Joscelin (great-uncle), and he could have claimed the regency of the kingdom, but it does not appear that he did so.[87] Meanwhile, in September 1185, another revolt in Constantinople resulted in the murder of the Emperor Andronikos Komnenos and the succession of Isaac II Angelos, who shortly afterwards agreed a treaty with Saladin.[88]

Only two more documents issued by King Baldwin V's government survive. One appears to have been a mutually beneficial private financial arrangement made between Joscelin and Raymond. None of the nobility of the kingdom witnessed it: the first and most eminent witness was the royal butler, Miles, followed by Walter Durus the marshal and other familiar non-noble witnesses, officers and burghers.[89] The charter is a further indication of Count Joscelin's wealth and influence in the region of Acre.

On 30 December 1185, Guy at last appeared witnessing a royal charter. Baldwin V issued at Acre a general confirmation of the donations made by his predecessors and other donors from the kingdom of Jerusalem to the Premonstratensian canons of the Church of St Samuel. The witnesses were: Bernard, bishop of Lydda; Odo, bishop of Sidon; Raymond, count of Tripoli; Guy, count of Jaffa and Ascalon; Count Joscelin, the king's seneschal; Baldwin, lord of Ramla; and Reynald, lord of Sidon.[90] Count Guy's approval would have been needed because the confirmation included property at Jaffa and Ascalon, but his presence in the witness list shows that his authority over the county was acknowledged by King Baldwin V's government. The fact that there are no surviving similar confirmation charters for other religious orders in the kingdom suggests that none of them thought that the king's authority would help to protect their holdings in the kingdom of Jerusalem – a reflection of the precariousness of the king and kingdom.

Nevertheless, the kingdom appeared to be at peace, and the truce with Saladin held. Neither Reynald de Châtillon or Guy de Lusignan raided into Saladin's territories in the winter of 1185–1186. Saladin was seriously ill at the time, but he eventually recovered sufficiently to receive envoys from Mosul and on 4 March 1186 concluded a treaty with the lord of Mosul, 'Izz al-Dīn, whereby the latter acknowledged Saladin as his overlord and promised to provide troops to Saladin as required.[91]

Saladin returned to Damascus on 23 May 1186, still in pain and feeling very unwell. The Qadi al-Fādil told him to make a vow to God that if he recovered he would no longer fight Muslims but would concentrate on the Holy War against the Franks, and promise that if he captured Reynald de Châtillon or Count Raymond of Tripoli he would kill them. Otherwise he would never have complete victory.[92] Even though the Franks had kept the truce which Saladin made with Count Raymond in spring 1185, clearly Saladin did not trust these two, their leading commanders.

Baldwin V died in the summer of 1186, probably on 13 September.[93] Born in the autumn or winter of 1177, he would have been nearly nine years old at his death.[94] Although the Yorkshire monk William of Newburgh later accused Count Raymond III of poisoning him, in fact he probably died of illness.[95] It was to counteract such accusations that Count Raymond had refused to have personal care of the king and he had been entrusted to his great-uncle's custody.

Like his father, he was buried in the chapel of the Latin kings in the church of the Holy Sepulchre, in a beautiful and elaborate stone tomb, which – as Jerusalem was lost to the Christians just over a year later – must have been commissioned by his mother and constructed within a few months. In initiating this memorial to her child she was carrying out a duty common to noblewomen in ensuring the commemoration of their husbands and children: her cousin-in-law Eleanor of Aquitaine would commission the tombs of her husband Henry and her son Richard at Fontevrault Abbey, Eleanor's daughter Countess Marie of Champagne had commissioned inscriptions on the tomb of her husband Count Henry I, 'the Liberal', who had died in 1181, and Eleanor's daughter Eleanor and her husband Alfonso VIII of Castile founded the Abbey of Las Huelgas de Burgos in 1187 as a dynastic mausoleum for their dead children and themselves. The sculpted images carved on Baldwin V's tomb express both sorrow and pride in the dead child, showing a dead young eagle, angels and Christ, as if the angels were conveying the soul of the child (the young eagle) to Heaven. The inscription, describing him as the seventh king of Jerusalem, hoped that he would possess paradise.[96]

Notes

1 WT 2: 1007–1008 (Bk 22 ch. 1); Lyons and Jackson, *Saladin*, pp. 146–147, 165; Phillips, *Life and Legend*, p. 135; Hamilton, *Leper King*, p. 159; Lewis, *Counts of Tripoli*, pp. 246–247.

112 Wife of Guy de Lusignan

2 Barber, *Crusader States*, p. 364; Harris, *Byzantium and the Crusades*, pp. 126–127.
3 WT 2: 1012 (Bk 22 ch. 5); IA, Part 2, pp. 351–352 (vol. 12.17).
4 Buck, *Principality of Antioch*, pp. 99–100, 213–215; Andrew D. Buck, 'The Noble Rebellion at Antioch, 1180–1182: A Case Study in Medieval Frontier Politics', *Nottingham Medieval Studies*, 60 (2016), 93–121; quotation from WT 2: 1015 (Bk 22 ch. 6).
5 WT 2: 1012 (Bk 22 ch. 5); BD, p. 173 (section 182).
6 *ULKJ* 2: 717–719 (no. 422); Hamilton, 'Women in the Crusader States', p. 167; Hamilton, *Leper King*, pp. 161–162; Mayer, 'Die Legitimität Balduins IV', pp. 69–70.
7 WT 2: 1012 (Bk 22 ch. 4); for the election of 1157 see 2: 840–841 (Bk 18 ch. 20). William himself could have expected to be a candidate for the position of patriarch, but his history implies that he was not interested in the post: Edbury and Rowe, *William of Tyre*, pp. 21–22; Edbury, 'Propaganda and Faction', p. 184.
8 Hamilton, *Leper King*, pp. 162–163; *Chronique d'Ernoul*, pp. 82–84 (ch. 8); 'L'Estoire de Eracles Empereur', pp. 58–60 (Bk 23 chs 38–39); *La Continuation de Guillaume de Tyr*, p. 50 (sections 37, 38).
9 Benjamin Z. Kedar, 'The Patriarch Eraclius', in *Outremer: Studies in the History of the Crusading Kingdom of Jerusalem presented to Joshua Prawer*, ed. Benjamin Z. Kedar, Hans Eberhard Mayer and R. C. Smail (Jerusalem, 1982), pp. 177–204, at p. 188; P. W. Edbury and J. G. Rowe, 'William of Tyre and the Patriarchal Election of 1180', *English Historical Review*, 93 (1978), 1–25, at 12.
10 Kedar, 'The Patriarch Eraclius', pp. 178–181, 184–186, 189–191; *Chronique d'Ernoul*, p. 85 (ch. 8). The *Estoire de Eracles* added that Eraclius excommunicated William, before poisoning him: 'L'Estoire de Eracles Empereur', p. 61 (Bk 23 ch. 39); *La Continuation de Guillaume de Tyr*, p. 51 (section 39).
11 Hamilton, *Leper King*, p. 160.
12 Edbury and Rowe, *William of Tyre*, p. 63, citing 'Cor nostrum' in Alexandri III Papæ, 'Epistolæ et Privilegia', in *PL* 200, cols 1294–1296 (no. 1504), at col. 1294. The bull was reissued by Lucius III in 1184 at the time of Patriarch Eraclius's mission to the West. On *Cor nostrum* see Phillips, *Defenders*, pp. 246–247, 256; Hamilton, *Leper King*, p. 164.
13 Harris, *Byzantium and the Crusades*, p. 127.
14 Hamilton, *Leper King*, p. 167.
15 *ULKJ* 2: 783–785, 851 (nos 457, 502).
16 *ULKJ* 2: 720–722, 785–786, 852 (nos 424, 459, 460, 503, 504).
17 IP 1, p. 336 (Bk 1 ch. 46). According to the 'L'Estoire de Eracles Empereur', p. 151 (Bk 25 ch. 10), the two daughters who died with Sybil were named were Alice ('Aelis') and Marie. As this work was compiled in the 1240s and there are no earlier records of their names, these names are doubtful. Marie and Alice were the names of the two eldest daughters of Sybil's younger half-sister Isabel: Marie was the daughter of Conrad of Montferrat while Alice was the daughter of Henry of Champagne: Guy Perry, *The Briennes: The Rise and Fall of a Champenois Dynasty in the Age of the Crusades, c. 950–1356* (Cambridge, 2018), p. 48.
18 LFWT, p. 50 (Bk 1 ch. 1); Philip of Novara, *Le Livre de Forme de Plait*, pp. 66–69, 227–229 and notes (sections 20–21); WT 2: 1058–1059 (Bk 22 ch. 30).
19 *ULKJ* 2: 719–720 (no. 423), p. 705 line 32 for Gillebert de Flori; for Geoffrey Tortus, see Mayer, 'Die Legitimität Balduins IV', 72; Peter Edbury, 'The "Livre" of Geoffrey le Tor and the "Assises" of Jerusalem', in *Historia administrativa y*

ciencia de la administración comparada. Trabajos en homenaje a Ferran Valls i Taberner, ed. M. J. Peláez, vol. 15 (Barcelona, 1990), pp. 4291–4298, at 4295.
20 *ULKJ* 2: 723–724 (no. 425).
21 *ULKJ* 2: 726–727 (no. 427).
22 WT 2: 1026 (Bk 22 ch. 15): *Arabes quosdam infra tempus federis contra legem pactorum cepisse diceretur et repetitos reddere negaverat.*
23 Hamilton, *Leper King*, pp. 170–171; Lyons and Jackson, *Saladin*, pp. 157–158, 159–161; Phillips, *Life and Legend*, pp. 140–141; WT 2: 1026 (Bk 22 ch. 15).
24 *ULKJ* 2: 728–730, 786 (nos 429, 461)
25 *ULKJ* 2: 730–733, 787, 852 (nos 430, 462, 505). On the *fondo* of Acre see David Jacoby, 'The *fonde* of Crusader Acre and Its Tariff: Some New Considerations', in *Dei gesta per Francos: Études sur les croisades dédiées à Jean Richard / Crusade Studies in Honour of Jean Richard*, ed. Michel Balard, Benjamin Z. Kedar, and Jonathan Riley-Smith (Aldershot, 2001), pp. 277–293; Pringle, *Churches*, 4: 6, 17 (figure 3).
26 Mayer, 'Die Legitimität Balduins IV', pp. 70–72.
27 WT 2: 1019–1020 (Bk 22, ch. 10); Lewis, *Counts of Tripoli*, p. 253; Hamilton, *Leper King*, pp. 167–169.
28 This view has been set out and critically deconstructed by Edbury, 'Propaganda and Faction', p. 179.
29 Hamilton, *Leper King*, pp. 172–179; Barber, *Crusader States*, pp. 177–178; Murray, '"Mighty against the Enemies of Christ"', p. 237; Lyons and Jackson, *Saladin*, pp. 165–171; Phillips, *Life and Legend*, pp. 143–146.
30 Harris, *Byzantium and the Crusades*, pp. 128–132.
31 Lyons and Jackson, *Saladin*, pp. 185–188; Phillips, *Life and Legend*, pp. 151–154; Hamilton, *Leper King*, pp. 179–185; Bernard Hamilton, 'The Elephant of Christ: Reynald of Châtillon', in *Religious Motivation: Biographical and Sociological Problems for the Church Historian; Papers read at the Sixteenth Summer Meeting and the Seventeenth Winter Meeting of the Ecclesiastical History Society*, ed. Derek Baker, Studies in Church History 15 (1978), 97–108, at 103–104 and note 49.
32 *ULKJ* 2: 789–791, 853 (nos 470, 507); Edbury, *John of Ibelin*, pp. 148, 154 (nos 48, 100).
33 *ULKJ*, 2: 742–745, 788, 852–853 (nos 437, 466, 506).
34 *ULKJ*, 2: 745–749 (no. 438), for the witnesses William de Furcis and Antelm de Lucca see 2: 707 (no. 413).
35 Barber, *Crusader States*, p. 280; Hamilton, *Leper King*, pp. 187–188; Lyons and Jackson, *Saladin*, pp. 198–204; Phillips, *Life and Legend*, pp. 149–150, 154.
36 WT 2: 1049–1050 (Bk 22 ch. 26).
37 WT 2: 1053–1054 (Bk 22 ch. 28); Murray, '"Mighty against the Enemies of Christ"', p. 237.
38 R.C. Smail, 'The Predicaments of Guy of Lusignan, 1183–87', in *Outremer: Studies in the History of the Crusading Kingdom of Jerusalem presented to Joshua Prawer*, ed. Benjamin Z. Kedar, Hans Eberhard Mayer and R. C. Smail (Jerusalem, 1982), pp. 159–176, at pp. 165–171; Barber, *Crusader States*, pp. 281–282; Hamilton, *Leper King*, pp. 189–192; Lewis, *Counts of Tripoli*, p. 255; Lyons and Jackson, *Saladin*, pp. 206–208; Phillips, *Life and Legend*, pp. 154–155. On the general tax see WT 2: 1043–1046 (Bk 22 ch. 24); Hamilton, *Leper King*, pp. 186–187; Kedar, 'The General Tax of 1183'.
39 WT 2: 1057 (Bk 22 ch. 30).

40 Pringle, *Churches*, 4: 177–230, with plan at p. 179; Pringle, *Secular Buildings*, pp. 103–104 (no. 227); Boas, *Crusader Archaeology*, p. 53; David Jacoby, 'Conrad, Marquis of Montferrat, and the Kingdom of Jerusalem (1187–1192)', in *Atti del Congresso Internazionale "Dai feudi monferrini e dal Piemonte ai nuovi mondi oltre gli Oceani", Alessandria, 2–6 aprile 1990* (Alessandria, 1993), pp. 187–238, at pp. 195, 202, 216.
41 WT 2: 1057–1059 (Bk 22 ch. 30); Edbury, 'Propaganda and Faction', p. 182; Hamilton, *Leper King*, pp. 192–195.
42 Simon John, 'Royal inauguration and liturgical culture in the Latin kingdom of Jerusalem, 1099–1187', *Journal of Medieval History*, 43.4 (2017), 485–504, at pp. 498–499; Sebastián Salvadó, 'Rewriting the Latin liturgy of the Holy Sepulchre: text, ritual and devotion for 1149', *Journal of Medieval History*, 43.4 (2017), 403–420, at pp. 414–415; M. Cecilia Gaposchkin, *Invisible Weapons: Liturgy and the Making of Crusade Ideology* (Ithaca and London, 2017), p. 146–147.
43 WT 2: 1055–1057 (Bk 22 ch. 29); Lyons and Jackson, *Saladin*, pp. 209–210; Phillips, *Life and Legend*, pp. 155–156.
44 WT 2: 1063 (Bk 23 ch. 1).
45 Edbury, 'Propaganda and Faction', p. 182.
46 *Chronique d'Ernoul*, pp. 98–103, 115–119.
47 Hamilton, *Leper King*, p. 241.
48 John, 'Royal inauguration', 498; Alexander Beihammer, 'Comnenian imperial succession and the ritual world of Niketas Choniates' *Chronike diegesis*', in *Court Ceremonies and Rituals of Power in Byzantium and the Medieval Mediterranean: Comparative Perspectives*, ed. by Alexander Beihammer, Stavroula Constantinou, and Maria G. Parani, The Medieval Mediterranean, 98 (Leiden, 2013), pp. 159–202, at pp. 166, 175, 176, 185, 187; Warren, *Henry II*, pp. 110–111.
49 Lois L. Honeycutt, 'Female Succession and the Language of Power in the Writings of Twelfth-Century Churchmen', in *Medieval Queenship*, ed. John Carmi Parsons (Stroud, 1994), pp. 189–201, at p. 196.
50 Mayer, 'Studies in the History of Queen Melisende of Jerusalem'; Murray, 'Constance, Princess of Antioch', p. 94; Buck, *Principality*, pp. 81–82.
51 *LFWT*, p. 51 (Bk 1 ch. 1).
52 Brundage, 'Marriage Law', p. 261.
53 WT 2: 1055–1057 (Bk 22 ch. 29); Hamilton, *Leper King*, pp. 192–193;
54 WT 2: 1059–1060 (Bk 22 ch. 31); Hamilton, *Leper King*, pp. 192–193, 195–196; Murray, '"Mighty against the Enemies of Christ"', p. 237; Barber, *Crusader States*, pp. 283–285; Lewis, *Counts of Tripoli*, p. 258; Lyons and Jackson, *Saladin*, pp. 209–211.
55 WT 2: 1062 (Bk 23 ch. 1).
56 Hamilton, *Leper King*, p. 197; Brundage, 'Marriage Law', p. 262; Avignon, 'Marché matrimonial clandestin', 522.
57 WT 2: 1062–1063 (Bk 23 ch. 1).
58 WT 2: 1063 (Bk 23 ch. 1).
59 WT 2: 1063 (Bk 23 ch. 1).
60 For Saladin's campaigns against the Franks in the summer of 1184 see Ralph of Diceto, 'Ymagines historiarum', 2: 27–28; Lyons and Jackson, *Saladin*, pp. 216–220; Phillips, *Life and Legend*, pp. 157–160.
61 Phillips, *Defenders*, pp. 252–263; Barber, *Crusader States*, pp. 286–288; Kedar, 'The Patriarch Eraclius', pp. 191–194; Mayer, 'Henry II of England', 731–734, quotation at p. 732; Warren, *Henry II*, pp. 604–607.

62 WT 2: 1063–1064 (Bk 23 ch. 1); Barber, *Crusader States*, p. 285; Lewis, *Counts of Tripoli*, p. 256; Hamilton, *Leper King*, p. 204 (date).
63 Lyons and Jackson, *Saladin*, pp. 156–157, 186.
64 Lyons and Jackson, *Saladin*, pp. 220–221; for a Frankish raid into Egypt in September 1184 see Phillips, *Life and Legend*, p. 161 and note 9.
65 *ULKJ* 2: 791–793, 853 (nos 471, 508); Mayer, 'Die Legitimität Balduins IV', pp. 84, 87, 88–89; Hamilton, *Leper King*, p. 214 note 17; Joseph Delaville Le Roulx, 'Inventaire de pièces de Terre Sainte de l'ordre de l'Hôpital', *Revue de l'Orient latin*, 3 (1895), 36–106, at p. 86 (no. 262).
66 WT 2: 1064 (Bk 23 ch. 1); Hamilton, *Leper King*, pp. 203–204, 205.
67 Lyons and Jackson, *Saladin*, pp. 221–222; Phillips, *Life and Legend*, p. 162.
68 Edbury, 'Ernoul, *Eracles*, and the Collapse of the Kingdom of Jerusalem', pp. 46–47.
69 *Chronique d'Ernoul*, pp. 115–116 (ch. 10).
70 *Chronique d'Ernoul*, pp. 116–117 (ch. 10); Hamilton, *Leper King*, pp. 205–207; Barber, *Crusader States*, pp. 289–290; Lewis, *Counts of Tripoli*, pp. 256–258; 'L'Estoire de Eracles Empereur', pp. 4–6 (Bk 23 chs 2–3); *La Continuation de Guillaume de Tyr 1184–1197*, ed. Margaret Ruth Morgan, Documents relatifs à l'histoire des Croisades 14 (Paris, 1982), pp. 19–20 (sections 2–3); translated in *The Conquest of Jerusalem and the Third Crusade: Sources in Translation*, ed. and trans. Peter W. Edbury, Crusade Texts in Translation 1 (Aldershot, 1996), pp. 11–145, at pp. 12–14; this point in the *Estoire de Eracles* will be discussed in the forthcoming new edition and study of the *Chronique d'Ernoul* and *L'Estoire de Eracles Empereur* by Peter Edbury and Massimiliano Gaggero.
71 *Chronique d'Ernoul*, p. 117 (ch. 10); Hamilton, *Leper King*, pp. 206–207; Lewis, *Counts of Tripoli*, pp. 256–258.
72 Susan B. Edgington, *Baldwin I of Jerusalem, 1100–1118*, Rulers of the Latin East (Abingdon, 2019), pp. 185–187.
73 On the *Chronique d'Ernoul*'s confusion over the succession arrangements see Kedar, 'The Patriarch Eraclius', p. 195.
74 *Chronique d'Ernoul*, pp. 117–118 (ch. 10); Hamilton, *Leper King*, pp. 207–209.
75 Hamilton, *Leper King*, p. 210; Barber, *Crusader States*, pp. 264, 365.
76 *LFWT*, p. 50 (Bk 1 ch. 1); *ULKJ* 2: 768–779 (nos 451–454); *Chronique d'Ernoul*, p. 129 (ch. 11).
77 Pringle, *Churches*, 4: 5, 8, 16, 173, plate III and figure 3.
78 *IP* 2, p. 234 (Bk 3 ch. 18).
79 For the city as a whole see Boas, *Crusader Archaeology*, pp. 32–42; Pringle, *Churches*, 4: 3–175; Pringle, *Secular Buildings*, pp. 15–17 (no. 5).
80 *ULKJ* 2: 769–773 (nos 451, 452); on Peter of Lydda see Mayer, *Die Kanzlei*, 2: 341–342, 403–410.
81 The later Latin continuation of William of Tyre's history describes Guy as bitterly resentful of his exclusion from power and describes him and Raymond as bitter enemies at this time, each deeply suspicious of whatever the other did: *LFWT*, p. 51 (Bk 1 ch. 1); but this was written after the Third Crusade, with considerable benefit of hindsight.
82 Barber, *Crusader States*, p. 365; Kedar, 'The Patriarch Heraclius', p. 194.
83 For his election: Roger of Howden, *Gesta*, 1: 319, 320, 321; for his departure: ibid. 2: 105–106. For his taking the cross: Holdsworth, 'Baldwin [Baldwin of Forde]', 444; Christopher J. Holdsworth, 'Baldwin of Forde, Cistercian and archbishop of Canterbury', *Annual Report* [Friends of Lambeth Palace Library] (1989), 13–31,

at 22; citing Roger of Howden, *Chronica*, 2: 302; Kathryn Hurlock, *Britain, Ireland and the Crusades, c. 1000–1300* (Basingstoke, 2013), p. 42.
84 William Marshal's biographer gives very little information about this expedition, beyond noting that it took place and that it resulted in Marshal giving himself to the Templars. For discussion see Nicholas L. Paul, 'In Search of the Marshal's Lost Crusade: The Persistence of Memory, the Problems of History and the Painful Birth of Crusading Romance', *Journal of Medieval History*, 40.3 (2014), 292–310.
85 Hugh M. Thomas, 'Mowbray, Sir Roger de (d. 1188), magnate', *Oxford Dictionary of National Biography*, ed. H. C. G Matthew and Brian Harrison (Oxford, 23 Sep. 2004), accessed 30 March 2021. https://www-oxforddnb-com.abc.cardiff.ac.uk/view/10.1093/ref:odnb/9780198614128.001.0001/odnb-9780198614128-e-19458
86 Hamilton, *Leper King*, p. 215; Roger of Howden, *Gesta*, 1: 359; Roger of Howden, *Chronica*, 2: 316; *Radulphi de Coggeshall Chronicon Anglicanum*, p. 21.
87 Hamilton, *Leper King*, p. 214; Pringle, *Secular Buildings*, pp. 98–99 (no. 215); Pringle, *Churches*, 2: 339 (no. 250); *Continuation de Guillaume de Tyr*, p. 24 (section 10).
88 Harris, *Byzantium and the Crusades*, pp. 134–156, 139.
89 *ULKJ* 2: 777–779 (no. 454).
90 *ULKJ* 2: 773–776 (no. 453).
91 Lyons and Jackson, *Saladin*, pp. 234–239; Phillips, *Life and Legend*, pp. 164–166.
92 Lyons and Jackson, *Saladin*, pp. 243, 246.
93 Barber, *Crusader States*, p. 293. For the date: *ULKJ* 2: 782; Vogtherr, 'Die Regierungsdaten der lateinischen Könige von Jerusalem', 67.
94 Hamilton, *Leper King*, p. 139, note 47.
95 Hamilton, *Leper King*, p. 216; William of Newburgh, *Historia rerum anglicarum*, 1: 255 (Bk 3 ch. 16). The Latin continuation also alluded to accusations that Raymond had caused the boy's death: *LFWT*, p. 58 (Bk 1 ch. 6).
96 Jaroslav Folda, *Crusader Art: The Art of the Crusaders in the Holy Land, 1099–1291*, (Aldershot, 2008), pp. 66–67; Zehava Jacoby, 'The Tomb of Baldwin V, King of Jerusalem (1185–1186), and the Workshop of the Temple Area', *Gesta*, 18.2 (1979), 3–14, at p. 8; drawing of the tomb printed in Elzearius Horn, *Ichnographiae locorum et monumentorum veterum Terrae Sanctae, Accurate delineatae et descriptae. E codice Vaticano, Lat. No. 9233 excerpsit*, ed. Girolamo Golubovich (Rome 1902), fromVatican Biblioteca Apostolica Vaticana, MS 9233 TII2, fol. 103v, online at: https://digi.vatlib.it/view/MSS_Vat.lat.9233.pt.2/0109 (accessed 30 March 2021). For women's role in burial and commemoration see, for example, Elisabeth van Houts, *Memory and Gender in Medieval Europe 900–1200* (Basingstoke, 1999), pp. 94–95, 97–100, 102–103; for some other mausolea commissioned by queens and noblewomen in Latin Europe see Bowie, *The Daughters*, pp. 194–196, 202, 204–205; Evergates, *Henry the Liberal*, pp. 166–169; for Queen Melisende's construction of her own and her mother's tomb see Nurith Kenaan-Kedar, 'Decorative architectural sculpture in crusader Jerusalem: the Eastern, Western, and Armenian sources of a local visual culture', in *The Crusader World*, ed. Adrian J. Boas (Abingdon, 2016), pp. 609–623, at pp. 610, 618–621.

6   Queen (1186–1187)

Coronation

Events moved swiftly following the death of the young Baldwin V. If the young king had been living at Acre, his body had to be brought to Jerusalem for burial. In addition (if the *Chronique d'Ernoul* reported the decisions of the council in spring 1185 correctly) Count Raymond should now send an embassy to the pope, Emperor Frederick Barbarossa and kings Philip of France and Henry of England to ask for their judgement on the succession.[1]

During the period that they had been jointly responsible for Baldwin V and his kingdom, Counts Raymond and Joscelin appear to have worked well together. The truce with Saladin had been upheld. Internally the kingdom was at peace. According to the *Chronique d'Ernoul*, when Baldwin V died, Joscelin urged Raymond to go to Tiberias rather than attending the king's funeral and told him that the Templars would take charge of the young king's corpse, taking it to Jerusalem and overseeing its burial.[2] It is odd that Raymond would not attend the royal funeral, but we might suppose that Joscelin feared that if Raymond went to Jerusalem for the funeral he would use the opportunity to seize the crown. As soon as Raymond had departed (according to the account in the *Chronique d'Ernoul*) Joscelin took over the castle at Acre and garrisoned it, and then he went to Beirut – which was under Raymond's control – entered the city and garrisoned it with knights and sergeants. Then he wrote to his niece Sybil, countess of Jaffa, and told her to go to Jerusalem with her barons and all her knights, so that when her son the king was buried they could seize the city and garrison it and she could take the crown; and he had already secured Acre and Beirut.[3]

The *Chronique d'Ernoul* accused Joscelin of treachery for telling Raymond to go to Tiberias and then seizing Acre and Beirut. However, Raymond's actions could also be interpreted as treacherous. To follow the arrangements reportedly made by King Baldwin IV, Raymond should have summoned the High Court or a general council of the barons of the kingdom to a royal city such as Jerusalem or Acre and made arrangements to send an embassy to Europe to consult on the succession. Instead (according to this account), he retreated to his wife's lordship of Tiberias, from where he summoned 'all the high men of the land and all the knights, on their homage and the oath that they had made to him, to come to him at Nablus'.[4] Nablus was not a centre of royal government: it was the lordship of Maria Komnene, widow of King Amaury, and her second husband Balian of Ibelin. Summoning the lords of the kingdom to Nablus rather than Jerusalem suggests that Raymond was planning to seize power in collaboration with the dowager queen and her husband, by putting her daughter Isabel on the throne.

The *Chronique d'Ernoul* placed Raymond's summons to the barons of the kingdom after Joscelin's takeover of Acre and Beirut and his letter to Sybil, but before Baldwin V's funeral, and explained Raymond's action by stating he was reacting to Joscelin's treachery. Alternatively, if Raymond sent out his summons to the barons of the kingdom first, Joscelin could have suspected that Raymond intended to stage a coup and crown Isabel, and responded by seizing Acre and Beirut and sending a letter to warn his niece Sybil. Whoever acted first, the result was that (according to the *Chronique d'Ernoul*) some of the barons of the kingdom went to Jerusalem to attend Baldwin V's funeral while some went to Nablus to respond to Raymond's summons.

This account is not convincing. Whatever their previous oaths regarding the procedure for choosing a successor, the nobles of the kingdom would normally attend the dead king's funeral. It is not clear from the *Chronique d'Ernoul* why the majority of the nobility of the kingdom did not attend the child king's funeral. As the truce with Saladin still held there was no immediate danger of invasion. In addition, this story requires Raymond to have acted with 'unbelievable political ineptitude' as Smail expressed it, in allowing Joscelin de Courtenay to persuade him not to attend the king's funeral and so allowing Joscelin to take the political and military initiative. Both Raymond and Joscelin were practised political campaigners and neither had any reason to trust the other's ambitions. At this point they should have been keeping an eye on each other, not allowing either to depart on business of his own. In short, these events are so unbelievable that they probably did not happen as stated in the *Chronique d'Ernoul*: something has been left out, or the order of events has been changed.[5]

The problem with establishing what did happen is that all the contemporary Christian sources reached their present form after Saladin's victories of 1187. Even the *Chronique d'Ernoul*, which at this point may be based on an account by Balian of Ibelin's servant Ernoul, is not an eyewitness account because as Ernoul was at the council at Nablus with Balian he would have had to rely on a second-hand view of events in Jerusalem. Each interested party blamed the others' actions for Saladin's success and their accounts of events differ accordingly. All commentators agreed that at some point after her son's funeral Sybil was crowned queen and that Count Raymond opposed Guy. But they disagreed over whether Guy was crowned with Sybil or later and the nature and extent of Raymond's opposition to Guy.[6]

'Imād al-Dīn and Ibn al-Athīr, who stood outside these debates, recorded that when the child king, nephew of the leper king, died, the sovereignty passed to his mother. She married a Frank who had come to Syria from the West (Ibn al-Athīr named him as Guy) and crowned him. 'Imād al-Dīn thought that she had previously been married to Count Raymond, confusing Sybil with Eschiva of Tiberias, and that the prince whom she now married tried to take Count Raymond's finest provinces from him; in response, Count Raymond went to Saladin and became one of his partisans, and would have converted to Islam had he not feared the reaction of his compatriots. Ibn al-Athīr did not believe that Count Raymond had gone so far. According to his account, Sybil summoned the patriarch, the priests and monks, the Hospitallers, the Templars and the barons and told them that she had handed royal power to her husband. Count Raymond, who had been the boy-king's guardian and had ruled the country because of his influence and excellent counsel, was also ambitious to be king. He was outraged and disappointed by what the queen had done, especially when he was then required to account for the money he had collected while he was regent for the child king. He maintained that he had spent it on the king, and he made his opposition to the new regime plain. Then he went to Saladin, allied with him, and asked him for his support to become king. Saladin promised to do this. Both authors agreed that several other Franks followed the count's example and so the Franks' unity was broken up. This, in the opinion of these external commentators, was one of the most important developments in enabling Saladin to conquer the Franks' territories.[7]

Although these Muslim accounts did not examine the details of the coronation process, they highlighted what the Franks' Muslim neighbours understood to be the main points: the crown being inherited through the king's mother, the king's mother exercising agency in passing on sovereignty by her own hand, and Count Raymond's anger leading him to make an alliance with Saladin.

Nearly all the Christian sources that discussed the matter agreed that something was amiss with the coronation, which they implied contributed towards Saladin's victories in the following year.[8] The *Chronique d'Ernoul* (followed by the various versions of the *Estoire de Eracles*) and the *Libellus de expugnatione terre sancte* recorded that most of the barons of the kingdom were not present and that they had been physically shut out of Jerusalem by the patriarch, the master of the Temple and Prince Reynald de Châtillon, who had closed the gates so that no one could go in or out. The only attendees named apart from these three were Joscelin de Courtenay, Baldwin V's great-uncle, and the Marquis William V of Montferrat, Baldwin V's paternal grandfather. As the author of the *Libellus* clearly used Ernoul's account as a source of information, these versions of events are probably based on a single source.[9] The *Chronique d'Ernoul* stated that the patriarch crowned Sybil, then told her that she needed a man to govern with her and gave her a second crown, which she placed on Guy's head as he knelt before her. But whereas previous kings of Jerusalem had been anointed as well as crowned – most recently Baldwin V had been anointed as well as crowned king on 20 November 1183 – the *Chronique d'Ernoul* stated only that Sybil and Guy were crowned.[10]

The *Libellus* simply reported that Sybil made her husband Guy de Lusignan king.[11] The 'Regni Iherosolymitani Brevis Historia' recorded that the master of the Temple, Prince Reynald, and Count Joscelin crowned Sybil and Guy, but made no mention of anointing.[12] A lack of anointing when the monarch of Jerusalem was normally anointed would have meant that Sybil's and Guy's position as monarchs was not fully validated, but the later *Estoire de Eracles* – which was otherwise generally hostile to Guy – added the information that Guy (but not, apparently, Sybil) was anointed after being crowned.[13]

Other near-contemporary accounts, by Roger of Howden, William of Newburgh, Guy of Bazoches, and the anonymous *Continuatio Aquicincinta* and Latin continuation of William of Tyre's history, suggest that all the princes of the kingdom were present along with the patriarch and the masters of the Temple and Hospital and that Sybil was crowned queen by right of inheritance. Then she crowned Guy, to the great displeasure of many of the nobles, especially the count of Tripoli.[14] Master Tolosanus, writing in Faenza, stated that the count of Tripoli, Count Reynald of Sidon, Hugh of Tiberias, Humphrey of Toron and many others were grieved at their new king's mediocrity and began to cause dissension in the kingdom.[15]

Roger of Howden, Guy of Bazoches and the Latin continuation of William of Tyre's history state that Sybil was required to divorce Guy de Lusignan before she could be crowned. An anonymous Latin poet and crusader writing during the siege of Acre between October 1189 and July 1190 also hinted at this without going into details.[16] The grounds stated for this divorce appear inadequate: although Guy was a good enough knight and noble, he was not up to the task of being king (Roger of Howden specified that he was not of sufficiently high birth). These accounts agree that the countess was reluctant to comply; the Latin continuation states that she was '*rarum quidem nostri seculi exemplum*' (a rare example to our age), a woman who placed love before a kingdom. Roger of Howden's *Gesta* depicted Sybil giving way because she saw that there was no other way to get the kingdom; in his later *Chronica* the patriarch and the Templars and Hospitallers gave her no choice. The Latin continuation depicted Sybil as agreeing only because the kingdom depended on her.

In the Latin continuation's version of events, those who held first place in the assembly appealed to Sybil on the basis of the desolation of the kingdom and the urgent necessity at this juncture, and even Guy begged her not to impede the kingdom's provision for his sake. Eventually she agreed on condition that the magnates should swear to accept as their lord and king whomever she chose (Roger of Howden agreed on this point), that Guy should remain count of Jaffa, and that their children should be legitimated (as had been done when her parents were divorced). When this was agreed, she received their liege homage and was crowned. Then it was announced that Saladin had invaded and was not far away. The queen called a general council of clergy and laity to elect a king, which Guy attended with the others. She then called out in the meeting that she chose him as her husband and gave him herself and the kingdom. Everyone was dumbfounded and asked how one astute woman had frustrated so many wise men. They had intended her to commit adultery, but she had managed matters so that she obtained a kingdom for her husband and a husband for herself.[17] Roger of Howden's *Chronica* remarked on her *mira calliditate* (amazing cleverness) in outmanoeuvring those who wanted the divorce.[18]

It is not easy to reconcile these accounts.[19] If Sybil had been required to divorce Guy before she would be crowned, this would explain the *Chronique d'Ernoul*'s description of Patriarch Eraclius telling her that she needed a man to govern with her and to choose the man to wear the second crown, which would not have been an issue unless Sybil had already been separated from her husband. It would not be the first time that a coronation of a ruler of Jerusalem had been made dependent on their first divorcing their spouse, as Amaury had been forced to divorce Agnes de Courtenay before his coronation in 1163. In that case the ostensible basis for the divorce was consanguinity, although in fact it may have been bigamy.[20] In 1190 Isabel would divorce Humphrey IV of Toron on the grounds that she had not consented to their marriage.[21] There were adequate grounds to annul Sybil's marriage to Guy: it had taken place during the Easter feast, when canonical law did not allow marriages, and Sybil had already been betrothed to Duke Hugh III of Burgundy. The accounts of the events of Sybil's coronation, however, do not mention any of these as grounds for the divorce: they indicate that the reason was that the nobles of the kingdom did not wish to be ruled by her husband. Elsewhere in the crusader states the nobility may also have claimed the right to influence the ruler's marriage, as in the early 1180s the nobility of the principality of Antioch apparently refused to accept Bohemond III's wife Sybil.[22]

But this is not the only problem with the account of the coronation set out in the *Chronique d'Ernoul*. Even if we assume that Ernoul's original account included a description of Sybil's divorce which was later taken out, the *Chronique d'Ernoul* indicates that the only members of the lay nobility of the kingdom of Jerusalem who were present were Count Joscelin and Reynald de Châtillon. They had previously been Guy's allies and were the least likely to have regarded him as unfit to be king. The situation would be more believable if the divorce had been demanded by the barons whom Master Tolosanus listed as opposing Guy: Count Raymond, Reynald of Sidon, Hugh of Tiberias and Humphrey of Toron – whose wife Isabel's claim to the crown was almost equal to Sybil's. Other obvious opponents of Guy's accession to the throne would have been Isabel's mother and step-father, Maria Komnene and Balian of Ibelin, who could have expected to benefit personally if Isabel became queen rather than Sybil. Baldwin of Ramla's later reluctance to do homage to Guy suggests that he could also have been one of those who demanded a divorce. But although the *Chronique d'Ernoul*'s description of the coronation implied that a divorce had been imposed on Sybil, it had already made clear that all those who would have been most likely to demand that she divorce Guy were at Nablus rather than at Jerusalem – so the story makes no sense.

Queen (1186–1187)

As the account of events in the *Chronique d'Ernoul* set out to vindicate Balian of Ibelin and his brother Baldwin of any blame for Saladin's conquests in 1187, the compiler had every incentive to omit the fact that they had tried to force Sybil to divorce Guy as a condition of her coronation and that she had circumvented them. This compiler would not have wanted to let readers know that Baldwin and Balian had been party to an attempt to force Sybil to commit adultery by leaving her legal husband and marrying another man, and so indicated that they were far away at Nablus throughout proceedings, played absolutely no role in the coronation, and had no clear idea of what was going on because the gates of Jerusalem had been shut and so they had to rely on a report by a spy who did not see the whole ceremony. Balian of Ibelin's reputation suffered enough through his association with Isabel's divorce from Humphrey of Toron in 1190, without further blackening his reputation by publicising his association with an earlier divorce.[23]

As for the other commentators: the Muslim observers were aware that Sybil had made her husband king and that Count Raymond was deeply angered and troubled by this development, but did not know details. In contrast, the Latin Christian writers who took part in the Third Crusade or who heard first-hand reports from those who were present had obtained a version of events favourable to Queen Sybil and Guy de Lusignan. None of them ever set eyes on Queen Sybil – the English contingent led by the archbishop of Canterbury did not reach Acre until after her death – but they would have seen Guy de Lusignan and could have obtained details of the coronation from his followers who accompanied him then and at the siege of Acre.[24]

Taking all these aspects into account, it is possible to reconcile the various versions of events at Sybil's coronation to a 'best fit' as follows. Count Raymond and all the barons of the realm attended King Baldwin V's funeral (as the nobility would normally attend a king's funeral) and then Count Raymond, still acting as regent, held a council of all the clerical leaders and lay nobles of the kingdom which decided that in view of the urgency of the situation they could not wait to obtain a judgement from the rulers of Europe but must choose an heir at once. The council chose Sybil as nearest heir and more experienced in government than her half-sister, but required her to divorce Guy and choose a different husband. The reason given for this requirement was that the king should be more noble and more competent than Guy, but in effect this requirement was a demand that the council should choose the king. Sybil outmanoeuvred the council by obtaining the barons' promise to accept whomever she chose, and then choosing Guy.

The nobles of the kingdom who were not prepared to accept her choice then re-assembled at Nablus and decided to put Isabel on the throne, but this plan failed when – as recounted by the *Chronique d'Ernoul* – Isabel's husband Humphrey of Toron decided to accept Sybil and Guy as monarchs. The *Chronique d'Ernoul* depicts Humphrey fleeing to Jerusalem by night and Sybil refusing to speak to him because he had not been at her coronation – suggesting that the council at Nablus had been a deliberate act of defiance by Count Raymond and most of the nobles of the kingdom. Humphrey apologised and explained that he had been retained against his will but had fled when the council wanted to make him king by force. Sybil then pardoned Humphrey and called on him to do homage to the king. The council at Nablus then broke up, with most of the lay nobles doing homage to Guy.

Only Count Raymond of Tripoli and Baldwin of Ramla refused to do homage. Count Raymond went to Tiberias, from where he opened negotiations with Saladin. Baldwin of Ramla sent his young son to King Guy do homage in his place and requested the barons to ask the king to put his son in seisin of his lordship and receive his homage. Guy refused to put a son in seisin of land for which the father had not done homage and said that if Baldwin did not do homage for Ramla he would take it into his own hands. So Baldwin did homage, but did not give Guy the accustomed kiss; then his son was vested with the land and did homage. Baldwin then took his leave of King Guy, entrusted his son and his lordship to the care of his brother Balian, and went into voluntary exile in the principality of Antioch, where in February 1187 he witnessed some documents in favour of the Hospitallers.[25]

It remains unclear whether those who demanded the divorce had a husband in mind for Sybil's third marriage. There were no obvious candidates: the other eminent nobles of the kingdom were either already married, or too closely related to Sybil, or both. Perhaps Count Raymond expected Sybil to take the title of queen while he continued to act as military commander. Roger of Howden claimed in his *Gesta* that Raymond had hoped to marry the queen, but he was already married and was related to Sybil within the prohibited degrees.[26]

Sybil's contemporaries depicted her choice of Guy as her husband and king as the action of a pious and devoted wife who regarded her marriage vows as sacrosanct. It is possible, however, that Sybil genuinely believed what she was later reported to have said: that Guy was the best king for the kingdom. In the autumn of 1183, at Saffūriyya, he had led the kingdom's army successfully, forcing Saladin to withdraw. If it became necessary to appeal for military aid from the West, Guy had a wide family network to call on, as well as his family's lords – the kings of England and counts of Poitou. The fact that none of the Frankish nobility emerged as the overall military leader of the Christian forces during the coming crises suggests that none of them was able to command the support of all the Franks of the crusader states. Guy, as a relatively new arrival in the crusader states, had the advantage of standing outside old family rivalries. However, because he stood outside the existing networks of control and influence he relied largely on outsiders – his own followers from Poitou – for support. As they now received the royal patronage that the warriors of the kingdom expected to receive from the king, there was resentment against the new regime. There had already been a hint of such resentment in autumn 1183, when Baldwin IV conferred the administration of the realm on Guy but made him promise not to alienate any property, and the author of the Lyon *Eracles* later hinted at rivalry between Guy's Poitevin supporters and the native Franks, describing the former taunting the latter, telling them that they could not prevent Guy from becoming king.[27]

Queen, but not regnant

Sybil's crowning of Guy would be her most famous action as queen. In so doing, she apparently transferred her authority and power to him: Ibn al-Athīr specifically stated as much.[28] Very few charters survive granted by Sybil as queen, and all of those that do were issued jointly with Guy; she apparently issued none (as queen) in her name alone.[29] It must be remembered, however, that those royal charters that survived Saladin's conquest of Jerusalem – those given to religious houses and the maritime cities, who carefully preserved records of their rights and privileges – may not be representative of the whole.

Sybil's grandmother Melisende had – after an initial struggle to establish her authority – governed equally with Fulk of Anjou. Yet even though it was Sybil's direct action which gave Guy the throne, Sybil does not appear to have ruled in tandem with Guy. It is not clear why Sybil did not attempt to emulate her grandmother and govern with her spouse. Her contemporary Queen Tamar of Georgia showed that it was possible for a woman, admittedly a woman who was not a Latin Christian, to rule in her own right with her husband responsible only for leading the army. When it was necessary to take up a position of leadership and act in her husband's place, Sybil did so, but only so far as was unavoidable, handing over the burden to a male relative as soon as possible.

Perhaps Sybil believed that her grandmother Melisende's joint rulership with her husband and then her son had been divisive and that the kingdom needed a single leader to face Saladin. It is also possible that she was not physically well enough to rule the kingdom in person. Her brother had been sick for much of his life; her son died young; perhaps she herself was also in poor health – and, if this were the case, it would help to explain why Stephen of Sancerre and Duke Hugh of Burgundy decided against marrying her after their initial enthusiasm and when they had had the opportunity to meet her or receive eyewitness reports from their relatives. But as contemporaries who saw her during her lifetime recorded nothing of her health or appearance this remains speculation. Perhaps she preferred to concentrate on producing a healthy male heir to the throne while her husband undertook the dangers of war and government.

Nevertheless, Sybil was not inactive. She did issue charters with Guy in which Guy stated that he, 'eighth king of the Latins in the holy city of Jerusalem by the grace of God' was acting with the 'assent and will' of his wife, venerable queen of the same kingdom (*ego Guido per dei gratiam in sancta civitate Ierusalem Latinorum rex octavus assensu et voluntate domne Sibelle uxoris mee eiusdem regni venerabilis regine*), or that he, king of the Latins, issued this charter with Lady Sybil his wife, queen of the same, or queen by the same grace (*ego Guido per dei gratiam in sancta civitate Iherusalem Latinorum rex VIIIus et domna Sibilla sponsa mea, eorundem venerabilis regina* or *per eandem venerabilis regina*), emphasising her royal authority and the fact that he held his authority only through her.[30] As previously noted, she was probably responsible for commissioning the intricately decorated tomb which formed a memorial for her son Baldwin V. The work would have been done by sculptors attached to a workshop in the Temple area of Jerusalem. She may also have overseen the final completion of the renovation and redecoration of the *Coenaculum* (or Cenacle, traditionally the 'upper room' where the Last Supper was held); this work was done in the 1180s before the fall of Jerusalem to Saladin in 1187. In this she would have been following the example of her grandmother Queen Melisende, who in addition to founding the Abbey of St Lazarus at Bethany had supported and substantially influenced at least five large building projects in Jerusalem during her reign, including the church of the Holy Sepulchre, the abbey church of St Anne, the Armenian cathedral of St James and the Armenian church of the Archangels. Noble and royal women in Europe at this period also patronised art in various forms, especially to create commemorative objects for themselves and their families.[31]

The royal palace in Jerusalem was a modern building, constructed in the 1160s adjoining the Tower of David. A drawing on a map of Jerusalem from the second half of the twelfth century shows a porticoed building with a gabled roof, a small domed tower on the south side and a large crenelated tower on the north, all enclosed by a crenelated fortification. But it is impossible to know whether this was based on personal observation or is simply a generic image of a royal palace, as nothing survives of the building above ground; only the site is certain, as fragments of its basements have been excavated.[32] However, Sybil and Guy – who to judge from their charters had spent most of their earlier married life in the maritime city of Ascalon – appear to have preferred to live at the royal castle in Acre, as their joint charters were all issued there.

They issued two charters at Acre in October 1186, shortly after their coronation, and Guy issued another in November in Acre, all confirming property to Sybil's uncle Joscelin de Courtenay, who (at least according to the *Chronique d'Ernoul*) had helped to secure Sybil's coronation. The first confirmed him in possession of Toron and Chastelneuf, which Humphrey IV of Toron had had to surrender in order to marry Sybil's and Baldwin IV's half-sister Isabel, which his sister Agnes de Courtenay had received from Baldwin IV, and which should have come to Sybil as Agnes's heir but which appear to have passed to Joscelin instead. Now that Sybil was queen, she confirmed her uncle in possession.

The second charter confirmed Joscelin's possession of the inheritable properties and revenues that King Baldwin IV had confirmed to him. Finally, in November Guy announced that Joscelin had given his eldest daughter in marriage to Guy's brother William de Valence and given them Toron, Chastelneuf (which he and Sybil had just given Joscelin) and Kabul and its appurtenances (which they had sold him on 1 February 1185). This property had all been held by Agnes de Courtenay and now passed to her niece as her dowry. The witness lists of all three documents were headed by Patriarch Eraclius, followed by the archbishops of Tyre, Caesarea and Nazareth; then the bishops of Lydda, Bethlehem and Beirut; the masters of the Temple and of the Hospital; then Prince Reynald de Châtillon, Aimery the constable (Guy's brother), Miles the king's butler, Peter de Creseca, Goscelin Hircus, Anselin Babini (missing from the November witness list), Geoffrey Tortus, and William de Molenbec (or Molembocca). Peter, archdeacon of Lydda and the king's chancellor, produced the charter.[33] Of the non-noble witnesses, Miles the butler, Goscelin Hircus – also known as Gotsuin Boccus– and William de Molenbec (spelt Molembecca or Molembucca in the charters of Baldwin V) had also served King Baldwin V's government, while Geoffrey Tortus had also witnessed Baldwin IV's documents and since 1182 had been a vassal of Joscelin de Courtenay. Peter de Creseca had witnessed charters for Kings Amaury and Baldwin IV and had been castellan of Jerusalem in 1178 and 1181. Anselin Babini or Dabini had witnessed one charter of Baldwin IV, in 1177.[34] These witness lists indicate that the leading clergy of the kingdom and the masters of the military-religious orders supported Guy, but only two of the leading nobles were associated with his government: his wife's uncle Joscelin and Reynald de Châtillon. Many of the administrative officers, however, continued to work for him, led by his brother Aimery, who was still constable. This meant that government could continue, provided there was no crisis which required Guy to get the agreement of all the nobles of the kingdom in council. But for the moment the truce with Saladin held.

At some point during their reign, that is, between 13 September 1186 and 20 October 1190, King Guy of Jerusalem and Queen Sybil his wife also gave one Walter le Bel (later *vicecomes* of Acre) the house of Barraguilla in Acre.[35] They issued no more charters together until November 1189, when they were besieging Acre. It may be a measure of the new monarchs' lack of power and authority that no general confirmation charters to religious houses issued in their names survive, indicating that none of the religious institutions in the kingdom thought that they would gain any security by obtaining such a confirmation. The Hospitallers, for example, retained records of other documents issued in the crusader states at this period, so if they had received any charters from the new queen and king they would have kept a record of them.[36]

Meanwhile, Count Raymond III of Tripoli had made a separate peace treaty with Saladin. 'Imād al-Dīn and Ibn al-Athīr indicated that Raymond would be a client ruler of Saladin, and both commentators added that many other Franks followed the count's example and made alliances or acts of obedience to Saladin. Their depiction of Count Raymond's actions and intentions offers some support to the contemporary Latin Christian writers who accused Raymond of wanting to become king himself and agreeing to betray King Guy to Saladin. As Lewis has pointed out, this was not the first time that a count of Tripoli had allied with a Muslim general. Raymond's parents had done so with Nūr al-Dīn in 1148 in order to achieve their political ends, and in the Middle East strategic alliances between Christian and Muslim lords were common. However, these had been agreements between autonomous lordships seeking local allies for mutual advantage, not voluntary submission to the ruler of an expanding empire that would fatally undermine others' resistance to that empire.[37]

The *Chronique d'Ernoul* stated that King Guy assembled the army at Nazareth to attack Count Raymond at Tiberias, but Balian of Ibelin persuaded him that this would be unwise, as Saladin would come to his defence, and it would be better to send a party of barons to negotiate with him. Guy agreed, but Count Raymond responded that he would not make peace until his castle that had been taken from him was returned, presumably a reference to Joscelin's seizure of Beirut.[38]

While Count Raymond III was effectively submitting his county to Saladin's overlordship, in the south of the kingdom Reynald de Châtillon had returned to his previous policy of attacking Muslim targets during the winter months. 'Imād al-Dīn wrote that every year Reynald waged war on Saladin, and the compliment was returned. He had gained a truce from Saladin, but as soon as this was agreed and caravans were once again crossing his lands, Reynald began to impose tolls on them as they went out and returned, and he attacked the roads and spread terror. One day he attacked an important caravan carrying rich merchandise and took everything to Kerak. 'We sent him a message condemning his behaviour and reproaching him for his perfidy and his robberies, but he only became more obstinate and damaging. The Sultan swore then that he would have his life.'[39] The author of the *Itinerarium peregrinorum* considered that Reynald's attack on the caravan had given Saladin a pretext for invading the kingdom of Jerusalem.[40] While Reynald was simply continuing his previous policy, Saladin's position had changed. Unlike earlier years when he had been preoccupied in fighting the Muslim rulers of Syria and further afield, Saladin was now looking for a pretext to break his truce with the kingdom of Jerusalem and capture the land from the Franks.[41]

The end of the truce

Shortly before 29 March (Easter day) 1187, Saladin assembled his troops and marched to besiege Reynald's fortress of Kerak. It was imperative for Guy to settle the breach with Count Raymond so that they could concentrate on driving Saladin's forces out of Transjordan, so he sent another delegation to Tiberias, led by Archbishop Joscius of Tyre and including the masters of the Temple and Hospital, Balian of Ibelin and Reynald of Sidon.[42] But meanwhile, Saladin's son al-Afdal sent a military force across Count Raymond's territory in Galilee to raid the region around Acre. By the terms of Raymond's agreement with Saladin he had to allow the force to pass through, but its passing coincided with the arrival of the peace delegation. The two met on 1 May 1187 at a place called the Spring of the Cresson, and the little Frankish force with the delegation was annihilated. The master of the Hospitallers, Brother Roger des Moulins, was among the dead. Balian of Ibelin, who had delayed at Nablus to deal with his own business and then had paused on the road to hear mass because 1 May is a holy day, missed the battle completely.[43]

Ernoul blamed the master of the Temple's pride for the defeat, on the basis that when he heard that the Muslim force was advancing through Galilee he should have waited until the danger was past. But equally Ernoul's master Balian was in an embarrassing position. If he had travelled with the main party rather than delaying at Nablus he could have brought his experience and authority to bear on the situation. He might have talked the master of the Temple out of attempting to proceed in the face of the hostile Muslim force, just as he had talked King Guy out of attacking Count Raymond the previous autumn. Given his previous association with Count Raymond, his deliberate hanging back behind the rest of the party might suggest that he knew something about the dangers on the road the rest of the party did not. His actions could be construed as cowardice or even treachery.

Latin Christians in Europe were informed of the defeat through a letter from Pope Urban III, which was based on a letter sent to him by Gerard de Ridefort, master of the Temple. The pope's letter depicted the battle as an act of Christian piety. In contrast, the *Itinerarium peregrinorum* presented the battle as an unexpected encounter between Saladin's invading forces and the masters of the military orders. William of Newburgh held Count Raymond as directly responsible for the defeat because his treaty with Saladin had allowed Saladin to invade.[44]

Only Balian of Ibelin and Archbishop Joscius of Tyre finally reached the castle of Tiberias, where they met Reynald of Sidon and Count Raymond. According to the *Chronique d'Ernoul*, the count was so appalled at what had occurred that he agreed to do whatever the envoys advised. They advised him to put the Muslims out of the city of Tiberias and come with them to the king. Peace was made, and King Guy held a council of all the nobles of the kingdom, at which Count Raymond advised King Guy to summon the army to the springs of Saffūriyya in Galilee (the same place that Baldwin IV had mustered the army in September 1183 when he delegated command to Guy) and to send for help from Prince Bohemond of Antioch, which the king did. The prince of Antioch, according to Ernoul, sent one of his sons with sixty knights. In fact Prince Bohemond had just made a peace treaty with Saladin's nephew Taqī al-Dīn, but that would have covered only his principality.[45]

If Guy was delighted by the reconciliation with Count Raymond, Saladin and his advisors were appalled. They had trusted Count Raymond and dealt with him in good faith: as Saladin wrote to Isaac II Angelos, 'we had not wished to use him, but to be of use to him'. Count Raymond had implored Saladin's support against King Guy, but now he abandoned Saladin and gave his support to Guy. Saladin suggested to Isaac that if he wanted to attack the Franks, the Muslims would support him. Meanwhile he himself had begun to muster his army. The Franks may have made diplomatic approaches to request at least an exchange of prisoners, but although some of Saladin's advisors were reluctant to risk an attack, Saladin knew that after so many years spent establishing his authority over Muslims he needed a decisive victory over the Franks to convince his subjects that he was an enthusiastic defender of Islam.[46]

Queen (1186–1187)

The Frankish army mustered at Saffūriyya, with the Holy Cross and additional fighting men hired from the money sent by King Henry II of England to the East to assist his planned crusade. But the Frankish army did not advance, adopting the same waiting game that Guy had played successfully in 1183. Taking the initiative in an attempt to force Guy to move, on 2 July 1187 Saladin attacked the town of Tiberias, which was defended by Lady Eschiva of Tiberias, Count Raymond's wife. The following day, the Frankish army left Saffūriyya to relieve the siege.[47]

The Muslim commentators did not know which of King Guy's advisors had persuaded him to move the army from Saffūriyya, imagining either of the king's formidable military commanders – Count Raymond or Prince Reynald de Châtillon – making a convincing case to advance.[48] Ernoul would have been with the army in the service of Balian of Ibelin but possibly not in the discussions between the commanders of the army. He depicted Count Raymond advising King Guy not to advance while the master of the Temple told the King that Count Raymond was a traitor. In addition to Count Raymond's earlier peace treaty with Saladin – and who knew whether he was still in treasonous correspondence with the Muslims? – the master had every reason to distrust Count Raymond after the disaster which had befallen the Templars and Hospitallers on 1 May, which was directly attributable to the count's treaty with Saladin.[49] Latin Christian commentators writing during the Third Crusade blamed either Count Raymond for betraying the Christian army to Saladin, the sins of the Franks more generally, or the physical conditions of the terrain where the battle was fought. Witnesses in the Holy Land wrote of a heroic charge by the Templars which was not followed up and a group of Frankish knights who defected to Saladin. The count of Tripoli, lord Balian and Reynald lord of Sidon got away.[50] Ernoul explained this: they had been in the rearguard, and they escaped to Tyre with the prince of Antioch's son and the knights who had accompanied him.[51]

A great deal of scholarly research has been carried out on what actually took place during the battle of Hattin on 4 July 1187, and there has been much discussion of how Saladin was able to defeat the Franks so decisively.[52] These discussions need not be repeated here, but R. C. Smail's assessment of Guy's predicaments is worth consideration in the context of the impact his defeat made on his wife.[53] If Guy had followed the strategy he had either adopted or had forced on him at Saffūriyya in the autumn of 1183, he might have forced Saladin to withdraw. But in July 1187 both Guy and Saladin desperately required a victory to consolidate their positions. Saladin had won many victories against Muslim princes but needed to demonstrate that he could also progress the cause of Islam against the Franks. Guy had to convince the nobles of the kingdom of Jerusalem that he could win victories as King Baldwin IV, Count Raymond and Prince Reynald de Châtillon had done. Neither of them could afford to retreat, and so a battle was inevitable – if not at Hattin, then later. The question is whether if Guy had remained at Saffūriyya on 3 July 1187, he could have forced Saladin to engage the Franks on more favourable ground and won a victory; and, if so, whether it would have been a sufficient victory to force Saladin to withdraw and make a truce or whether Saladin would have returned within a few weeks.

The news that reached Sybil after the Battle of Hattin was dire. The relic of the Holy Cross, the holy talisman through whose help (in the words of the *Itinerarium peregrinorum*) the Franks had always been the victors in battle, had been lost; a terrible psychological blow to the whole of Latin Christendom.[54] Virtually all the fighting men of the kingdom had been captured or killed, including most of those who had supported Sybil's coronation in 1186. Prince Reynald de Châtillon was dead, slain by Saladin's own hand as the sultan had sworn. Her husband, her brother-in-law Aimery de Lusignan, her father-in-law the Old Marquis of Montferrat, and the master of the Temple had all been captured, as had her brother-in-law Humphrey of Toron and at least one member of the royal household, Miles of Colaverdo.[55] It is not clear whether Sybil's uncle Joscelin de Courtenay was also a prisoner. It appears that he escaped, because in July or early August 1187 he was listed as a witness to a document issued at Tyre, alongside the count of Tripoli, Reynald of Sidon and Balian.[56] In contrast, the lords who were probably behind the attempt to force her to divorce Guy were certainly still at large: her stepfather Balian of Ibelin, her cousin Count Raymond of Tripoli and her mother's widower Reynald of Sidon.

Notes

1 *Chronique d'Ernoul*, p. 117 (ch. 10).
2 *Chronique d'Ernoul*, pp. 129–130 (ch. 11).
3 *Chronique d'Ernoul*, p. 130 (ch. 11).
4 *Chronique d'Ernoul*, p. 130 (ch. 11).
5 See Lewis, *Counts of Tripoli*, pp. 258–260, for a survey of this account of events and the questions it throws up.
6 *Chronique d'Ernoul*, pp. 130–139 (ch. 11: and see p. 149 (ch. 12) for claim of authorship); 'Libellus', pp. 108–111; 'Regni Iherosolymitani Brevis Historia', pp. 137–138; Roger of Howden, *Gesta*, 1: 358–359; Roger of Howden, *Chronica*, 2: 315–316; Guy of Bazoches, 'Cronosgraphia', Paris, Bibliothèque nationale, MS Lat. 4998, fols 35r–64v, at fol. 63vb; *LFWT*, pp. 64–67; William of Newburgh, *Historia rerum anglicarum*, 1: 255–256 (Bk 3 ch. 16); 'Continuatio Aquicinctina', p. 424; *Magistri Tolosani Chronicon Faventinum*, p. 105; 'Versus ex libro magistri Ricardi', 458–459 (lines 31–62); 'L'Estoire de Eracles Empereur', pp. 25–34 (Bk 23 chs 17–23); *La Continuation de Guillaume de Tyr*, pp. 31–35 (sections 17–21); *L'Estoire de la Guerre Sainte*, pp. 404–405 (lines 2441–2472); *The History of the Holy War*, 1: 39–40, 2: 66–67 (lines 2437–2467). Ralph of Diceto pointed out that Guy was consecrated king of Jerusalem because his wife was the only daughter and heir of King Amaury: Ralph of Diceto, 'Ymagines historiarum', 2: 47. *IP* 1, p. 253 (Bk 1 ch. 5) mentions the conflict between King Guy and Count Raymond but does not mention the coronation.
7 IA, p. 316 (vol. 11.527); 'Imād al-Dīn in Abū Shāma, 'Le Livre des Deux Jardins', in *Recueil des historiens des croisades. Historiens orientaux*, vol. 4, ed. l'Académie des inscriptions et belles-lettres (Paris 1898), pp. 257–258.

8 An exception is Arnold of Lübeck, writing before 1214, who believed that only the master of the Hospital had any doubts about Guy's coronation, but also believed that no one even knew Sybil was married to Guy until she told the patriarch after Baldwin V's death: 'Arnoldi abbatis S. Iohannis Lubecensis Cronica Slavorum', ed. J. M. Lappenberg, in *Monumenta Germaniae Historica Scriptores in Folio*, 21, ed. Georg Heinrich Pertz (Hanover, 1869), pp. 100–250, at pp. 164–165; Leila Werthschulte, 'Arnold of Lübeck', in *Encyclopedia of the Medieval Chronicle*, ed. Graeme Dunphy, 2 vols (Leiden, 2010), 1: 110–111.

9 'Libellus', pp. 36–37, 108–109 (I); *Chronique d'Ernoul*, pp. 130 (erroneously naming William V of Montferrat as 'Boniface'), 132 (ch. 11); Kane, 'Wolf's Hair', 95–112.

10 John, 'Royal inauguration'; WT 2: 1058 (Bk 22 ch. 30): *decoratus est unctione et sollempniter coronatus*; *Chronique d'Ernoul*, p. 134 (ch. 11).

11 'Libellus', pp. 110–111 (I).

12 'Regni Iherosolymitani Brevis Historia', pp. 137–138.

13 'L'Estoire de Eracles Empereur', p. 29 (Bk 23 ch. 17); *La Continuation de Guillaume de Tyr*, p. 33 (section 18).

14 Roger of Howden, *Gesta*, 1: 358–359; Roger of Howden, *Chronica*, 2: 315–316; Guy of Bazoches, 'Cronosgraphia' fol. 63vb; *LFWT*, pp. 64–67; William of Newburgh, *Historia rerum anglicarum*, 1: 255–256 (Bk 3 ch. 16); 'Continuatio Aquicinctina', p. 424.

15 *Magistri Tolosani Chronicon Faventinum*, p. 105.

16 Roger of Howden, *Gesta*, 1: 358–359; Roger of Howden, *Chronica*, 2: 315–316; Guy of Bazoches, 'Cronosgraphia', fol. 63vb; *LFWT*, pp. 64–67; 'Versus ex libro magistri Ricardi', p. 458 (lines 37–42).

17 *LFWT*, pp. 64–65 (Bk 1 ch. 10).

18 Roger of Howden, *Chronica*, 2: 316.

19 Kedar, 'The Patriarch Eraclius', pp. 196–198, sets out some of the contradictions.

20 Mayer, 'The Beginnings of King Amalric of Jerusalem'; Edbury, 'The Crusader Town and Lordship of Ramla', pp. 11–12.

21 *IP* 1, p. 354 (Bk 1 ch. 63).

22 Buck, *Principality of Antioch*, pp. 99–100.

23 *IP* 1, pp. 353–354 (Bk 1 ch. 63).

24 Highlighted by Kedar, 'The Patriarch Eraclius', pp. 196–197.

25 *Chronique d'Ernoul*, pp. 134–139, 141 (chs 11, 12); Buck, *Principality of Antioch*, p. 239; *Cartulaire général*, 1: 491, 496 (nos 782, 783).

26 Roger of Howden, *Gesta*, 1: 359.

27 WT 2: 1049 (Bk 22 ch. 26); *La Continuation de Guillaume de Tyr*, p. 53 (section 41).

28 Woodacre, 'Questionable Authority', p. 395; IA, p. 316 (vol. 11.527).

29 *ULKJ*, nos 473, 474, 476, 477, 478, 479, 480, *481, 482, pp. 798.3, 800.30.40.41, 807.23, 810.35, 814.14, 817.36, 820.30, 821.17.19, 824.5); Mayer and Sode, *Die Siegel*, p. 152.

30 Charters issued with Sybil's *assensu et voluntate*: *ULKJ* 2: 798, 800 (nos 473, 474) or as king with Sybil: *ULKJ* 2: 807, 810, 814, 817, 820, 824 ('queen of the same': nos 476, 477; 'queen': no. 478; 'queen by the same grace': 479, 480, 482).

31 Folda, *Crusader Art*, pp. 66–67; Jacoby, 'The Tomb of Baldwin V', 11; Kenaan-Kedar, 'Decorative architectural sculpture', pp. 609–623; Van Houts, *Memory and Gender*, pp. 102–103.

32 Boas, *Crusader Archaeology*, p. 20; Adrian Boas, 'Some Reflections on Urban Landscapes in the Kingdom of Jerusalem: Archaeological Research in Jerusalem and Acre', in *Dei gesta per Francos: Études sur les croisades dédiées à Jean Richard / Crusade Studies in Honour of Jean Richard*, ed. Michel Balard, Benjamin Z. Kedar, and Jonathan Riley-Smith (Aldershot, 2001), pp. 241–260, at pp. 251–252.

33 *ULKJ* 2: 796–803, 854 (nos 473, 474, 475, 510, 511); Mayer, 'Die Legitimität Balduins IV', 76, 84–87, 89.

34 For Geoffrey Tortus as Joscelin's vassal see Mayer, 'Die Legitimität Balduins IV', 72. For these individuals as witnesses see their entries in *ULKJ* 4: 1611, 1637, 1640, 1664, 1671, 1694.

35 *ULKJ* 2: 821–822, 856 (nos *481, *5170. See also *ULKJ* 2: 836–837 (no. *489); Guy and Sybil later took this gift back, as in February 1191 or, more likely, 1192, Guy gave Walter the house which belonged to Turgissus in Acre in exchange. This may be the 'Turginus' to whom Sybil and Guy had sold land in the casal of Gesehale at some time between 24 September and 24 December 1180: *ULKJ* 2: 783–785, 851 (nos *457 *502).

36 *Cartulaire général*, 1: 510, 514, 516, 4: 327 (nos 819, 827, 830).

37 IA, p. 316 (vol.11.527); 'Imād al-Dīn in Abū Shāma, pp. 257–258; Lewis, *Counts of Tripoli*, pp. 264–266; Phillips, *Life and Legend*, p. 168.

38 *Chronique d'Ernoul*, pp. 141–142 (ch. 12).

39 'Imād al-Dīn in Abū Shāma, p. 259; similar in IA, pp. 316–317 (vol. 11. 527–528).

40 *IP* 1, pp. 253–254 (Bk 1 ch. 5).

41 Lewis, *Counts of Tripoli*, pp. 266–267.

42 Barber, *Crusader States*, p. 297; Lyons and Jackson, *Saladin*, pp. 248–249; Phillips, *Life and Legend*, pp. 169–170; *Chronique d'Ernoul*, pp. 143–144 (ch. 12).

43 *Chronique d'Ernoul*, pp. 144–152 (ch. 12); Barber, *Crusader States*, pp. 298–299; Lyons and Jackson, *Saladin*, pp. 249–250; Phillips, *Life and Legend*, pp. 170–171; Denys Pringle, 'The Spring of the Cresson in Crusading History', in *Dei gesta per Francos*, ed. Balard, Kedar, and Riley-Smith, pp. 231–240.

44 Pope Urban III's letter of 3 September 1187, translated in *The Conquest of Jerusalem and the Third Crusade: Sources in Translation*, ed. and trans. Peter W. Edbury, Crusade Texts in Translation 1 (Aldershot, 1996), pp. 156–157; *IP* 1, pp. 248–249 (Bk 1 ch. 2); William of Newburgh, *Historia rerum anglicarum*, 1: 256 (Bk 3 ch. 16).

45 *Chronique d'Ernoul*, pp. 152–154 (ch. 12); Barber, *Crusader States*, p. 299; Lyons and Jackson, *Saladin*, p. 252; Phillips, *Life and Legend*, p. 172. For Latin European views, see *IP* 1, p. 253 (Bk 1 ch. 5); William of Newburgh, *Historia rerum anglicarum*, 1: 256 (Bk 3 ch. 16).

46 Lyons and Jackson, *Saladin*, pp. 250–259, esp. pp. 251–252 for Saladin's letter to Isaac Angelos; Phillips, *Life and Legend*, pp. 172–173.

47 Murray, '"Mighty Against the Enemies of Christ"', p. 238; Mayer, 'Henry II of England', 735–736; Phillips, *Life and Legend*, pp. 173–177; 'Libellus', pp. 134–135.

48 Lyons and Jackson, *Saladin*, p. 258.

49 *Chronique d'Ernoul*, pp. 158–162 (ch. 13).

50 *IP* 1, p. 257 (Bk 1 ch. 5); 'Epistola Januensium ad Urbanum papam', in Roger of Howden, *Gesta*, 2: 11–12; summarised in *RRH Additamenta*, pp. 45–46, no. 664a; RRR no. 1241, accessed 15 April 2021; letter to Lord Archumbald, master of the

Hospitallers of Italy, and the brothers, translated in *The Conquest of Jerusalem and the Third Crusade: Sources in Translation*, ed. and trans. Peter W. Edbury, Crusade Texts in Translation 1 (Aldershot, 1996), pp. 160–162, and notes 14, 15; Latin text in 'Chronica collecta a Magno Presbitero', in *MGH SS*, vol. 17, ed. Georg Heinrich Pertz (Hanover, 1861), pp. 476–523, at p. 508; *RRH*, p. 176, no. 661; RRR no. 1237, accessed 15 April 2021; *RRH*, p. 175 (no. 658); RRR no. 1229, accessed 15 April 2021; *Radulphi de Coggeshall Chronicon Anglicanum*, p. 21; Lewis, *Counts of Tripoli*, p. 269.

51 *Chronique d'Ernoul*, pp. 169–170 (ch. 14).

52 For example, Lyons and Jackson, *Saladin*, pp. 255–266; Phillips, *Life and Legend*, pp. 177–186; Benjamin Z. Kedar, 'The Battle of Hattin Revisited', in *The Horns of Ḥaṭṭīn*, ed. B. Z. Kedar (Jerusalem and London, 1992), pp. 190–207; John France, *Hattin* (Oxford, 2015); Steve Tibble, *The Crusader Armies 1099–1187* (New Haven and London, 2018), pp. 321–344; Phillips, *Life and Legend*, pp. 172–186.

53 Smail, 'The Predicaments of Guy of Lusignan', pp. 173, 176.

54 'Cuius presidio nostri semper in bellis exstitere victores': *IP* 1, p. 258 (Bk 1 ch. 5); Murray, '"Mighty Against the Enemies of Christ"', pp. 217–218; Penny J Cole, 'Christian perceptions of the battle of Hattin (583/1187)', *Al-Masāq: Journal of the Medieval Mediterranean*, 6.1 (1993), 9–39.

55 *Chronique d'Ernoul*, p. 173 (ch. 15); 'L'Estoire de Eracles Empereur', p. 66 (Bk 23 ch. 44); 'Libellus', pp. 158–159 (XIV); see also *La Continuation de Guillaume de Tyr*, p. 55, section 43, which adds Hue de Gibelet (Jubail) to the list of prisoners.

56 The Lyon *Eracles* states that he escaped from Hattin with Balian of Ibelin and went to Acre: *La Continuation de Guillaume de Tyr*, p. 56 (section 44); *ULKJ* 3: 1339–1343 (no. 769); and see 'Regni Iherosolymitani Brevis Historia', p. 145. After this he did not appear as a witness to a charter until April 1190: *ULKJ* 1: 812–814 (no. 478).

7 Sybil versus Saladin (1187–1189)

After Hattin

What did Sybil do when she heard that Saladin had defeated the army of her kingdom at Hattin, imprisoned her husband and most of her allies and executed her long-standing supporter Prince Reynald de Châtillon and the Templar and Hospitaller knights captured at the battle?[1]

None of the sources for this period between Hattin and the beginning of the Third Crusade provide a complete picture of events, and all present problems of interpretation. The *Chronique d'Ernoul* (and the various versions of the *Estoire de Eracles* which follow it) is apparently based on Ernoul's first-hand eyewitness account, but it is impossible to know how much it has been altered from Ernoul's original. The *Libellus de expugnatione terrae sanctae* is partly founded on eyewitness accounts, but rather than setting out to exculpate the Ibelin brothers, the objective of the *Chronique d'Ernoul*, this compiler regarded Balian as partly to blame for the surrender of Jerusalem. Contemporary European writers recorded information from appeals for aid, eyewitness reports or what they later heard as participants in the Third Crusade, but their information was incomplete, and they tended to be hostile towards the Frankish nobility. The *Itinerarium peregrinorum* set out to justify the position of Queen Sybil and King Guy, hinting at the queen's interactions with her brother-in-law Conrad of Montferrat but brushing over details. The Latin continuation of William of Tyre's history, writing over a decade after events, attempted to reconcile a range of accounts but was not completely successful.[2] For writers who took part in the Third Crusade and set out to record it for posterity, such as Ambroise and 'Monachus', the events between the battle of Hattin and the beginning of King Guy's siege of Acre in August 1189 were only a prelude to the crusade. They set out Saladin's conquests, described Conrad of Montferrat's defence of Tyre and the captivity and release of King Guy, how Conrad refused to work with Guy, and how the Third Crusade got underway; but they barely mention, or completely omit, Queen Sybil.[3]

None of the surviving appeals for aid after the battle of Hattin were sent in Sybil's name; they were dispatched by the ecclesiastical leaders, the secular nobles and members of the orders of the Temple and Hospital. Probably the leaders of the various Christian churches represented in Jerusalem also informed their co-religionists of events. Certainly the world chronicle composed by Michael, patriarch of the Syrian Orthodox Church 1166–1199, included an account of the battle and Saladin's subsequent conquests.[4] The chronicle of Constable Smpad of Cilician Armenia, probably written after his younger brother Het'um became king of Cilician Armenia in 1226, contained a great detail of information on the battle of Hattin, although slightly muddled.[5] The Muslim commentators provide the most complete account of the events of 1187–1189, but as they regarded the Franks as religious enemies and the majority wrote in praise of Saladin, unsurprisingly their accounts are far from objective.

It is not clear where Sybil was immediately after Hattin. She was not at Tyre, where the fugitives from the battle assembled, because a generous privilege issued to the Genoese by 'the barons of the kingdom of Jerusalem with the archbishops and commanders of the Temple and Hospital' at some point between 10 July and 6 August indicates that she was elsewhere. Because they had been quick to defend the city after Hattin and were willing to serve the lord king and queen, the Genoese received free entry and exit from Tyre for their goods and property, and those giving the privilege undertook that this would be ratified by the king and queen. The witnesses included the count of Tripoli, Count Joscelin the seneschal of the kingdom, Reynald lord of Sidon, Balian, Walter of Caesarea, 'and a great many other men of the king and queen'. Count Raymond and the barons of the kingdom went on to give further privileges to the Genoese, and also to the Pisans, in recognition of their assistance in the defence against Saladin and to ensure their future help.[6] But where was the queen?

Sybil's and Guy's charters indicate that they had been living at Acre rather than Jerusalem, but if Sybil was at Acre she would have had to leave when the city surrendered to Saladin without a fight on 9 July. The Lyon *Eracles* blamed the quick capitulation on Count Joscelin of Edessa.[7] The *Chronique d'Ernoul*, followed by the *Estoire de Eracles*, stated that Sybil was in Jerusalem after the defeat at Hattin, with just two knights in the city who had escaped from the battle.[8] Sybil might have gone to Jerusalem after Acre was surrendered. But if she did go to Jerusalem, she then left the city, because two western writers (Ralph of Coggeshall and the author of the Latin continuation of William of Tyre's History) recorded that she went to her city of Ascalon and made it ready to resist a siege.[9]

It is not inherently unlikely that Sybil would have defended her city. Queens and noblewomen in twelfth-century Latin Christendom acted as military leaders in defence of their lands when necessary.[10] Queen Melisende initiated military action in her kingdom, and her younger sister Alice may have had her own military policies.[11] Women in the crusader states were often involved in fighting, in raiding the enemy or in self-defence to repel raiders.[12] Military service was a duty for Frankish noblewomen holding fiefs, although they were not expected to fight in the field in person; a lord would expect an heiress to marry and for her husband to perform the military service due.[13]

136 *Sybil versus Saladin (1187–1189)*

Noblewomen oversaw the defence of fortresses. Cecilia of le Bourcq, widow of Roger of Salerno, prince of Antioch, one of the major landholders in the principality of Antioch and styled 'Lady of Tarsus', may have helped to organise the defence of Antioch in 1119 after her husband's death in battle against the Muslim Il-ghazi ibn Artuk of Mardin.[14] The *Chronique d'Ernoul* told a story of Stephanie de Milly sending food and a personal message to Saladin while he was besieging her castle of Kerak in November–December 1183; Stephanie could have been involved in commanding the defence.[15] Eschiva de Bures, lady of Galilee, defended her castle of Tiberias against Saladin's besieging force for around a week from c. 27 June to 5 July 1187, surrendering only after King Guy's relief force was defeated at Hattin on 4 July.[16] Citing the *Estoire de Eracles*, some modern historians have claimed that after the battle of Hattin Maria Komnene also defended her city of Nablus against Saladin, but in fact the *Estoire de Eracles* does not state this; it indicates that she evacuated Nablus in the face of Saladin's approach and went to Jerusalem, where her husband Balian found her.[17]

After capturing Acre, Saladin's forces captured a series of towns and fortresses including Nablus, Caesarea and Jaffa. The castle of Toron or Tibnīn surrendered on 26 July, Sidon on 29 July, Jubail (or Gibelet, in the county of Tripoli), and then Beirut on 6 August. Saladin then headed south to clear the road to Egypt, bypassing Tyre, which he judged would be difficult to capture because the Frankish commanders had taken refuge there.[18] Meanwhile another of Sybil's relatives arrived at Tyre, whose actions would have a substantial impact on the course of the war and Sybil's own future.[19]

When Marquis William V of Montferrat came to the East after his grandson Baldwin V became sole king of Jerusalem, his second son Conrad also took the cross. However, the offer of a marriage alliance from Emperor Isaac II Angelos took Conrad, a widower, to Constantinople instead, where he was betrothed to the emperor's sister Theodora. The emperor relied on him to organise Constantinople's defences during an attempted military coup in 1187, but subsequently Conrad left the city. The Genoese writer of the 'Regni Iherosolymitani Brevis Historia' wrote that Conrad departed because he had made too many enemies in Constantinople in putting down the coup, while the Byzantine historian Niketas Choniates wrote that Conrad thought he had not been sufficiently rewarded for his efforts. In any case, Conrad set out on his sworn pilgrimage to the Holy Land with (according to the 'Brevis Historia') his Genoese counsellor Ansaldo Bonvicino and in a Genoese ship belonging to one Balduino Erminio. When his ship arrived off Acre, he realised that the city had fallen to the Muslims, evaded capture, and sailed back up the coast to Tyre, where he took over command of the city.[20]

Conrad had an obvious legal basis for assuming command of one of the last cities of the kingdom remaining under Frankish control. He was the younger brother of William Longsword, Sybil's first husband, who may have been intended to take over the government of the kingdom before his early death in 1177. Conrad was the nearest surviving direct male relative of the last anointed king of Jerusalem to rule in his own right, Baldwin V, and much more closely related to the child king than the regent Count Raymond of Tripoli. Described by the contemporary eyewitness author of the *Itinerarium peregrinorum* as 'an extraordinary man of action who was strenuous in all his endeavours', if Conrad had arrived in the kingdom when King Baldwin V was alive, he could have expected to take on the regency.[21]

According to Bahā' al-Dīn ibn Shaddād, two years later Conrad would tell Guy de Lusignan that he was the lieutenant of the kings across the sea in his command of Tyre and he could not give it up to Guy without their permission.[22] The 'Brevis Historia' provides an explanation for this statement: the count of Tripoli, Count Joscelin, Reynald lord of Sidon, Pagan of Haifa, the lord of Caesarea, 'and other princes of that land' unanimously placed the city of Tyre into Conrad's custody until the coming of any of the four crowned heads, viz., the Emperor Frederick, the king of France, the king of England or William, king of Sicily.[23] This list echoes the Frankish nobles' earlier oath to King Baldwin IV to consult the pope, the emperor and the kings of France and England on the succession to the kingdom of Jerusalem, but now consulting the king of Sicily rather than the pope. The *Itinerarium peregrinorum* indicated that the city of Tyre was entrusted to Conrad on condition that it should be handed over to the heirs of the king and the kingdom, which this author interpreted as meaning it should be given to Guy.[24]

Other writers, however, did not know of any formal agreement by which Count Raymond and the Frankish nobility entrusted Tyre to Conrad. The *Chronique d'Ernoul* (followed by the *Estoire de Eracles*) and Ibn al-Athīr believed that Count Raymond had abandoned Tyre and gone to Tripoli.[25] Ibn al-Athīr believed that when Conrad arrived at Tyre there was no one to lead the defence. The *Chronique d'Ernoul* recorded that Reynald of Sidon was in command with the castellan of Tyre, but as they realised they could not hold out against Saladin they negotiated terms of surrender. Conrad then arrived, Reynald of Sidon and the castellan of Tyre fled at night by ship to Tripoli, and Conrad took over defence of Tyre by popular request. Saladin besieged Tyre but was forced to withdraw.[26]

The sieges of Ascalon and Jerusalem

Meanwhile, according to the the *Estoire de Eracles*, Balian of Ibelin had found his wife Maria at Jerusalem and planned to go to Ascalon and take his wife and children there. As Ralph of Coggeshall and the Latin continuation of William of Tyre state that Sybil went to Ascalon, then either Balian's intention was that he and his family would travel with his stepdaughter Sybil from Jerusalem to her city of Ascalon, or she was already at Ascalon with her children and Balian intended that Maria and their children should take refuge with her.[27] But Balian and Maria did not go to Ascalon; Saladin attacked it as part of his strategy to clear the Franks from the road to Egypt.

All commentators agreed that the defenders of Ascalon surrendered in return for Saladin's promise to release King Guy. Saladin brought King Guy out before the city walls and he pleaded with the defenders to hand over the city in return for his freedom.[28] This was a particularly effective tactic, because as Guy had been count of Ascalon and had been in residence in the city for some years, he would have been personally known to many of the defenders of the city and could have appealed to them as their personal lord and friend. It would have had even more impact if Guy's wife were commanding the defence – as Ralph of Coggeshall and the Latin continuator of William of Tyre state she was.[29] Roger of Howden, who took part in the Third Crusade, did not mention Sybil's defence of the city but stated that she personally surrendered it to redeem her husband King Guy from prison.[30]

These three writers indicated that it was a long siege: Ralph of Coggeshall thought that Sybil surrendered the city in the following year, 1188. He placed the start of the siege in the summer of 1187 and stated: 'later in the following year she surrendered the city to Saladin for the redemption of her husband, and thus she liberated him from Saladin's prison'.[31] Roger of Howden placed the surrender of Ascalon in 1189.[32] The Latin continuator of William of Tyre's history had Saladin besieging the city but, finding that the queen was there and the city was fully prepared for a siege, passed on to besiege Jerusalem. He returned after capturing Jerusalem; but knowing that the queen was there and he already planned to take Ascalon in return for the king's release, he went on to besiege Tyre. After failing to capture Tyre he returned to Ascalon. As he could not commit to a long siege, he offered to release King Guy and a hundred knights in return for the city. According to this writer, Sybil at last surrendered the city because she was afraid Saladin would treat her husband as he had treated Reynald of Châtillon and kill him. Given that these events are depicted as taking place after Saladin abandoned the siege of Tyre at the start of January 1188, this writer indicated that Ascalon fell early in spring 1188.[33]

In fact, however, Ascalon was surrendered to Saladin on 4 September 1187, only two months after the battle of Hattin. The date is certain because the *Itinerarium peregrinorum* refers to an eclipse which occurred on the day of the surrender.[34] The confusion over the date Ascalon was surrendered may have been because Saladin did not immediately release Guy. He returned the captive king to prison and did not free him until the end of March 1188 (according to the *Chronique d'Ernoul*) or May (according to the *Itinerarium peregrinorum*).[35] The Templars surrendered Gaza on the same basis – that the master of the order would be released in exchange – but the master was not released until early summer 1188.[36]

According to the *Chronique d'Ernoul* (followed by the *Estoire de Eracles*), after he captured Ascalon Saladin told Sybil to go to Nablus to join King Guy, because he did not want her to be in Jerusalem while he besieged it.[37] This reflects the Latin Christian legend that later developed around Saladin depicting him as the ideal chivalric lord, more honourable than Christians,[38] but there was no reason why Sybil should have obeyed any instructions from Saladin. In fact, the Muslim commentators 'Imād al-Dīn and Ibn al-Athīr recorded that Sybil was in Jerusalem during Saladin's siege and only left for Nablus to see her husband – with Saladin's permission – after the city surrendered. They noted that there was also a pious Greek lady living in Jerusalem whom Saladin allowed to depart with her entourage and property and indicated that Stephanie de Milly, lady of Transjordan, was in Jerusalem during the siege as well.[39] Ibn al-Athīr stated that Saladin had allowed the defenders of Ascalon and their women and children to leave with all their possessions for Jerusalem after they surrendered.[40] He does not mention that Queen Sybil and her daughters were in Ascalon, but if Sybil was among these refugees this would explain how she came to be at Jerusalem during the siege of that city.

Saladin's siege of Jerusalem began on 20 September 1187.[41] The Latin Christian writers recorded that the city was full of refugees and there were hardly any trained fighting men in it.[42] In contrast, the Muslim commentators believed that it was full of fighting men.[43] 'Imād al-Dīn and Ibn al-Athīr understood that the patriarch of Jerusalem, 'revered by the Franks and more important than their king', was leading the defence, and negotiations for surrender were conducted by Balian of Ibelin 'whose standing in their eyes was equal to that of the king'. 'Imād al-Dīn also mentioned the Hospitallers and Templars and other barons who had escaped from Hattin.[44] 'Imād al-Dīn and Ibn al-Athīr depicted Saladin rejecting the peace overtures of several of the Franks' leaders who approached him to ask for terms. Balian of Ibelin obtained terms of surrender only by threatening that the inhabitants of Jerusalem would destroy the Muslim holy sites, kill their Muslim prisoners and then go down fighting to the last man. In response to these dire threats, Saladin agreed to allow the Franks to ransom themselves. Men should pay ten dinars (the Frankish texts state bezants), women five and a child of either sex two. Those who could not pay within forty days would be enslaved. The city was surrendered on 2 October 1187.[45]

The *Chronique d'Ernoul*, followed by the *Estoire de Eracles*, agreed with the Muslim writers that the most active leader of the siege defences was Balian of Ibelin while the Patriarch Eraclius was also influential, as were the Templars and Hospitallers. The *Chronique d'Ernoul* explains that when Balian had arrived in Jerusalem to take his wife Maria and their children to safety, he had been asked by the patriarch to stay and assume military command of the city. He did so, knighting the sons of the burghers of the city and raising money to pay fighting men by stripping silver from the church of the Holy Sepulchre. He also obtained from Saladin an escort for his wife and children to safety in Tripoli, but he remained in the city until it fell. The Lyon *Eracles* gave him the formal title of *baili* in Jerusalem and added a story of how he negotiated safe conduct from Saladin for the sons of Baldwin of Ramla and Raymond of Gibelet. The *Chronique d'Ernoul* insisted that Balian wrung the best possible terms of surrender from Saladin and went to great expense to ensure as many of the population as possible were ransomed.[46]

The *Libellus de expugnatione terrae sanctae*, which makes clear that here it is based on eyewitness evidence, wrote of 'the lord patriarch and other great men of the city' (*domini patriarche et ceterorum magnorum ciuitatis*) in command of the defence. The *homines Ierusalem inhabitantes* (people dwelling in

Jerusalem) sent envoys to Saladin asking for terms, but he refused. They then sent Balian, and Rainer of Nablus and Thomas Patricius (both associates of Balian and former witnesses of documents for King Amaury) to offer Saladin 100,000 besants, but he refused again. They sent another embassy comprising these and others, urging Saladin to set his own terms or else they would hold out until he was destroyed. Saladin then agreed terms. The author commented that the terms only pleased the lord patriarch and the wealthy. The people of the city in general were unhappy because any man without ten bezants was left helpless, and they declared that they would have preferred to die defending the city rather than be enslaved. Who could imagine, declared the author, that Christians could voluntarily surrender the Holy Places to non-Christians, without hard fighting and heavy bloodshed? May those worst of merchants who had sold the holy city and Christ perish like Judas did when his body burst open and spilled his entrails on the ground. Let the children and wives of those who did not wish to defend Christ's inheritance be orphans and widows in a foreign land![47]

Ralph of Diceto, dean of London, writing shortly after events, recorded that Eraclius, patriarch of Jerusalem, Balian of Nablus and Reynald, lord of Sidon, negotiated the terms of surrender and handed over Jerusalem, Ascalon, Darum, Gaza, Nablus, Jaffa and other fortresses and cities to Saladin. In his view they had some excuse for the surrender as they acted to ransom King Guy and the master of the Temple. The king's brother (Aimery de Lusignan) was freed immediately, while the king and the master were freed after Easter.[48]

However, the near-contemporary account in the *Itinerarium peregrinorum*, followed by the Latin continuation of William of Tyre's history, did not mention Balian's role in negotiating the ransom terms. These works stated that the patriarch and Queen Sybil were pre-eminent in the city of Jerusalem while it was under siege from Saladin and surrendered only because the cowardly and fearful common people urged them to do so.[49] By placing Sybil at Jerusalem during Saladin's siege of the city, the Latin continuation contradicted its earlier and later assertions that she was leading the defence of Ascalon which in this version of events continued from before Saladin's siege of Jerusalem until early 1188. Apart from showing that this author never succeeded in reconciling the various versions of events brought together in this work, this also suggests that the author was anxious not to give Balian any credit for events in Jerusalem and to show that Sybil had no choice in its surrender.

Given that the Muslim sources agree that Balian negotiated the terms of surrender, the *Chronique d'Ernoul* appears justified in assigning him the leading role in negotiations. But the *Libellus* and the *Itinerarium peregrinorum* indicate that contemporaries were far from happy with Balian's solution. The *Libellus* equates Balian and his fellow negotiators with Judas Iscariot who sold Christ to His enemies while the *Itinerarium peregrinorum* suggests that the city could have been defended if the inhabitants had been united in their resistance. Both authors indicate that the city was lost because of the sin of its inhabitants.[50] In the face of such savage criticism, the author of the *Chronique d'Ernoul* tried to explain and justify Balian's actions, although the fact that Balian played no further leadership role within the kingdom, supporting rather than leading, suggests that his surrender of the city ruined his reputation among Latin Christians generally: he was now the man who had sold the holy city to its enemies. This writer was also anxious to show that Sybil had no role in and no responsibility or credit for what occurred and took care to depict her as being out of the city during the siege.

As the Muslim sources record that Sybil was in Jerusalem during the siege, there is no reason to doubt that she was there. As queen of Jerusalem she would have had authority in the city. So why did she not take a leading role in negotiations with Saladin?

In the Latin Christian West, kings would meet as equals on neutral ground to negotiate, for example on a river, on an island or at a border.[51] Yet this was not the custom in the Muslim Levant at this time. When Richard of England suggested a face-to-face meeting with Saladin, Saladin replied (in the words of his qadi, Bahā' al-Dīn ibn Shaddād):

> When princes meet, their subsequent enmity is disgraceful. When something is arranged, then it is good to meet … [but not] … until something is settled and a firm basis established. At that point there can be a meeting which will be followed by friendship and love.[52]

Saladin did not deal face to face with enemy commanders but expected to deal with an intermediary. Balian of Ibelin was the ideal person to take on this role. As the husband of Queen Sybil's stepmother Maria Komnene, he was Sybil's nearest male relative who was not in Saladin's prison, apart from Conrad of Montferrat at Tyre. With Sybil's husband a captive, Balian was *in loco parentis* of the temporarily widowed queen and thus the obvious male figure to act on her behalf. He was also an experienced military commander who was respected by the Muslims. According to the *Chronique d'Ernoul*, he was known personally to Saladin: he had been in contact with him to obtain assurance of safe conduct to come to Jerusalem to take his wife and children to safety, and he had obtained an escort from Saladin to guide his wife and their children to Tripoli.

If Sybil did exercise authority during Saladin's siege of Jerusalem, she delegated the task of negotiating peace terms to her stepfather. Nonetheless, the *Libellus*'s eyewitness account indicates that Balian was not the only negotiator; other individuals were involved on the Frankish side, including negotiators chosen by the people living in the city (*homines Ierusalem inhabitantes*), and the patriarch also played a command role. In any case, the Latin Christian sources which mention Sybil's presence indicate that she could not save the city because the majority, or at least those with influence in the city, wanted to surrender.

The Muslim commentators rejoiced that the holy city was restored to Muslim hands and that Saladin had purified its holy places from Frankish filth while the *Itinerarium peregrinorum* lamented: 'there is no sorrow like this sorrow, when they possess the [Holy] Sepulchre but persecute the one who was buried there'.[53]

Former queen of Jerusalem

Reports of the fall of Jerusalem were rapidly sent to the West. In mid-October Prince Bohemond III of Antioch dispatched the archbishop of Tarsus, chancellor of the principality of Antioch, to the West to plead for help and wrote 'to all Christians' with news of the battle of Hattin, where Saladin captured the king and True Cross, and that Ascalon and Jerusalem had been lost, although Antioch still held out against the enemy.[54] In the same month Joscius, archbishop of Tyre, led an embassy to Europe to seek help from the leaders of Latin Christendom. According to Bahā' al-Dīn ibn Shaddād, Conrad of Montferrat

> produced a picture of Jerusalem on a large sheet of paper, depicting the Sepulchre to which they come on pilgrimage and which they revere. The tomb of the Messiah is there, where he was buried after his crucifixion, as they assert .... He pictured the tomb and added a Muslim cavalryman on horseback trampling on the Messiah's tomb, upon which the horse had staled. This picture he publicised overseas in the markets and assemblies, as the priests, bareheaded and dressed in sackcloth, paraded it, crying doom and destruction. Images affect their hearts, for they are essential to their religion. There multitudes of people, whom God alone could number, were roused up.[55]

Bahā' al-Dīn ibn Shaddād did not specifically state that Archbishop Joscius of Tyre took this piece of visual propaganda with him on his preaching campaign, but his description of it being shown in markets and assemblies would fit with Joscius's campaign, as would the account of its powerful impact. After hearing Joscius's appeal, King William II of Sicily began to prepare an expedition, equipping a fleet under the command of his admiral, Margaritus of Brindisi. Joscius then went on to Rome, where he met the pope, now Pope Gregory VIII, who on 29 October had issued a call to crusade. Opening with the words 'Audita tremendi' ('hearing, we tremble'), Gregory had called all Christians to repentance so that they could deal with the enemies of Christendom. Gregory had not then heard about the fall of Jerusalem, but Joscius's news would only strengthen the impact of his letter.

Within a month, Count Richard of Poitou, eldest surviving son of King Henry II of England, had taken the cross.[56] The author of the *Itinerarium peregrinorum* later claimed that he was the first to do so, although in fact Archbishop Baldwin of Canterbury had been the first of Richard's later travelling companions to take the cross, back in March 1185.[57] But Gregory VIII did not live to see the results of his call to crusade. He died on 20 December 1187, and it was his successor Pope Clement III who continued his plans.[58]

Sybil versus Saladin (1187–1189) 143

While ambassadors from the crusader states sought help in the West, what of Sybil and the refugees from the city of Jerusalem? Ibn al-Athīr and 'Imād al-Dīn stated that after Jerusalem fell, Saladin:

> set free the queen of Jerusalem .... He also released her wealth and her retinue. She sought permission to go to her husband, at this time confined in the citadel at Nablus. Saladin gave her permission, so she went to him and remained there with him.[59]

The *Itinerarium peregrinorum* confirmed this account up to a point, stating that after the surrender of Jerusalem Queen Sybil set off with the Templars, the Hospitallers, the patriarch and a large group of exiles for the city of Antioch by way of Nablus, where Saladin allowed her a brief meeting with Guy, in contrast to the longer stay indicated by the Muslim commentators. According to the *Itinerarium peregrinorum*, Sybil then intended to embark for Europe – perhaps on Guy's advice. Like the chancellor of Antioch and Archbishop Joscius of Tyre, she could have gone to seek help for her husband and her kingdom. But she was unable to set sail because Conrad of Montferrat had her ship carried away to Tyre by force: *navem ... marchisus violenter Tyrum abduxerit*. Regrettably, 'in the interests of brevity', the author gives no more details about this incident, not even stating from which port Sybil intended to embark.[60] In the kingdom of Jerusalem, only the port of Tyre was still in Christian hands, but as Conrad took the ship to Tyre it clearly had been somewhere else. As Saladin had captured all the ports on the Syrian-Palestinian coastline south of Tripoli during the summer of 1187, Sybil was probably at Tripoli when she tried to embark for the West.[61]

At Tyre, Conrad had strengthened the city's defences by enlisting the support of the maritime powers. In October, at the Hospitallers' house in Tyre, he issued a series of legal documents with the agreement of the ecclesiastical leaders, the temporary leaders of the Templars and Hospitallers, Brothers Terricus and Burellus, and the knights and burghers of Tyre. He confirmed the property and rights that the Pisans held at Tyre (confirmed to them in July or early August by Count Raymond of Tripoli) and (if they were recovered by the Christians) at Jaffa and Acre. He also rewarded with various rights and privileges the burghers of Saint-Gilles, Montpellier, Marseille, Barcelona and Nîmes, who had helped to defend Tyre, and if other cities were recovered by the Christians they would have the same rights there. The witnesses included the commander of the Templars at Tyre and five of his brothers, the Hospitaller prior of Saint-Gilles and two of his brothers, and eighteen laymen including Lord Hugh of Tiberias and his brother Ralph, Lord Walter of Caesarea, Lord Elias *vicecomes* of Nazareth, Eustace *vicecomes* of Lajjun, Hubert Nepos, the marquis's seneschal, Ansaldo Bonuicino (Conrad's Genoese counsellor), Ansaldo's brother Baldwin, and Bernard de Templo *vicecomes* in Tyre. The charters were drawn up by Conrad's scribe Bandinus.[62]

To judge from these documents, Conrad was receiving assistance from the Pisans and the representatives of other mercantile cities of southern Europe and many of the Frankish nobility. Walter of Caesarea had been one of the lords who witnessed Count Raymond's charter to the Genoese in July or early August 1187, while the brothers Hugh and Ralph of Tiberias may have been captured at Hattin but if so had been ransomed. Conrad also had friendly relations with the Genoese and the Hospitallers and Templars were working with him: he issued these documents in the Hospitallers' house at Tyre, and – according to Conrad's later letter to Archbishop Baldwin of Canterbury – they had given him money that King Henry of England had deposited with them. The Hospitallers and Templars also provided him with ships.[63]

In sending Archbishop Joscius to the West to seek help and issuing confirmations and privileges to European merchants at Tyre, Acre and Jaffa, Conrad was acting as if he were regent of the kingdom. As the previous regent (Count Raymond of Tripoli) was now dead, Conrad could claim the regency by right. It was in this context that he took Sybil's ship to Tyre and prevented her from crossing to Europe. Perhaps his view was that the queen must not abandon the Christians of the crusader states: as the crowned head of the kingdom she must stay in the East to act as a focus for warriors arriving from the West and to lend her authority to the Christian leaders of what remained, particularly himself as her brother-in-law. It was sufficient for Archbishop Joscius to go overseas as an ambassador for the kingdom; the queen should not go in person.

The *Itinerarium peregrinorum* does not indicate what Sybil did next, only implying that she continued on her way to Antioch. The Latin continuation states that after surrendering Ascalon to Saladin (in spring 1188) she went to the count of Tripoli.[64] By this time the count of Tripoli was the son of Prince Bohemond III of Antioch, perhaps explaining the confusion over Sybil's destination. As it was probably from Tripoli that she tried and failed to embark for the West, it is most likely that Sybil remained at Tripoli. Hamilton suggested that she stayed in Tripoli with her stepmother Maria Komnene, but this is not specifically supported by the contemporary writers.[65] The later *Chronique d'Ernoul* and the *Estoire de Eracles* state that Sybil was at Tripoli when Saladin was besieging the city in summer 1188.[66] Sybil had, then, left the kingdom of Jerusalem; and she did not return until spring 1189. Perhaps she had handed over responsibility for defending her kingdom to her brother-in-law Conrad while she went to a place of safety with her daughters and gathered troops, although no contemporary recorded as much.

On 11 November 1187 Saladin began to besiege Tyre, attacking by both land and sea. According to the *Itinerarium peregrinorum* he brought out Conrad's father, William V of Montferrat, and offered to release him in return for the surrender of Tyre. Unlike Sybil and the defenders of Ascalon at the sight of the captive King Guy, Conrad refused to be moved and even fired a crossbow at his father – although the *Itinerarium peregrinorum* insisted that he fired to miss. When Saladin threatened to kill the old Marquis, Conrad retorted that then 'that wicked man would have a good end' and he himself would have a martyr as a father. The *Chronique d'Ernoul* (which placed this scene during Saladin's earlier siege in August that year) and most versions of the *Estoire de Eracles* omitted the crossbow but had Conrad retorting that his father was old and had already lived too long; the Lyon *Eracles* also depicted Conrad firing a crossbow at his father. In any case, on the night of 29–30 December the defenders sallied out of the city in boats and broke up Saladin's blockade in a sea battle. Saladin's land forces attempted an assault, but Conrad had the city's land gates thrown open and a body of knights led by Hugh of Tiberias and his brothers charged out and threw down their attackers. At the beginning of January 1188, Saladin withdrew.[67]

This was the first victory that the Franks had won against Saladin since the end of the truce the previous spring and Conrad was quick to exploit it, writing to King Béla III of Hungary that month with news of Saladin's victories, the loss of the Holy Cross and Saladin's conquest of Jerusalem but also describing how he repulsed Saladin's siege of Tyre and listing the fortresses which still held out against the invader. He also wrote to the Emperor Frederick and other kings, barons and important people of Europe, as well as the cities of Genoa and Pisa. Similarly, Brother Terricus, temporary commander of the Templars who had been in Tyre since the aftermath of Hattin, wrote to King Henry of England with the news of not only the fall of Jerusalem but also Conrad's successful defence of Tyre with the help of the Hospitallers and Templars and listing the fortresses which still held out.[68]

In Europe preparations for a crusade proceeded apace. On 21 January 1188 King Henry II of England and King Philip II of France took the cross at Gisors after a sermon by Archbishop Joscius of Tyre. They were followed by Duke Hugh III of Burgundy, Count Philip of Flanders and many others. Henry set about making preparations, sending letters to the Emperor Frederick Barbarossa, the Emperor Isaac Angelos and King Béla of Hungary to arrange passage for his army through their territories and the means of supplying his troops with provisions. He also wrote to patriarchs Aimery of Antioch and Eraclius of Jerusalem to inform them that he and his son had taken the cross and would soon set out. Early in February, Archbishop Baldwin of Canterbury and Bishop Gilbert of Rochester preached the crusade at a council at Geddington in Northamptonshire before the king and his nobles, and many clergy and laity took the cross. Henry also raised a tax, the so-called Saladin tithe, on everyone who did not take the cross. In March, Archbishop Baldwin set out on a preaching tour of Wales to raise recruits for the crusade.[69] On 27 March 1188 the Emperor Frederick Barbarossa held an assembly of his nobles at Mainz at which he took the cross, followed by his ecclesiastical and secular nobility. Frederick went on to negotiate terms with Emperor Isaac Angelos to allow his army to pass through the Byzantine Empire and purchase provisions.[70]

Perhaps it was while she was in Tripoli in spring 1188 that Sybil wrote to Emperor Frederick Barbarossa, warning him that the emperor of Constantinople was in a conspiracy with Saladin:

> To her venerable and most illustrious lord Frederick, by the grace of God most victorious emperor of Rome and most friendly champion of the Holy Cross, Sybil, former queen of Jerusalem, his most humble one, greatly humiliated in God's name. [This form of address indicates that

she wrote before Guy's release from prison, and could even suggest she had given up her claim to the kingdom to her brother-in-law; but it could also simply mean that as Jerusalem had been lost she could no longer be queen of it.]

Spare the subjected and conquer the proud. I, your most humble maid-servant (as I said above) am compelled to tell your highness and supreme excellency of the grief of the whole city and of the disgrace of the holy Christians. For the emperor of Constantinople, persecutor of God's Church, has entered into a conspiracy with Saladin, the seducer and destroyer of the holy Name, against the name of Our Lord Jesus Christ.

I make this known, which I am indeed unable to say without tears: in order to make a perverse concord and reconciliation, Saladin, the aforesaid enemy of Christ, has sent to the Greek emperor and to the persecutor of the holy Name many presents very pleasing to worldly people. For the slaughter and destruction of the Christians wishing to exalt the name of God, he sent 600 measures of poisoned grain and added a very large container of wine, filled with such a malignant poison that when he wanted to test its evil efficacy he called a man, who was killed by the odour alone when the container was opened.

Along with the rest I am compelled to tell my lord another thing. The aforesaid emperor, in order to increase our misfortunes and magnify the destruction of the Christians, does not permit wheat or other necessary victuals to be carried from his country to Jerusalem. Whence the wheat which might be sent by himself and others is also shut up in the city of Constantinople.

However, at the end of this tearful letter, I tell you truthfully that you must believe the most faithful bearer of this letter. For he himself witnesses what he has seen with his own eyes and heard with his own ears. This is the reason that, with my head bowed to the ground and with bent knees, I ask your Magnificence that, as you are the head of the world and a wall for the house of Israel, you should never believe the emperor of Greece.[71]

The letter survives only as a copy in the account of Frederick Barbarossa's crusade by Tageno, dean of Passau cathedral. Tageno indicated that the emperor received the letter in autumn or winter 1189, suggesting that Sybil wrote it in summer 1189. However, the fact that she wrote it in her own name alone rather than in conjunction with her husband Guy suggests that it was written while Guy was still a prisoner: so, before summer 1188. In addition, its strong anti-Byzantine stance would be more appropriate while Sybil was staying with her cousins of Tripoli and Antioch, rather than if she were with Guy *en route* to besiege Acre as she was in the summer of 1189. Sybil's host in Tripoli – the son of Prince Bohemond III of Antioch – would have profoundly distrusted the Byzantines after the murder of his aunt Maria in 1182 by the usurper Andronikos. Even though the Byzantine regime had changed since

1182, if Sybil wrote as a guest of Prince Bohemond's son in Tripoli or of Prince Bohemond in Antioch she would have been writing in a milieu that was suspicious of the Byzantine emperor's influence. Moreover, the interests of her stepmother Maria Komnene may be reflected in the letter – especially if Sybil were staying with her in Tripoli, as Hamilton suggested; Maria would have been hostile towards Isaac Angelos, who had overthrown the Komnenos family.[72]

Sybil's accusations echo the hostility of a letter sent to the West in 1188 or 1189 by French envoys in Constantinople.[73] It was true that the Byzantine emperor had a treaty with Saladin and that Saladin had encouraged him to attack the Franks.[74] On the other hand, Isaac was not hostile to the Latin Christians. He had negotiated with the Pisans and Genoese to compensate them for the damage they had suffered in 1182 and 1187 when their representatives in Constantinople were attacked and killed, and he would later negotiate similarly with the Venetians. His second wife, Margaret (called Maria by the Byzantines), was the daughter of King Béla of Hungary and Agnes of Antioch. He had betrothed his sister Theodora to Conrad of Montferrat – although Conrad apparently left Constantinople before the marriage took place. He employed Latin Christian mercenaries and had relied on Conrad of Montferrat to put down a military rebellion. He responded favourably to King Henry of England's requests for safe passage and markets for his crusade army when it passed through his empire and sent two ministers of his palace to negotiate terms. There is no evidence that he had entered a conspiracy against the Franks: his negotiations with Saladin would have related to the already-existing mosque in Constantinople and Byzantine claims to a protectorate over the Holy Places of Jerusalem.[75] Isaac may have failed to send food aid to the Franks, but at a time of scarcity that grain would be needed in his own empire.

If Sybil had wanted Byzantine aid, she might have preferred aid from Isaac Angelos rather than the Komnenoi, who were more likely to support her younger sister Isabel, a Komnene through her mother. But her letter makes clear that the suzerainty that the Byzantine emperor had exercised over the Frankish rulers of the crusader states in the time of John and Manuel Komnenos had ended and she had no wish to restore it. Her letter in effect warned the Latin emperor that any agreement he might make with the Greek emperor relating to the crusader states would be unacceptable to the Franks.

Meanwhile, her brother-in-law continued to strengthen Tyre. In May 1188, at the castle of Tyre, Conrad issued further privileges to the Pisans. One document confirmed to the Pisans of the *Societas Vermiliorum* all their property at Acre, including property which had belonged to Henry le Buffle and to Joscelin of Edessa. The witnesses included Lord Pagan of Haifa; Lovell, former castellan of Tyre; and Bernard de Templo, *vicecomes* of Tyre. With the Templars (led by Brother Terricus) and the Hospitallers (led by Brother Burellus), and Reynald of Sidon, Walter of Caesarea and all the military men then assembled in Tyre, Conrad also gave a range of property and rights to the members of the Pisan *Societas Vermiliorum* in recognition of their help in defending Tyre.[76]

Giving such liberties and confirming ownership of property in a city that was currently in Saladin's hands, Conrad was acting as if he were the king. With the support of the Templars and Hospitallers, significant members of the nobility, two of the powerful Italian mercantile cities, and smaller trading powers, he was a power to be reckoned with. His propaganda campaign in the West would soon bring a large force of warriors to the Holy Land, enabling him to lead an effective fightback against Saladin.

There was one obvious action that Saladin could take to thwart Conrad by shattering his support base: he released King Guy from prison. He also released Gerard de Ridefort, master of the Templars, and Marquis William V of Montferrat.

Reunion with Guy: taking the war to the enemy

The *Itinerarium peregrinorum* recorded that Guy had to promise Saladin in exchange for his release that he would abjure the kingdom and cross the sea into exile, but the clergy of the kingdom judged that an oath given under duress is invalid and absolved him. This author described Guy meeting Sybil at the island of Arwad (or Ruad), just offshore from Tortosa, at the beginning of May 1188 in an emotional meeting of kisses, tearful embraces and joy at their escape from the disasters that had befallen them. They then spent a year in Antioch and Tripoli, gathering an army of crusaders who had come to help recover Jerusalem.[77] As regards his oath, Guy could argue that he had crossed the sea by going to Arwad to meet Sybil.

According to the *Chronique d'Ernoul* and the *Estoire de Eracles*, it was Sybil herself who prompted Guy's release. Saladin had left Damascus in mid-May to campaign in the region around Tripoli, capturing fortresses and settlements, but he did not capture Tripoli. It is unclear from the Muslim commentators whether he intended to besiege that strongly defended city or only set out to weaken it by capturing its hinterland and surrounding fortresses. In any case, on 1 July he set off north towards Tortosa.[78] In contrast, the *Chronique d'Ernoul* depicts Saladin undertaking a full siege of Tripoli, which was relieved by the ships sent by King William of Sicily under his admiral Margaritus and troops sent by Conrad of Montferrat from Tyre. As increasing numbers of ships arrived to relieve Tripoli, Saladin decided to withdraw. However, before he left, Sybil – who was in Tripoli – demanded that he should keep the undertakings he had given regarding her husband when he departed from Ascalon. Saladin replied that he would so do willingly and sent to Damascus with instructions that the king and ten knights, such as he chose from the prison, be escorted to Tortosa.[79] Once again, the *Chronique d'Ernoul* depicted Saladin as the chivalrous and generous lord who acted to aid a lady in distress.

The *Chronique d'Ernoul* stated that Saladin also ordered his people to release Marquis William of Montferrat, take him to Tyre, and present him to his son Conrad. Those released with the king included the master of the Temple, Aimery the constable (the king's brother), and the marshal of the kingdom of Jerusalem. Saladin then also released Humphrey of Toron to his mother, the widow of Prince Reynald of Kerak.[80]

The actual timing of these releases is unclear. Imād al-Dīn had inserted into his narrative of events early in 1188 an account of how after Saladin's capture of Jerusalem the queen had joined Stephanie de Milly, lady of Kerak, and her daughter-in-law Isabel in pleading with Saladin for the release of King Guy and Humphrey of Toron and that Saladin had agreed to release Humphrey in return for the surrender of Kerak and Montreal (Shaubak) – but their defenders had refused to surrender the fortresses.[81] Kerak did not surrender until November 1188, and according to Bahā' al-Dīn ibn Shaddād, Humphrey was then released.[82] The *Itinerarium peregrinorum*, however, stated that Humphrey was not released until Montreal surrendered (at the end of April or early May 1189), and this was also implied by 'Imād al-Dīn.[83] The Muslim commentators do not record when King Guy and Master Gerard de Ridefort were released, implying that it was shortly after the surrender of Jerusalem in October 1187.[84] If the master of the Templars was released while Saladin was besieging Tortosa, as claimed by the *Chronique d'Ernoul*, it is strange that he was able to go immediately to join his brothers in the Templars' tower at Tortosa and defy Saladin as described by 'Imād al-Dīn.[85]

Having captured the town of Tortosa but not the Templars' tower, Saladin continued his march north towards Jabala.[86] As the army passed along the narrow coastal road below the Hospitallers' castle of Marqab it was attacked by the fleet sent by King William of Sicily under admiral Margaritus, which was patrolling the coast. Saladin's army managed to pass and reached Jabala on 15 July 1188; the fortress surrendered to Saladin on the following day.[87] Saladin progressed up the coast, capturing the port of Latakia and a series of fortresses. He could then have besieged Antioch, but instead went north and besieged the Templar castles of Darbsak and Baghras (or Gaston), which surrendered on 26 September 1188. Saladin could now have besieged Antioch, but instead Antioch's leaders negotiated an eight-month truce, agreeing to surrender after this period if no relief forces had arrived from the West.[88]

The *Itinerarium peregrinorum*, written within three years of these events, stated that King Guy went to Antioch after his release and meeting with Sybil at Arwad Island. However, the edited, expanded and continued version of this work, probably written by Richard de Templo and known as the *Itinerarium peregrinorum et gesta regis Ricardi*, as well as the *Estoire de la Guerre Sainte*, probably written by Ambroise, claimed further that the prince of Antioch specifically invited him.[89] If this were true, it would have been in hopes that Guy would attract military aid to the principality to help the fight against Saladin. One of the arrivals in the East was Guy's older brother Geoffrey de Lusignan, who brought additional warriors with him. Ambroise and Richard de Templo agreed that Geoffrey de Lusignan went first to Tyre, but as Conrad would not admit him to the city he came on to Tripoli, where he found his brother.[90] These sources do not record whether Sybil had accompanied Guy, but as she had previously been in Tripoli and possibly Antioch,

Prince Bohemond and his sons were her cousins, and she and her daughters were later with Guy at the siege of Acre, it is reasonable to assume that she travelled with Guy throughout.

Guy's release considerably undermined Conrad of Montferrat's position, as many who had accepted Conrad as *de facto* regent of the kingdom regarded his regency as ended when the king was released. In a newsletter to Archbishop Baldwin of Canterbury which Conrad wrote on 20 September, probably in 1188, he complained that because he had protected Tyre from Saladin, Guy de Lusignan the former king of Jerusalem, the Templars and the magnates of the kingdom of Jerusalem envied and disparaged him and deprived him of resources. (Guy would be 'former king of Jerusalem' for the same reason that Sybil was 'former queen': as Jerusalem had been lost to Saladin, Guy could no longer be its king.) The master of the Temple had taken from him the alms that King Henry had sent to aid the Holy Land. However, the Hospitallers were still helping him to defend Tyre with their share of the king of England's alms and their own resources. He was sending to the archbishop Master Bandanus (or Bandinus), his chancellor and trusted secretary, and John, a doughty knight and confidant. Baldwin should acknowledge them as his *speciales legatos* and not hesitate to believe what they told him on Conrad's behalf.[91]

Conrad wrote on similar lines to Emperor Frederick Barbarossa, asking him to hurry up and come to the East because the Muslims were terrified of his coming. He complained about the actions of the former king Guy and about a Templar who had done him much more damage than the Muslims and had taken from him the silver which the king of England had sent to help the Christians. The letter may have prompted Frederick to hasten his preparations.[92]

During the winter the castles of Kerak, Safad and Belvoir (Kaukab) surrendered to Saladin's besieging forces; Montreal would surrender in late spring 1189. Meanwhile, Antioch had been reinforced by the Sicilian fleet under Margaritus. Saladin deferred renewing his attack on Antioch while he negotiated with Reynald of Sidon, who had offered to surrender his castle of Beaufort (or al-Shaqīf) on certain conditions.[93] While these negotiations were in train, Saladin was informed that King Guy had led an army to Tyre. According to Bahā' al-Dīn ibn Shaddād, Guy tried to gain admission to the city, but Conrad retorted that he was the lieutenant of the kings across the sea and he could not give it up to Guy without their permission. (As the Genoese 'Brevis Historia' indicated, these 'kings' were the emperor and the kings of France, England and Sicily.) 'Imād al-Dīn had heard something similar about Conrad's reaction to Guy's arrival, and many of the Latin Christian sources confirm that Conrad refused to admit Guy to Tyre. The *Chronique d'Ernoul* specifically states that both the king and the queen came to Tyre and describes their joint dismay at Conrad's refusal to admit them to the city.[94] Certainly if Sybil had believed that her brother-in-law was acting as her regent while she was in safely at Tripoli with her daughters, gathering troops for the fight back against Saladin, she would have been taken aback by his refusal to admit her into Tyre and his denial of her authority over the city.

Sybil versus Saladin (1187–1189)   151

The Latin Christian sources depict a stand-off which Guy resolved by deciding to lead his small army to besiege Acre. The *Itinerarium peregrinorum* and Ambroise state that Guy was at Tyre for four months before setting off for Acre (which would have meant that he was camped outside Tyre from late April to late August), whereas the *Chronique d'Ernoul* has Guy immediately sending a messenger to Tripoli to the knights of King William of Sicily instructing them to bring their fleet to Acre because he was going to besiege it.[95]

These sources indicated that the Christian forces were divided. A letter from 'Theobald the prefect and Peter Leonis' to the pope, included by Ralph of Diceto in his work, states that the king of Jerusalem, the Templars, Hospitallers, archbishop of the Pisans and many Pisans began the siege of Acre against the will of the lord marquis (that is, Conrad of Montferrat, although in fact he was not yet marquis as his father was still alive) and the archbishop of Ravenna and of other Christians. The *Itinerarium peregrinorum* stated that the Pisans rebelled against Conrad and came to join the king; Ambroise agreed that they joined him but did not mention a revolt and added that noble Germans and the Tiberias brothers also came out of Tyre and joined the king. The Pisans must have decided that they should support the crowned king, but the loss of Pisan financial and naval assistance was a great blow to Conrad after all his efforts to win their support. Roger of Howden recorded that King Guy had the support of the Templars and Hospitallers, as well as all the Christians of the region who had scattered from fear of the infidel, and he began the siege of Acre on the advice of Patriarch Eraclius.[96]

So far as the Muslim commentators could judge, the Franks and crusaders were a far more unified force than the Latin Christian commentators believed. Bahā' al-Dīn ibn Shaddād and 'Imād al-Dīn concurred that after their initial disagreement the king and Conrad agreed to work together against the Muslims. Ibn al-Athīr also reported that Saladin believed that the king had come to terms with Conrad and that they proposed to unite their forces against Saladin. At the same time, Saladin did not want to move his army because he hoped to obtain the surrender of Beaufort. Eventually he realised that Reynald of Sidon was playing for time with no intention of surrendering the castle, whereupon he had Reynald arrested and sent him as a prisoner to Damascus. Meanwhile, the Franks undertook a number of engagements against Saladin's forces, which culminated in their army moving off to besiege Acre.[97]

The siege of Acre began on 28 August 1189, and would continue for nearly two years.[98] Roger of Howden recorded that King Guy lodged with the queen and their daughters on 'Thoron', the ancient tell (Tel 'Akko) to the east of the city, with the sea on one side and the mound top on the other.[99] Guy's brothers Geoffrey and Aimery were encamped near him.[100]

Meanwhile in Europe, the kings whom Conrad claimed to represent had been planning their expeditions to the East. Emperor Frederick Barbarossa set out on his crusade early in May 1189.[101] The plans of Kings Henry II of England and Philip II of France, and Count Richard of Poitou, were delayed by war followed by the death of Henry II on 6 July 1189 and the succession of Richard as king of England. King William of Sicily died in November that year.[102] Some groups of French crusaders set off before the kings: Stephen of Sancerre, Sybil's former betrothed, and his brother Theobald of Blois arrived in the summer of 1190 with their nephew Count Henry II of Champagne.[103] Sybil's cousin Philip of Flanders and her former betrothed Duke Hugh III of Burgundy travelled with Philip II of France and would not reach the East until after Easter 1191, after Sybil's death.[104] Until the arrival of the kings across the sea, there was no hope of a resolution to the dispute between Conrad and Guy.

Notes

1 Earlier versions of this chapter were published as: Helen J. Nicholson, 'Queen Sybil of Jerusalem as a military leader', in *Von Hamburg nach Java. Studien zur mittelalterlichen, neuen und digitalen Geschichte zu Ehren von Jürgen Sarnowsky*, ed. Jochen Burgtorf, Christian Hoffart and Sebastian Kubon (Göttingen, 2020), pp. 265–276; and Helen J. Nicholson, 'Defending Jerusalem: Sybil of Jerusalem as a military leader', *Medieval Warfare Magazine*, 9.4 (Oct/Nov 2019), 6–13.
2 For some of these problems of interpretation see Kane, 'Between parson and poet'; Kane, 'Wolf's Hair'; Edbury, 'Ernoul, *Eracles*, and the Collapse of the Kingdom of Jerusalem'; Nicholson, 'The Construction of a Primary Source'.
3 *L'Estoire de la Guerre Sainte*, pp. 406–415 (lines 2488–2786); *The History of the Holy War*, 1: 40–45, 2: 67–71 (lines 2484–2781); 'Versus ex libro magistri Ricardi', 460–474 (lines 101–607); 'Monachi Florentini', pp. cvi–cviii (lines 1–58).
4 *Chronique de Michel le Syrien, patriarche Jacobite d'Antioche (1166–1199)*, ed. and trans. J.-B. Chabot, 5 vols (Paris, 1899–1924), 3: 403–05, 407; Weltecke, Dorothea, 'Michael the Great (the Syrian, the Elder), in *Encyclopedia of the Medieval Chronicle*, ed. Graeme Dunphy, 2 vols (Leiden, 2010), 2: 1110–11.
5 Sirarpie der Nersessian, 'The Armenian Chronicle of the Constable Smpad or of the "Royal Historian"', *Dumbarton Oaks Papers*, 13 (1959), 141,143–68, at 150–53.
6 *ULKJ* 3: 1339–46 (nos 769, 770, 771); Jacoby, 'Conrad, Marquis of Montferrat', pp. 190–191, 194–196, 203–204. In August Count Raymond also confirmed the Pisans' rights in his own lands: *RRH*, p. 176, no. 662.
7 Lyons and Jackson, *Saladin*, pp. 267–268; Phillips, *The Life and Legend*, pp. 187–188; *La Continuation de Guillaume de Tyr*, p. 56 (section 44). This story does not appear in the *Chronique d'Ernoul*, p. 174 (ch. 15), or 'L'Estoire de Eracles Empereur', p. 68 (Bk 23 ch. 45).
8 '*Encore estoit li roine, li feme al roi Guion, en Jherusalem*': *Chronique d'Ernoul*, p. 175 (ch. 13); 'L'Estoire de Eracles Empereur', p. 70 (Bk 23 ch. 46).
9 Ralph of Coggeshall, *Chronicon anglicanum*, p. 22; *LFWT*, p. 74 (Bk 1 ch. 15).
10 See above, Introduction, pp. 000–000.
11 *WT* 2: 720, 761, 838 (Bk 16 ch. 4, Bk 17 ch. 1, Bk 18 ch. 19); Buck, 'Women in the Principality of Antioch', p. 101.
12 Some examples in *An Arab-Syrian Gentleman and Warrior in the Period of the Crusades: Memoirs of Usāmah ibn-Munqidh*, trans. Philip K. Hitti (repr. Princeton, 1987), pp. 158–159; Usama ibn Munqidh, *The Book of Contemplation: Islam and the Crusades*, trans. Paul M. Cobb (London, 2008), pp. 141–142.

13 Edbury, 'Women and the Customs of the High Court of Jerusalem', p. 286.
14 Asbridge, 'Alice of Antioch', p. 31.
15 *Chronique d'Ernoul*, pp. 103–105 (ch. 9); Barber, *The Crusader States*, p. 419 n.108.
16 Barber, *The Crusader States*, pp. 299, 301, 307; *Chronique d'Ernoul*, p. 174 (ch. 13); 'L'Estoire de Eracles Empereur', p. 68 (Bk 23 ch. 45); *Continuation de Guillaume de Tyr*, p. 56 (section 44); Ralph of Coggeshall, *Chronicon anglicanum*, p. 22).
17 Ligato, *Sibilla regina crociata*, p. 206; citing Sylvia Schein, 'Rulers and Ruled: Women in the Crusader Period', in *Knights of the Holy Land: The Crusader Kingdom of Jerusalem*, ed. Silvia Rozenberg (Jerusalem, 1999), pp. 61–67, at pp. 66–67; Sylvia Schein, 'Women in Medieval Colonial Society: The Latin Kingdom of Jerusalem in the Twelfth Century', in *Gendering the Crusades*, ed. Susan B, Edgington and Sarah Lambert (Cardiff, 2001), pp. 140–153, at p. 147, citing 'L'Estoire de Eracles Empereur', p. 68 (Bk 23 ch. 46); see also 'Libellus', pp. 174–175, 178–179 (XVIII, XIX); IA, p. 326 (vol. 11.540); BD, p. 75 (section 79); 'Imād, pp. 35–36 – none of which mention Maria Komnene defending Nablus.
18 Lyons and Jackson, *Saladin*, pp. 267–271; Phillips, *The Life and Legend*, pp. 188–189; Lewis, *Counts of Tripoli*, pp. 270–271.
19 IA, pp. 328–329 (vol. 11.544). For the timing of Conrad of Montferrat's arrival at Tyre – late July or early August 1187 – see Jacoby, 'Conrad, Marquis of Montferrat', p. 190.
20 Hamilton, *Leper King*, p. 214; Harris, *Byzantium and the Crusades*, pp. 140, 162; Marianne McLeod Gilchrist, 'Getting away with murder: Runciman and Conrad of Montferrat's career in Constantinople', *The Mediæval Journal*, 2.1 (2012), 15–36, at pp. 18–21; Jacoby, 'Conrad, Marquis of Montferrat', pp. 190, 204; 'Regni Iherosolymitani Brevis Historia', pp. 144–145; IA, pp. 328–329 (vol. 11.544); *IP* 1, pp. 261–262 (Bk 1 ch. 7).
21 '*vir quidem singularis industrie et ad quevis aggredienda strenuus*': *IP* 1, p. 262 (Bk 1 ch. 7).
22 BD, p. 91 (section 98).
23 '*unanimiter ciuitatem Tyri in eius custodiam posuerunt usque ad aduentum alicuius ex istis quatuor coronatis*': 'Regni Iherosolymitani Brevis Historia', p. 145.
24 '*cui tamen civitas eo tenore commissa fuerat, ut regi et regni heredibus redderent*': *IP* 1, p. 305 (Bk 1 ch. 26).
25 *Chronique d'Ernoul*, p. 178 (ch. 16); IA, p. 328 (11.543); Lyons and Jackson, *Saladin*, p. 269; 'L'Estoire de Eracles Empereur', p. 72 (Bk 23 ch. 47).
26 *Chronique d'Ernoul*, pp. 179, 182–183 (ch. 16); 'L'Estoire de Eracles Empereur', pp. 73, 76–78 (Bk 23 chs 48–51). The Lyon *Eracles* gives a slightly different account: *La Continuation de Guillaume de Tyr*, pp. 59, 61–62 (sections 46, 48–49). See also *IP* 1, pp. 262–263 (Bk 1 ch. 8); *LFWT*, pp. 73–74 (Bk 1 ch. 15): the Latin continuation combines the account in the *Itinerarium peregrinorum* with some details in the *Chronique d'Ernoul*.
27 'L'Estoire de Eracles Empereur', p. 68 (Bk 23 ch. 46); The Lyon *Eracles*, in contrast, stated that Balian intended to take his wife and their children to Tripoli: *Continuation de Guillaume de Tyr*, p. 57 (section 45).
28 IA, pp. 329–330 (11.545); 'Imād al-Dīn in Abū Shāma, pp. 312–313; *IP* 1, p. 263 (Bk 1 ch. 8); 'Libellus', pp. 186–191 (XXI); *Chronique d'Ernoul*, pp. 184–183 (ch. 16); 'L'Estoire de Eracles Empereur', pp. 78–78 (Bk 23 ch. 51); *La Continuation de Guillaume de Tyr*, p. 62 (section 49); Lyons and Jackson, *Saladin*, pp. 271–272; Phillips, *The Life and Legend*, p. 188.

154   *Sybil versus Saladin (1187–1189)*

29 Ralph of Coggeshall, *Chronicon anglicanum*, p. 22: '*Regina vero, Guidonis regis uxor, recepit se cum familia et duabus filiabus suis in civitate Aschalona, et eam munivit victualibus et bellatoribus; sed postmodum anno sequenti tradidit civitatem Salaadino pro redemptione mariti sui, et sic liberavit eum a carcere Saladini*'; *LFWT*, p. 74 (Bk 1 ch. 15): '*Regina enim cum filiabus suis illic erat, et urbem, quantum temporum patiebatur angustia et moles miseriarum, viris, armis et victualibus communierat*'.
30 '*Eodem anno Sibylla regina Jerusalem dedit Saladino Scalonam pro redemptione Widonis de Lezinun, regis Jerusalem, mariti sui*': Roger of Howden, *Gesta*, 2: 93; virtually the same words in Roger of Howden, *Chronica*, 3: 20.
31 Ralph of Coggeshall, *Chronicon anglicanum*, p. 22.
32 Roger of Howden, *Gesta*, 2: 93; Roger of Howden, *Chronica*, 3: 20, under 1189.
33 *LFWT*, pp. 74, 78, 89–90 (Bk 1 ch. 15, Bk 2 chs 1, 9).
34 William Stubbs in Roger of Howden, *Chronica*, 3: cvi, n. 5.
35 *IP* 1, p. 263 (Bk 1 ch. 8); *Chronique d'Ernoul*, p. 185 (ch. 16); 'L'Estoire de Eracles Empereur', p. 79 (Bk 23 ch. 51); *La Continuation de Guillaume de Tyr*, p. 62 (section 49).
36 'Libellus', pp. 186–187; Lyons and Jackson, *Saladin*, p. 272. Gerard de Ridefort was free by July 1188: 'Imād, p. 124.
37 *Chronique d'Ernoul*, p. 185 (ch. 16); 'L'Estoire de Eracles Empereur', p. 79 (Bk 23 ch. 51); *La Continuation de Guillaume de Tyr*, p. 62 (section 49).
38 Margaret Jubb, *The Legend of Saladin in Western Literature and Historiography* (Lewiston, 2000), pp. 19–31, 44–47.
39 'Imād al-Dīn in Abū Shāma, pp. 332–333; IA, p. 333 (11.550).
40 IA, p. 330 (11.546).
41 IA, p. 331 (11.547); 'Libellus', pp. 198–199 (XXIII); Lyons and Jackson, *Saladin*, p. 273; Phillips, *The Life and Legend*, p. 190.
42 *IP* 1, p. 264 (Bk 1 ch. 9); 'Libellus', pp. 198–199, 204–205 (XXIII); *Chronique d'Ernoul*, pp. 175–176, 215 (chs 15, 18); 'L'Estoire de Eracles Empereur', pp. 70–71, 86 (Bk 23 chs 46, 56).
43 IA, p. 330 (11.546–47); 'Imād al-Dīn in Abū Shāma, pp. 320–321; BD, p. 77 (81).
44 IA, p. 330 (11.546) (including quotations); 'Imād al-Dīn in Abū Shāma, p. 330.
45 IA, pp. 332–334 (11.548–49); 'Imād al-Dīn in Abū Shāma, pp. 327–329.
46 *Chronique d'Ernoul*, pp. 175–176, 186–187, 214–231 (chs 15, 16, 18); 'L'Estoire de Eracles Empereur', pp. 70–71, 81, 85–87, 88–98, 100 (Bk 23 chs 46, 54, 56, 59–62, 64); *La Continuation de Guillaume de Tyr*, pp. 57, 63, 65–73 (sections 45, 49, 52–59).
47 'Libellus', pp. 204–213 (XXIII–IV); paraphrased translation from pp. 210, 212. For Renier of Nablus and Thomas son of *Johannes Patricius*, burgher of Jerusalem see Edbury, *John of Ibelin*, pp. 18, 145–146; Kane, 'Wolf's Hair', 110–111; Keagan Brewer and James H. Kane, 'Introduction' in *The Conquest of the Holy Land by Salāh al-Dīn*, ed. and trans. Brewer and Kane, pp. 1–107, at 41–42 and n. 188; *ULKJ* 1: 337, 361, 435, 2: 575, 610, 632 (nos 150, 179, 236, 333, 349, 363); *Cartulaire général*, 1: 341, 363, 364 (nos 495, 530, 531).
48 Ralph of Diceto, 'Ymagines historiarum', 2: 56.
49 *IP* 1, p. 263, 264 (Bk 1 chs 8, 9); *LFWT*, p. 75 (Bk 1 ch. 16).
50 *IP* 1, p. 265 (Bk 1 ch. 9); 'Libellus', pp. 208–209 (XXIV); Kane, 'Wolf's Hair', 112.
51 Julia Barrow, 'Chester's earliest regatta? Edgar's Dee-rowing revisited', in: *Early Medieval Europe*, 10.1 (2001), 81–93; Paul Dalton, 'Sites and Occasions of

Peacemaking in England and Normandy, c. 900–c. 1150', *Haskins Society Journal*, 16 (2005), 12–26.
52 BD, pp. 193–194; cited in Thomas Asbridge, 'Talking to the Enemy: the role and purpose of negotiations between Saladin and Richard the Lionheart during the Third Crusade', *Journal of Medieval History*, 39.3 (2013), 275–296, at p. 279.
53 BD, pp. 77–78 (sections 81–82); IA, pp. 332–334 (11.549–553); 'Imād al-Dīn in Abū Shāma, pp. 330, 333–334; *IP* 1, p. 265 (Bk 1 ch. 9).
54 *RRH*, p. 176 (no. 663), RRR no. 1247, accessed 23.04.21.
55 BD, p. 125 (sections 136–37) (D. S. Richards's translation).
56 Barber, *Crusader States*, pp. 324–325; Mayer, 'Henry II of England', 737–738. For 'Audita Tremendi' see *Crusade and Christendom: Annotated Documents in Translation from Innocent III to the Fall of Acre, 1187–1201*, ed. Jessalynn Bird, Edward Peters, and James M. Powell (Philadelphia, 2013), pp. 4–9.
57 *IP* 1, pp. 276–277 (Bk 1 ch. 17), and note 2, citing Giraldus Cambrensis, 'De principis instructione liber', in *Giraldi Cambrensis Opera*, 8 vols, ed. James F. Dimock, J. S. Brewer, and George F. Warner, Rolls Series 21 (London, 1861–91), 8: 239.
58 Barber, *Crusader States*, pp. 324–325.
59 IA, p. 333 (11.550); similarly in 'Imād al-Dīn in Abū Shāma, p. 332.
60 *IP* 1, p. 23 (Bk 1 ch. 10).
61 For brief descriptions of both Antioch and Tripoli, see Boas, *Crusader Archaeology*, p. 42.
62 *ULKJ* 2: 859–77 (nos 519, 520, 521, 522); Jacoby, 'Conrad of Montferrat', pp. 196–199. On Conrad's charters and Bandinus see Mayer, *Die Kanzlei*, 2: 434–91.
63 Jacoby, 'Conrad of Montferrat', pp. 191–192, 204–205, 211–212; Ralph of Diceto, 'Ymagines historiarum', 2: 61; Roger of Howden, *Gesta*, 2: 41; trans. Edbury, *The Conquest of Jerusalem and the Third Crusade*, pp. 166, 169 (nos 5b, 6a); 'Otoboni scribae Annales', in *MGH SS*, vol. 18, ed. Georg Heinrich Pertz (Hanover, 1863), pp. 96–114, at p. 101, line 50. For King Henry's money helping the defence of Tyre see also *IP* 1, p. 269 (Bk 1 ch. 12).
64 *LFWT*, p. 90 (Bk 2 ch. 9).
65 Hamilton, 'Women in the Crusader States', p. 172.
66 'L'Estoire de Eracles Empereur', pp. 120–121 (Bk 24 chs 11–12).
67 Lyons and Jackson, *Saladin*, pp. 279–283; Phillips, *The Life and Legend*, pp. 206–209; *IP* 1, pp. 266–269 (Bk 1 ch. 10); *Chronique d'Ernoul*, p. 183 (ch. 16); 'Estoire de Eracles Empereur', pp. 77–78 (Bk 23 ch. 50); *Continuation de Guillaume de Tyr*, pp. 61–62 (section 49); trans. in *Conquest of Jerusalem*, pp. 53–54.
68 'Otoboni scribae Annales', p. 102, lines 1–4; *RRH*, pp. 178–179, 181 (nos 669, 670, 676 note 1), RRR nos 1255, 1256, accessed 26 April 2021.
69 Ralph of Diceto, 'Ymagines historiarum', 2: 51–54; Roger of Howden, *Gesta*, 2: 33, 38–39; William of Newburgh, *Historia rerum anglicarum*, 1: 272 (Bk 3 ch. 23); *RRH*, p. 180 (no. 673); RRR no. 1254, accessed 26 April 2021; Bradbury, *Philip Augustus*, pp. 77–78; Warren, *Henry II*, pp. 607–608; Rhodes, *The Crown and the Cross*, p. 147; Peter W. Edbury, 'Preaching the Crusade in Wales', in *England and Germany in the High Middle Ages. In Honour of Karl J. Leyser*, ed. Alfred Haverkamp and Hanna Vollrath (Oxford, 1996), pp. 221–233; Hurlock, *Britain, Ireland and the Crusades*, 41–44, 56–58, 106–8. For those who joined the crusade see now Stephen Bennett, *Elite Participation in the Third Crusade* (Woodbridge, 2021).

70 *The Crusade of Frederick Barbarossa: The History of the Expedition of the Emperor Frederick and Related Texts*, trans. G. A. Loud, Crusade Texts in Translation 19 (Farnham, 2010), pp. 16–18, 47–48.

71 Slightly adapted from the translation in *Letters of the Crusaders*, trans. Munro, pp. 21–22; Latin text in 'Tagenonis decani Pataviensis', p. 410. Summaries in *RRH*, p. 182 (no. 681); *RRR* no. 1267. Accessed 28 April 2021 (both dating the letter to summer 1189).

72 Hamilton, 'Women in the Crusader States', p. 172.

73 The report from the envoys that King Philip of France had sent to the Emperor Isaac of Constantinople was dated by Diceto to 1189 and by Roger of Howden to 1188: Ralph of Diceto, 'Ymagines historiarum', 2: 58–60; Roger of Howden, *Gesta*, 2: 51–53; *RRH*, p. 183 (no. 688), (date given as November 1189); *RRR* no. 1274, accessed 28 April 2021 (date given as c. 1189). The St Albans chronicler Roger of Wendover later combined the French envoys' letter with a letter from Conrad of Montferrat to Archbishop Baldwin of Canterbury written in around September 1188: *Rogeri de Wendover Liber qui dicitur Flores Historiarum ab anno domini MCLIV, annoque Henrici Anglorum regis secundi primo; The Flowers of History by Roger of Wendover from the Year of Our Lord 1154, and the first year of Henry the second, king of the English*, ed. Henry G. Hewlett, 3 vols, Rolls Series 84 (London, 1886), 1: 153–54. In fact Conrad's letter did not discuss Emperor Isaac.

74 Lyons and Jackson, *Saladin*, pp. 251–252.

75 Harris, *Byzantium and the Crusades*, pp. 139–141; Jacoby, 'Conrad of Montferrat', p. 215; Ralph of Diceto, 'Ymagines historiarum', 2: 53.

76 *ULKJ* 2: 877–85 (nos 523, 524); Jacoby, 'Conrad of Montferrat', pp. 199–200.

77 *IP* 1, pp. 268–269, 304 (Bk 1 chs 10, 11, 25).

78 Lyons and Jackson, *Saladin*, pp. 286–287; Barber, *The Crusader States*, p. 316.

79 *Chronique d'Ernoul*, pp. 251–253 (ch. 21); 'L'Estoire de Eracles Empereur', pp. 120–221 (Bk 24 chs 11–12).

80 *Chronique d'Ernoul*, p. 253 (ch. 21); 'L'Estoire de Eracles Empereur', p. 121 (Bk 24 chs 11–12).

81 'Imād, pp. 105–107.

82 Lyons and Jackson, *Saladin*, p. 291; Phillips, *The Life and Legend*, p. 215; BD, p. 88.

83 *IP* 1, p. 275 (Bk 1 ch. 15); 'Imād, p. 107. Saladin received the news that Shaubak had fallen on 5 May 1189: 'Imād al-Dīn in Abū Shāma, p. 397; Lyons and Jackson, *Saladin*, p. 295.

84 'Imād, p. 106; IA, p. 60 (vol. 12.28); BD, p. 91 (section 98).

85 'Imād, pp. 124–125.

86 'Imād, pp. 124–125.

87 'Imād, pp. 125–127; Roger of Howden, *Gesta*, 2: 54; Lyons and Jackson, *Saladin*, p. 287.

88 Lyons and Jackson, *Saladin*, pp. 288–291; Phillips, *The Life and Legend*, p. 213; *IP* 1, pp. 269–270 (Bk 1 ch. 13).

89 *IP* 1, p. 269; *IP* 2, pp. 25–26 (Bk 1 ch. 11); *L'Estoire de la Guerre Sainte*, pp. 411–412 (lines 2669–2686), and see pp. 65–92 on authorship; *The History of the Holy War*, 1: 43 (lines 2664–2680), 2: 70.

90 Ralph of Diceto, 'Ymagines historiarum', 2: 54–55; Roger of Howden, *Gesta*, 2: 34; *IP* 1, p. 305; *IP* 2, pp. 26, 60 (Bk 1 chs 11, 25); *L'Estoire de la Guerre Sainte*, pp. 411–412, 414 (lines 2669–2686, 2751–2752); *The History of the Holy War*, 1: 43, 44 (lines 2664–2680, 2746–2748), 2: 70, 71; Vasselot, 'A Crusader Lineage', 110.

91 Ralph of Diceto, 'Ymagines historiarum', 2: 60–62, trans. Edbury, *The Conquest of Jerusalem and the Third Crusade*, pp. 168–169 (no. 6a); *RRH*, p. 181 (no. 676); RRR no. 1260, accessed 27 April 2021.

92 'Continuatio I', in *Chronica Regia Coloniensis (Annales maximi Coloniensis)*, ed. Georg Waitz, Scriptores Rerum Germanicarum in usum scholarum ex Monumentis Germaniae Historicis recusi (Hanover, 1880), pp. 128–169, at p. 141 (section 38); *RRH*, p. 181 (no. 676), note 1.

93 Lyons and Jackson, *Saladin*, pp. 291–293, 295–296; Phillips, *The Life and Legend*, pp. 217–218; *IP* 1, pp. 271–272 (Bk 1 ch. 14).

94 BD, p. 91 (section 98); 'Regni Iherosolymitani Brevis Historia', p. 145; 'Imād, p. 163; *IP* 1, pp. 305–306; *Chronique d'Ernoul*, pp. 256–257 (ch. 22); 'Estoire de Eracles Empereur', pp. 123–124 (Bk 24 ch. 13); *IP* 2, p. 60 (Bk 1 ch. 26); *L'Estoire de la Guerre Sainte*, pp. 412–413 (lines 2705–2728); *The History of the Holy War*, 1: 43–44 (lines 2700–2723), 2: 70–71; Roger of Howden, *Gesta*, 2: 93; Roger of Howden, *Chronica*, 3: 20; William of Newburgh, *Historia rerum anglicarum*, 1: 265 (Bk 3 ch. 20).

95 *IP* 1, pp. 305–307; *Chronique d'Ernoul*, p. 257 (ch. 22); 'Estoire de Eracles Empereur', pp. 124–125 (Bk 24 chs 13–14); *IP* 2, pp. 60–62 (Bk 1 ch. 26); *L'Estoire de la Guerre Sainte*, pp. 413–414 (lines 2743–2755); *The History of the Holy War*, 1: 43 (lines 2739–2750), 2: 71.

96 Ralph of Diceto, 'Ymagines historiarum', 2: 70; *IP* 1, pp. 306–307; *IP* 2, pp. 61–62 (Bk 1 ch. 26); *L'Estoire de la Guerre Sainte*, p. 413 (lines 2729–2742); *The History of the Holy War*, 1: 44 (lines 2724–2737), 2: 71; Roger of Howden, *Gesta*, 2: 93; Roger of Howden, *Chronica*, 3: 20; Jacoby, 'Conrad of Montferrat', p. 200.

97 'Imād, pp. 163–168; BD, pp. 91–97 (sections 98–104); IA, pp. 360–365 (12.27–35).

98 *IP* 1, pp. 306–307 (Bk 1 ch. 26).

99 '*Gwydo rex Jerosolimitanus cum regina et filiabus suis hospitatus est in Thorono subtus versus mare, versus caput montis*': Roger of Howden, *Gesta*, 2: 95; similar in his *Chronica*, 3: 22.

100 Ralph of Diceto, 'Ymagines historiarum', 2: 80.

101 'The History of the Expedition of the Emperor Frederick', in *The Crusade of Frederick Barbarossa: The History of the Expedition of the Emperor Frederick and Related Texts*, trans. G. A. Loud, Crusade Texts in Translation 19 (Farnham, 2010), pp. 33–134, at p. 47.

102 Warren, *Henry II*, pp. 621–626; Bradbury, *Philip Augustus*, p. 77; *IP* 1, p. 278 (Bk 1 ch. 17).

103 *L'Estoire de la Guerre Sainte*, p. 437 (lines 3509–3514); *The History of the Holy War*, 1: 56 (lines 3504–3508), 2: 81 and note 256;

104 Rhodes, *The Crown and the Cross*, pp. 162–165; *IP* 2, p. 213 (Bk 3 ch. 4); *L'Estoire de la Guerre Sainte*, p. 470 (lines 4527–4532); *The History of the Holy War*, 1: 73 (lines 4521–4526), 2: 94.

8 The siege of Acre and the end of the reign (1189–1190)

The siege of Acre

None of the surviving sources record Sybil playing any military role in the siege of Acre: she did not take part in military councils or muster troops.[1] However, she and Guy issued a number of documents during the course of the siege, at least one of which confirmed rights earlier conferred by Conrad of Montferrat as lord of Tyre.[2] These documents asserted their position as rulers of the whole of the kingdom, and tried to ensure the loyalty of those to whom they granted property, rights and privileges. Like Conrad's donations, they were so generous that it is questionable whether they would all have been carried out after the crusade.[3] In fact that situation did not arise, as none of these three survived as ruler of the kingdom until the end of the Third Crusade.

In September 1189 Conrad was still at Tyre, giving a house to a Genoese burgher who had served him at Tyre in a document witnessed first by Ansaldo Bonvicino, Conrad's Genoese counsellor who had accompanied him from Constantinople in the summer of 1187. Ansaldo was followed by Oberto Malocello, from a prominent Genoese family, and three other witnesses not otherwise known.[4] However, the letter from Theobald the prefect and Peter Leonis informed the pope that seven days from the end of September Conrad and the archbishop (of Ravenna) set out by water from Tyre to Acre with a thousand knights and 20,000 infantry to help the Christians at Acre. The *Itinerarium peregrinorum* stated that it was Landgrave Ludwig of Thuringia, recently arrived in the East, who had persuaded Conrad to come to Acre.[5] Among the other eminent crusaders arriving from France – especially Champagne and Flanders – and elsewhere in north-west Europe at this time was the renowned knight James of Avesnes, lord of Condé and Guise. At some point before late summer 1190, James and Landgrave Ludwig took over command of the crusader army from King Guy, although he retained the status of king.[6]

Saladin's forces had taken up a position outside the besiegers' encampment, so that the besiegers were themselves besieged.[7] With the reinforcements from Tyre and the newly arrived crusaders, the crusade army was sufficiently large to attempt a direct assault on Saladin's surrounding army.

DOI: 10.4324/9781315205960-9

The siege of Acre and the end of the reign 159

On 4 October, the crusader army attacked Saladin's forces, but after initial success the Acre garrison counterattacked from the rear, and the crusaders' ranks were broken. After suffering heavy losses, the crusaders retreated to their camp.[8] They held off from further assaults while they fortified their own camp and concentrated on blockading the city, while further reinforcements arrived from the West.[9]

Guy and Sybil set about building up their support network. On 19 November 1189, they confirmed the concession of privileges Count Raymond of Tripoli had made in summer 1187 to the Pisans at Tyre, which had already been confirmed in November 1187 by Conrad of Montferrat – but their document did not mention Conrad's. The witnesses were Guy's brothers Geoffrey de Lusignan and Aimery the royal constable; then Sybil's stepfather Balian of Ibelin; two of the Tiberias brothers, Hugh and William; Geoffrey Tortus (whom we have met before witnessing documents for Baldwin IV and for Guy and Sybil); Galgan de Chenecheé (from the Lusignan area, who would go on to witness further charters for Guy); and one Alelmus Bellus (who witnessed other documents for King Guy at this time but is otherwise unknown).[10] On the same day Guy and Sybil confirmed to the Pisans the property that Conrad had confirmed in Acre in October 1187. The same men witnessed this document, except that one Lord Gazellus of Tyre (a crown vassal who had also witnessed charters for King Baldwin IV) was second in the list after Geoffrey de Lusignan; Geoffrey Tortus's son Geoffrey joined him; and Alelmus Bellus was missing.[11] These witness lists indicate that Sybil and Guy had brought together some of the individuals who had previously worked with them and King Baldwin IV and that they were beginning to recreate a royal household of individuals who were habitually present supporting their actions.

Over the winter of 1189–1190, Conrad returned to Tyre to repair and maintain his fleet, and Saladin took the opportunity to reprovision his military garrison at Acre from the sea. As the siege continued, the *Itinerarium peregrinorum* recorded that Conrad and King Guy reached a compromise through the advice of the princes: Conrad would continue to hold Tyre and would have Beirut and Sidon (currently held by Saladin); and he would promote the interests of the king and the kingdom. Having reached this agreement, Conrad brought his fully equipped fleet back to Acre shortly before Easter (which in 1190 fell on 25 March). With control of the sea, the crusaders could prevent supplies reaching the besieged garrison of Acre. An attempt by the besieged to break the naval blockade was defeated in a sea battle, but the besiegers were unable to make any progress in breaching Acre's walls.[12]

Efforts continued by both Conrad and Sybil and Guy to build support among the maritime powers who could give them control of the sea and ensure the continuation of the kingdom's trade. On 10 April 1190, Guy and Sybil gave and confirmed to the people of Amalfi full tax exemption on their trade and shipping at Acre and allowed them to have a court at

Acre with their own officials to exercise jurisdiction, just as the Venetians, Pisans and Genoese already had. The donation was witnessed by Count Joscelin the royal seneschal (his first appearance in the records since summer 1187), Hugh of Tiberias, Geoffrey Tortus, Galgan de Chenenché and Alelmus Bellus (who had all witnessed the documents issued by Sybil and Guy in November 1189), Rainer of Gibelet (who would appear later in Guy's service on Cyprus), Antelm of Lucca (a burgher of Acre who had witnessed documents for Baldwin IV and Baldwin V), and Raymond of Nephin (who also witnessed charters for the counts of Tripoli; his family had long been in royal service).[13] The royal household of long-standing royal officers, servants and advisors was still operating around the king and queen.

The following day at Tyre, Conrad, now styling himself as lord of Tyre, Sidon and Beirut, gave the Genoese (represented by Guido de Spinola, commander of the Genoese fleet that had arrived in the East in spring 1190) privileges and property in thanks for their help in the defence of Tyre and now in the siege of Acre. The first two witnesses were Ansaldo Bonvicino (who was now castellan of Tyre) and his brother Balduin; the other witnesses whose families can be identified were from Genoa or Piedmont. Although Conrad's charter appears very generous, it was in fact a compromise that redefined Genoese rights and limited rather than expanded them. Conrad extended Genoese fiscal privileges but defended his own interests so that the Genoese would not be completely independent of the lord of Tyre.[14] As part of this compromise, on Conrad's request, three days later Archbishop Joscius gave the Genoese the right to found a new chapel, whose chaplain would be subject to the archbishop of Tyre. Guido de Spinola was one of the witnesses of this concession.[15]

On 29 April 1190, the castle of Beaufort surrendered to Saladin, and Reynald of Sidon was released from prison in Damascus. He and the garrison of the castle went to Tyre. One of those who had reportedly entrusted Conrad with the command of Tyre in summer 1187, Reynald would later act as Conrad's negotiator with Saladin in collaboration with Balian of Ibelin.[16]

Two weeks after their previous concession, Sybil and Guy had given concessions to the citizens of the city of Marseille in return for their service to the siege of Acre. Many of the witnesses were the same as those for the charter of 10 April: Count Joscelin, royal seneschal; Hugh of Tiberias, Geoffrey Tortus, Galgan de Chenenché, and Alelmus Bellus. But Aimery, royal constable, joined the noble witnesses, and the last three witnesses of 10 April were replaced by Raymond Babin, who had witnessed a charter of King Baldwin IV, Count Guy and Countess Sybil in 1181.[17] Ten days later, Guy and Sybil confirmed the rights of the Genoese in Acre (again represented by Guido de Spinola) in return for their support for the siege of Acre. The charter covered all the Genoese had had in Acre before its conquest, especially their freedom to come and go by sea and land without paying dues. Like Conrad's charter to the Genoese at Tyre, the royal couple conceded very little that was new but did give the Genoese freedom of movement and fiscal exemption, which they had not previously had at Acre. The document was witnessed by Conrad lord of Tyre and by Aimery, royal constable; Count Joscelin, seneschal of the kingdom; Hugh of Tiberias, Geoffrey Tortus, Galgan de Cheneché, and one Gazellus – probably the Lord Gazellus of Tyre who had witnessed Sybil's and Guy's confirmation to the Pisans in November 1189.[18]

This was Sybil's final public action as queen. She issued no more charters and was not mentioned again by contemporary commentators until they noted her death and the death of her two surviving daughters in late summer or autumn that year. By this time another of the kings from whom Conrad claimed his authority had died: Emperor Frederick Barbarossa drowned on 10 June 1190, on his way through Cilician Armenia. His army, under the command of his son Duke Frederick of Swabia, continued its march and reached Antioch on 21 June, where Prince Bohemond welcomed them. In late August, the duke and the remainder of the German crusader army went on to Tripoli. According to the *Itinerarium peregrinorum*, the princes of the crusader army at Acre wanted him to remain at Tripoli and attack Saladin's territory, and sent Conrad of Montferrat, who was related to the duke, to deliver their request. Conrad, who wanted the duke's support in his plans to take over the throne of Jerusalem, told the duke that the princes were jealous of him and wanted to keep the glory of capturing Acre for themselves. So the duke came to Acre, where he initiated new attacks on Saladin's forces but also proved a disruptive force in the Christian army.[19]

If the *Itinerarium peregrinorum*'s interpretation of events is correct, Conrad had been planning his coup for some time, in anticipation of Sybil's death. Contemporary commentators who did not arrive – or whose informants did not arrive – in the East until the summer of 1191 were not certain when Sybil and her daughters died.[20] Their main interest in her death was that as Guy de Lusignan's claim to the throne died with her, Conrad then launched his own bid for the throne.

Sybil probably died in October 1190. Archbishop Baldwin of Canterbury and his party of English clergy and warriors arrived at Tyre on 16 September after a voyage from Marseille. They stayed there for around a month recovering from sickness and then travelled on to Acre, arriving on 12 October. At this point the archbishop sent a letter to the monks of Canterbury reporting that he was well and that the kings of England and France were expected to arrive soon.[21] As he did not mention that the queen had died, it is likely that Sybil was still alive at that date. On 21 October, Archbishop Baldwin's chaplain wrote to the monks of Canterbury to report on the sorry state of the crusading army. He listed a number of deaths of eminent persons: first on the list was the queen of Jerusalem.[22] Sybil died, then, between 16 and 21 October 1190.[23] Conrad of Montferrat challenged Guy de Lusignan for the crown of Jerusalem almost as soon as Sybil was dead.

The chaplain did not record the cause of any of the deaths he listed. Sybil could have died of sickness, in childbirth or from some accident, but the fact that both of her daughters died at around the same time indicates that they all three died from illness.[24] Other leading figures in the siege had become ill: Landgrave Ludwig set off for home during the summer of 1190 because of illness but died on the way. (Count Henry II of Champagne replaced him as leader of the army – the eldest son of the Count Henry who had come to Jerusalem on pilgrimage in 1179–1180.)[25] Stephen of Sancerre died around the same time as Sybil.[26] Patriarch Eraclius also fell ill in autumn 1190; Archbishop Baldwin took over his duties but then became ill himself and died, and the patriarch probably also died around the same time.[27]

According to the *Itinerarium peregrinorum* (here an eyewitness of these events), Conrad brought a complaint that Guy was not up to managing affairs of state and had no right to the throne because another daughter of King Amaury was still alive: Isabel, Sybil's younger half-sister. He persuaded the princes of the army that Isabel's marriage to Humphrey IV of Toron was invalid because she had been underage (only eleven) when she married him and she had not given her own consent to the marriage.[28]

The princes of the army then summoned Humphrey to bring his wife before the council, but when he did so she was taken from him and put into safe custody while the princes debated the case for a divorce. Ralph of Diceto states that the bishop of Acre 'and a certain other bishop of the land of Jerusalem' were judges in the divorce case.[29] The *Itinerarium peregrinorum* explains that the patriarch was too ill to get involved, but the archbishop of Canterbury, acting for him, absolutely opposed the divorce. Reynald of Sidon, Pagan of Haifa, Balian of Ibelin and his wife Maria Komnene, Isabel's mother, told Isabel to bring an action for divorce against Humphrey on the basis that she had always opposed the marriage and never consented to it. On this basis the archbishop could not prevent the divorce. The princes agreed to give Conrad the kingdom and the girl.[30]

Conrad needed ecclesiastical dispensation in order to marry Isabel, as she was half-sister of his deceased brother William's wife Sybil. The later accounts by Ambroise and Richard de Templo claim that Conrad was already married twice over, with wives in Montferrat and Constantinople; on the other hand, the contemporary Byzantine historian Niketas Choniates states Conrad's first wife was dead while the second marriage either never took place or was annulled after Conrad left Constantinople.[31] The archbishop excommunicated those contracting and those consenting to the marriage, but after his death on 19 November the wedding went ahead.[32]

The *Itinerarium peregrinorum* does not make clear exactly when the conflict between Conrad of Montferrat and King Guy reached its climax, but implies that it was late October or early November 1190, as it was before the archbishop cried out to God about the sinful state of the army, which was a little over a fortnight before his death on 19 November.[33] If Conrad brought his complaint about King Guy to the princes' council before the end of October, within two weeks at the most of Sybil's death, he and his supporters must have been planning his move for some time. This at least suggests that Sybil's death was expected by those around her.[34]

The corpses of Sybil and her daughters would have been buried outside the crusaders' camp, probably in the cemetery of St Nicolas, which lay between the walls of Acre and the ancient tell where Guy was camped and was the burial place of many of the Christians who died during the siege.[35] Their remains could have been exhumed and reburied in the cathedral church of the Holy Cross in Acre after the city was captured by the crusade army in July 1190; this was where Henry of Champagne, Sybil's successor as ruler of the kingdom, was buried after his death in 1197. However, no contemporary mentioned her final resting place and even the site of the cathedral is now uncertain.[36]

According to Roger of Howden in his *Gesta*, Guy refused to accept the decision of the princes to give the kingdom to Conrad while he was still alive, but Conrad expelled Guy and took the kingdom. In his *Chronica*, Roger added that Guy offered to defend his right to the kingship in the court of the kings of France and England (who were expected to arrive in the East shortly), but Conrad did not wish to wait so long and took over all the rights of the kingdom, expelling King Guy.[37] The Latin continuation of William of Tyre's history stated that after the princes of the army decided to give both Isabel and the kingdom to Conrad, Guy retired in confusion to the county of Tripoli to await the arrival of the king of England. According to this account, Guy hoped to recover the kingdom with the king's help as he was related to almost all the greater nobles of Aquitaine, many of whom were said to be coming with the king of England.[38] Certainly the evidence for Guy's location in the winter of 1190–91 is unclear, as most of the charters he issued in 1190–1192 did not give the year of issue and the narrative accounts do not mention him.[39]

However, Conrad did not remain in Acre after his marriage to establish his authority as king: he and Isabel withdrew to Tyre. During the following winter months the crusading army at Acre suffered famine and disease (the duke of Swabia was one of those who died) and some blamed Conrad for not sending supplies from Tyre, although perhaps the weather was against him. Conrad did not style himself 'king of Jerusalem' in a confirmation of the Pisans' privileges that he issued at Tyre with his wife Isabel 'daughter of the illustrious Amaury, former king of Jerusalem' (*quondam illustris Amalrici regis Ierosolimitani filia*) on 3 March 1191: he continued to use the title 'Lord of Tyre' (*Tyri domnus*). However, the first of the kings across the sea to arrive in the East endorsed Conrad as king. Conrad was one of those accompanying King Philip of France when he arrived at Acre on 20 April 1191; and when on 9 May Conrad and Isabel issued a confirmation of the Venetians' privileges in the kingdom of Jerusalem, confirmed by (among others) King Philip of France, Count Philip of Flanders, and Duke Leopold of Austria, Conrad styled himself 'king-elect of Jerusalem' (*rex Ierosolimorum electus*') while Isabel was again 'daughter of the illustrious Amaury, former king of Jerusalem'.[40]

So both the king of France and the great maritime trading power of Venice had declared for Conrad. Perhaps it was when Philip arrived at Acre that Guy retreated to Tripoli. His next appearance in the Latin Christian accounts of the crusade was on 11 May 1191, when he arrived on Cyprus to meet King Richard of England. Roger of Howden – who was with King Richard's crusade – recorded that Guy arrived with his brother Geoffrey de Lusignan; Humphrey of Toron; Raymond (presumably Bohemond III), prince of Antioch; Bohemond his son, the count of Tripoli; and Leon, brother of Rupen of the Mountain – who had succeeded his brother as ruler of Cilician Armenia. They offered the king their service and swore to be his faithful men.[41] Guy and Geoffrey had been Richard's vassals when he was count of Poitou. Guy had lost his kingdom and Humphrey of Toron had lost his wife to Conrad of Montferrat, and they would both have hoped that the king of England could win them redress. Bohemond and his son were Richard's relations – Bohemond's father Raymond of Poitiers had been uncle of Eleanor of Aquitaine, Richard's mother. Bohemond may have hoped to co-ordinate his own campaigns against Saladin in north Syria with Richard's campaigns in the south. Leon had sent troops to the crusader camp at Acre and negotiated with the Emperor Frederick Barbarossa to raise Cilician Armenia to a kingdom; perhaps he hoped that assisting King Richard would help to bring that about.[42]

King Richard and his army arrived at Acre 8 June 1191, and Richard championed Guy's claim to the kingdom. Roger of Howden, who may have been a witness of these events, recorded that Guy made a formal complaint against Conrad, accusing him of taking both the revenues and the rights of the kingdom by force and unjustly. The revenues were entrusted to the Templars and Hospitallers until a judicial decision could be reached. Geoffrey de Lusignan accused Conrad in the kings' court of breaking faith, perjury and treachery against the king and the whole Christian army and gave a pledge to pursue his challenge. Conrad refused to fight and left the court, pursued by jeers, but no one laid a hand on him in case the people protested, and Conrad departed for Tyre.[43] After Acre was surrendered to the crusade army on 12 July 1191, Kings Philip and Richard worked out a compromise whereby Conrad would continue to hold Tyre and have Beirut and Sidon when they were recaptured, but he would succeed to the throne only if Guy died first.[44] Following a serious epidemic in the crusader camp, which attacked both kings and among others killed Count Philip of Flanders, King Philip set off back to France on 31 July 1191, leaving Hugh III of Burgundy as leader of the French contingent. Hugh III never returned to the West, as he died of illness at Acre in August 1192.[45]

Guy made a number of charitable donations for the salvation of his late wife's soul, including one to the Hospitallers and one to the German hospital at Acre (later became the Teutonic Order) issued at Acre in January. This was probably January 1192, as both gifts involved property within Acre which he could only have given away after the recapture of Acre, and the donation to the Hospitallers named the new master, Garnier of Nablus, who arrived at Acre with King Richard in June 1191. The lists of witnesses show that Guy still retained the circle of supporters and officials he had had before Conrad's challenge to his position in October/November 1190. His donation to the Hospitallers was witnessed first by his brothers Geoffrey de Lusignan (who was now count of Jaffa) and Aimery the constable, then by Hugh Martin the marshal (a Poitevin who later accompanied Guy to Cyprus as his marshal), Galgan de Cheneché, Walter le Bel, *vicecomes* of Acre, Renier (or Rainer) of Gibelet, John Borgungus (who would later witness charters for Henry of Champagne as ruler of the kingdom), Baldoin of Cyprus (possibly the man rewarded by Baldwin IV and Sybil in 1178 for his long service for King Amaury), Thomas Chamberlain (who would be *vicecomes* of Acre under Henry of Champagne), and Philip Moresin (a burgher of Acre). His donation to the German hospital was witnessed by the bishop of Acre and the two new masters of the Temple and Hospital, then Geoffrey de Lusignan count of Jaffa and Aimery the constable; then two members of the military religious orders, followed by Hugh of Tiberias; Guillaume Fortis (from Tripoli; he had served Count Raymond III); Hugh Martini, the marshal; Galgan de Cheneché; Walter le Bel, *vicecomes*; and Renier de Gibelet, who had all witnessed charters for Guy in the past. After six Pisan witnesses were two more familiar names, Alelmus Bellus and Baldoin of Cyprus. Guy did not mention his and Sybil's daughters in either of these donations, nor in a later donation for Sybil's soul made when he was lord of Cyprus.[46]

In these documents Guy still held the title of king, but this would not long continue. In spring 1192 the crusader army elected Conrad of Montferrat as king. After Conrad was assassinated in April 1192, Count Henry II of Champagne married Isabel and ruled as king, although he was never crowned. Guy became ruler of Cyprus, which he had helped King Richard to conquer in May–June 1191. The Treaty of Jaffa between Richard and Saladin on 2 September 1192, ensured the continuing existence of the Frankish kingdom, albeit now with Acre rather than Jerusalem as its capital.[47]

Sybil's later reputation

With the benefit of hindsight, commentators in Europe assessed and reassessed Saladin's conquests in the Holy Land and who was to blame for the loss of Jerusalem and the kingdom. Building on brief references in the work of Roger of Howden, in the early thirteenth century the author of the Latin continuation of William of Tyre's history developed Sybil's role considerably, giving a much fuller and more sympathetic description of her response to the crisis than in Roger of Howden's work. Whereas Roger of Howden depicted Sybil's divorce of Guy, her coronation and her giving the crown to Guy as occurring in succession on the same day, the Latin continuation had Guy departing to his own (*ad sua*) after Sybil's coronation without hope of having his wife or the kingdom. Only later, in response to news of Saladin's approach, did the queen summon the ecclesiastical and secular nobles to elect a king and then she chose Guy. The Latin continuation also expanded Roger of Howden's brief account of Sybil's defence of Ascalon to cover several months, as if it were virtually the equal of Conrad's defence of Tyre. Although Sybil eventually had to surrender the city, the Latin continuation showed that in an impossible situation she took the best action to help her people and her husband. Following the *Itinerarium peregrinorum*, this author also set her alongside the patriarch in command of Jerusalem when it was under siege from Saladin, agreeing to surrender the city only because the common people insisted.[48]

The next generation of writers primarily remembered Sybil for her determination not to give up her husband to satisfy the demands of her nobles. Writing from 1232 to the 1250s, Aubrey or Alberich of Troisfontaines repeated Guy of Bazoches's account of Sybil's response on being told she must divorce Guy because he was not sufficiently noble to be king: she did not want any other than the man whom God had joined to her, because it was not permitted to her to confer the crown which he ought to wear on anyone other than him to whom she had promised her fidelity.[49]

Writing between around 1220 and 1236, Roger of Wendover, chronicler of St Alban's Abbey, followed the Latin continuation's version of Sybil's coronation, with Guy departing to his own after Sybil's coronation without hope of having his wife or the kingdom. Meanwhile, the news came that Saladin's army was nearby, at which the queen summoned the ecclesiastical and secular nobles to elect a king and chose Guy.[50] Roger of Wendover's successor Matthew Paris, writing between 1240 and 1259, copied this account into his *Chronica Majora* and his *Historia Anglorum*. In his summarised history, the *Flores historiarum*, he mentioned only that Sybil succeeded to the throne as the sole surviving heir when her son Baldwin died.[51]

These works' sympathetic view of King Guy and Queen Sybil was in sharp contrast to the *Chronique d'Ernoul* and the *Estoire de Eracles*, which were written during the same period. As at least one version of the latter was produced in Acre, it was probably this version of the history of the crusader states and of Sybil's life that would have been the best known in her homeland. It blackened her memory, depicting her usurping the crown, and denigrated her supporters.[52] But around a decade after the Lyon *Eracles* was compiled, a writer in the north-east of France devised a sympathetic version of Sybil's role in the Third Crusade, depicting the Frankish nobility of the Latin East as traitors and Saladin as defending her interests.[53]

The so-called *Récits d'un ménestrel de Reims* (stories from a minstrel of Reims) was written in 1260. This is a fictionalised history of France, Flanders, England and the Holy Land compiled in French prose.[54] Here Sybil becomes a wronged heroine and her husband Guy a tragic hero, and rather than being Baldwin IV's sister she is sister of King Amaury. Guy inherits the kingdom of Jerusalem as Sybil's husband and rules for a while, but then the nobles of the kingdom (the marquis of Montferrat, the count of Tripoli, the lord of Beirut and the lord of Sidon) become jealous of him and persuade the

The siege of Acre and the end of the reign 167

patriarch to tell the queen that she should abandon her husband because he is not suited to be king. The patriarch tells her that she must leave her husband; otherwise the kingdom will fall to Saladin. Shocked, the queen says that she does not wish to act against God or her husband. The council of barons arranges for the queen to come to the church of Holy Cross in Acre, and she is told to give the crown to one of the barons, who will then be king. The queen makes the patriarch and barons swear never to force her to take another husband, and then puts the crown on Guy's head. The patriarch and barons are amazed because each had hoped to be king. They call a council and contact Saladin, intending to betray the king to Saladin. The count of Tripoli negotiates with him, and he and Saladin drink each other's blood as a sign of their alliance. Guy is betrayed into Saladin's hands and taken to prison in Babylon. Saladin captures Acre. The queen is at Tyre, which is governed by '*li baus de Sur*', and she has no power. Saladin conquers the whole of the Holy Land except for Tyre.

Saladin tells Guy that his barons betrayed him and releases him and those knights the king chooses. Guy then takes his little army to Tyre, but the '*bau*' will not admit him. Meanwhile, the queen is trapped in Tyre, but she and one of her damsels escape down a rope lowered from the battlements by night. She goes to the king's tent, wakes him and they are joyfully reunited. After the forces of the Third Crusade, led by King Philip of France and King Richard of England, recapture Acre, Sybil and Guy are restored to their position as rulers of the kingdom and live out their lives for another fourteen years. In an echo of this story, in the early fourteenth century the author of the verse *Le Pas Saladin* depicted King Guy telling the king of France that Count Raymond betrayed him because he wanted Guy's wife, sister of King Amaury, but she would never agree because she loved Guy truly and loyally. In these works Sybil and her husband had become a small part of the European legend of Saladin as a chivalric hero.[55]

In respect to Sybil's appearance in legend, some scholars have suggested that Chrétien de Troyes's story of the Holy Grail, *Le Conte du Graal*, which was dedicated to Count Philip of Flanders, was an allegory of Philip's pilgrimage to the Holy Land in 1177. Baldwin IV, the leper king, would have become the wounded king of the Grail Castle, and Sybil, Philip's widowed cousin, would be the bereaved female cousin who berates the hero Percival for failing to speak out to aid the king at the Grail Castle. While this theory would explain some of the puzzling features of Chrétien's classic work, and Wolfram von Eschenbach may also have intended a similar crusade allegory in his *Parzival*, such fictional treatments do not appear to have any impact on depictions of Sybil in contemporary historical works.[56]

It was Archbishop William of Tyre's account of events, translated and continued in the *Estoire de Eracles*, which became the most widely known version of the history of the crusader states and of Sybil's role in history.[57] Writing between 1300 and 1321, the crusade theorist Marino Sanudo used a slightly amended version of this for his summary of the history of the crusader states and the crusades: Baldwin IV gave his sister Sybil in marriage to

William Longsword and then, after his death, to Guy of Lusignan, and because he was weakened by his illness he entrusted Guy with the direction of the whole kingdom. Then, when Guy incurred his wrath, he took it back and had his nephew Baldwin associated with him in the government, placing the boy in the safekeeping of the count of Tripoli. Baldwin IV died in 1185, followed by his nephew in 1186. The kingdom passed to Sybil by right of inheritance and she saw to it that Guy was anointed king, without getting the count's agreement. He was very angry, especially as he had hoped for the kingdom himself; and he made a truce with Saladin, so that the kingdom was dangerously divided. Later in his narrative, Sanudo noted that on Sybil's death the kingdom passed to her sister Isabel, and noted Isabel's divorce and remarriage to Conrad of Montferrat.[58]

In the early 1320s, Nicholas Trevet – Dominican friar, theologian and historian – incorporated a slightly muddled summary into his *Annales sex regum Angliae*: in 1181 Baldwin, king of Jerusalem, gave his sister to the noble knight Guy de Lusignan, who fathered a son from her, whom they hoped would be the future heir of the kingdom. Under 1186, he noted that 'Guy of Jaffa, born in Poitou, having Sybil the only daughter and heir of King Amaury as wife, was made king of Jerusalem in August'. Under 1191, he discussed the genealogy of the kings of Jerusalem (based on that in the *Itinerarium peregrinorum*) to explain why King Guy was competing with the 'Marquis' (in fact Conrad, son of the Marquis) for the kingdom, and explained that Baldwin the leper had designated the son of his sister Sybil as his heir, but when the child Baldwin and his father died, Sybil married Guy, who became king through his wife's paternal right. But when she and their children died, Amaury's surviving daughter from his second marriage inherited the kingdom, and because the Marquis had married her, he tried to expel Guy from the kingdom.[59]

Two centuries later, Sebastian Münster included in his description of the Holy Land in Book Five of his *Cosmographia* a similar but even briefer reference to Sybil as the sister of Baldwin IV whose husband became king on Baldwin's death. First published in 1544, the *Cosmographia* was expanded and translated from German into Latin, Italian, Czech and French, and its description of the Holy Land grew to include mention of Baldwin V's coronation and death, followed by the accession of Guy as Sybil's husband.[60]

It was Münster's *Cosmographia* that the English clergyman Thomas Fuller, in his *Historie of the Holy Warre*, a history of the crusades completed in 1639, credited with the information that 'Sibyll', mother of the infant Baldwin V, in order to defeat Raymond earl of Tripoli, who wanted to be the young king's protector, 'first murdered all natural affection in herself, and then by poison murdered her son; that so the crown in her right might come to her husband Guy'.[61] In fact, the story was from François de Belleforest's considerably expanded French version of the *Cosmographia*, published in 1575. Belleforest did not give a source for the story beyond '*dit on*': 'it is said', or 'they say', an admission that this was only rumour. Perhaps because he had no source for it, the story is not in his *Grandes annales et histoire générale de France* of

1579.[62] Like successive redactors of the *Estoire de Eracles*, the inventor of this story seems to have been 'striving for literary effect by painting the protagonists in more lurid colours'.[63] Perhaps Sybil's name – redolent of classical legend and associated with seduction and occult arts – suggested this tale to Belleforest.[64]

Conclusion

In his 1982 appraisal of Patriarch Eraclius, Benjamin Kedar commented: 'it is noteworthy that ... historians have exhibited a tendency to opt at every juncture for the alternative least complimentary to the patriarch's reputation, as if in response to some variety of Gresham's Law'[65] – so that bad history drives out good. R. C. Smail noted the same tendency among historians writing about King Guy.[66] Queen Sybil's reputation has been similarly affected, so that a story apparently invented by François de Belleforest and presented as rumour could be repeated as fact sixty-five years later by Thomas Fuller and called unjust almost two hundred years after that by Joseph-François Michaud, blaming this sixteenth-century story on the attitudes of the late twelfth century. Nearer Sybil's own day, the story in the *Chronique d'Ernoul* that she was for a short time in love with Baldwin of Ramla was repeated as fact in the latter part of the twentieth century by (for example) Jonathan Riley-Smith and Régine Pernoud.[67]

Setting aside the colourful legends, the Sybil that has emerged in this study was both typical of contemporary elite women – in that her life comprised education followed by marriage, childbirth, widowhood, remarriage and further childbirth, wielding authority as an administrator of land, supporting her husband in war and the aftermath of defeat – and exceptional, in that she was an heir to the kingdom of Jerusalem who succeeded in making good her claim. Yet although Sybil became queen, it is debatable whether she can be said to have ruled or exercised power over her kingdom.

Access to power by elite women in twelfth-century Latin Christendom has focussed considerable scholarly attention in recent years, along with the question of how power should be defined: is it simply having agency to act, or does it involve commanding and controlling others?[68] Sybil may appear to have had little agency for much of her life, as her childhood and marriages were controlled by her family, she reportedly delegated her authority as queen to her second husband and she was unable to retain her kingdom in the face of Saladin's invasion. On the other hand, the witness lists to her charters as countess of Jaffa and Ascalon indicate that she had a household made up of established officials who would have exercised authority on her behalf. She was able to exercise patronage in a donation to the military-religious Order of Mountjoy and she co-operated in or gave her consent to other gifts and sales to religious orders or individuals. She also acted as a patron of culture: she probably commissioned her son's tomb and she may have overseen the final completion of the renovation and redecoration of the Cenacle in the church of the Holy Sepulchre. Unlike her grandmother Melisende and many queens and noblewomen in the Latin Christian West she did not found a religious house, but in view of Saladin's conquests and the short time she was queen she scarcely had the opportunity to do so. Like her grandmother and other elite women in the West, she did act as a military commander in a time of emergency, and she negotiated with Saladin on her husband's behalf. In this respect she exercised leadership and authority.

Until her son's death Sybil was seldom mentioned by the narrative records. But in the time of crisis for the kingdom that followed Baldwin V's death, when the nobles of the kingdom may have vowed to wait for the decision of four rulers of Europe on who should rule the country yet a leader was needed at once to face the threat from Saladin, it was Sybil who stepped forward to take on the responsibility of government. Although her action was opposed by a part of the nobility and her insistence on retaining Guy as her husband was unacceptable to some, most accepted it as the best option in the circumstances. There were no obvious alternative candidates for her hand and (as became evident over the following months) no single leader who could unite all the Franks against Saladin.

Sybil's contemporaries and writers of the next generation depicted her as a resourceful, lively and determined woman who enforced her right to the throne of Jerusalem, circumvented attempts by first her brother and then her nobles to force her to divorce Guy de Lusignan, garrisoned and defended Ascalon against Saladin, escaped from Jerusalem when her brother might have tried to detain her and (in fiction) from Tyre down a rope over the battlements under cover of night, with only one of her ladies-in-waiting accompanying her. Yet she failed to hold on to her kingdom, and the question arises how far she was to blame for its collapse.

During Sybil's childhood, the kingdom of Jerusalem appeared to be strong; her father came close to conquering Egypt, and his alliance (or client-kingship) with the Byzantine emperor ensured a powerful protector for the kingdom. Marriage alliances with the Byzantines and the Christian nobility of Armenia rooted the royal family of Jerusalem securely within the region and ensured a network of support in time of need. Alliances between local Christian and Muslim rulers opposed powerful aggressors such as the rulers of Damascus, Mosul and Aleppo and maintained some sort of balance of power. But the change in Byzantine policy under Andronikos Komnenos shattered the kingdom's relationship with Constantinople, while the rise of Saladin transformed the multiplicity of Muslim lordships in northern Syria into a single empire. By 1186, when Sybil won the throne of Jerusalem, there was no longer a network of Christian support in the East to come to the kingdom's aid. Count Raymond of Tripoli apparently planned to become a client king of Saladin, but voluntarily submitting the holy places of Jerusalem to Muslim overlordship would never have been acceptable to the Christian kings of Europe, who were outraged at the surrender of Jerusalem to Saladin in 1187.

As a child Sybil's future prospects appeared excellent: as the eldest child of King Amaury of Jerusalem and as a member of the dynasty that claimed

The siege of Acre and the end of the reign 171

descent from Godfrey de Bouillon and the other heroes of the First Crusade, we might expect that she would have been an attractive marriage prospect. Yet European noblemen did not queue up to seek her hand. One reason for this might have been that commanding the defence of the kingdom of Jerusalem in the face of aggressive Muslim expansionism was a daunting prospect for any warrior, no matter how ambitious. Moreover, as her brother Baldwin's illness became generally known in Europe, Sybil's potential husbands may have wondered whether she and her children would be similarly afflicted. In addition, as her brother Baldwin and his council made clear to Philip of Alsace in autumn 1177, outside aid was unwelcome in the kingdom except on the terms they dictated. Robert VI of Béthune, Philip of Alsace's candidate for Sybil's hand, might have made a more effective count of Jaffa and Ascalon, regent of the kingdom and king consort than Guy de Lusignan, but Baldwin – aged only sixteen at the time of Count Philip's crusade – preferred to marry his sister to a man he knew.

If King Baldwin IV had supported his elder sister as the heir who – given that Baldwin V was very young and in uncertain health – would almost certainly inherit the kingdom, it might have been possible for Sybil to unite the nobles of the kingdom behind her as her brother had done. But his contradictory and changing policies left her rights of inheritance unclear and the nobles of the kingdom divided. He married her to one of his household knights, then attempted to divorce them; he appointed her husband as procurator, then shortly afterwards deposed him and appointed her son as his co-ruler, and then appointed another procurator, then finally appointed two regents, one to care for the young king Baldwin V and the other to govern. If he made further arrangements for the succession after Baldwin V they were unworkable. By marrying his younger half-sister to a leading noble of the kingdom but forcing the bridegroom to surrender his inherited estates in return, King Baldwin IV ensured that both his sisters and their husbands and supporters had grievances against him. While his measures reduced any threat that he would be overthrown during his lifetime, they boded badly for the kingdom after the death of his immediate heir.

Given the rivalries between the leading nobles of the kingdom and Saladin's need to win a decisive victory over the Franks, no one could have prevented Saladin from taking Jerusalem and conquering most of Sybil's kingdom; Sybil was doomed to failure as queen. Not only did she lose Jerusalem, but she also failed in the most fundamental function of a noblewoman: she failed to provide an heir for herself, as both her son Baldwin and her daughters died in childhood. On the other hand, in the face of disaster she did not abandon her kingdom and flee to Europe, nor did she retire to a religious house. Instead, she stayed in the crusader states and did all she could to oppose the invader. She tried to defend Ascalon, she remained in Jerusalem until it was surrendered to Saladin, she obtained her husband's release from Saladin's prison, and by accompanying him in the months that followed she gave him the authority to continue as king of Jerusalem. As husband of the eldest daughter of King Amaury of Jerusalem and as a crowned king, Guy had a stronger claim to royal authority than Conrad of Montferrat: crusaders from Europe rallied to him and the representatives of the Italian maritime cities supported him so that he could begin the fightback against Saladin which was continued by the Third Crusade and enabled the kingdom of Jerusalem to continue to exist until 1291. When Sybil died, Guy's authority died with her; but she had ensured that her kingdom would not die, at least for another century.

Notes

1 There has been extensive scholarly study of the siege of Acre, which will not be repeated here. Recent studies include: John H. Pryor, 'A Medieval Siege of Troy: The Fight to the Death at Acre, 1189–1191 or The Tears of Ṣalāḥ al-Dīn', in *The Medieval Way of War: Studies in Medieval Military History in Honor of Bernard S. Bachrach*, ed. Gregory I. Halfond (Farnham, 2015), 97–115; John D. Hosler, *The Siege of Acre, 1189–1191: Saladin, Richard the Lionheart, and the Battle that Decided the Third Crusade* (New Haven and London, 2018).
2 *ULKJ* 2: 804–808, 809–812, 812–814, 815–818, 819–821, 822–824 (nos 476, 477, 478, 479, 480, 482), Sybil confirms: *ULKJ* 2: 854, 855, 856 (nos 512, 513, 514, 515, 516, 518).
3 On this question in relation to Conrad's concessions: Jacoby, 'Conrad of Montferrat', p. 224.
4 *ULKJ* 2: 886–888 (no. 525; see p. 887 for the witnesses); 'Regni Iherosolymitani Brevis Historia', p. 144; Jacoby, 'Conrad of Montferrat', pp. 205–206.
5 Ralph of Diceto, 'Ymagines historiarum'. 2: 70; *IP* 1, pp. 310, 311 (Bk 1 ch. 29).
6 *IP* 1, pp. 309–312, 333–334 (Bk 1 chs 27–29, 43); Hosler, *Siege of Acre*, p. 19.
7 *IP* 1, p. 308 (Bk 1 ch. 27).
8 *IP* 1, pp. 312–316 (Bk 1 chs 29–30); Hosler, *Siege of Acre*, pp. 27–38; Lyons and Jackson, *Saladin*, pp. 302–304; Phillips, *The Life and Legend*, pp. 225–228.
9 *IP* 1, p. 316 (Bk 1 ch. 31); *L'Estoire de la Guerre Sainte*, p. 425 (lines 3125–3134); *The History of the Holy War*, 1: 50 (lines 3116–3128), 2: 76–77; Hosler, *Siege of Acre*, pp. 41–44.
10 Original, as confirmed by Conrad in October 1187: *ULKJ* 2: 859–865 (no. 519); confirmation: *ULKJ* 2: 809–812, 855 (nos 477, 513), esp. p. 807 lines 10–13 on Galgan de Cheneché, and p. 810 lines 24–27.
11 Original donation in *ULKJ* 2: 872–877 (no. 522); confirmation in *ULKJ* 2: 804–808, 854 (nos 476, 512), and pp. 699 lines 22–24 on Gazellus of Tyre.
12 *IP* 1, pp. 321–324, 325–327 (Bk 1 chs 34, 36); BD, p. 108 (sections 117–118); Jacoby, 'Conrad of Montferrat', p. 206; Lyons and Jackson, *Saladin*, pp. 309–310; Phillips, *The Life and Legend*, pp. 231–233.
13 *ULKJ* 2: 812–814, 855 (nos 478, 514), esp. p. 707 lines 5–7 on Antelm de Luca and p. 813 lines 38–46 on Rainer de Gibelet and Raymond of Nephin; Jacoby, 'Conrad of Montferrat', p. 213.
14 *ULKJ* 2: 888–894 (no. 526); Jacoby, 'Conrad of Montferrat', pp. 207–209.
15 *ULKJ* 2: 894–896 (no. 527); Jacoby, 'Conrad of Montferrat', p. 209.
16 BD, pp. 108, 194 (sections 117, 202); *IP* 2, p. 337 (Bk 5 ch. 24); *Estoire de la Guerre Sainte*, p. 606 (lines 8707–8714); *The History of the Holy War*, 1: 141 (lines 8686–8693), 2: 149; Lyons and Jackson, *Saladin*, p. 310; Phillips, *The Life and Legend*, pp. 272, 274; 'Regni Iherosolymitani Brevis Historia', p. 145.

The siege of Acre and the end of the reign 173

17 *ULKJ* 2: 815–818, 855 (nos 479, 515), and p. 722 (no. 424) for Raymund Babin.
18 *ULHJ* 2: 819–821, 855 (nos 480, 516); Jacoby, 'Conrad de Montferrat', p. 209.
19 'The History of the Expedition of the Emperor Frederick', pp. 115–118; *IP* 1, pp. 301–303, 334–335 (Bk 1 chs 24, 44); BD, p. 125 (section 136); 'Imād, p. 250 (section 287).
20 *IP* 1, pp. 335, 336, 352; *IP* 2, pp. 95, 97, 119 (Bk 1 chs 45, 46, 63); repeated in *LFWT*, pp. 129–130 (Bk 3 chs 14–15); Ambroise states that Sybil and the two daughters of King Guy, *dreiz heirs de la terre* (line 3906/3900), died just after the end of August 1190: *Estoire de la Guerre Sainte*, p. 450 (lines 3897–3904); *The History of the Holy War*, 1: 63 (lines 3891–3898), 2: 86; *Chronique d'Ernoul*, p. 267 (ch. 24); states that the queen and four children died; the Colbert-Fontainebleau version of the 'L'Estoire de Eracles Empereur', p. 151 (Bk 25 ch. 10) places Sybil's death shortly after 15 July, stating that she and her two daughters Aelis and Marie died *en cele saison*; other versions of the text state simply that immediately after her death, Conrad moved to get Humphrey of Toron divorced from Isabel: see the texts on the lower part of p. 154. The death of Sybil and her daughters is also noted by Roger of Howden, *Gesta*, 2: 141, 147; Roger of Howden, *Chronica*, 3: 70; *LFWT*, p. 129 (Bk 3 ch. 14); other writers mentioned only the queen's death: Ralph of Diceto, 'Ymagines historiarum', 2: 86; William of Newburgh, *Historia rerum anglicarum*, 1: 363 (Bk 3 ch. 24).
21 *Epistolæ Cantuarienses: the Letters of the Prior and Convent of Christ Church, Canterbury From A.D. 1187 to A.D. 1199*, in *Chronicles and Memorials of the Reign of Richard I*, ed. William Stubbs, Rolls Series 38 (London, 1865), p. 328 (no. 345); RRH no. 1286, accessed 30 April 2021.
22 *Epistolæ Cantuarienses*, pp. 328–329 (no. 346); RRR no. 1287, accessed 30 April 2021.
23 For discussion of the date see Vogtherr, 'Die Regierungsdaten', 68–70; see also Kedar, 'The Patriarch Eraclius', p. 204.
24 This is stated by *LFWT*, p. 129 (Bk 3 ch. 14).
25 *IP* 1, pp. 333–334 (Bk 1 ch. 43).
26 *Epistolæ Cantuarienses*, p. 329 (no. 346).
27 *IP* 1, pp. 349, 353 (Bk 1 chs 61, 63); Gervase of Canterbury gives the date of the archbishop's death: *The Historical Works of Gervase of Canterbury*, ed. William Stubbs, 2 vols, Rolls Series 73, (London 1870–1880), 1: 488, and states that he was buried at Acre; Kedar, 'The Patriarch Eraclius', p. 204.
28 *IP* 1, p. 352 (Bk 1 ch. 63).
29 Ralph of Diceto, 'Ymagines historiarum', 2: 86.
30 *IP* 1, pp. 353–354 (Bk 1 ch. 63). The *Estoire de Eracles* recorded that at her divorce Isabel returned to Humphrey the castles of Toron, Châteauneuf and everything he had given her brother in order to marry her: Mayer, 'Die Legitimität Balduins IV', 77 note 40.
31 Gilchrist, 'Getting away with murder', 18 and n. 18 (death of Conrad's first wife) and 21–22 (second wife).
32 *IP* 2, pp. 122–123 (Bk 1 ch. 63); *L'Estoire de la Guerre Sainte*, pp. 457–458 (lines 4127–4140, 4151–4165); *The History of the Holy War*, 1: 66–67 (lines 4121–4138, 4145–4159), 2: 89; *LFWT*, p. 134 (Bk 3 ch. 19). The exact date of the wedding is not clear. Ambroise, *IP* 2 (as cited above), and Ralph of Diceto state that on the day of the wedding, those returning from the wedding feast were ambushed: Ralph of Diceto, 'Ymagines historiarum', 2: 86. Baha al-Din ibn Shaddad and

'Imād al-Dīn al-Isfahāni record an ambush on 22 November when 'the king's treasurer, a certain number of French and their chief fell into captivity', which could be the same occasion: BD, pp. 139–140; 'Imād, pp. 268–269 (sections 306–308). The verse account of the siege of Acre by 'Monachus' indicates that the ambush occurred on 24 November: 'Monachus Florentinus', p. cxxiv, line 522 and n. 1.

33   *IP* 1, p. 357 (Bk 1 ch. 65).
34   *IP* 1, p. 3535 (Bk 1 ch. 46).
35   Pringle, *Churches*, 4: 151; Ralph of Diceto, 'Ymagines historiarum', 2: 81.
36   Pringle, *Churches*, 4: 35–40, at pp. 36, 39.
37   Roger of Howden, *Gesta*, 2: 142; Roger of Howden, *Chronica*, 3: 71.
38   *LFWT*, p. 133 (Bk 3 ch. 18).
39   *ULKJ* 2: pp. 824–825, 828–831, 832–840 (nos 483–484, 486, 488–491),
40   Barber, *Crusader States*, pp. 338–339, 344; Hosler, *Siege of Acre*, pp. 98–108; Jacoby, 'Conrad of Montferrat', pp. 201, 214, 217; Roger of Howden, *Gesta*, 2: 161; *IP* 2, p. 213 (Bk 3 ch. 4); *ULKJ* 2: pp. 896–904 (nos 529, 530).
41   Roger of Howden, *Gesta*, 2: 165; Roger of Howden, Chronica, 3: 108.
42   Buck, *Principality of Antioch*, p. 57; Boase, 'The History of the Kingdom', pp. 15, 17.
43   Roger of Howden, *Gesta*, 2: 170–171; Roger of Howden, *Chronica*, 3: 113–114.
44   Barber, *Crusader States*, pp. 343–346; Hosler, *Siege of Acre*, pp. 113, 118–119, 135, 141–142; Roger of Howden, *Gesta*, 2: 184; Roger of Howden, *Chronica*, 3: 124–125; *IP* 2, pp. 235–226 (Bk 3 ch. 20).
45   Hosler, *Siege of Acre*, pp. 140–141; Rhodes, *The Crown and the Cross*, pp. 167, 172–173.
46   *ULKJ* 2: pp. 828–831, 832–835 (nos 486, 488), and p. 827 lines 15–20 for Hugh Martini the Marshal, pp. 943 and 952 for Johannes Borgundus, p. 830 lines 23–25 and p. 835 for Baldoin of Cyprus, p. 953 for Thomas Camerarius, p. 834 lines 38–42 for William Fortis, 4: 1673 for Philip Moresin; Mayer, *Die Kanzlei*, 2: 917.
47   Barber, *Crusader States*, pp. 352–354; Lyons and Jackson, *Saladin*, pp. 348–360; Phillips, *The Life and Legend*, pp. 283–295.
48   Hans Eberhard Mayer, 'Das IP 1 und die Continuatio Willelmi Tyri', in *IP* 1, pp. 152–161; Helen J. Nicholson, 'Introduction', in *Chronicle of the Third Crusade*, trans. Nicholson, pp. 1–17, at pp. 3–4; Kane, 'Between parson and poet', 65–69; *LFWT*, pp. 64–65, 74, 75, 78, 89–90 (Bk 1 chs 10, 15, 16, Bk 2 chs 1, 9).
49   'Chronica Albrici Monachi Trium Fontium', ed. Paul Scheffer-Boichorst, in *MGH SS*, vol. 23, ed. Georg Heinrich Pertz (Hanover, 1874), pp. 631–950, at pp. 859–860; Régis Rech, 'Alberich of Troisfontaines [Aubrey]', in *Encyclopedia of the Medieval Chronicle*, ed. Graeme Dunphy, 2 vols (Leiden, 2010), 1: 23.
50   *Rogeri de Wendover Liber*, 1: 138–139; Lisa M. Ruch, 'Roger of Wendover', in *Encyclopedia of the Medieval Chronicle*, ed. Graeme Dunphy (Leiden, 2010), 2: 1291.
51   [Matthew Paris] *Matthæi Parisiensis monachi Sancti Albani Chronica majora*, ed. Henry Richards Luard, 7 vols, Rolls Series 57 (London, 1872–1883), 2: 325–326; Matthew Paris, *Historia Anglorum, sive, ut vulgo dicitur, Historia minor. Item, ejusdem Abbreviatio chronicorum Angliæ*, ed. Frederic Madden, 3 vols, Rolls Series 44 ((London, 1866–1869), 1: 439; Matthew Paris, *Flores historiarum*, ed. Henry Richards Luard, 3 vols, Rolls Series 95 (London, 1890), 2: 97; Lisa M. Ruch, 'Matthew Paris', in *Encyclopedia of the Medieval Chronicle*, ed. Dunphy, 2: 1093–1095.

52 Rubin, *Learning in a Crusader City*, pp. 191–192; Edbury, 'Ernoul, *Eracles*, and the Collapse of the Kingdom of Jerusalem', pp. 45, 56, 60, 62.
53 *Récits d'un ménestrel de Reims au treizième siècle*, ed. Natalis de Wailly (Paris, 1876), pp. 14–26, 30, 36–37 (parts VII–X sections 28–49, 56, 69), available online at: https://gallica.bnf.fr/ark:/12148/bpt6k1123107; Helen J. Nicholson, '"La roine preude femme et bonne dame": Queen Sybil of Jerusalem (1186–1190) in History and Legend, 1186–1300', *The Haskins Society Journal*, 15 (2004), 110–124.
54 *Récits d'un ménestrel de Reims*, ed. Wailly, p. xxxii.
55 *Le Pas Saladin: An Old French Poem of the Third Crusade*, ed. Frank E. Lodeman (Baltimore, 1897), pp. 8, 10 (lines 65–76, 294–299); Jubb, *Legend of Saladin*, 134–141, 167.
56 Helen Adolf, 'An Historical Background for Chrétien's Perceval', *PMLA*, 58.3 (1943), 597–620; Armel Diverres, 'The Grail and the Third Crusade: Thoughts on *Le Conte del Graal* by Chrétien de Troyes', in *Arthurian Literature X*, ed. Richard Barber (Cambridge, 1990), pp. 13–109; Nicholson, *Love, War and the Grail*, pp. 112, 114, 117–118, 131.
57 R. H. C. Davis,, 'William of Tyre', in *Relations between East and West in the Middle Ages*, ed. Derek Baker (Edinburgh, 1987), pp. 64–76, at p. 71.
58 Marino Sanudo Torsello, *The Book of the Secrets of the Faithful of the Cross: Liber Secretorum Fidelium Crucis*, trans. Peter Lock, Crusade Texts in Translation 21 (Farnham, 2011), pp. 273–274, 312.
59 *F. Nicholai Triveti de ordine Frat. Prædicatorum, Annales sex regum Angliæ*, ed. Thomas Hog (London, 1845), pp. 95, 106, 124–125; Lisa M. Ruch, 'Trevet, Nicholas', in *Encyclopedia of the Medieval Chronicle*, ed. Graeme Dunphy, 2 vols (Leiden, 2010), 2: 1445–1446; *IP* 1, pp. 335–337 (Bk 1 ch. 46).
60 Sebastian Münster, *Cosmographia* (Basel, 1544), p. dciij ('Das funfft buch', pp. dc–dcv under 'Das heylig gelope land'. The greatly extended Latin edition of 1572 mentioned Baldwin V as Baldwin the leper's nephew and son of his sister Sibylla from her first husband Guilelmo marquis of Montferrat: Sebastian Münster, *Cosmographiae vniversalis lib. VI* (Basel, 1572), p. 1169 (Book 5, under 'Terra Sancta': 'Gesta sub Baldvino VII Rege Leproso, cap. XLI', and 'Gesta sub Guidone VIII Rege Ierosolymitano, cap. XLII'); likewise, the Italian edition of 1575 mentions Baldwin V as Sybil's son who died shortly after his uncle: Sebastian Münster, *Cosmographia vniuersale* (Cologne, 1575), p. 1082 (under Book 5, 'Terra Santa' (pp. 1076–1098).
61 Thomas Fuller, *The Historie of the Holy Warre*, 3rd edn (Cambridge, 1640), p. 102 (Bk 2 ch. 43), citing: *Cosmog. Lib. 5.in terra sancta*.
62 François de Belle-forest and Sebastian Münster, *La cosmographie vniuerselle de tout le monde*, 2 vols (Paris, 1575), vol. 2, col. 1076 (Bk 5 ch. 21). The story does not appear in François de Belle-forest, *Les grandes annales et histoire générale de France, dès la venue des Francs en Gaule, jusques au règne du roy trés-chrestien Henry III* (Paris, 1579), p. 552 verso (l'an M. CLXXXVII, Philippe Auguste Livre III ch. LXII).
63 Peter Edbury, 'Gerard of Rideford and the Battle of Le Cresson (1 May 1187): The Developing Narrative Tradition', in *On the Margins of Crusading: The Military Orders, the Papacy and the Christian World*, ed. Helen J. Nicholson, Crusades Subsidia 4 (Farnham, 2011), pp. 45–60, at p. 49.
64 Mora-Lebrun, 'Les metamorphoses de la Sibylle'.
65 Kedar, 'Patriarch Eraclius', p. 180.
66 Smail, 'The Predicaments of Guy of Lusignan'.

176 *The siege of Acre and the end of the reign*

67 Jonathan Riley-Smith, *The Feudal Nobility*, p. 105; Pernoud, *La femme*, p. 147.
68 To give just a few examples, some of which have been cited already in this book: Mary Erler and Maryanne Kowaleski, eds, *Women and Power in the Middle Ages* (Athens, GA, 1988); Mary C. Erler and Maryanne Kowaleski, eds, *Gendering the Master Narrative: Women and Power in the Middle Ages* (Ithaca, NY, 2003); Susan M. Johns, *Noblewomen, Aristocracy and Power in the twelfth-century Anglo-Norman Realm* (Manchester, 2003); *Mächtige Frauen? Königinnen und Fürstinnen im europäischen Mittelalter (11.–14. Jahrhundert)*, ed. Claudia Zey with Sophei Caflisch and Philippe Goridis, Vorträge und Forschungen 81 (Ostfildern, 2015); Heather J. Tanner, ed., *Medieval Elite Women and the Exercise of Power, 1100–1400: Moving beyond the Exceptionalist Debate* (Cham, 2019).

Bibliography

Primary Sources

Unpublished

Guy of Bazoches, 'Cronosgraphia', Paris, Bibliothèque nationale, MS Lat. 4998, fols 35r–64v, https://gallica.bnf.fr/ark:/12148/btv1b10723143m/f71.item.r=Latin%204998

Published

Abū Shāma, 'Le Livre des deux jardins', in *Recueil des Historiens des Croisades, Historiens Orientaux*, ed. l'Académie des Inscriptions et Belles-Lettres, 4 vols (Paris, 1898)
[Ambroise] *L'Estoire de la Guerre Sainte*, ed. Catherine Croizy-Naquet, Classiques français du Moyen Âge 174 (Paris, 2014)
[Ambroise] *The History of the Holy War: Ambroise's* Estoire de la Guerre Sainte, ed. and trans. Marianne Ailes and Malcolm Barber, 2 vols (Woodbridge, 2003)
'Annales Magdeburgensis', in *Monumenta Germaniae Historica Scriptores in Folio*, ed. Georg Heinrich Pertz, vol. 16 (Hanover, 1859), pp. 105–96
'Annales Palidenses auctore Theodore monarcho', in *Monumenta Germaniae Historica Scriptores in Folio*, ed. Georg Heinrich Pertz, vol. 16 (Hanover, 1859), pp. 48–98
'Annales Rodenses', in *Monumenta Germaniae Historica Scriptores in Folio*, ed. Georg Heinrich Pertz, vol. 16 (Hanover, 1859), pp. 688–723
'Arnoldi abbatis S. Iohannis Lubecensis Cronica Slavorum', ed. J. M. Lappenberg, in *Monumenta Germaniae Historica Scriptores in Folio*, ed. Georg Heinrich Pertz, vol. 21 (Hanover, 1869), pp. 100–250
'Assises de la cour des bourgeois', ed. Le Comte Beugnot, in *Recueil des historiens des croisades: Lois*, 2 vols (Paris, 1843)
'Auctarium Affigemense', ed. D. L. C. Bethmann, *Monumenta Germaniae Historica Scriptores in Folio*, ed. Georg Heinrich Pertz, vol. 6 (Hanover, 1844), pp. 398–405
'Auctarium Aquicinense', ed. D. L. C. Bethmann, *Monumenta Germaniae Historica Scriptores in Folio*, ed. Georg Heinrich Pertz, vol. 6 (Hanover, 1844), pp. 392–398
[Bahā' al-Dīn Ibn Shaddād] *The Rare and Excellent History of Saladin or al-Nawādir al-Sulṭāniyya wa'l-Maḥāsin al-Yūsufiyya by Bahā' al-Dīn Ibn Shaddād*, trans. D. S. Richards. Crusade Texts in Translation 7 (Aldershot, 2002)
[Benjamin of Tudela] *The Itinerary of Benjamin of Tudela*, ed. Marcus Nathan Adler (London, 1907)

178   Bibliography

Cartulaire général de l'ordre des Hospitaliers de S. Jean de Jérusalem, ed. Joseph Delaville le Roulx, 4 vols (Paris, 1894–1906)

The Chanson d'Antioche: An Old French Account of the First Crusade, trans. Susan B. Edgington and Carol Sweetenham, Crusade Texts in Translation 22 (Farnham, 2011)

Chrétien de Troyes, *Les Romans de Chrétien de Troyes édités d'après la copie de Guiot (Bibl. nat. fr. 794) I: Erec et Enide*, ed. Mario Roques, Classiques français du Moyen Âge 80 (Paris, 1981)

Christine de Pisan, *The Treasure of the City of Ladies or the Book of the Three Virtues*, trans. Sarah Lawson (Harmondsworth, 1985)

Christine de Pizan, *The Book of the City of Ladies*, trans. Rosalind Brown-Grant (Harmondsworth, 1999)

'Chronica Albrici Monachi Trium Fontium', ed. Paul Scheffer-Boichorst, in *Monumenta Germaniae Historica Scriptores in Folio*, ed. Georg Heinrich Pertz, vol. 23 (Hanover, 1874), pp. 631–950

'Chronica collecta a Magno Presbitero', in *Monumenta Germaniae Historica Scriptores in Folio*, ed. Georg Heinrich Pertz, vol. 17 (Hanover, 1861), pp. 476–523

Chronicle of the Third Crusade: See *Itinerarium peregrinorum et gesta regis Ricardi*

Chronique d'Ernoul et de Bernard le trésorier, ed. L. de Mas Latrie (Paris, 1871)

Chronique de Michel le Syrien, patriarche Jacobite d'Antioche (1166–1199), ed. and trans. J.-B. Chabot, 5 vols (Paris, 1899–1924)

Codice diplomatico della Repubblica di Genova, ed. C. Imperiale di Sant'Angelo, 3 vols (Rome, 1936–1942)

Codice diplomatico del Sacro Militare Ordine Gerosolimitano, ed. Sebastiano Paoli, 2 vols (Lucca, 1733–1737)

The Conquest of Jerusalem and the Third Crusade: Sources in Translation, ed. and trans. Peter W. Edbury, Crusade Texts in Translation 1 (Aldershot, 1996)

'Continuatio Aquicinctina', ed. D. L. C. Bethmann, in *Monumenta Germaniae Historica Scriptores in Folio*, ed. Georg Heinrich Pertz, vol. 6 (Hanover, 1844), pp. 405–38

La Continuation de Guillaume de Tyr 1184–1197, ed. Margaret Ruth Morgan, Documents relatifs à l'histoire des Croisades 14 (Paris, 1982)

Crusade and Christendom: Annotated Documents in Translation from Innocent III to the Fall of Acre, 1187–1201, ed. Jessalynn Bird, Edward Peters and James M. Powell (Philadelphia, 2013)

The Crusade of Frederick Barbarossa: The History of the Expedition of the Emperor Frederick and Related Texts, trans. G. A. Loud, Crusade Texts in Translation 19 (Farnham, 2010)

Earldom of Gloucester Charters: The Charters and Scribes of the Earls and Countesses of Gloucester to A.D. 1217, ed. Robert B. Patterson (Oxford, 1973)

Epistolæ Cantuarienses: The Letters of the Prior and Convent of Christ Church, Canterbury From A.D. 1187 to A.D. 1199, in *Chronicles and Memorials of the Reign of Richard I*, ed. William Stubbs, vol. 2, Rolls Series 38 (London, 1865)

'L'Estoire de Eracles Empereur et la Conqueste de la Terre d'Outremer', in *Recueil des historiens des croisades, Historiens occidentaux*, ed. l'Académie des Inscriptions et Belles-Lettres, vol. 2 (Paris, 1859)

[Gervase of Canterbury] *The Historical Works of Gervase of Canterbury*, ed. William Stubbs, 2 vols, Rolls Series 73 (London, 1870–1880)

Horn, Elzearius, *Ichnographiae locorum et monumentorum veterum Terrae Sanctae, Accurate delineatae et descriptae. E codice Vaticano, Lat. No. 9233 excerpsit*, ed. Girolamo Golubovich (Rome 1902)

[Ibn al-Athīr] *The Chronicle of Ibn al-Athīr for the Crusading Period from al-Kāmil fī'l-ta'rīkh*, part 2: *The Years 541–589/1146–1193: The Age of Nur al-Din and Saladin*, trans. by D. S. Richards, Crusade Texts in Translation 15 (Farnham, 2007)

'Imād al-Dīn al-Isfahānī, *Conquête de la Syrie et de la Palestine par Saladin (al-Fath al-qussî fî l-fath al-qudsî)*, trans. Henri Massé, Documents relatifs à l'histoire des Croisades 10 (Paris, 1972)

Das Itinerarium peregrinorum: Eeine zeitgenössische englische Chronik zum dritten Kreuzzug in ursprünglicher Gestalt, ed. Hans Eberhard Mayer, Schriften der Monumenta Germaniae historica (Deutsches Institut für Erforschung des Mittelalters) 18 (Stuttgart, 1962)

Itinerarium peregrinorum et gesta regis Ricardi, auctore, ut videtur, Ricardo, canonico Sanctæ Trinitatis Londoniensis, ed. William Stubbs, vol. 1 of *Chronicles and Memorials of the Reign of Richard I*, Rolls Series 38 (London, 1864), pp. 1–450, trans. as: 'Itinerary of Richard I and others to the Holy Land', in *Chronicles of the Crusades* (London, 1882), pp. 65–339; and as *Chronicle of the Third Crusade: A Translation of the* Itinerarium Peregrinorum et Gesta Regis Ricardi, trans. Helen J. Nicholson, Crusade Texts in Translation 3 (Aldershot, 1997)

John of Ibelin, *Le Livre des Assises*, ed. Peter W. Edbury (Leiden, 2003)

Kohler, Ch., ed., 'Chartes de l'Abbaye de Notre-Dame de la Vallée de Josaphat en Terre-Sainte (1108–1291). Analyses et extraits', *Revue de l'Orient Latin*, 7 (1899), 108–222

Die lateinische Fortsetzung Wilhelms von Tyrus, ed. Marianne Salloch (Leipzig, 1934)

'Libellus de expugnatione Terrae Sanctae per Saladinum', in *The Conquest of the Holy Land by Ṣalāḥ al-Dīn: A Critical Edition and Translation of the Anonymous Libellus de expugnatione terre sancte per Saladinum*, ed. and trans. Keagan Brewer and James H. Kane, Crusade Texts in Translation (London, 2019), pp. 108–245

Magister Tolosanus, *Chronicon Faventinum [AA. 20 av. C.-1236]*, ed. Giuseppe Rossini, Rerum Italicarum Scriptores: Raccolta degli Storici Italiani dal cinquecento al millecinquecento, ed. L. A. Muratori, new revised edn ed. Giosue Carducci, Vittorio Fiorini and Pietro Fedele, 28.1 (Bologna, 1936)

'Magni presbyteri annales Reicherspergenses', ed. Wilhelm Wattenbach, in *Monumenta Germaniae Historica Scriptores in Folio*, ed. Georg Heinrich Pertz, vol. 17 (Hanover, 1861), pp. 439–534

Marino Sanudo Torsello, *The Book of the Secrets of the Faithful of the Cross: Liber Secretorum Fidelium Crucis*, trans. Peter Lock, Crusade Texts in Translation 21 (Farnham, 2011)

Matthew Paris, *Chronica majora*, ed. Henry Richards Luard, 7 vols, Rolls Series 57 (London, 1872–1883)

Matthew Paris, *Flores historiarum per Matthaeum Westmonasteriensem collecti*, ed. Henry Richards Luard, 3 vols, Rolls Series 95 (London, 1890)

Matthew Paris, *Historia Anglorum, sive, ut vulgo dicitur, Historia minor. Item, ejusdem Abbreviatio chronicorum Angliæ*, ed. Frederic Madden, 3 vols, Rolls Series 44 (London, 1866–1869)

Minstrel of Reims see *Récits d'un ménestrel de Reims*

'Monachus Florentinus de expugnatione civitatis Acconensis', in Roger of Howden, *Chronica*, vol. 3 pp. cv–cxxxvi

F. Nicholai Triveti de ordine Frat. Prædicatorum, Annales sex regum Angliæ, ed. Thomas Hog (London, 1845)

180 Bibliography

Odo of Deuil, *De Profectione Ludovici VII in Orientem. The Journey of Louis VII to the East*, ed. and trans. Virginia Gingerick Berry (New York, 1948)

Le Pas Saladin: An Old French Poem of the Third Crusade, ed. Frank E. Lodeman (Baltimore, 1897)

Philip of Novara, *Le Livre de Forme de Plait*, ed. and trans. Peter W. Edbury (Nicosia, 2009)

Radulphi de Coggeshall Chronicon Anglicanum, ed. Joseph Stevenson, Rolls Series 66 (London, 1875)

Ralph of Diceto, 'Ymagines historiarum', in *Radulfi de Diceto Decani Lundoniensis opera historica: The Historical Works of Master Ralph de Diceto, Dean of London*, ed. William Stubbs, 2 vols, Rolls Series 68 (London, 1876), 1: 291–440, 2: 3–174

Récits d'un ménestrel de Reims au treizième siècle, ed. Natalis de Wailly (Paris, 1876)

Regesta regni Hierosolymitani, MXCVII–MCCXCI, ed. Reinhold Röhricht, 2 vols (Innsbruck, 1893–1904). New edition: Revised Regesta Regni Hierosolymitani Database, online at: http://crusades-regesta.com

'Regni Iherosolymitani Brevis Historia', in *Annali Genovesi di Caffaro et de' suoi continuatori del MXCIX al MCCXCIII*, New edition, ed. Luigi Tommaso Belgrano, Fonti per la Storia d'Italia, 5 vols (Genoa, 1890–1929), 1: 125–49

[Robert of Torigny] *The Chronicle of Robert of Torigni, Abbot of the Monastery of St Michael-in-peril-of-the-sea*, in *Chronicles of the Reigns of Stephen, Henry II, and Richard I*, ed. Richard Howlett, Rolls Series 82, vol. 4 (London, 1889)

Roger of Howden, *Chronica Magistri Rogeri de Houedene*, ed. William Stubbs, 4 vols, Rolls Series 51 (London, 1868–1871)

[Roger of Howden] *Gesta regis Henrici secundi: The Chronicle of the Reigns of Henry II and Richard I, A.D. 1169–1192*, ed. William Stubbs, 2 vols, Rolls Series 49 (London, 1867)

Rogeri de Wendover Liber qui dicitur Flores Historiarum ab anno domini MCLIV, annoque Henrici Anglorum regis secundi primo; The Flowers of History by Roger de Wendover from the Year of Our Lord 1154, and the first year of Henry the second, king of the English, ed. Henry G. Hewlett, 3 vols, Rolls Series 84 (London, 1886)

'Sibylla regina Hierusalemitana epistola Friderico Imp.' in 'Tagenonis decani Pataviensis, Descriptio Expeditionis Asiaticæ contra Turcas Friderici Imp.', in *Rerum Germanicarum Scriptores aliquot insignes*, vol. 1, ed. Marquard Freher, 3rd edition revised Burchard Gotthelf Struve (Strassburg, 1717), p. 410; trans. in *Letters of the Crusaders*, trans. Dana Carleton Munro (Philadelphia, 1902), pp. 21–22

Sicardi Episcopi Cremonensis Cronica, ed. O. Holder-Egger, in *Monumenta Germaniae Historica Scriptores in Folio*, vol. 31 (Hanover, 1903), pp. 22–181

Tolosanus, see Magister Tolosanus

Die Urkunden der lateinischen Könige von Jerusalem, ed. Hans Eberhard Mayer, 4 vols, Monumenta Germaniae historica. Diplomata regum Latinorum Hierosolymitanorum (Hanover, 2010)

Usama ibn Munqidh, *The Book of Contemplation: Islam and the Crusades*, trans. Paul M. Cobb (London, 2008)

[Usāmah ibn-Munqidh] *An Arab-Syrian Gentleman and Warrior in the Period of the Crusades: Memoirs of Usāmah ibn-Munqidh*, trans. Philip K. Hitti (repr. Princeton, 1987).

'Versus ex libro magistri Ricardi canonici Sancti Victoris Parisiensis', in 'Ein zeitgenössisches Gedicht auf die Belagerung Accons', ed. Hans Prutz, *Forschungen zur deutschen Geschichte*, 21 (1881), 449–94

Wace, *The Hagiographical Works*: *The* Conception Nostre Dame *and the Lives of St Margaret and St Nicholas*, trans. Jean Blacker, Glyn S. Burgess and Amy V. Ogden (Leiden, 2013)

William of Newburgh, *Historia rerum anglicarum*, in *Chronicles of the Reigns of Stephen, Henry II and Richard I*, ed. Richard Howlett, Rolls Series 82 (London, 1884–1889)

Willelmi Tyrensis Archiepiscopi Chronicon/Guillaume de Tyr, *Chronique*, ed. R. B. C. Huygens, 2 vols, Corpus Christianorum Continuatio Mediaeualis 63, 63A (Turnhout, 1986)

Secondary works

Adolf, Helen, 'A Historical Background for Chrétien's Perceval', *PMLA*, 58.3 (1943), 597–620

Asbridge, Thomas S., *The Creation of the Principality of Antioch 1098–1130* (Woodbridge, 2000)

Asbridge, Thomas, 'Alice of Antioch: A case study of female power in the twelfth century', in *The Experience of Crusading, volume two: Defining the Crusader Kingdom*, ed. Peter Edbury and Jonathan Phillips (Cambridge, 2003), pp. 29–47

Asbridge, Thomas, 'Talking to the Enemy: The role and purpose of negotiations between Saladin and Richard the Lionheart during the Third Crusade', *Journal of Medieval History*, 39.3 (2013), 275–96

Avignon, Carole, 'Marché matrimonial clandestin et officines de clandestinité à la fin du Moyen Âge: l'exemple du diocèse de Rouen', *Revue historique*, 312.3/655 (2010), 515–49

Baldwin, John W., *The Government of Philip Augustus: Foundations of French Royal Power in the Middle Ages* (Berkeley, 1986)

Barber, Malcolm, *The Crusader States* (New Haven and London, 2012)

Barrow, Julia, 'Chester's earliest regatta? Edgar's Dee-rowing revisited', *Early Medieval Europe*, 10.1 (2001), 81–93

Bassett, Hayley, 'Regnant Queenship and Royal Marriage between the Latin Kingdom of Jerusalem and the Nobility of Western Europe', in *A Companion to Global Queenship*, ed. Elena Woodacre (Leeds, 2018), pp. 39–52

Bell, David N., *What Nuns Read: Books and Libraries in Medieval English Nunneries* (Kalamazoo, MI, 1995)

Belleforest, François de and Sebastian Münster, *La cosmographie vniuerselle de tout le monde*, 2 vols (Paris, 1575)

Belleforest, François de, *Les grandes annales et histoire générale de France, dès la venue des Francs en Gaule, jusques au règne du roy trés-chrestien Henry III* (Paris, 1579)

Boas, Adrian, 'Some Reflections on Urban Landscapes in the Kingdom of Jerusalem: Archaeological Research in Jerusalem and Acre', in *Dei gesta per Francos: Études sur les croisades dédiées à Jean Richard/Crusade Studies in Honour of Jean Richard*, ed. Michel Balard, Benjamin Z. Kedar and Jonathan Riley-Smith (Aldershot, 2001), pp. 241–60

Boas, Adrian J., *Archaeology of the Military Orders. A survey of the urban centres, rural settlements and castles of the military orders in the Latin East (c. 1120–1291)* (Abingdon, 2006)

Boas, Adrian J., *Crusader Archaeology: The Material Culture of the Latin East*, 2nd edition (Abingdon, 2017)

182 *Bibliography*

Boase, T. S. R. (ed.), *The Cilician Kingdom of Armenia* (Edinburgh and London, 1978)
Bom, Myra Miranda, *Women in the Military Orders of the Crusades* (Basingstoke, 2012)
Bouchard, Constance Brittain, *"Those of my Blood": Constructing Noble Families in Medieval Francia* (Philadelphia, 2001)
Bowie, Colette, *The daughters of Henry II and Eleanor of Aquitaine* (Turnhout, 2014)
Bradbury, Jim, *Philip Augustus, King of France 1180–1223* (London, 1998)
Brigitte-Porëe, P., 'Les moulins et fabriques à sucre de Palestine et de Chypre: Histoire, geographie et technologie d'une production croisée et médiévale', in *Cyprus and the Crusades: Papers given at the International Conference 'Cyprus and the Crusades', Nicosia, 6–9 September, 1994*, ed. N. Coureas and J. Riley-Smith (Nicosia, 1995), pp. 377–510
Bronstein, Judith, Elisabeth Yehuda and Edna J. Stern, 'Viticulture in the Latin Kingdom of Jerusalem in the Light of Historical and Archaeological Evidence', *Journal of Mediterranean Archaeology*, 33.1 (2020), 55–78
Brooke, Christopher N. L., *The Medieval Idea of Marriage* (Oxford, 1989)
Brundage, James A., *Medieval Canon Law* (London, 1995)
Brundage, James A., 'Marriage Law in the Latin Kingdom of Jerusalem', in *Outremer: Studies in the history of the Crusading Kingdom of Jerusalem presented to Joshua Prawer*, ed. B. Z. Kedar, H. E. Mayer and R. C. Smail (Jerusalem, 1982), pp. 258–71
Buck, Andrew D., 'The Noble Rebellion at Antioch, 1180–82: A Case Study in Medieval Frontier Politics', *Nottingham Medieval Studies*, 60 (2016), 93–121
Buck, Andrew D., 'Politics and diplomacy in the Latin East: The principality of Antioch in historiographical perspective', *History Compass*, 15.9 (2017)
Buck, Andrew D., *The Principality of Antioch and its Frontiers in the Twelfth Century* (Woodbridge, 2017)
Buck, Andrew D., 'Women in the Principality of Antioch: Power, Status, and Social Agency', *Haskins Society Journal*, 31 (2019), 95–132
Buckingham, Hannah, and Denys Pringle, 'The Fortifications: Grid 20 Fortification Tower', in *The Leon Levy Expedition to Ashkelon, Ashkelon 8: The Islamic and Crusader Periods*, ed. Tracy Hoffman (Pennsylvania, 2019), pp. 76–90
Cadden, Joan, *Meanings of Sex Difference in the Middle Ages: Medicine, Science, and Culture* (Cambridge, 1993)
Cheney, C. R., ed., revised by Michael Jones, *A Handbook of Dates for Students of British History* (Cambridge, 2000)
Chibnall, Marjorie, *The Empress Matilda: Queen Consort, Queen Mother, and Lady of the English* (Oxford, 1991)
Chibnall, Marjorie, 'The Empress Matilda as a Subject for Biography', in *Writing Medieval Biography 750–1250: Essays in Honour of Professor Frank Barlow*, ed. David Bates, Julia Crick, and Sarah Hamilton (Woodbridge, 2006), pp. 185–94
Ciggaar, Krijnie N., 'Robert de Boron en Outremer? Le Culte de Joseph d'Arimathie dans le monde byzantin et en Outremer', *Polyphonia Byzantina: Studies in Honour of Willem J. Aerts*, ed. Hero Hokwerda, Edmé R. Smits and Marinus M. Woesthuis (Groningen, 1993), pp. 145–59
Cole, Penny J., 'Christian perceptions of the battle of Hattin (583/1187)', *Al-Masāq: Journal of the Medieval Mediterranean*, 6.1 (1993), 9–39
Corbet, Patrick, 'Entre Aliénor d'Aquitaine et Blanche de Castille. Les princesses au pouvoir dans la France de l'Est', in *Mächtige Frauen? Königinnen und Fürstinnen im*

europäischen Mittelalter (11.–14. Jahrhundert), ed. Claudia Zey with Sophei Caflisch and Philippe Goridis, Vorträge und Forschungen 81 (Ostfildern, 2015), pp. 225–47

Corner, David, 'The *Gesta Regis Henrici Secundi* and *Chronica* of Roger, Parson of Howden', *Bulletin of the Institute of Historical Research*, 56/134 (1983), 126–44

Crouch, David, 'At Home with Roger of Howden', in *Military Cultures and Martial Enterprises in the Middle Ages: Essays in Honour of Richard P. Abels*, ed. John D. Hosler and Steven Isaac (Woodbridge, 2020), pp. 156–76

Dalton, Paul, 'Sites and Occasions of Peacemaking in England and Normandy, c. 900–c. 1150', *Haskins Society Journal*, 16 (2005), 12–26

D'Angelo, Edoardo, 'A Latin School in the Norman Principality of Antioch?', in *People, Texts and Artefacts: Cultural Transmission in the Medieval Norman Worlds*, ed. David Bates, Edoardo D'Angelo, and Elisabeth van Houts (London, 2017), pp. 77–88

Davis, R. H. C., 'William of Tyre', in *Relations between East and West in the Middle Ages*, ed. Derek Baker (Edinburgh, 1973), pp. 64–76

DeAragon, RāGena C., 'Power and Agency in Post-Conquest England: Elite Women and the Transformations of the Twelfth Century', in *Medieval Elite Women and the Exercise of Power, 1100–1400: Moving beyond the Exceptionalist Debate*, ed. Heather J. Tanner (Cham, 2019)

Delaville, Le Roulx, Joseph, 'Inventaire de pièces de Terre Sainte de l'ordre de l'Hôpital', *Revue de l'Orient latin*, 3 (1895), 36–106

Diverres, Armel, 'The Grail and the Third Crusade: Thoughts on *Le Conte del Graal* by Chrétien de Troyes', in *Arthurian Literature X*, ed. Richard Barber (Cambridge, 1990), pp. 13–109

Dutton, Kathryn, '*Ad erudiendum tradidit*: The Upbringing of Angevin Comital Children', in *Anglo-Norman Studies XXXII: Proceedings of the Battle Conference 2009*, ed. C. P. Lewis (Woodbridge, 2010), pp. 24–39

Eastmond, Antony, 'Royal Renewal in Georgia: The Case of Queen Tamar', in *New Constantines: The Rhythm of Imperial Renewal in Byzantium, 4th–13th Centuries*, ed. Paul Magdalino (Aldershot, 1994), pp. 283–93

Eastmond, Antony, *Tamta's World: The Life and Encounters of a Medieval Noblewoman from the Middle East to Mongolia* (Cambridge, 2017)

Edbury, P. W., and J. G. Rowe, 'William of Tyre and the Patriarchal Election of 1180', *English Historical Review*, 93 (1978), 1–25

Edbury, Peter W., and John Rowe, *William of Tyre: Historian of the Latin East* (Cambridge, 1988)

Edbury, Peter W., 'The "Livre" of Geoffrey le Tor and the "Assises" of Jerusalem', in *Historia administrativa y ciencia de la administración comparada. Trabajos en homenaje a Ferran Valls i Taberner*, ed. M. J. Peláez, vol. 15 (Barcelona, 1990), 4291–98, reprinted in Peter Edbury, ed., *Kingdoms of the Crusaders: From Jerusalem to Cyprus* (Aldershot, 1999), article X.

Edbury, Peter W., *The Kingdom of Cyprus and the Crusades, 1191–1374* (Cambridge, 1991)

Edbury, Peter W., 'Propaganda and Faction in the Kingdom of Jerusalem: The Background to Hattin', in *Crusaders and Muslims in Twelfth-Century Syria*, ed. M. Shatzmiller (Leiden, 1993), pp. 173–89

Edbury, Peter W., 'Law and Custom in the Latin East: *Les Letres dou Sepulcre*', in *Intercultural Contacts in the Medieval Mediterranean: Studies in Honour of David*

Jacoby, ed. B. Arbel, *Mediterranean Historical Review*, 10 (1995), 71–76; reprinted in Peter Edbury, ed., *Kingdoms of the Crusaders: From Jerusalem to Cyprus* (Aldershot, 1999), article IX

Edbury, Peter W., 'Preaching the Crusade in Wales', in *England and Germany in the High Middle Ages. In Honour of Karl J. Leyser*, ed. Alfred Haverkamp and Hanna Vollrath (Oxford, 1996), pp. 221–33

Edbury, Peter W., *John of Ibelin and the Kingdom of Jerusalem* (Woodbridge, 1997)

Edbury, Peter W., 'Women and the customs of the High Court of Jerusalem according to John of Ibelin', in *Chemins d'outre-mer: Études d'histoire sur la Méditerranée médiévale offertes à Michel Balard*, ed. D. Coulon, C. Otten-Froux, P. Pagès and D. Valérian (Paris, 2004), pp. 285–92; reprinted in Peter W. Edbury, ed., *Law and History in the Latin East* (Farnham, 2014), article V

Edbury, Peter, 'Gerard of Ridefort and the Battle of Le Cresson (1 May 1187): The Developing Narrative Tradition', in *On the Margins of Crusading: The Military Orders, the Papacy and the Christian World*, ed. Helen J. Nicholson, Crusades Subsidia 4 (Farnham, 2011), pp. 45–60

Edbury, Peter, 'Ernoul, *Eracles*, and the Beginnings of Frankish Rule in Cyprus, 1191–1232', in *Medieval Cyprus: A Place of Cultural Encounter*, ed. Sabine Rogge and Michael Grünbart, Schriften des Instituts für Interdisziplinäre Zypern-Studien, 11 (Münster, 2015), pp. 29–51

Edbury, Peter W., 'Ernoul, *Eracles*, and the Collapse of the Kingdom of Jerusalem', in *The French of Outremer: communities and communications in the Crusading Mediterranean*, ed. Laura K. Morreale and Nicholas L. Paul (New York, 2018), pp. 44–67

Edbury, Peter W., 'The Crusader Town and Lordship of Ramla (1099–1268)', in *Ramla: City of Muslim Palestine, 715–1917*, ed. Andrew Petersen and Denys Pringle (Oxford, 2021), pp. 7–17

Edgington, Susan B., *Baldwin I of Jerusalem, 1100–1118*, Rulers of the Latin East (Abingdon, 2019)

Ellenblum, Ronnie, 'Frontier Activities: the Transformation of a Muslim Sacred Site into the Frankish Castle of Vadum Iacob', *Crusades*, 2 (2003), 83–97

Evergates, Theodore, ed., *Aristocratic Women in Medieval France* (Philadelphia, 1999)

Evergates, Theodore, *Henry the Liberal, Count of Champagne, 1127–1181* (Philadelphia, 2016)

Evergates, Theodore. *Marie of France: Countess of Champagne, 1145–1198* (Philadelphia, 2019)

Fleming, Peter, *Family and Household in Medieval England* (Basingstoke, 2001)

Folda, Jaroslav, 'Manuscripts of the *History of Outremer* by William of Tyre: a Handlist', *Scriptorium*, 27.1 (1973), 90–95

Folda, Jaroslav, *Crusader Art: The Art of the Crusaders in the Holy Land, 1099–1291* (Aldershot, 2008)

Forey, Alan, 'The Order of Mountjoy', *Speculum*, 46 (1971), 250–66

France, John, *Hattin* (Oxford, 2015)

Frappier, Jean, *Les Chansons de geste du cycle de Guillaume d'Orange*, 2 vols (Paris, 1955, 1965)

Fuller, Thomas, *The Historie of the Holy Warre*, 3rd edition (Cambridge, 1640)

Gaposchkin, M. Cecilia, *Invisible Weapons: Liturgy and the Making of Crusade Ideology* (Ithaca and London, 2017)

Geldsetzer, Sabine, *Frauen auf Kreuzzügen, 1096–1291* (Darmstadt, 2003)

Gerish, Deborah, 'Holy War, Royal Wives, and Equivocation in Twelfth-Century Jerusalem', in *Noble Ideals and Bloody Realities: Warfare in the Middle Ages*, ed. Niall Christie and Maya Yazigi, History of Warfare 37 (Leiden, 2006), pp. 119–44

Gerish, Deborah, 'Royal Daughters of Jerusalem and the demands of holy war', *Leidschrift: Historisch Tijdschrift*, 27.3 (2012), 89–112

Gilchrist, Marianne McLeod, 'Getting away with murder: Runciman and Conrad of Montferrat's career in Constantinople', *The Mediæval Journal*, 2.1 (2012), 15–36

Gilchrist, Roberta, *Gender and Material Culture: The Archaeology of Religious Women* (London, 1994)

Gilchrist, Roberta, *Contemplation and Action: the Other Monasticism* (London, 1995)

Gillingham, John, 'Roger of Howden on Crusade', in *Medieval Historical Writing in the Christian and Islamic Worlds*, ed. David O. Morgan (London, 1982), pp. 60–75

Gillingham, John, 'Love, Marriage and Politics in the Twelfth Century', *Forum for Modern Language Studies*, 25 (1989), pp. 292–303

Gillingham, John, *Richard I*, Yale English Monarchs (New Haven and London, 1999)

Gordo Molina, Angel G., 'Urraca de León y Teresa de Portugal. Las Relaciones de Fronteras y el Ejercicio de la Potestad Femenina en la Primera Mitad del Siglo XII. Jurisdicción, *Imperium* y Linaje', *Intus-Legere Historia*, 2.1 (2008), 9–23

Goridis, Philippe, '*Rex factus est uxorius*: Weibliche und männliche Herrschaftsrollen in Outremer', in *Kreuzzug und Gender*, ed. Ingrid Baumgärtner and Melanie Panse, *Das Mittelalter. Perspektiven mediävistischer Forschung*, 21.1 (Berlin, 2016), pp. 22–39

Hamilton, Bernard, 'Women in the Crusader States: the queens of Jerusalem, 1100–1190', in *Medieval Women*, ed. Derek Baker, Studies in Church History Subsidia 1 (Oxford, 1978), pp. 143–74

Hamilton, Bernard, 'The Elephant of Christ: Reynald of Châtillon', in *Religious Motivation: Biographical and Sociological Problems for the Church Historian; Papers read at the Sixteenth Summer Meeting and the Seventeenth Winter Meeting of the Ecclesiastical History Society*, ed. Derek Baker, Studies in Church History 15 (1978), 97–108

Hamilton, Bernard, *The Latin Church in the Crusader States: The Secular Church* (London, 1980)

Hamilton, Bernard, 'The Titular Nobility of the Latin East: the Case of Agnes of Courtenay', in *Crusade and Settlement. Papers read at the First Conference of the Society for the Study of the Crusades and the Latin East and presented to R. C Smail*, ed. Peter W. Edbury (Cardiff, 1985), pp. 197–203

Hamilton, Bernard, *Religion in the Medieval West* (London, 1986)

Hamilton, Bernard, 'Manuel I Comnenus and Baldwin IV of Jerusalem', in *Kathēgētria: essays presented to Joan Hussey on her 80th birthday*, ed. J. Chrysostomides (Camberley, 1988), pp. 353–75

Hamilton, Bernard, 'Miles of Plancy and the Fief of Beirut', in *The Horns of Ḥaṭṭīn*, ed. B. Z. Kedar (Jerusalem and London, 1992), pp. 136–46

Hamilton, Bernard, *The Leper King and his Heirs: Baldwin IV and the Crusader Kingdom of Jerusalem* (Cambridge, 2000)

Hamilton, Bernard, and Andrew Jotischky, *Latin and Greek Monasticism in the Crusader States* (Cambridge, 2020)

Handyside, Philip, *The Old French William of Tyre*, The Medieval Mediterranean 103 (Leiden, 2015)

Bibliography

Hanley, Catherine, *Matilda: Empress, Queen, Warrior* (New Haven and London, 2019)

Harris, Jonathan, *Byzantium and the Crusades*, 2nd edition (London, 2014)

Hartmann, Florian, 'Sicard of Cremona [Sicardus episcopus Cremonensis]', in *Encyclopedia of the Medieval Chronicle*, ed. Graeme Dunphy (Leiden, 2010), 2: 1357

Hartmann, Florian, 'Tolosanus', in *Encyclopedia of the Medieval Chronicle*, ed. Graeme Dunphy (Leiden, 2010), 2: 1430–31

Hay, David J., *The Military Leadership of Matilda of Canossa, 1046–1115* (Manchester, 2008)

Hodgson, Natasha R., *Women, Crusading and the Holy Land in Historical Narrative* (Woodbridge, 2007)

Hodgson, Natasha, 'Conflict and Cohabitation: Marriage and Diplomacy between Latins and Cilician Armenians, c. 1097–1253', in *The Crusades and the Near East: Cultural Histories*, ed. Conor Kostick (Abingdon, 2011), pp. 83–106

Holdsworth, Christopher J., 'Baldwin of Forde, Cistercian and archbishop of Canterbury', *Annual Report* [Friends of Lambeth Palace Library] (1989), 13–31

Holdsworth, Christopher, 'Baldwin [Baldwin of Forde] (c. 1125–1190), archbishop of Canterbury', in *Oxford Dictionary of National Biography*, ed. H. C. G. Matthew, and Brian Harrison, 60 vols (Oxford, 2004), 3: 442–45

Holt, Peter Malcolm, *Early Mamluk Diplomacy, 1260–1290: Treaties of Baybars and Qalāwūn with Christian Rulers* (Leiden, 1995)

Hosler, John D., *The Siege of Acre, 1189–1191: Saladin, Richard the Lionheart, and the Battle that Decided the Third Crusade* (New Haven and London, 2018)

Huneycutt, Lois, 'Tamar of Georgia (1184–1213) and the Language of Female Power', in *A Companion to Global Queenship*, ed. Elena Woodacre (Leeds, 2018), pp. 27–38

Hurlock, Kathryn, *Britain, Ireland and the Crusades, c. 1000–1300* (Basingstoke, 2013)

Jacoby, David, 'Knightly Values and Class Consciousness in the Crusader States of the Eastern Mediterranean', *Mediterranean Historical Review*, 1.2 (1986), 158–86

Jacoby, David, 'Conrad, Marquis of Montferrat, and the Kingdom of Jerusalem (1187–1192)', in *Atti del Congresso Internazionale "Dai feudi monferrini e dal Piemonte ai nuovi mondi oltre gli Oceani", Alessandria, 2–6 aprile 1990* (Alessandria, 1993), pp. 187–238

Jacoby, David, 'The *fonde* of Crusader Acre and Its Tariff: Some New Considerations', in *Dei gesta per Francos: Études sur les croisades dédiées à Jean Richard/Crusade Studies in Honour of Jean Richard*, ed. Michel Balard, Benjamin Z. Kedar and Jonathan Riley-Smith (Aldershot, 2001), pp. 277–93.

Jacoby, Zehava, 'The Tomb of Baldwin V, King of Jerusalem (1185–1186), and the Workshop of the Temple Area', *Gesta*, 18.2 (1979), 3–14

John, Simon, 'Royal Inauguration and Liturgical Culture in the Latin kingdom of Jerusalem, 1099–1187', *Journal of Medieval History*, 43.4 (2017), 485–504

Johns, Susan M., *Noblewomen, Aristocracy and Power in the twelfth-century Anglo-Norman Realm* (Manchester, 2003)

Jordan, Erin L., 'Hostage, Sister, Abbess: The Life of Iveta of Jerusalem', *Medieval Prosopography*, 32 (2017), 66–86

Jordan, Erin, 'Corporate Monarchy in the Twelfth-Century Kingdom of Jerusalem', *Royal Studies Journal*, 6.1 (2019), 1–15

Jordan, Erin L., 'Women of Antioch: Political Culture and Powerful Women in the Latin East', in *Medieval Elite Women and the Exercise of Power, 1100–1400: Moving beyond the Exceptionalist Debate*, ed. Heather J. Tanner (Cham, 2019), pp. 225–46

Jotischky, Andrew, *Crusading and the Crusader States* (Harlow, 2004)

Jubb, Margaret, *The Legend of Saladin in Western Literature and Historiography* (Lewiston, 2000)

Kane, James H., 'Wolf's Hair, Exposed Digits, and Muslim Holy Men: *The Libellus de expugnatione Terrae Sanctae per Saladinum* and the *Conte* of Ernoul', *Viator*, 47.2 (2016), 95–112

Kane, James H., 'Between Parson and Poet: A Re-examination of the Latin Continuation of William of Tyre', *Journal of Medieval History*, 44.1 (2018), 56–82

Kedar, Benjamin Z., 'The General Tax of 1183 in the Crusading Kingdom of Jerusalem: Innovation or Adaptation?' *English Historical Review*, 89 (1974), 339–45

Kedar, Benjamin Z., 'The Patriarch Eraclius', in *Outremer: Studies in the History of the Crusading Kingdom of Jerusalem presented to Joshua Prawer*, ed. Benjamin Z. Kedar, Hans Eberhard Mayer and R. C. Smail (Jerusalem, 1982), pp. 177–204

Kedar, Benjamin Z., 'Gerard of Nazareth, a Neglected Twelfth-Century Writer in the Latin East: A Contribution to the Intellectual and Monastic History of the Crusader States', *Dumbarton Oaks Papers*, 37 (1983), 55–77

Kedar, Benjamin Z., 'Genoa's Golden Inscription in the Church of the Holy Sepulchre: A Case for the Defence', in *I comuni italiani nel Regno Crociato di Gerusalemme. Atti del colloquio di Gerusalemme, 24–28 maggio 1984*, ed. G. Airaldi and B. Z. Kedar (Genoa, 1986), pp. 317–35, at pp. 110–11, reprinted in Benjamin Z. Kedar, ed., *The Franks in the Levant, 11th to 14th Centuries* (Aldershot, 1993), article III

Kedar, Benjamin Z., 'The Battle of Hattin Revisited', in *The Horns of Ḥaṭṭīn*, ed. B. Z. Kedar (Jerusalem and London, 1992), pp. 190–207

Kenaan-Kedar, Nurith, 'Decorative Architectural Sculpture in Crusader Jerusalem: The Eastern, Western, and Armenian Sources of a local visual culture', in *The Crusader World*, ed. Adrian J. Boas (Abingdon, 2016), pp. 609–23

Khamisy, Rabei G., 'Frankish Viticulture, Wine Presses, and wine production in the Levant: New Evidence from Castellum Regis (Mi'ilyā)', *Palestine Exploration Quarterly*, 153.3 (2020), 191–221

King, Edmund, 'Eustace, count of Boulogne (c. 1129–1153), claimant to the English throne', in *Oxford Dictionary of National Biography*, ed. H. C. G. Matthew and Brian Harrison (Oxford, 23 Sep. 2004); accessed 17 Mar. 2021: https://www-oxforddnb-com.abc.cardiff.ac.uk/view/10.1093/ref:odnb/9780198614128.001.0001/odnb-9780198614128-e-46704

Kool, Robert, 'Coins', in *The Leon Levy Expedition to Ashkelon, Ashkelon 8: The Islamic and Crusader Periods*, ed. Tracy Hoffman (Pennsylvania, 2019), pp. 523–74

Kool, Robert, 'Civitas regis regvm omnivm: Inventing a royal seal in Jerusalem, 1100–1118', in *Crusading and Archaeology: Some Archaeological Approaches to the Crusades*, ed. Vardit R. Shotten-Hallel and Rosie Weetch, Crusades Subsidia 14 (Abingdon, 2020), pp. 245–62

Korpiola, Mia, 'Introduction: Regional Variations and Harmonization in Medieval Matrimonial Law', in *Regional Variations in Matrimonial Law and Custom in Europe, 1150–1600*, ed. Mia Korpiola (Leiden, 2011), pp. 1–20

Lambert, Sarah, 'Queen or Consort: Rulership and Politics in the Latin East, 1118–1228', in *Queens and Queenship in Medieval Europe: Proceedings of a Conference held at King's College London, April 1995*, ed. Anne J. Duggan (London, 1997), pp. 153–69

Lambert, Sarah, 'Images of Queen Melisende', in *Authority and Gender in Medieval and Renaissance Chronicles*, ed. Juliana Dresvina and Nicholas Sparks (Newcastle Upon Tyne, 2012), pp. 140–64

LaMonte, John L., 'The Lords of Le Puiset on the Crusades', *Speculum*, 17.1 (1942), 100–118

La Porta, Sergio, '"The Kingdom and the Sultanate Were Conjoined": Legitimizing Land and Power in Armenia during the 12th and Early 13th Centuries', *Revue des études arméniennes*, 34 (2012), 73–118

Lewis, Kevin James, 'Countess Hodierna of Tripoli: From Crusader Politician to "Princess Lointaine"', *Assuming Gender*, 3.1 (2013), 1–26

Lewis, Kevin James, *The Counts of Tripoli and Lebanon in the Twelfth Century: Sons of Saint-Gilles*, Rulers of the Latin East (Abingdon, 2017)

Leyser, Henrietta, *Medieval Women: A Social History of Women in England, 450–1500* (London, 1995)

Ligato Giuseppe, *Sibilla regina crociata: guerra, amore e diplomazia per il trono di Gerusalemme* (Milan, 2005)

Lyons, Malcolm Cameron, and D. E. P. Jackson, *Saladin: The Politics of the Holy War* (Cambridge, 1982)

MacEvitt, Christopher, *The Crusades and the Christian World of the East: Rough Tolerance* (Philadelphia, 2008)

Martin, Therese, 'The Art of a Reigning Queen as Dynastic Propaganda in Twelfth-Century Spain', *Speculum*, 80.4 (2005), 1134–71

Mayer, Hans Eberhard, 'Studies in the History of Queen Melisende of Jerusalem', *Dumbarton Oaks Papers*, 26 (1972), 93, 95–182

Mayer, Hans Eberhard, *Das Siegelwesen in den Kreuzfahrerstaaten* (Munich, 1978)

Mayer, Hans Eberhard, 'Carving up Crusaders: the early Ibelins and Ramlas', in *Outremer: Studies in the History of the Crusading Kingdom of Jerusalem presented to Joshua Prawer*, ed. B. Z. Kedar, H. E. Mayer and R. C. Smail (Jerusalem, 1982), pp. 101–18

Mayer, Hans Eberhard, 'Henry II of England and the Holy Land', *English Historical Review*, 97 (1982), 721–39

Mayer, Hans Eberhard, 'The Double County of Jaffa and Ascalon: One Fief or Two?', in *Crusade and Settlement. Papers read at the First Conference of the Society for the Study of the Crusades and the Latin East and presented to R. C. Smail*, ed. Peter W. Edbury (Cardiff, 1985), pp. 181–90

Mayer, Hans Eberhard, 'Die Legitimität Balduins IV. von Jerusalem und das Testament der Agnes von Courtenay', *Historisches Jahrbuch*, 108 (1988), 63–89, reprinted in Hans E. Mayer, ed., *Kings and Lords in the Latin Kingdom of Jerusalem* (Aldershot, 1994), article IX

Mayer, Hans Eberhard, 'The Beginnings of King Amalric of Jerusalem', in *The Horns of Ḥaṭṭīn*, ed. Benjamin Z. Kedar (Jerusalem and London, 1992), pp. 121–35

Mayer, Hans Eberhard, *Die Kanzlei der lateinischen Könige von Jerusalem*, 2 vols, Monumenta Germaniae Historica, Schriften, 40 (Hanover, 1996)

Mayer, Hans Eberhard, and Claudia Sode, *Die Siegel der lateinischen Könige von Jerusalem*, Monumenta Germaniae Historica, Schriften, 66 (Wiesbaden, 2014)

Mays, S. A., M. P. Richards and B. T. Fuller, 'Bone Stable Isotope Evidence for Infant Feeding in Mediaeval England', *Antiquity*, 76 (2002), 654–56

Michaud, Joseph-François, *Histoire des Croisades séconde partie, contenant l'histoire des seconde et troisième croisades, deuxième volume* (Paris, 1814)

Möhring, Hannes, 'Joseph Iscanus, Neffe Balduins von Canterbury, und eine anonyme englische Chronik des Dritten Kreuzzugs: Versuch einer Identifikation', *Mittellateinisches Jahrbuch*, 19 (1984), 184–90

Mora-Lebrun, Francine, 'Les metamorphoses de la Sibylle au XIIe siècle', *Bien Dire et Bien Aprandre*, 24 (2006), 11–24

Münster, Sebastian, *Cosmographia* (Basel, 1544)

Münster, Sebastian, *Cosmographiae vniversalis lib. VI* (Basel, 1572)

Münster, Sebastian, *Cosmographia vniuersale* (Cologne, 1575)

Murray, Alan V., '"Mighty Against the Enemies of Christ": The Relic of the True Cross in the Armies of the Kingdom of Jerusalem', in *The Crusades and their Sources: Essays Presented to Bernard Hamilton*, ed. John France and William G. Zajac (Aldershot, 1998), pp. 217–38

Murray, Alan V., *The Crusader Kingdom of Jerusalem: A Dynastic History 1099–1125* (Oxford, 2000)

Murray, Alan V. (general editor), *The Crusades: An Encyclopedia* (Santa Barbara, 2006)

Murray, Alan V., 'Kingship, Identity and Name-giving in the Family of Baldwin of Bourcq', in *Knighthoods of Christ: Essays on the History of the Crusades and the Knights Templar presented to Malcolm Barber*, ed. Norman Housley (Aldershot, 2007), pp. 27–38

Murray, Alan V., 'Women in the Royal Succession of the Latin Kingdom of Jerusalem (1099–1291)', in *Mächtige Frauen? Königinnen und Fürstinnen im europäischen Mittelalter (11.–14. Jahrhundert)*, ed. Claudia Zey, Vorträge und Forschungen 81 (Ostfildern, 2015), pp. 131–62

Murray, Alan V., 'Constance, Princess of Antioch (1130–1164): Ancestry, Marriages and Family', in *Anglo-Norman Studies XXXVIII: Proceedings of the Battle Conference 2015*, ed. Elisabeth van Houts (Woodbridge, 2016), pp. 81–95

Nersessian, Sirarpie der, 'The Armenian Chronicle of the Constable Smpad or of the "Royal Historian"', *Dumbarton Oaks Papers*, 13 (1959), 141, 143–68

Nicholas, Karen S., 'Countesses as Rulers in Flanders', in *Aristocratic Women in Medieval France*, ed. Theodore Evergates (Philadelphia, 1999), pp. 111–37

Nicholson, Helen J., *Love, War and the Grail: Templars, Hospitallers and Teutonic Knights in Medieval Epic and Romance, 1150–1500* (Leiden, 2001)

Nicholson, Helen J., '"La roine preude femme et bonne dame": Queen Sybil of Jerusalem (1186–1190) in History and Legend, 1186–1300', *The Haskins Society Journal*, 15 (2004), 110–24

Nicholson, Helen J., 'The True Gentleman? Correct Behaviour towards Women according to Christian and Muslim writers: from the Third Crusade to Sultan Baybars', in *Crusading and Masculinities*, ed. Natasha R. Hodgson, Katherine J. Lewis and Matthew M. Mesley, Crusades Subsidia 13 (Abingdon, 2019), pp. 100–12

Nicholson, Helen J., 'The Construction of a Primary Source. The Creation of *Itinerarium Peregrinorum* 1', *Cahiers de recherches médiévales et humanistes/Journal of Medieval and Humanistic Studies*, 37 (2019), 143–65

Nicholson, Helen J., 'Defending Jerusalem: Sybil of Jerusalem as a military leader', *Medieval Warfare Magazine*, 9.4 (Oct/Nov 2019), 6–13

Nicholson, Helen J., 'Queen Sybil of Jerusalem as a military leader', in *Von Hamburg nach Java. Studien zur mittelalterlichen, neuen und digitalen Geschichte. Festschrift zu Ehren von Jürgen Sarnowsky*, ed. Jochen Burgtorf, Christian Hoffarth and Sebastian Kubon (Göttingen, 2020), pp. 265–76

Bibliography

Oksanen, Eljas, *Flanders and the Anglo-Norman World, 1066–1216* (Cambridge, 2012)

Orme, Nicholas, *Medieval Children* (New Haven and London, 2001)

Park, Danielle E. A., *Papal Protection and the Crusader: Flanders, Champagne, and the Kingdom of France, 1095–1222* (Woodbridge, 2018)

Parsons, John Carmi, 'Mothers, Daughters, Marriage, Power: Some Plantagenet Evidence, 1150–1500', in *Medieval Queenship*, ed. John Carmi Parsons (Stroud, 1994), pp. 63–78

Paul, Nicholas L., 'In Search of the Marshal's Lost Crusade: The Persistence of Memory, the Problems of History and the Painful Birth of Crusading Romance', *Journal of Medieval History*, 40.3 (2014), 292–310

Pernoud, Régine, *La femme au temps des Croisades* (Paris, 1990)

Perry, Guy, *The Briennes: The Rise and Fall of a Champenois Dynasty in the Age of the Crusades, c. 950–1356* (Cambridge, 2018)

Phillips, Jonathan, *Defenders of the Holy Land: Relations between the Latin East and the West, 1119–1187* (Oxford, 1996)

Phillips, Jonathan, 'Armenia, Edessa and the Second Crusade', in *Knighthoods of Christ: Essays on the History of the Crusades and the Knights Templar presented to Malcolm Barber*, ed. Norman Housley (Aldershot, 2007), pp. 39–50

Phillips, Jonathan, *The Life and Legend of the Sultan Saladin* (London, 2019)

Pick, Lucy K., *Her Father's Daughter: Gender, Power and Religion in the Early Spanish Kingdoms* (Ithaca and London, 2017)

Pogossian, Zaroui, 'Women, Identity, and Power: A Review Essay of Antony Eastmond, *Tamta's World*', *Al-ʿUṣūr al-Wusṭā: The Journal of Middle East Medievalists*, 27 (2019), 233–66

Pringle, Denys, *The Churches of the Crusader Kingdom of Jerusalem: A Corpus*, 4 vols (Cambridge, 1993–2009)

Pringle, Denys, *Secular Buildings in the Crusader Kingdom of Jerusalem: An archaeological gazetteer* (Cambridge, 1997)

Pringle, Denys, 'Templar Castles between Jaffa and Jerusalem', in *The Military Orders*, vol. 2: *Welfare and Warfare*, ed. Helen Nicholson (Aldershot, 1998), pp. 89–109

Pringle, Denys, 'The Spring of the Cresson in Crusading History', in *Dei gesta per Francos: Études sur les croisades dédiées à Jean Richard/Crusade Studies in Honour of Jean Richard*, ed. Michel Balard, Benjamin Z. Kedar and Jonathan Riley-Smith (Aldershot, 2001), pp. 231–40

Pringle, Denys, 'The Walls of Ascalon in the Byzantine, Early Islamic and Crusader Periods. A Preliminary Report on Current Research', in *Guerre et paix dans le Proche-Orient médiéval (x^e–xve siècle)*, ed. Mathieu Eychenne, Stéphane Pradines and Abbès Zouache (Cairo, 2019), pp. 449–79

Pringle, Denys, 'The Survey of the Walls of Askhelon', in *The Leon Levy Expedition to Ashkelon, Ashkelon 8: The Islamic and Crusader Periods*, ed. Tracy Hoffman (Pennsylvania, 2019), pp. 98–221

Pryor, John H., 'A Medieval Siege of Troy: The Fight to the Death at Acre, 1189–1191 or The Tears of Ṣalāḥ al-Dīn', in *The Medieval Way of War: Studies in Medieval Military History in Honor of Bernard S. Bachrach*, ed. Gregory I. Halfond (Farnham, 2015), pp. 97–115

Rech, Régis, 'Alberich of Troisfontaines [Aubrey]', in *Encyclopedia of the Medieval Chronicle*, ed. Graeme Dunphy (Leiden, 2010), 1: 23

Reilly, Bernard F., *The Kingdom of León-Castilla under Queen Urraca 1109–1126* (Princeton, 1982)

Reiner, Eichanan, 'Jews in the Crusader Kingdom of Jerusalem', in *Knights of the Holy Land: The Crusader Kingdom of Jerusalem*, ed. Silvia Rozenberg (Jerusalem, 1999), pp. 48–59

Rezak, Brigitte Bedos, 'Women, Seals, and Power in Medieval France, 1150–1350', in *Women and Power in the Middle Ages*, ed. Mary Erler and Maryanne Kowaleski (Athens, GA, 1988), pp. 61–82

Rhodes, Hilary, *The Crown and the Cross: Burgundy, France, and the Crusades, 1095–1223*, Outremer: Studies in the Crusades and the Latin East 9 (Turnhout, 2020)

Riley-Smith, Jonathan, *The Feudal Nobility and the Kingdom of Jerusalem, 1174–1277* (Basingstoke, 1973)

Riley-Smith, Jonathan, 'The Crusading Heritage of Guy and Aimery of Lusignan', in *Cyprus and the Crusades: Papers given at the International Conference 'Cyprus and the Crusades', Nicosia, 6–9 September, 1994*, ed. N. Coureas and J. Riley-Smith (Nicosia, 1995), pp. 31–45

Riley-Smith, Jonathan, *The First Crusaders 1095–1131* (Cambridge, 1997)

Rubanovich, Julia, 'Re-writing the episode of Alexander and Candace in medieval Persian literature: patterns, sources, and motif transformation', in *Alexander the Great in the Middle Ages: Transcultural Perspectives*, ed. Markus Stock (Toronto, 2015), pp. 123–52

Ruch, Lisa M., 'Matthew Paris', in *Encyclopedia of the Medieval Chronicle*, ed. Graeme Dunphy (Leiden, 2010), 2: 1093–95

Ruch, Lisa M., 'Roger of Wendover', in *Encyclopedia of the Medieval Chronicle*, ed. Graeme Dunphy (Leiden, 2010), 2: 1291

Ruch, Lisa M., 'Trevet, Nicholas', in *Encyclopedia of the Medieval Chronicle*, ed. Graeme Dunphy (Leiden, 2010), 2: 1445–46

Salvadó, Sebastián, 'Rewriting the Latin liturgy of the Holy Sepulchre: Text, ritual and devotion for 1149', *Journal of Medieval History*, 43.4 (2017), 403–20

Sans, María Echániz, *Las Mujeres de la Orden Militar de Santiago en la Edad Media* (Salamanca, 1992)

Schein, Sylvia, 'Between East and West: The Jews in the Latin Kingdom of Jerusalem 1099–1291', in *East and West in the Crusader States: Context, Contacts, Confrontations: Acta of the Congress Held at Hernen Castile in May 1993*, ed. Krijnie N. Ciggaar, Adelbert Davids and Herman G. Teule, Orientalia Lovaniensia analecta 75 (Leuven, 1996), pp. 31–37

Schein, Sylvia, 'Rulers and Ruled: Women in the Crusader Period', in *Knights of the Holy Land: The Crusader Kingdom of Jerusalem*, ed. Silvia Rozenberg (Jerusalem, 1999), pp. 61–67

Schein, Sylvia, 'Women in Medieval Colonial Society: The Latin Kingdom of Jerusalem in the Twelfth Century', in *Gendering the Crusades*, ed. Susan B. Edgington and Sarah Lambert (Cardiff, 2001), pp. 140–53

Shadis, Miriam, 'Unexceptional Women: Power, Authority, and Queenship in Early Portugal', in *Medieval Elite Women and the Exercise of Power, 1100–1400: Moving beyond the Exceptionalist Debate*, ed. Heather J. Tanner (Cham, 2019), pp. 247–70

Siberry, Elizabeth, *Criticism of Crusading 1095–1274* (Oxford, 1985)

Sinibaldi, Micaela, 'Karak Castle in the Lordship of Transjordan: Observations on the Chronology of the Crusader-period Fortress', in *Bridge of Civilisations: The Near East and Europe c. 1100–1300*, ed. Peter Edbury, Denys Pringle and Balázs Major (Oxford, 2019), pp. 97–114

Smail, R.C., 'The Predicaments of Guy of Lusignan, 1183–87', in *Outremer: Studies in the History of the Crusading Kingdom of Jerusalem presented to Joshua Prawer*, ed. Benjamin Z. Kedar, Hans Eberhard Mayer and R. C. Smail (Jerusalem, 1982), pp. 159–76

Spufford, Peter, with Wendy Wilkinson and Sarah Tolley, *Handbook of Medieval Exchange* (London, 1986)

Stalls, William Clay, 'Queenship and the Royal Patrimony in Twelfth-Century Iberia: The Example of Petronilla of Aragon', in *Queens, Regents and Potentates*, ed. Theresa M. Vann (Dallas, TX, 1993), pp. 49–61

Tanner, Heather J., ed., *Medieval Elite Women and the Exercise of Power, 1100–1400: Moving beyond the Exceptionalist Debate* (Cham, 2019)

Tessera, Miriam Rita, 'Philip Count of Flanders and Hildegard of Bingen: Crusading against the Saracens or Crusading against Deadly Sin?' in *Gendering the Crusades*, ed. Susan B. Edgington and Susan Lambert (Cardiff, 2001), pp. 77–93

Thomas, Hugh M., 'Mowbray, Sir Roger de (d. 1188), magnate', in *Oxford Dictionary of National Biography*, ed. H. C. G. Matthew and Brian Harrison (Oxford, 23 Sep. 2004), accessed 30 Mar. 2021: https://www-oxforddnb-com.abc.cardiff.ac.uk/view/10.1093/ref:odnb/9780198614128.001.0001/odnb-9780198614128-e-19458

Tibble, Steve, *The Crusader Armies 1099–1187* (New Haven and London, 2018)

Truax, Jean A., 'Anglo-Norman Women at War: Valiant Soldiers, Prudent Strategists or Charismatic Leaders?' in *The Circle of War in the Middle Ages: Essays on Medieval Military and Naval History*, ed. Donald J. Kagay and L. J. Andrew Villalon (Woodbridge, 1999), pp. 111–25

Tsurtsumia, Mamuka, 'Commemorations of crusaders in the manuscripts of the Monastery of the Holy Cross in Jerusalem', *Journal of Medieval History*, 38.3 (2012), 318–34

Turner, Ralph V., 'The Children of Anglo-Norman Royalty and their Upbringing', *Medieval Prosopography*, 11.2 (1990), 17–52

Turner, Ralph V., *Eleanor of Aquitaine* (New Haven and London, 2009)

Tyerman, Christopher, *God's War: A New History of the Crusades* (London, 2006)

Van Houts, Elisabeth, *Memory and Gender in Medieval Europe 900–1200* (Basingstoke, 1999)

Vasselot, Clément de, 'L'Ascension des Lusignan: les réseaux d'une famille seigneuriale (Xe–XIIe siècle), *Cahiers de civilisation médiévale*, 58 (2015), 123–37

Vasselot de Régné, Clément de, 'A Crusader Lineage from Spain to the Throne of Jerusalem: The Lusignans', *Crusades*, 16 (2017), 95–114

Vincent, Nicholas, 'Isabella of Angoulême: John's Jezebel', in *King John: New Interpretations*, ed. S. D. Church (Woodbridge, 1999), pp. 165–219

Vogtherr, Thomas, 'Die Regierungsdaten der lateinischen Könige von Jerusalem', *Zeitschrift des Deutschen Palästina-Vereins (1953)*, 110.1 (1994), 51–81

Warlop, E., *The Flemish Nobility before 1300* (Courtrai, 1975–1976), originally published as *De Vlaamse Adel voor 1300* (Handzame, 1968), translated by J. B. Ross and H. Vandermoere.

Warren, W. L., *Henry II* (London, 1973)

Wathelet-Willem, Jeanne, 'Guibourc, femme de Guillaume', in *Les Chansons de geste du cycle de Guillaume d'Orange*, vol. 3: *Les moniages; Guibourc. Hommage à Jean Frappier*, ed. Philippe Ménard and Jean-Charles Payen (Paris, 1983), pp. 335–55

Weltecke, Dorothea, 'Michael the Great (the Syrian, the Elder)', in *Encyclopedia of the Medieval Chronicle*, ed. Graeme Dunphy (Leiden, 2010), 2: 1110–11

Werthschulte, Leila, 'Arnold of Lübeck', in *Encyclopedia of the Medieval Chronicle*, ed. Graeme Dunphy (Leiden, 2010), 1: 110–111

Whalen, Logan E. (ed.), *A Companion to Marie de France* (Leiden, 2011)

Woodacre, Elena, 'Questionable Authority: Female Sovereigns and their Consorts in Medieval and Renaissance Chronicles', in *Authority and Gender in Medieval and Renaissance Chronicles*, ed. Juliana Dresvina and Nicholas Sparks (Newcastle Upon Tyne, 2012), pp. 376–406

Unpublished secondary works

Crowley, Heather E., 'The Impact of the Franks on the Latin Kingdom of Jerusalem: Landscape, Seigneurial Obligations and Rural Communities in the Frankish East', unpublished PhD thesis, Cardiff University, 2016

Index

Acre: city of 10, 12, 33–34, 49n46, 55, 61, 62, 63, 70, 72, 76, 80–81, 85, 89n38, 93, 96, 98–99, 104–105, 106, 108, 109–110, 117–118, 125, 126, 127, 135, 136, 143, 144, 147, 158–167; siege of (1189–1191) 2, 5, 14, 16, 33–34, 46, 85, 95, 120, 122, 126, 134, 146, 150, 151–152, 158–165, 167
Adela of Champagne, queen of France 44, 79, 82
Adela of Normandy, countess of Blois 44
Adelaide of Maurienne, queen of France 59, 70
Ademar de Leron, lord of Caesarea 10
al-'Ādil 97
Advent 101
al-Afdal 127
Afonso Henriques, king of Portugal 19
Agnes (Anna) of Antioch, queen of Hungary 41, 57, 147
Agnes de Courtenay: ancestry and family 7, 29–30; divorce 2, 34–35, 121; land holdings 93, 96, 106, 125; marriage (to Amaury 30, 34–35; to Hugh of Ibelin 30, 35, 40, 55, 75; to Reynald of Sidon) 40, 52, 55, 80, 82, 83, 95; mother of Sybil 12, 32, 40; power and influence 53, 55, 57, 81, 84, 93–94, 96–97, 101; William II, archbishop of Tyre's views of 57, 85, 93–94, 96, 101
Agnes, daughter of Henry le Buffle 57–58
Agnes (Anna) of France, Byzantine empress 78, 82, 92, 98
Agnes of Waiblingen 59
agriculture 61–62
Aimery; *see also* Aymeri
Aimery of Limoges, patriarch of Antioch 11, 92, 145

Aimery de Lusignan 56, 84; royal constable 18, 83–84, 85, 95, 96, 98, 126, 130, 140, 148, 151, 159, 160, 161, 165
Alelmus Bellus 159–160, 165
Aleppo 7, 20, 30, 35, 41, 52, 57, 78, 95–96, 97, 98, 99, 100, 170
Alexander III, pope 11, 35, 43, 94
Alexios II Komnenos, Byzantine emperor 78, 82, 92, 98
Alfonso VIII, king of Castile 43, 111
Alice, princess of Antioch 3, 12, 20, 135
Alice of France, countess of Chartres 44
Alix of Lorraine 79–80
Almodis de Lusignan 56, 84, 86
Amalfi 15, 159–160
Amaury (Amalric), king of Jerusalem: appearance 8; count of Jaffa and Ascalon 29, 58, 63–64; death 30, 53; divorce 2, 34–36, 45, 107, 121; and Egypt 41–42, 54, 170; family 7, 29, 31, 52, 54, 55; father of Sybil 30, 31, 39, 42–44, 63, 74, 81, 107, 162, 166–167, 168, 170; heir to kingdom of Jerusalem 1, 5, 9, 13, 34–35, 58, 108, 162, 163–164; and Manuel Komnenos 40–43, 45, 170; marriage (to Agnes de Courtenay 29–30, 34–35, 121; to Maria Komnene) 36, 40, 42, 45, 75, 118); reforms 59; and William II, archbishop of Tyre 10–11, 34; former witnesses and officials 70, 79, 126, 140, 165
Amaury of Nesle, patriarch of Jerusalem 20, 31, 72, 77, 93
Ambroise 134, 149, 151, 162
Anchin, Benedictine abbey *see Continuatio Aquicincinta*
Andronikos Komnenos, Byzantine emperor 98, 107, 110, 146, 170

Ansaldo Bonvicino, castellan of Tyre 136, 143, 158, 160
Anselin Babini (Dabini) 126
Anthelm (Antelm) of Lucca 81, 99, 160
Antioch: city of 6, 20, 136, 142, 143, 144, 149–150, 161; patriarch of 11, 145; principality of 1, 3, 6, 18, 20, 30, 35, 38, 40, 41, 53–54, 57, 76, 78, 82, 87, 92–93, 94, 99, 103, 107, 121, 123, 128, 136, 142, 146–147, 148, 164
Aragon 19, 62
Armenia, Armenians 6–7, 20, 97, 125; *see also* Cilician Armenia
Arnold of Torroja, master of the Temple 101, 104, 105
Artah, battle of (1164) 41, 52, 56, 78, 84
Arthur, legendary king 2, 12, 14, 38, 167
Arwad (Ruad) 148, 149
Ascalon 1, 2, 9, 12, 13, 16, 29, 42, 57, 58, 60–65, 70, 72, 76–77, 78, 81, 85, 97, 104, 109, 125, 135, 137–139, 140, 142, 144, 148, 166, 170, 171
Assises de la Cour de Bourgeois 86
Aubrey (Alberich) of Troisfontaines 166
Audita tremendi 142
Aymeri de Narbonne, epic hero 38, 73

Bahā' al-Dīn ibn Shaddād 15, 93, 137, 141, 142, 149, 150, 151
Balduino Erminio 136
Baldwin, brother of Ansaldo Bonvicino 143
Baldwin I (of Boulogne), count of Edessa, king of Jerusalem 6–7, 44, 71, 108, 109
Baldwin II (de Bourcq), count of Edessa, king of Jerusalem 7, 9, 19, 20, 32, 35, 44, 53, 54, 55, 58, 59, 63
Baldwin, count of Hainaut 19, 31
Baldwin III, king of Jerusalem 9, 19, 20, 29, 30, 31, 32, 34, 41, 69–70, 97, 102
Baldwin IV (the leper king), king of Jerusalem: appearance 8; and Baldwin V 101–102, 107–108; and Bohemond III, prince of Antioch 54, 76, 82–83, 87, 92, 94, 96–97; and Byzantine empire 63, 76, 94, 97–98; childhood 10–11, 30–32, 35–36, 43; death 109; family 7, 70–71; and Guy de Lusignan 82–87, 94–96, 98–106, 171; heir to the kingdom of Jerusalem 30, 34–35, 53; illness 43, 45, 53, 58, 64–65, 69, 71, 72, 82, 94, 96, 99–100, 102, 107; and Isabel of Jerusalem 93, 94, 125; in legend, 166–167; military activity 57, 76–77, 80, 87, 97, 102, 103, 129; minority 53–57; and his mother 40, 81, 82, 93, 95, 96, 101; and Philip of Alsace 70–74, 76, 78–79; and Raymond III, count of Tripoli, 54, 56–57, 76, 78, 82–83, 87, 93, 94, 96–97, 98–99, 101–103, 105–107; regents of 56–57, 69, 72–73, 94, 95, 99, 101, 103, 106–107, 123, 128; succession arrangements 101–102, 107–108, 117, 137; and Sybil 1–2, 3, 17, 58, 70, 74, 76, 79, 80–81, 82–83, 85, 87, 94, 96, 98, 102, 103–104, 166–168, 171; truces 92, 107; views of, contemporary 14, 94; and William II, archbishop of Tyre 10–12, 72–74, 78–79, 82–83, 86, 94, 96; and William Longsword 58–59, 64; former witnesses and officials 159, 160, 165
Baldwin V, king of Jerusalem 2, 9, 16, 35, 64, 70, 77, 79, 81, 95, 98, 101–103, 107–111, 117–119, 122, 125–126, 136–137, 160, 166, 168, 169, 170, 171
Baldwin of Antioch 57, 93
Baldwin (Baldoin) of Cyprus 79, 165
Baldwin of Forde, archbishop of Canterbury 13, 109–110, 142, 144, 145, 150, 161–162
Baldwin of Ibelin, lord of Ramla 1, 2, 12, 14, 40, 55, 56, 61, 63, 70, 75–76, 80, 83, 85, 87, 94–95, 96, 98, 100, 101, 110, 121–122, 123, 139, 169
Baldwin (Baldus) de Samosac (Semunsac) 63, 70, 98
Balian (Barisan) of Ibelin, lord of Nablus 12–13, 55, 56, 61, 75, 77, 83, 96, 98, 100, 101, 108, 109, 118, 121–122, 123, 127–130, 134–137, 139–141, 159–160, 162
Bandinus, chancellor of Conrad of Montferrat 143, 150
Banyas 43, 93
Barcelona 15, 143
Barraguilla, house of at Acre 126
Barziyya (Bourzey), fortress 92
Beatrice, countess of Edessa 30, 68n42
Beaufort (al-Shaqīf) 150, 151, 161
Bedouin 98, 105–106
Beirut 55, 80, 108, 117–118, 126, 127, 136, 159, 160, 164, 166
Béla III, king of Hungary 41, 57, 145, 147
Belleforest, François de 168–169
Belvoir (Kaukab), fortress 105, 150
Benjamin of Tudela 61

196 Index

Bernard de Templo, *vicecomes* in Tyre 143, 147
Bernard the Treasurer *see Chronique d'Ernoul et de Bernard le Trésorier*
Bertram of Jaffa (Bertrand of Caruana) 81, 98
Bethany *see* St Lazarus of
Bethlehem: bishop of 77, 126; church of the Nativity in 40; town of 61
Béthune *see* Robert V
Bohemond I, prince of Antioch 6
Bohemond II, prince of Antioch 20
Bohemond III, prince of Antioch 6, 18, 35, 41, 53–54, 57, 76, 78, 82–83, 86–87, 92–93, 97, 99, 100, 101, 103, 121, 128, 129, 142, 144, 150, 161, 164
Bohemond IV, count of Tripoli 144, 146–147, 164
Bologna 10, 11, 46, 94
Boulogne, comital family of 6–8, 28n62, 44, 70, 71, 108
Brindisi 105, 142
Burellus, grand commander of the Hospital of St John of Jerusalem 143, 147
Burgundy 18, 45, 59, 79, 81; *see also* Hugh III
Byzantine empire 6, 7, 9, 10, 20, 30, 40–43, 45, 46, 56, 62–63, 64, 72, 76, 78, 87, 92–93, 94, 97–98, 102, 105, 136, 145–147, 162, 170; *see also* Alexios Komnenos; Andronikos Komnenos; Isaac II Angelos; Manuel Komnenos
Byzantium (Constantinople), city of 7, 42, 45, 52, 62, 76, 78, 82, 83, 92, 94, 98, 107, 110, 136, 146–147, 158, 162

Caesarea 10, 75, 79, 125, 136; *see also* Eraclius, Hugh, lord of, Juliana, Walter, lord of
Cairo 58, 73, 80
Canterbury, archbishop of *see* Baldwin of Forde
captives *see* prison
castellan, office of 63, 70, 77, 80, 81, 95, 96, 98, 126, 137, 147, 160
Castile 3, 18–19, 43–44, 111
Cecilia of le Bourcq, princess of Antioch 136
Celestine II, pope 32–33
Celestine III, pope 93
Chastelneuf 93, 96, 98, 110, 125
Chrétien de Troyes 38, 73, 167
Christine de Pizan (Pisan) 30, 37, 70

Chronique d'Ernoul et de Bernard le Trésorier 9, 12–15, 35, 75–76, 83–85, 93–94, 102, 105, 107–109, 117–119, 121–122, 125, 127–129, 134–141, 144, 148–151, 166, 169
chivalric ideals 2, 12, 38, 60, 72–73, 76, 138, 148
Cilician Armenia 45, 46, 93, 94, 105, 107, 135, 161, 164, 170; *see also* Leon I; Leon II; Mleh; Rupen
Cistercian order 13, 45, 62
Clement III, pope 142, 151, 158
Conrad III, king of Germany 41, 59
Conrad of Montferrat 14, 15, 112n17, 134, 136–137, 141, 142–145, 147–152, 158–166, 168, 172
Constance, princess of Antioch 3, 6, 12, 20, 35, 41, 57, 69, 103
Constance of France 70
Constantinople *see* Byzantium
Continuatio Aquicincta 14, 64, 120
Cosmographia 168
Cresson *see* Spring of the Cresson
Cross *see* Holy Cross
Crusade: First 6–7, 17, 18, 38, 40, 44, 171; Second 18, 19, 31, 40, 44, 60, 64–65, 82, 110; Third 5, 13–14, 34, 46, 122, 129, 134, 138, 142–146, 148–152, 158–165, 166–167, 171–172
Curginus *see* Turginus
Cyprus 34, 46, 79, 98, 160, 164, 165

Damascus 1, 42, 53, 58, 73, 80, 93, 95, 97, 100, 106, 111, 148, 151, 160, 170
Darum 105, 140
divorce 2, 13, 17, 34–35, 39, 45, 48n29, 92–93, 103–104, 105, 120–123, 130, 162, 165–167, 168, 170, 171, 173n30

Easter 71, 78, 81, 82–87, 94, 97, 101, 103–104, 121, 127, 140, 152, 159
Edessa: city 6–7, 29; county 6–7, 30, 34, 40, 63, 68n42, 87, 97; *see also* Joscelin I; Joscelin II; Joscelin III
education 36–39, 52
Egypt 6, 7, 34, 40, 41–43, 46, 52, 54, 61, 63, 72–73, 76, 87, 92, 97–98, 115n64, 136, 137, 170
Eilat 95, 98
Eleanor, duchess of Aquitaine, queen of France, queen of England 1, 3, 36, 44, 48n29, 49n39, 52, 111, 164
Eleanor of England (Leonor), queen of Castile 43–44, 111

Index 197

England 10, 13, 19, 38, 43, 70, 71, 74, 86, 110, 122, 161, 166, 168; *see also* Henry II king of England, Matilda of England, Richard I
Eracles see Estoire de Eracles empereur
Eraclius: archbishop of Caesarea 79, 93; patriarch of Jerusalem 9, 84, 93–94, 97, 99, 103, 104–105, 107, 108, 109–110, 119–121, 125, 131n8, 139–141, 143, 145, 151, 162, 166–167, 169
Eremburge of Maine, countess of Anjou 7, 20, 31, 36
Ernoul 12, 118, 121, 128–129, 134; *see also Chronique d'Ernoul et de Bernard le Trésorier*
Eschiva, daughter of Baldwin of Ibelin lord of Ramla 56
Eschiva de Bures, lady of Tiberias and Galilee 52–53, 80, 87, 96, 108, 117, 119, 129, 136
Estoire de Eracles empereur 9, 12, 15, 93–94, 107, 110, 112n10, 112n17, 119–120, 123, 134–139, 144–145, 148, 166, 167, 169, 173n20
Estoire de la guerre sainte see Ambroise
Eustace III, count of Boulogne 28n62, 108

al-Fādil 92, 111
Farrukh-Shah 53, 95
Flanders, counts of *see* Philip of Alsace, Sybil, Thierry
Fontevrault abbey 33, 36, 111
France: kingdom of 7, 9–10, 11–12, 30, 38, 44, 45, 46, 55, 56, 70, 72, 74, 78, 81–82, 86, 102, 147, 158, 164, 166; kings of, *see* Louis VI, Louis VII, Philip II
Frederick, archbishop of Tyre 10, 43–44, 46
Frederick, duke of Swabia 161, 163
Frederick Barbarossa, emperor 37, 40, 42, 45, 56, 58, 79, 105, 107–108, 117, 137, 145–147, 150–151, 161, 164
Fulk V, count of Anjou, king of Jerusalem 1, 7, 13, 19, 20, 31, 32–33, 44, 55, 58, 59, 60, 71, 124
Fuller, Thomas 168–169

Galgan de Cheneché 159–161, 165
Gaza 61, 138, 140
Gazellus of Tyre 159, 161
Genoa, Genoese 14, 15, 55, 59, 100, 109, 135, 136, 143–144, 145, 147, 158, 160–161
Geoffrey de Lusignan 1, 84, 149, 151, 159, 164–165

Geoffrey Tortus (Le Tor) 95, 96, 98, 126, 159, 160–161
Geoffrey of Tours, burgher of Jerusalem 70
Georgia *see* Tamar
Gerard, lord of Sidon 40, 55
Gerard of Nazareth 38
Gerard of Remille (Ramini, Rumeilei) 63, 77
Gerard de Ridefort: master of the Temple 119–120, 126, 127–130, 138, 140, 148–149, 150; royal marshal 81
Gibelet (Jubail) 11, 133n55, 136; *see also* Rainer of Gibelet
Gillebert *see* Giselbert
Girard *see* Gerard
Giselbert de Floriaco (Gillebert de Flori), *vicecomes* of Acre 81, 95
Godfrey de Bouillon 7–8, 28n62, 44, 71, 76, 171
Gotsuin (Goscelin, Gosohuin) Boccus (Hircus, Ircus) 80, 98, 126
Greek Orthodox Church 7, 61, 139
Gregory VIII, pope 142
Guibert, brother of Bertram (Bertrand) of Jaffa 81, 98
Guido de Spinola 160
Guillaume; *see also* William
Guillaume Fortis 165
Guillaume d'Orange, epic hero 38, 73
Gumushtekin, atabeg of Aleppo 57
Guy, brother of Walter, lord of Beirut 80
Guy of Bazoches 120, 166
Guy de Lusignan: charters of 15, 94–95, 98, 106, 109, 124–126, 158–161; children 95, 112n17, 161–163, 165; coronation 18, 94, 118–124, 131n8, 165–166; count of Jaffa and Ascalon 85, 94–98, 103–106, 108–110, 138; divorce proposals 103–104, 120–123, 170, 171; early career 56, 84, 85, 91n70; household 98, 126, 159–161, 165; king of Jerusalem 1–4, 18, 124–130, 134, 148–152, 159–165, 171–172; marriage to Sybil 74, 75, 82–87; military record 18, 98, 99–101, 123, 127, 128–130, 149, 150–151, 158; modern scholars') 15–18; prisoner of Saladin 130, 134, 137–138, 140, 144, 148–149; regent of Baldwin IV 99–102; relationship with Sybil 104, 120–122, 124, 138, 143, 148–150, 164–167; and Reynald de Châtillon 95, 98, 101, 106, 111; and Richard I of England 163–164; views of

(contemporary 12–14, 79, 102, 115n81); visual depictions 8–9

Haifa *see* Pagan, lord of Haifa
Harim 41, 78, 95; battle of (1164) *see* Artah
Hattin, battle of (1187) 10, 17, 33, 110, 129–130, 134–136, 139, 142, 144, 145
Henry I (the liberal), count of Champagne 3, 42, 44, 52, 79–80, 82, 111, 162
Henry II, count of Champagne 3, 112n17, 152, 162, 163, 165
Henry, duke of Louvain 100
Henry (the Lion), duke of Saxony and Bavaria 52
Henry II, king of England 1, 7, 8, 19, 42, 43–44, 52, 55, 56, 71, 73–74, 78, 84, 102, 105, 107–108, 111, 117, 129, 142, 144, 145, 147, 150, 151–152
Henry le Buffle 45, 57–58, 147
Hildegard, abbess of Bingen 71–72
Hodierna, countess of Tripoli 3, 20, 31, 35, 41, 126
Holy Cross, the 33, 76–77, 97, 100, 103, 129–130, 142, 145
Holy Cross, cathedral of Acre 163, 167
Holy Sepulchre: canons of 31, 32–33, 62; church of 9, 40, 77, 101, 108, 109, 111, 125, 139, 142, 169
Hospital of St John of Jerusalem (Hospitallers) 10, 52, 56, 61, 64, 70, 71, 72, 77, 81, 83, 94, 96, 100, 101, 104–105, 107, 108, 109–110, 119–120, 123, 126, 127, 129, 131n8, 134–135, 139, 143–145, 147–148, 149, 150, 151, 164–165
hospitals 61, 164
Hugh III, duke of Burgundy 45, 79–82, 85, 87, 103–104, 121, 124, 145, 152, 164
Hugh, lord of Caesarea 75
Hugh de Beauchamp 110
Hugh VIII le Brun de Lusignan 41, 56, 82, 84
Hugh of Ibelin, lord of Ramla 30, 35, 40, 55, 75
Hugh Martin the marshal 165
Hugh of Tiberias 53, 80, 90n47, 120, 121, 143–144, 145, 151, 159–161, 165
Humphrey (Henfrid, Humfrey) II of Toron 54–55, 57, 72, 80
Humphrey III of Toron 54, 58, 93
Humphrey IV of Toron 9, 62, 74, 93, 94, 96, 103, 120, 121–123, 125, 130, 149, 162, 164, 173n30
Husām al-Dīn Lu'lu 98

Ibelin 29, 55, 60; *see also* Baldwin of; Balian of; Hugh of; John of
Ibn al-Athīr 15, 18, 118–119, 124, 126, 137, 138–141, 143, 151
Ibn Jubayr (Jubair) 93, 106
Ibn al-Kardabus 19
Il-ghazi ibn Artuk of Mardin 136
'Imād al-Dīn al-Iṣfahānī 15, 16, 118–119, 126, 127, 138–141, 143, 149, 150, 151
Inab, battle of (1149)
Isaac II Angelos, Byzantine emperor 37, 110, 128, 136, 145–147, 156n73
Isabel I, queen of Jerusalem 2, 13, 35, 42, 45, 52, 57, 64, 74, 85, 93, 103, 108, 112n17, 118, 121–122, 125, 147, 149, 162–165, 168, 173n30
Isabel (Elizabeth), widow of Hugh of Caesarea 75
Isabel de Courtenay, sister of Agnes and Joscelin III 22n10
Isabel (Elizabeth) of Montlhéry, lady of Courtenay 7
Isabel of Toron 62, 94
Itinerarium peregrinorum 13, 64, 95, 127, 128, 130, 134, 137, 138, 140–145, 148–149, 151, 158–159, 161–162, 166, 168
Itinerarium peregrinorum et gesta regis Ricardi 16, 149, 162
Iveta (Yveta) of Jerusalem, abbess of the Abbey of St Lazarus of Bethany 31–34, 36, 39
'Izz al-Dīn Mas'ūd of Mosul 96, 111

Jabala 103, 149
Jacob's Ford *see* Vadum Iacob
Jaffa: city of 9, 15, 29, 55, 57, 59, 60–62, 63, 64, 80, 81, 104, 110, 136, 140, 143, 144, 165; county of *see* Amaury king of Jerusalem, Guy de Lusignan, Sybil queen of Jerusalem, William Longsword
Jerusalem: Byzantine protectorate over 40, 147; city of 6, 9, 10, 13, 32, 34, 45, 64, 78, 80, 82–83, 99–100, 104, 117–118, 122, 125, 126, 135, 136, 137, 165–166, 170; kingdom of 1, 3, 5, 6, 9–12, 15, 29, 38, 53, 58, 59, 60–61, 64, 69, 73–74, 101, 105, 144, 166–167, 170–172; laws and customs of 45–46, 69–70, 78, 86; patriarch of ,11, 34; *see also* Amaury of Nesle, Eraclius; Saladin's capture of 1, 8, 10, 13, 134, 138–143, 145, 146, 148–150, 171

Jews 6, 61
Joanna of England, queen of Sicily 36, 109
John, bishop of Banyas 43, 44
John, dragoman of Chastelneuf 98
John, knight of Conrad of Montferrat 150
John Borgungus 165
John of Ibelin, lord of Jaffa 45, 60
John Komnenos, Byzantine emperor 6, 22n10, 147
Joscelin I de Courtenay, count of Edessa 1, 34
Joscelin II de Courtenay, count of Edessa 7, 29–30, 68n42
Joscelin III de Courtenay, titular count of Edessa 22n10, 34–35, 41, 57, 63, 80, 81, 83, 94, 95–97, 98, 100, 101, 106, 107–110, 117–121, 125–126, 127, 130, 135, 137, 147, 160–161
Joscelin de Samosac (Semunsac, Somesac), castellan of Ascalon 63–64, 68n42, 70, 77, 81, 96, 98
Joscius: archbishop of Tyre 127, 128, 142, 143, 144, 145, 160; bishop of Acre 79
Jubail *see* Gibelet
Juliana, lady of Caesarea 10, 23n20

Kabul, casal 106, 125
Kaukab, casal 106; *see also* Belvoir
Kerak (Karak) 58, 101–104, 105, 127, 136, 149, 150
Knights Hospitaller *see* Hospital of St John of Jerusalem
Knights Templar *see* Temple, order of the
Komnenoi *see* Alexios, Andronikos, John, Manuel, Maria, Theodora

Latakia (Laodicea) 38, 103, 149
Lateran Council: Fourth (1215) 86; Third (1179) 11, 79–80
Latin continuation of William of Tyre's history 12, 81, 103, 109, 115n81, 116n95, 120–121, 134, 135, 137–138, 140, 144, 163, 165–166
Leon (Levon) I of Cilician Armenia 7
Leon II of Cilician Armenia 164
Libellus de expugnatione Terrae Sanctae per Saladinum 13, 119–120, 134, 139–141
Livre des Assises see John of Ibelin
Livre de Forme de Plait see Philip of Novara

Louis VI, king of France 59, 70
Louis VII, king of France 7, 13, 42, 44, 45, 46, 48n29, 59, 71, 72, 78, 79, 80, 81–82, 92
Lucius III, pope 105, 112n12
Ludwig III, Landgrave of Thuringia 158, 162
Lydda 109, 110, 126

Manuel Komnenos, Byzantine emperor 6, 20, 30, 36, 40–43, 46, 56, 57, 63, 68n42, 72, 76, 78, 82, 83, 92–93, 103, 147, 170
Marash 30
Margaret (Maria) of Hungary, Byzantine empress 147
Margaritus of Brindisi, admiral of Sicily 142, 148, 149, 150
Maria of Antioch, Byzantine empress 6, 41, 56, 57, 78, 92, 94, 98, 146
Maria Komnene, queen of Jerusalem 13, 36, 40, 42, 43, 45, 52, 53, 56–57, 64, 75, 77, 83, 93, 108, 118, 121, 136, 137, 139, 141, 144, 147, 162
Maria the Porphyrogenita 92, 94, 98
Marie of Champagne, duchess of Burgundy 79
Marie of France, countess of Champagne 1, 3, 36, 44, 111
Marie de France, poet 38
Marino Sanudo 167–168
Marj Uyun, battle of (1179) 80, 83
Maron (Maroun er-Ras) 96
marriage 2, 3, 6, 7, 8–9, 16, 18–20, 23n21, 29, 30, 32, 34–36, 39, 40–42, 43–46, 52–53, 54, 56–60, 71, 73–74, 75, 78–80, 82–83, 85–86, 92–94, 98, 103–104, 123, 125, 136, 147, 162, 165, 169, 170–171; marriage law 17, 69–70, 76, 86, 103; *see also* divorce
Marseille 143, 160, 161
Matilda, abbess of the Abbey of St Lazarus 32
Matilda, countess of Boulogne, queen of England 28n62, 44
Matilda of Canossa 19
Matilda of England (the empress) 3, 19, 36
Matthew Paris 36, 109, 166
Medina 98
Melisende, queen of Jerusalem 1–2, 3, 7, 9, 11–12, 19–20, 29, 31, 32–34, 35, 38, 41, 44, 59, 93, 97, 102, 124–125, 135, 169
Melisende of Montlhéry 7, 54

Melisende of Tripoli 41, 56
Michael, patriarch of the Syrian Orthodox Church 135
Michaud, Joseph-François 16, 169
Miles de Colouardino (Colaverdo), royal butler 95, 96, 110, 126, 130
Miles of Plancy, lord of Transjordan 54–55, 58, 65
Minstrel of Reims 2, 166–167
Mirabel (Majdal Yaba) 29, 60
Mleh of Cilician Armenia 45, 46
Monachus, archbishop of Caesarea 134, 174n32
Montferrat *see* Conrad, Renier, William V, William Longsword
Montgisard, battle of (1177) 77, 78, 100
Montpellier 143
Montreal (Shaubak, Shobak) 58, 149–150
Morphia (Morfia), countess of Edessa, queen of Jerusalem 7, 9, 32, 53
Mosul 7, 15, 96, 97, 98, 100, 106, 107, 111, 170
Mountjoy, military religious order of 9, 62–63, 169
Münster, Sebastian 168

Nablus 54, 56–57, 75, 105, 118, 121–123, 127–128, 136, 138, 140, 143, 165; *see also* Balian of Ibelin
Nazareth 38, 56, 99, 125, 127, 143
Nicholas Trevet 168
Niketas Choniates 136, 162
Nîmes 143
Nūr al-Daulak Balak 32
Nūr al-Dīn, ruler of Aleppo and Damascus 30, 40, 41–42, 46, 52–53, 56, 75, 78, 84, 97, 126

Oberto Malocello 158
Odo (Eudes) of Saint-Amand, master of the Temple 72, 77, 80
Osto of Tiberias 53, 151

Pagan (Pain), lord of Haifa 80, 137, 147, 162
Le Pas Saladin 167
Patrick, earl of Salisbury 84, 91n70
Peter, archdeacon of Lydda 109, 126
Peter de Courtenay, brother of Louis VII 7, 80
Peter de Creseca, castellan of Jerusalem 126
Peter Leonis 151, 158
Peter de Lusignan 56

Petronilla, vice-countess of Acre 80
Philip II (Augustus), king of France 81–82, 105, 107–108, 117, 145, 147, 151–152, 156n73, 163–164, 167
Philip of Alsace, count of Flanders 1, 7, 31, 42, 55, 69, 70–79, 87, 97, 110, 145, 152, 163, 164, 167, 171
Philip de Milly, lord of Nablus and Transjordan 54, 58
Philip Moresin 165
Philip of Novara 45–46, 53, 57, 69–70, 81
pilgrims 12, 31–32, 33, 39–40, 42–43, 46, 52, 70, 73, 82, 136, 142, 162, 167
Pisa, Pisans 15, 59, 61, 100, 109, 135, 143, 145, 147, 151, 159–161, 163, 165
poison 14, 16, 64, 111, 146, 168
Poitou 56, 82, 84, 123, 142, 151, 164, 168
Portugal 3, 18–19
prison, prisoners 1, 2, 14, 17, 20, 30, 32, 35, 41, 52, 55, 56, 57, 69, 80, 82, 83, 84, 97, 106, 110, 111, 128, 130, 133n55, 134, 138, 139, 141, 144, 146, 148, 151, 160, 167, 171, 174n32

queenship 2–3, 9–10, 16–20, 111, 124–126, 135–136, 144, 169–172

Rainald of Mongisard 98
Rainald of Soissons 98
Rainer; *see also* Renier
Rainer (Renier) of Gibelet 160, 165
Rainer of Nablus 140
Ralph, brother of William of Tyre 80
Ralph of Coggeshall 13, 135, 137–138
Ralph of Diceto 13, 77, 140, 151, 162
Ralph de Mauleon 100
Ralph (Raoul) of Tiberias 53, 143–144, 151
Ramadan 103
Ramla 29, 40, 60, 70, 75, 77, 123; *see also* Baldwin of Ibelin, Hugh of Ibelin
ransom 32, 41, 52, 57, 63, 81, 82, 83, 90n47, 110, 139–140, 144
Ravenna 151, 158
Raymond II, count of Tripoli 126
Raymond III, count of Tripoli: and coronation of Sybil 117–123, 130; and Guy de Lusignan 84, 85–86, 101, 103, 115n81, 119, 126–130, 159, 165; after Hattin and death 130, 135, 137, 143–144, 159, 165; heir to the kingdom of Jerusalem 35, 53, 119; and Manuel Komnenos 41, 56; marriage 52–53, 87, 96, 119; military record

Index   201

56, 80, 100, 103, 129–130; prisoner of Nūr al-Dīn 41, 52; regent for Baldwin IV 11, 54–57, 101–103, 105–107; regent for Baldwin V 16, 18, 107–111, 116n95, 117, 119, 168; relations with Baldwin IV 76, 78, 82–83, 87, 93, 94, 96–97, 98–99, 101; and Saladin 1, 17, 56, 92, 107, 119, 126–128, 170; traitor 13, 17, 126, 129, 166–167
Raymond, lord of Gibelet 139
Raymond, prince of Antioch, son of Bohemond III 128–129
Raymond Babin 160
Raymond of Nephin 160
Raymond of Poitiers, prince of Antioch 6, 69, 164
Raymond of Scandalion 95
Récits d'un ménestrel de Reims see Minstrel of Reims
Regni Iherosolymitani Brevis Historia 55, 120, 136
Renier de Gibelet *see* Rainer of Gibelet
Renier of Montferrat 92, 94, 98
Reynald, lord of Marash 30
Reynald, lord of Sidon 35, 40, 52, 55, 80–82, 83, 95–96, 100, 101, 110, 120–121, 127–128, 129–130, 135, 137, 140, 147, 150–151, 160, 162, 166
Reynald de Châtillon, prince of Antioch, lord of Transjordan 35, 41, 57, 62–63, 69, 70, 73, 76, 78, 80, 83, 93, 94, 95–96, 98, 100, 101, 103, 106, 111, 119–121, 126, 127, 129–130, 134, 138, 149
Reims *see* Minstrel of
Richard I, count of Poitou, king of England 1, 109, 111, 141, 142, 151–152, 164–165, 167
Richard Animal 36
Richard de Templo *see Itinerarium peregrinorum et gesta regis Ricardi*
Robert V, advocate of Béthune 71, 73–74, 78
Robert VI, advocate of Béthune 73–74, 171
Robert de Picquigny (Piquigni, Pinqueni) 70, 81
Robert of St Albans, fictional Templar 84
Robert of Torigni, Abbot of Mont-St-Michel 13, 77, 84
Rodrigo Alvarez, count 62
Roger of Howden 13, 71, 84–85, 87, 120–121, 123, 138, 151, 163, 164, 165–166

Roger des Moulins, master of the Hospital 72, 101, 104–105, 108, 109–110, 120, 126, 127, 131n8
Roger de Mowbray 110
Roger of Salerno, prince of Antioch 34, 136
Roger de Verdun 77, 81
Roger of Wendover 156n73, 166
Ruad *see* Arwad
Rupen III of Cilician Armenia 93, 94, 164

Safad (Saphet) 150
Saffūriyya (Saforie, Sepphoris) 99, 102, 123, 128–129
St Anne, monastery of 32, 125
St Elias (al-Taiyiba) 110
Saint-Gilles 70, 143
St John of Jerusalem, Hospital of *see* Hospital of St John of Jerusalem
St Lazarus of Bethany, abbey of 31–33, 36–40, 52, 56, 71, 125
St Nicolas, cemetery of 163
Saladin, sultan of Egypt and Damascus: and Aleppo 57, 95–96, 99–100; and Antioch 99, 107, 128, 149–150, 164; and Balian of Ibelin 139–141; and Byzantine empire 107, 110, 128, 146–147; captures Jerusalem 1, 10, 13, 16, 139–142, 171; and Cilician Armenia 107; conquest of kingdom of Jerusalem 1, 33, 53, 62, 69, 75, 83, 127–130, 134–151, 160, 169–171; and Conrad of Montferrat 137, 142, 144–145, 148, 150; and Damascus, 53, 73, 97, 100, 106, 111; in Egypt 42, 46, 52, 53, 76, 137; and Guy de Lusignan 17, 97–98, 100, 106, 130, 137–138, 148–151; and Hattin, battle of (1187) 10, 129–130, 134; legends about 54, 84, 138, 148, 165–167; and Marj Uyun, battle of (1179) 80–81, 83; and Montgisard, battle of (1177) 61, 76–78, 100; and Mosul 98, 100, 106, 107, 111; prisoners of 80, 83, 110, 128, 130, 134, 137–138, 140, 148–149, 151, 160; and Raymond III count of Tripoli 1, 17, 56, 76, 87, 103, 107, 111, 119, 123, 126–129, 170; and Reynald de Châtillon 58, 63, 95–96, 98, 101, 102, 103, 105, 106, 111, 127, 130, 134, 138; and Saffūriyya, battle at (1183) 99–100; and Sybil queen of Jerusalem 2, 8, 138, 143, 148–149, 170, 171; and

Third Crusade 149–151, 158–161, 164, 165; truces 17, 56, 92, 96, 97, 107, 109, 111, 117, 118, 126–127, 149, 165; views of, contemporary 12, 15, 135
as-Salih, prince of Aleppo 78, 95
Saone (Sahyūn) 30
scribes 70, 98, 143
seals 9–10, 20n20, 20n21, 40, 63, 80
Sebastian Münster *see* Münster, Sebastian
Shawar 41–42
Shirkuh 41–42, 43
Shobak *see* Montreal
sibyls 30–31, 170
Sicard, bishop of Cremona 14, 58–59
Sicily 44, 54, 56, 137, 150; *see also* Joanna of England, William II king of Sicily
Sidon 55, 58, 81, 110, 136, 159–160, 164; *see also* Reynald of Sidon
Smpad the constable 135
Spring of the Cresson, battle of (1187) 14, 127–128
Stephanie de Courtenay 34
Stephanie de Milly, lady of Transjordan 54, 57–58, 62, 93, 136, 139, 149
Stephen, count of Sancerre 13, 44–46, 52, 54, 57, 58, 60, 79, 80, 124, 152, 162
sugar production 62, 96, 109
swan-maiden, legend of 8
Sybil, princess of Antioch 92–93, 121
Sybil, queen of Jerusalem: appearance 8–9; and Ascalon 1, 63, 64, 77, 104, 135, 137–138, 166, 171; and Baldwin IV 58, 64, 70, 73, 76, 79, 80–81, 82–83, 84, 85, 87, 94, 96, 98, 102–104, 171; birth 5; charters 2, 15, 63–64, 70, 77, 81, 94, 96, 98, 106, 109, 124, 125–126, 158–161; children 2, 5, 64, 77, 79, 81–82, 95, 102–103, 104, 108, 111, 112n17, 139, 144, 150, 151, 161–162, 165, 171, 173n20; and Conrad of Montferrat 136–137, 143–144, 150; coronation 5, 9, 117–123; countess of Jaffa and Ascalon 9–10, 57, 60, 62–65, 69–70, 76, 94–96, 103–104, 105, 106, 108, 109, 117, 169; death 1, 76, 161–162, 163; divorce attempts 2, 103–104, 120–123, 165–167, 171; education 32, 36–39; family 1, 3, 7–8, 19, 52, 70–71, 78–79; heir to the kingdom of Jerusalem 2, 5, 17–18, 30, 34–35, 42, 44, 53, 58, 79, 81, 98, 102, 107, 118–119, 122, 158; household 39, 63–64, 70, 77, 81, 98, 117, 125–126, 159–161, 169; infancy 32, 34; and Isabel of Jerusalem 52, 147, 149; in legend 166–167; letter-writing 5, 37, 145–147; loss of Jerusalem 1, 139, 140–141, 143; marriage (to Guy de Lusignan 1–2, 8–9, 16–18, 74, 75, 82–87, 104, 120–122, 124, 130, 138, 143, 146, 148–150, 164–167; to William Longsword of Montferrat 39, 57, 58–65, 162); marriage proposals 42–44, 46, 57, 58, 73–76, 79–80, 82, 83, 85, 87, 123, 170–171; military activity 1, 2, 69, 76, 77, 103, 105, 135, 137–138, 140–141, 151, 170, 171; name viii, 30–31, 170; and her parents 7–8, 29–30, 34–36, 39–40, 81, 96, 106; patronage (of art 2, 111, 125, 169; of religious orders 62–63, 169); queen 3, 9, 18, 20–21, 124–126, 135–152, 158–161, 171–172; and Saladin 1, 2, 8, 130, 138, 143, 148–149, 170, 171; seal 5, 9–10, 63; views of (contemporary 2, 8–15, 118–123, 126, 134, 165–167, 170; modern scholars' 15–18); widowhood 65, 69–70, 74; and William II, archbishop of Tyre 10–12, 32, 44, 46, 58–60, 73–74, 78–79, 97, 104
Sybil of Anjou, countess of Flanders 3, 19, 20, 31–32, 34, 36, 37–38, 39, 70–71, 78

Tageno, dean of Passau 146
Tamar the Great, queen of Georgia 1, 3, 20, 124
Taqī al-Dīn, lord of Hama 107, 128
Temple, order of the (Templars), 54, 61, 62, 71, 72, 77, 80, 81, 84, 100, 101, 104, 105, 107, 109, 110, 117, 119–120, 126, 127–130, 134–135, 138, 139–140, 143–145, 147–149, 150, 151, 164, 165
Templum Domini (Dome of the Rock, Lord's Temple) 9, 108, 125
Teresa, queen of Portugal 3, 18–19
Terricus, grand commander of the order of the Temple 143, 145, 147
Teutonic order 164–165
Theobald (Thibaut) V, count of Blois and Chartres 42, 44, 79, 152
Theobald the prefect 151, 158
Theodora Angela 136, 147
Theodora Komnene, princess of Antioch 57, 87, 92
Theodora Komnene, queen of Jerusalem 9, 34, 41

Thierry of Alsace, count of Flanders 19, 31–32, 42, 44, 46, 70
Thomas Chamberlain, *vicecomes* of Acre 165
Thomas Patricius 140
Tiberias 89, 96, 106, 108, 117, 123, 127–129, 136; *see also* Eschiva de Bures, Hugh of Tiberias
Tolosanus of Faenza 14, 64, 120, 121
Torgis 98
Toron (Tibnin, Turon) 93, 95, 96, 106, 125, 136, 173n30; *see also* Humphrey II of Toron, Humphrey III of Toron, Humphrey IV of Toron
Tortosa 11, 148, 149
Tower of David 9, 125
Transjordan, lordship of 58, 62, 76, 93, 95, 98, 103, 127; *see also* Miles of Plancy; Reynald de Châtillon; Stephanie de Milly
Tripoli: city of 6, 11, 83, 96, 137, 139, 141, 143, 144, 145–147, 148, 149, 150–151, 161, 165; county of 1, 18, 20, 41, 55, 56, 84, 92, 94, 107, 108, 136, 148, 163–164; counts of *see* Bohemond IV, Hodierna, Raymond II, Raymond III
Turginus (Curginus) 81
Tyre: archbishop of *see* Joscius, William II archbishop; city 10, 15, 70, 80, 93, 95, 96, 100, 102, 108, 129, 130, 135, 136–137, 138, 141, 143–145, 147, 148–151, 158–161, 163–164, 166, 167, 170; lord of *see* Conrad of Montferrat

Urban III, pope 84, 128
Urraca, queen of Castile 3, 19

Vadum Iacob (Jacob's Ford) 80
Venice, Venetians 59, 100, 109, 147, 160, 163, 164
Verdun 43, 77, 81
vicecomes, office of 63, 64, 80, 81, 95, 98, 126, 143, 147, 165

Wace 38
Walter, lord of Beirut 80
Walter, lord of Caesarea 100, 135, 137, 143–144, 147
Walter le Bel, *vicecomes* of Acre 126, 165
Walter Durus, royal marshal 110
Walter of St Omer 52
William, archbishop of Reims 44
William II, archbishop of Tyre: his attitudes towards (Baldwin IV 10–11, 34, 35–36, 43, 53, 86, 94, 96–97, 99, 102; Guy de Lusignan 82, 85, 97, 99–101, 103–106; legends 8; outsiders 12, 13, 46, 52, 60, 72–74, 78–79, 80, 82; Raymond III count of Tripoli 11, 55, 56, 96, 101–102, 105–106; Sybil queen of Jerusalem 10–12, 17, 32, 44, 46, 58–60, 73–74, 78–79, 97, 82, 104, 107); career 10–11, 31, 34, 42, 44, 79, 82; his history of the kingdom of Jerusalem 10–12, 17, 30, 38, 167; *see also Estoire de Eracles empereur*, Latin continuation
William, bishop of Acre 10
William, count of Nevers 45
William, count of Saône 45
William I, king of England 36, 44
William II, king of Sicily 42, 54, 56, 137, 142, 148, 149, 150, 151, 152
William of Béthune 73–74
William Fortis *see* Guillaume
William de Furcis, burgher of Acre 81, 99
William Longsword of Montferrat, count of Jaffa and Ascalon 14, 39, 56, 57, 58–65, 72, 75, 77, 79, 84, 92, 136, 162, 168
William de Lusignan *see* William de Valence
William de Mandeville, earl of Essex 73–74, 78
William Marshal 110
William de Molembec (Molenbec, Molembecca, etc.) 81, 98, 126
William of Montferrat, count of Jaffa and Ascalon *see* William Longsword
William V (the old marquis) of Montferrat 57, 59–60, 84, 92, 110, 119, 130, 136, 144–145, 148, 151
William of Newburgh 13, 16, 111, 120, 128
William Rufus, *vicecomes* of Ascalon 63–64, 81, 98
William of Saone (Sahyūn) 30
William of Saône 45
William of Tiberias 53, 151, 159
William of Tyre; *see also* William II archbishop
William of Tyre, witness for Amaury count of Jaffa 63–64
William de Valence (de Lusignan) 56, 125
wine production 62
Wolfram von Eschenbach 167

Zengi of Mosul 7, 29–30, 97

Printed in the United States
by Baker & Taylor Publisher Services